What is Clinical Psychology?

What is Clinical Psychology?

FOURTH EDITION

Edited by

John Hall

Research and Development Director,
Health and Social Care Advisory Service; and
Professor of Mental Health, Brookes University, Oxford, UK

Sue Llewelyn

Course Director, Oxford Doctoral Course in Clinical
Psychology, University of Oxford, Oxford, UK

OXFORD
UNIVERSITY PRESS

OXFORD
UNIVERSITY PRESS

Great Clarendon Street, Oxford OX2 6DP

Oxford University Press is a department of the University of Oxford.
It furthers the University's objective of excellence in research, scholarship,
and education by publishing worldwide in

Oxford New York

Auckland Cape Town Dar es Salaam Hong Kong Karachi
Kuala Lumpur Madrid Melbourne Mexico City Nairobi
New Delhi Shanghai Taipei Toronto

With offices in

Argentina Austria Brazil Chile Czech Republic France Greece
Guatemala Hungary Italy Japan Poland Portugal Singapore
South Korea Switzerland Thailand Turkey Ukraine Vietnam

Oxford is a registered trade mark of Oxford University Press
in the UK and in certain other countries

Published in the United States
by Oxford University Press Inc., New York

First edition published 1987
Second edition published 1992
Third edition published 1999
Reprinted 2000, 2001, 2003 (twice), 2004, 2005
Fourth edition published 2006

British Library Cataloguing in Publication Data

Data available

Library of Congress Cataloging in Publication Data

Data available

Typeset by Newgen Imaging Systems (P) Ltd., Chennai, India
Printed in Great Britain
on acid-free paper by
Ashford Colour Press Ltd., UK

ISBN 0–19–856689–1 978–0–19–856689–2

10 9 8 7 6 5 4 3 2 1

Preface to the fourth edition

Over the years many people, including those we see as clients, psychology graduates thinking of training as clinical psychologists, colleagues in other health or social care professions, and friends, have asked us about our work. What exactly *is* a clinical psychologist? What *do* you do? Are you the same as a psychiatrist, or a psychotherapist?

It was to answer these questions that this book has been written, for three main groups of readers:

- Psychology students and psychology graduates wanting to understand the work of clinical psychologists, perhaps because they are considering a career in clinical psychology
- Members of a range of health and social care professions whose work has a significant psychological content, and who want to understand the potential contribution of clinical psychology to their own work
- Members of the public with an interest in psychological approaches to understanding both health and ill-health, reflecting the increasing 'psychologisation of everyday life' that influences many issues of public interest and concern, such as bringing up children, substance misuse, and long-term disabling conditions.

There are now a number of professional groups offering psychological therapies to the public. These groups include counsellors, psychotherapists, and members of other professions, such as nursing, who have taken further training in these therapies. There are also a number of groups of applied psychologists working in health care, such as health psychologists, both in Britain and other countries. It is significant that clinical psychologists are overwhelmingly the largest of these applied psychologists groupings in health care, in most developed countries. Their work is thus both numerically important, and is also significant since a number of the other groups have grown from clinical psychology, and have derived both their theories and practice largely from clinical psychology.

There are many volumes now available in the general area of psychology as applied to personal problems and health, reflecting the growing general interest in this area, as also illustrated by numerous television programmes and magazine articles. While much of this material is attractively produced, not all of it is well informed. We take the view that books on clinical psychology should be based on an appreciation of the broad range of psychological knowledge now available and on sound evidence of what is likely to be effective for specific conditions and problems, and should also reflect what is likely to be available, in practice, to most people.

It is now 20 years since the first edition of this book was conceived. Over that period the number of more specialized books published concerning applied psychology has also increased markedly. These volumes can be categorized in a number of ways. One group of books offers relatively detailed accounts of theory and practice, often focusing on a particular problem, or approach to treatment. Another group includes texts on abnormal psychology, or health psychology, designed for teaching purposes. What these books do not do is describe the day-to-day current practice of clinical psychologists, and of those colleagues working closely with them.

In earlier editions we made the point that the majority of text books on clinical psychology and related areas were North American. While that remains the case, there is now so much good material also originating from British, European, Australian, and other authors that it is no longer necessary to stress that point. The growth in the research and theoretical underpinnings of the profession that derive from British and European work is reflected in many of the chapters of this book. Alongside the conceptual basis of clinical psychology, the ways in which clinical services are delivered are increasingly similar to the range of models found in Europe, especially north-west Europe and Scandinavia. The accounts of clinical work in the chapters of this book accordingly will be similar to accounts of work in such countries as the Netherlands and Australia, and there are many examples given here of work in those and other countries.

The book is written as a number of chapters, each describing the work of clinical psychologists with different patients or user groups, with different presenting problems, and in different settings. This approach to writing the chapters closely reflects much of the current practice, and many readers may have a primary interest in particular user groups or types of problem. We do accept, however, that separating the chapters by client group in this way is not strictly in line with the current emphasis on the clinical, academic, research, personal, and professional competencies which clinical psychologists aim to develop through training, and which should be demonstrated in all work across different settings, with a range of client groups. We have nevertheless aimed to show in each chapter how this range of competencies can be applied in various settings with different groups of clients. In each successive edition of this book we have also added new chapters reflecting the continuing emergence of clinical specialities—in this edition we have for the first time a chapter on eating disorders. There is also a new chapter addressing cross-cultural and international issues in clinical psychology practice. There are clinical psychologists who work predominantly or specifically with one client group, such as with children, or with people with neurological problems and disabilities, while there are others who work for multi-agency services which cut across client or age groups, such as those who work for family services. We have therefore tried to reflect this diversity in the book. In addition, in localities or countries with less well-developed clinical psychology services, individual psychologists tend to be less specialized, and will see people with a wider range of needs, and this has also been explored.

Each chapter is written by practitioners with both clinical experience, with the group of users or clients about whom they are writing, and other knowledge and skills. Some practitioners are also active researchers, or active teachers and trainers, on topics related to their chapters. There is inevitably some overlap between chapters, and this reflects the fact that many people may have multiple problems and ask for help for more than one problem at the same time, but also reinforces the common theoretical and practice themes, or competencies, which can be applied across different specialities.

Clinical psychologists do not work in an organizational vacuum, so their work must be related to national health and social care policies as well as to the work of other health and social care agencies and other professionals operating simultaneously. The health care system of Britain, the National Health Service, is still by far the largest employer of clinical psychologists in Britain, and to that extent is different from most other countries where there is a more diverse range of agencies providing health care services. However, the range of employers has increased everywhere quite apart from the growth in private practice, and there continue to be developments in government policy that are likely to further increase that range of providers and opportunities for innovative practice. Of special interest, for example, is the number of policy statements from the British Department of Health specifically encouraging the development in each locality of a range of effective psychological therapies. Initiatives such as these impinge on the work of clinical psychologists and therefore we have included coverage of them in many chapters.

The book does not need to be read from beginning to end, although most readers will find it helpful to start with the first chapter. At the end of each chapter there is a short list of further reading on the material covered by each chapter. These suggested reading lists have been chosen to be reasonably accessible to the non-specialist reader. A glossary of key terms is included at the end of the book to explain some of the technical and organizational terms used. There are also two appendices describing the current procedure for applying for clinical psychology training in the United Kingdom and working as a clinical psychologist abroad.

It is now 60 years since clinical psychology began as an identifiable profession in Britain. In preparing this fourth edition, we continue to be conscious of the ongoing growth of the profession, most significantly in terms of the range of approaches and practice the profession now encompasses, but also in terms of numerical growth. Clinical psychology continues to be an exciting, although demanding, career.

The first three editions of this book were edited by John Marzillier and John Hall. We thank John Marzillier for all of his thoughtful contributions to those earlier editions; his place has now been taken by Susan Llewelyn, who is also John's successor as Course Director for the Oxford University doctoral training course in clinical psychology. We have received a number of comments on the previous editions, and on the proposal for this edition, and they have helped to shape this volume. We thank all the chapter authors for their contributions to this present volume. We also thank those chapter authors who have contributed to those earlier editions, including Ron Blackburn and Ray Hodgson, and two chapter authors who had contributed to all the previous three editions, Jeff Garland and Dorothy Fielding. The influence of the book, and of all of their contributions, has meant that the previous Spanish translation of the book has now been joined by a Japanese translation from the University of Tokyo Press in 2003.

Oxford JNH
2006 SL

Contents

Contributors

Sarah Allcock
Centre for Applied Social and Psychological Development,
Canterbury Christ Church University College, Southborough
Tunbridge Wells TN3 0TG
E-mail: s.allock@salomons.org.uk

Kirsty Ashby
Addictions Division,
South London and Maudsley NHS Trust,
Marina House,
Camberwell, London SE5 8RS
E-mail: kirsty.ashby@slam.nhs.uk

Richard Barker
The Reaside Clinic, Birmingham & Solihull Mental Health NHS Trust,
Birmingham B45 9BE
E-mail: richard.barker@bsmht.nhs.uk

John Cape
Camden & Islington Mental Health and Social Care Trust,
St. Pancras Hospital, 4 Pancras Way,
London NW1 0PE
E-mail: j.cape@ucl.ac.uk

Katherine Carpenter
Department of Clinical Neuropsychology,
Russell Cairns Unit, Radcliffe Infirmary, Oxford OX2 6HE
E-mail: katherine.carpenter@orh.nhs.uk

Helen Combes
Shropshire & Staffordshire Clinical Training Programme,
Mellor Building,
Staffordshire University,
Stokc on Trent ST4 2DE
E-mail: helen.combes@staffs.ac.uk

Chris Cullen
Psychology Department,
Dorothy Hodgkin Building,
University of Keele, Keele,
Staffs ST5 5BG
E-mail: chris.cullen@northstaffs.nhs.uk

Jane Fossey
Fulbrook Centre,
Churchill Hospital,
Headington, Oxford OX3 7LE
E-mail: jane.fossey@oxmhc-tr.nhs.uk

John Hall
School of Health and Social Care,
Oxford Brookes University,
Jack Straws Lane, Oxford OX3 0FL
E-mail: john.hall@brookes.ac.uk

Alison Jones
Addictions Division,
South London and Maudsley NHS Trust,
Marina House,
Camberwell, London SE5 8RS
E-mail: alison.jones@slam.nhs.uk

Paul Kennedy
National Spinal Injuries Centre,
Stoke Mandeville Hospital,
Aylesbury, Bucks HP21 8AL
E-mail: paul.kennedy@smh.nhs.uk

Gary Latchford
Clinical Psychology Training Programme,
Academic Unit of Psychiatry,
University of Leeds,
15 Hyde Terrace, Leeds LS2 9LT
E-mail: g.latchford@leeds.ac.uk

Tony Lavender
Centre for Applied Social and Psychological Development,
Salomons Centre,
Canterbury Christ Church University College, Southborough
Tunbridge Wells TN3 0TG
E-mail: t.lavender@salmons.org.uk

Susan Llewelyn
Oxford Doctoral Course in Clinical Psychology,
Isis Education Centre,
Warneford Hospital,
Oxford OX3 7JX
E-mail: susan.llewelyn@hmc.ox. ac.uk

John McGovern
Cheadle Royal Hospital,
100 Wilmslow Road,
Cheadle,
Cheshire SK8 3DG
E-mail: jmcgovern@affinityhealth.co.uk

Yvonne Millar
Northern Health Centre,
580 Holloway Road,
London N7 6LB
E-mail: yvonne.millar@nhs.net

Chris Moore
Edenfield Centre, Bolton,
Salford & Trafford Mental Health NHS Trust,
Manchester M25 3BL
E-mail:
christopher.moore@bstmht.nhs.uk

Irene Sclare
South London and Maudsley NHS Trust,
Michael Rutter Centre, Maudsley Hospital,
De Crespigny Park,
London SE5 8AZ
E-mail: irene.sclare@slam.nhs.uk

Hannah Turner
Eating Disorder Service,
Hampshire Partnership NHS Trust,
Eastleigh Community Enterprise Centre,
Unit 3, Barton Park, Eastleigh,
Southampton S050 6RR
E-mail: hmt@soton.ac.uk

Andy Tyerman
Community Head Injury Service,
The Camborne Centre,
Jansel Square Aylesbury,
Bucks HP21 7ET
E-mail: andy.tyerman@voa-pct. nhs.uk

Shamil Wanigaratne
Addictions Division,
South London and Maudsley NHS Trust,
Marina House,
Camberwell, London SE5 8RS
E-mail:
shamil.wanigaratne@slam. nhs.uk

Chapter 1

What is clinical psychology?

John Hall and Sue Llewelyn

Introduction

What is psychology?

Although almost everyone is familiar with the term 'psychology', and we all more or less know that it refers to 'what makes people tick', the exact meaning remains complex and is still evolving. Psychology as a term originally derived from the Greek *psyche* meaning 'mind' or 'spirit', and *logos*, meaning 'study'. Early approaches to studying what we now think of as psychology were not distinguished from philosophy, when thinkers such as Descartes, Berkeley, Locke, and Hume, tried to understand how mental processes worked through philosophical discourse and analysis. More recently thinkers such as Freud and William James made use of forms of self-analysis and observation to develop theories about the mind. Over the years a more scientific approach began to dominate, and modern psychology became primarily concerned with trying to understand behaviour and mental function through empirical analysis and experimentation. During this time much use has been made of the study of animals, in an attempt to understand the fundamental processes involved in learning, memory, motivation, emotion, perception and social interaction, and much progress has thereby been made in getting closer to being able to predict and account for behaviour and functioning in both animals and humans. In recent years major advances have been made by focusing on cognitive processes, so that twenty-first century psychology is now dominated by the cognitive approach. Hence the main focus of interest and research now centres on how people make sense of their experiences (via cognitions), and how our brains and senses process information (both past and present) to allow us to function. Although there are still vigorous debates about this, most psychologists now make at least some use of the metaphor of humans as information-processors, and seek to understand how we translate our experiences and memories into current actions or thoughts.

In parallel with this, there is also recognition that as humans we are embodied, and as such we need to understand our biological functioning, which is intimately concerned with our psychological functioning. Hence psychologists also pay attention to the effects of physiological and biological processes such as the nervous and sensory system, on our experience, development, and behaviour. Any study of human emotion or motivation, for example, must take into account hormonal and endocrinal factors, and the role they play in the genesis and experience of feeling and desires. Likewise developmental factors, including ageing, and physical changes such as pregnancy, also have impact upon our psychological experiences.

Last but by no means least, psychology additionally recognizes the crucial role played by our social context in influencing our functioning. We are social animals, who do not live in isolation, and we exist within social relationships. Our interactions with others make us who we are, and can potentially be enormously enriching and constructive, or may equally be damaging and destructive. Although much social psychology also makes use of the cognitive metaphor of humans as sense-makers or information-processors, it points out that social and cultural factors also have a huge impact upon our individual sense-making, and how we communicate with each other.

As a result of recognition of the importance of all these factors, the most inclusive model which now underpins modern psychology is probably a biopsychosocial model. What this means is that humans, as thinking, feeling, behaving, developing, perceiving, and communicating beings, are understood to exist within bodies as well as within social relationships. Hence any understanding of 'how people tick' has to take into account social and biological factors as well as internal cognitive and psychological factors. Clinical psychology calls upon all these aspects of psychology when attempting to understand human behaviour, and as seen later, makes use of the biopsychosocial model when attempting to formulate and intervene to resolve human problems.

What is clinical psychology?

The application of psychological principles

From the earliest development of formal psychological methodology and theory in the late nineteenth century, the curiosity of the early psychologists led them to apply those principles to everyday practical problems. The German Emil Kraepelin, better known as a psychiatrist than as a psychologist, was an experimental psychologist of distinction, and in the 1890s was carrying out studies as to what happened when people carry out continuous work without a break. He checked the amount of work done on a simple adding task in successive short intervals of time, and built up the classic 'work curve', showing the opposing effects of practice and fatigue, and the warming-up period. C.S. Myers, a leading figure in early British psychology, from his appointment as Director of the Psychological Laboratory at Cambridge from 1912 was interested in the role of psychology in practical problems. He was later psychological consultant to the British Forces in the First World War, where he contributed to the use of the term 'shell shock', and he was later the first Director of the National Institute of Industrial Psychology from 1921.

This interaction between dominant theories and the range of experimental and other methodologies associated with them, and current perceived practical problems, has continued to be a feature of the development of both academic psychology and applied psychology. Early books such as Cyril Burt's The Young Delinquents, first published in 1925, had an enormous impact on teachers, probation officers, reaching a growing readership between the academic and the popular. The main areas of application were in the fields of education, work, and mental health—it is no accident that the first three sections or special interest groups within the British Psychological Society were the Education, Occupational, and Medical Sections.

From this sort of perspective, applied psychologists can be seen as occupying social roles such as toolmaker, constructing psychological instruments, such as personality tests, for the better good of all. The range of applications of psychology has become very broad. Conventional divisions into the fields of occupational, child, and forensic psychology—including of course clinical, counselling, and health psychology—are necessarily arbitrary, and do not highlight the communalities that may exist between these divisions in terms of theory, method, and the problems that are addressed.

Nikolas Rose, a significant commentator on the social impact of psychology in the twentieth century, has suggested (1999) that psychology has been more than just applied, but has changed the way in which people think about themselves, and the way in which society can be controlled. The four areas he addresses are: the government of military forces and civilians in times of war; the regulation of the factory and economic life; new ways of understanding child development and family relationships; and the rise of the psychotherapies. Rose's pungent and inspirational critique suggests that the applications of psychology are not simply value-free technologies, but have had a profound impact on the very nature of our society.

These reflections suggest that a bland definition of applied psychology as the practice and profession of the application of psychological knowledge and theories to human needs and problems is not enough. A purist model of the application of a science suggests that this interaction between theory and practice is logical and progressive, whereas it may in fact be led by the personal opinions and prejudices of individuals influenced by wider cultural trends, with unanticipated social consequences.

The debate on appealing to evidence

A major debate has existed for many years, and continues to exist, around the relationship between psychological theory and method, and the practices that are supposed to derive from those theories. This debate goes to the heart of what sort of evidence should inform applied psychological practice. Should the choice of a particular therapy be informed by the score a person has obtained on a standardized measure of, say, depression? Or should it be informed by the subjective opinion of the clinician or indeed of the person themselves where they are unlikely to know which therapy has been demonstrated to be most effective in a recent systematic review? The argument reflects a debate about the probabilities of benefit for a person based on their position along certain putative dimensions, as opposed to knowledge derived from unique study of that individual. A related issue is how to determine whether a treatment has been effective. The choice of outcome measures for different forms of psychological therapy has become hotly contested, reflecting a tension between the two different types of knowledge.

There is therefore a tension between professional action based on claims of technical rationality, and professional action that allows discretion on the basis that we can never fully understand another person, and that users of services must ultimately make their own choices. This argument also relates to the issue of the power and control exercised by professionals, on the basis of their knowledge and skill. This tension has only been exacerbated by the development, on the one hand of systematic reviews and meta-analyses, and on the other hand by the growth of the user movement in mental health. Clinical psychology has historically looked to evidence-based practice to support the development of the profession—but one implication of evidence-based practice is that it supports practice by competent practitioners from any professional background, if they are carrying out the treatment correctly—the treatment fidelity argument. One issue facing any clinical psychologist is therefore their stance on what theories and thus evidence they see as legitimately informing their practice, and whether in fact their practice is based on fidelity to that model.

The beginnings—the early development of clinical psychology in the United States and in Britain

The first use of the term 'clinical psychology' was by Lightner Witmer to describe the practice of a university clinic for children at the University of

Pennsylvania in the United States in 1907. The work of this clinic, which had started in 1896, was mainly for 'retarded children' and for children with physical defects associated with delayed development, which would nowadays be regarded as an example of educational psychology. Nevertheless, it stands as an example of applying psychology to individual problems, so illustrating the clinical approach.

Other clinics for children in the United States were established in the early 1900s, so that by 1914 there were 26 psycho-education clinics in the United States. Research laboratories and clinics for the mentally ill, and for the mentally deficient, were also established in the early twentieth century. While two of the early roles of clinical psychologists—those as remedial educators and researchers—were thus identifiable by 1910, there was as yet no idea of a separate profession of clinical psychology. Although a short-lived and small American Association of Clinical Psychologists existed between 1917 and 1919, it was not until the mid-1930s that formal training for a distinct profession of clinical psychology began in the United States, with the introduction of both approved internships and tentative plans for training curricula.

As in the United States, the application of psychology to individual problems began in Britain before the existence of an identifiable profession. The creation of the British Psychological Society (BPS) in 1901 both defined what psychology and psycholog*ists* then were. The ten founders of the Society established it as an academic and scientific learned society, with a membership limited to those who were recognized teachers of psychology, or who had 'published work of recognisable value'. The Society remained very small until the end of the First World War, when the categories of those eligible to become members were expanded in 1920 to bring in those working in three fields of applied psychology—medical psychology, educational psychology, and occupational psychology—without, however, the requirement for those members to possess a formal qualification in psychology.

The most significant of these applications for the future of clinical psychology was the growth of the child guidance movement. This was stimulated by Clifford Beers, an American who in 1908 both wrote a book and founded a society to promote a set of activities aimed at promoting mental health by working with children and families, which he termed 'mental hygiene'. Beers emphasized the importance of seeing his clients as people with needs, and hence the importance of early intervention and preventive work.

Mental hygiene soon became an international movement, which together with the 'new psychology'—psychoanalysis—informed the development of child guidance clinics in Britain. This was started by the children's department of the Tavistock Clinic in 1926, whose clinics were staffed by doctors and social workers, and also psychologists whose role was 'the carrying out of psychological tests, and the ascertainment of intelligence quotients'. By 1939 there were 22 local education child guidance clinics, and also by the mid-1930s there were a number of voluntary agencies concerned with mental health in the broader sense. There are a few references to psychologists working in hospitals for the mentally ill or for those with learning difficulties in the 1930s, and a few publications by them, but at the outbreak of the Second World War most 'clinical work' was done by educational psychologists. There was no recognizable profession of clinical psychology.

British psychology before the war was very limited, and reading through the main British psychology journals from the mid-1930s onwards emphasises both the very small size of the body of academic psychologists and the very limited range of theoretical underpinning of the experimental work carried out. However, the journals already give some indication of concerns about clinical topics. It is perhaps surprising that British psychology did not develop at the same pace as in America and Germany, as certainly developments both in philosophy and science, and the prosperity of the country, would have allowed that—the blame for this has been placed on the conservatism of British universities. The very small proportion of the population who were Honours graduates in *any* discipline, and the slow development of psychology in universities in Britain, also limited the growth of psychology as a discipline. Academic psychology remained small right up to the end of the Second World War: there were 717 BPS members in 1927, and only 811 in 1941.

There could hardly have been a worse period to start a new profession in Britain than in the 1940s in the middle of the Second World War. During the war, national priority was given to every activity directed at survival of the state through military action. Yet during the war major social welfare policies were being prepared, of which the Beveridge report, commissioned in 1941 and published in December 1942, was the most significant, in laying the foundations of a comprehensive health and welfare system.

The small numbers of senior academic psychologists, mostly male, either joined the armed forces, or worked on psychological problems generated by the war. The only significant group of psychologists still working with the problems of the civilian population were those working in the child guidance clinics who were overwhelmingly female. They were aware of the potential implications of the Beveridge report, and Dr Lucy Fildes had chaired an informal committee of educational psychologists in 1943, within which had arisen the suggestion that they should form a group within the BPS. This group, known as the Committee of Professional Psychologists (Mental Health), the CPP (MH), had its first meeting in December 1943.

From the beginnings of the work of the committee in 1944, planning was taking place nationally for the new post-war social and health structures. Before the NHS had even been proposed, the CPP (MH) were engaged in the agreement of conditions of service for educational psychologists with a range of local authority and private employers. By the end of their first full year of existence, the committee had met 8 times, and had discussed pay, qualifications, training, contact with Government, and prepared a number of memoranda. The Ministry of Health and other bodies responded to these approaches, and endorsed some of the proposals put to them.

The incorporation of the term 'mental health' in the title of the committee had two significant implications. It implied acceptance of the mental hygiene model of education and practice, and it carried with it reference to the officially recognized and funded umbrella organization, the National Association for Mental Health. The terms 'mental hygiene' and 'mental health' were themselves powerful and contemporary rhetoric. Joining the two terms 'professional' and 'mental health' invoked two prestige-laden ideas into the title of the new organization.

The Labour Government elected in 1945 was committed to implementing the Beveridge report, and so rapidly passed the National Health Service Act in 1946, which was implemented in 1948. No one then knew the real expense of the existing health services, and so had no knowledge of the cost of the forthcoming NHS, and at the outset of the NHS, there was only limited recognition of the parlous state of mental and mental handicap hospitals. Alongside the battle for resources ran another struggle, to induce members of the medical profession to join the new health service. Aneurin Bevan, the Labour Minister of Health responsible for creating the NHS, met with nurses, and with other professional organizations in their approximate order of importance and relevance. In this climate it was highly unlikely that the concerns of psychologists would be seen as a priority. But what is highly significant is that the process by which psychology became professionalized in Britain arose from two institutions—the NHS and the BPS—actively engaging with each other; clinical psychology in Britain was born in the cradle of the NHS.

The development of clinical psychology in Britain from the late 1940s

When the BPS Council in 1945 said that the term 'clinical psychologist' was 'not necessarily meaningless, but . . . liable to too much ambiguity and misunderstanding to be used by the Society' it was then an entirely reasonable position for them to take, for three reasons. The number of people in 1945 carrying out activities, which would later be seen as typical of clinical psychologists, were so few that they could hardly be called a professional group. Individuals moved freely between work with children and adults (and indeed into occupational psychology) so there was nothing distinctive about the term. Also the terms 'clinical' or 'medical' psychology were already used by members of the mostly medically qualified members of the Medical Section of the BPS.

From the mid-1940s a number of interlinked conceptual, practice, and setting traditions can be identified, most of them closely associated with specific institutions and people that guided the early development of clinical psychology. The first, numerically largest, and conceptually most consistent, was the Child Guidance and educational psychology tradition, noted above, which was based on a mental hygiene and educational premise, influenced by Cyril Burt's work, and carried out in child guidance clinics and schools. A significant proportion of these child guidance or educational psychologists moved into adult work with no additional training, including some of those who became the most influential leaders of the profession, such as May Davidson, who took this tradition with them.

A second tradition, and the one which is most often, but in many respects erroneously seen as the archetypal model of clinical psychology, is that of the Maudsley Hospital, London, linked closely with the ideas of Hans Eysenck. Before the Second World War there was a tradition of psychologists working at the Maudsley in different roles, including Philip Vernon, and J. Blackburn, publishing from the Central Pathological Laboratory. Eysenck had moved to the Maudsley in 1945, and was appointed as head of the department of psychology, later becoming the first professor of clinical psychology in Britain. The Maudsley was a unique institution, and as a small neurosis teaching hospital was atypical compared with other psychiatric hospitals in England. Eysenck advocated a strictly scientific role for clinical psychologists, and he personally never saw any patients at the Maudsley. Eysenck continues to be important for a number of classic papers criticizing the then current psychiatric and psychotherapy practice, and by his popular books on general psychology. He is widely seen as a prophetic figure in British psychology, and promoted the image of himself as the founding father of British clinical psychology. Eysenck's voice is quoted as representative of all clinical psychology, even by critical observers such as Nikolas Rose, but he represented one, and only one, way of conceptualizing a psychologist's role, and played no part in the professionalization of clinical psychology.

A third tradition, also based within the Maudsley Hospital, was the more exploratory tradition led by MB (Monte) Shapiro. He was appointed to the Maudsley independently of Eysenck. While Eysenck was the nominal head of the whole psychology department, he had no routine involvement in training, which was in fact the responsibility of Shapiro. All contemporary commentators on Maudsley training and practice place Shapiro at the centre of both activities, and stress the impact of his critical but person-centred systematic approach.

Another significant influence was the Tavistock Clinic, established in 1929 as one of the first independent outpatient clinics in Britain, which was committed to psychodynamic and psychoanalytic ideas. The annual report for 1937 showed two psychologists working as 'non-medical technical staff'. After 1943, when J.R. Rees became Medical Director, the Clinic grew significantly to become the main British training and research centre for psychodynamic therapy. Susan Isaacs had worked there, and Herbert Phillipson was the Head Psychologist there from 1946, supervising the expansion of the Tavistock as a training and practice base for those clinical psychologists who wished to work with an explicitly psychodynamic approach.

All four of the traditions so far described were London based. Another grouping emerged in the setting of the Crichton Royal Hospital, Dumfries in rural lowland Scotland, a highly unlikely spot for an innovative psychiatric institution, but which was more representative of British psychiatric hospitals than either the Maudsley Hospital or Tavistock Clinic. John Raven was invited in 1943 to set up a department of psychological research at the Crichton Royal, two years before Eysenck was appointed to the Maudsley. Raven espoused a humanistic psychology, reflecting his concern with patients as persons, coupled with systematic investigation. The Crichton was an important training place for a number of eminent clinical psychologists, including the Quaker pacifist Ralph Hetherington, and Graham Foulds who later worked at the Medical Research Council Unit for Epidemiological Studies at Edinburgh.

Two other groups both informed later developments. First, Oliver Zangwill worked as an experimental neuropsychologist at the Cambridge Psychological Laboratory from the 1930s, then in Edinburgh, clinically, in the early 1940s, and then in his highly prestigious position as Professor back at Cambridge from 1952. Psychologists working in neuropsychology held a distinctive position, as neurology had higher standing as a medical speciality than psychiatry, and there continued to be a very close relationship between academic psychology and clinical neuropsychology, especially in the leading academic centres of Cambridge, London, and Oxford. Second, educational psychologists were heavily involved in the 'ascertainment' of mental handicap, but were not directly attached to the mental handicap institutions. John Raven had worked at the Colchester mental handicap research project in the 1930s in a research capacity before his move to Dumfries. H.C. Gunzburg, a German émigré, was working at Monyhull Hospital in Birmingham from the 1940s as a training officer since he could not be officially recognized as a psychologist. From 1950 Alan and Ann Clarke had started their pioneering work at the Manor Hospital, Epsom, on understanding the learning potential of those with learning disabilities. A number of psychologists were working in what was then known as mental deficiency, even if for only part of their time, and were aware of the value of remedial education in that setting.

It is noteworthy that of the seven training courses that were first approved in 1957, four were for work with children only, and only the Dumfries course in south-western Scotland was not in London. None of the heads of the training courses had any training in the United States. Even in 1966 over half of the initial members of the then new Division of Clinical Psychology had not received a formal training. Certainly in 1958 there would have been a very wide range of theoretical perspectives among psychologists working in the National Health Service (NHS), with a correspondingly wide range of views on what constituted the future for clinical psychologists.

The developing role of clinical psychologists

Any developing profession must have one or more core functions or tasks that are required or expected of its members. For psychologists working clinically in the 1940s, this was unquestionably that of psychometrician. Psychometric tests had been developed both in the United States and France, and psychometric skills were sought most obviously in work with children, with adults with learning disabilities, and to a much lesser degree with adults with mental illness. The demand for competent psychometrists exceeded the supply of psychologists, so that even before the war nurses would act as testers, if no psychologist was available or willing to perform the function. A major, but unremarked, modification of the psychometrician role emerged as new physical and psychosocial treatments were introduced into the large psychiatric hospitals from the early 1950s, requiring psychologists to adopt the role of treatment evaluator.

An expected but not necessarily required task was also that of remedial educator for those working with children, and rehabilitator for those working with adults. Psychologists might also contribute to group work, such as that carried out at the wartime Emergency Military Hospitals, particularly but not only at Mill Hill and Belmont Hospitals, which offered a foundation for Bion and Foulkes' work with groups. These approaches laid the foundation for the later therapeutic community movement. Another expected task was that of teacher—to both trainee nurses and trainee psychiatrists. The task of researcher was not necessarily expected omit away from teaching hospitals, although many psychologists aspired to become independent researchers, rather than simply methodological or statistical supporters of medical research. There was clearly a tension between psychiatrists' expectations of psychologists that they could perhaps do some research, and the expectations of some psychologists, most prominently Eysenck, that they were primarily scientists.

Up until 1950, the CPP (MH) consisted mainly of psychologists working with children, in either a clinical or educational capacity. There was no separate professional body for psychologists working with adults, but as the numbers of these grew slowly, so the question of their professional organization became more pressing. In 1950 psychologists working with adults could be co-opted onto CPP (MH), and the committee continued to be concerned with issues relating to both clinical and educational psychologists. In 1952 the first Whitley Circular was issued by the Ministry of Health, agreeing the qualifications and conditions of service for psychologists working in the NHS. Conditions for those psychologists employed by Education Authorities were the separate concern of the Soulbury Committee. By 1954 CPP (MH) had discussed the separation of the committee into educational and clinical sections, and by 1957 this had been achieved, with the creation of educational and clinical sections within the new BPS 'Division of Professional Psychologists'. At long last, in the same year, the Ministry of Health formally approved the first training courses in clinical psychology.

Although academic psychology in the United Kingdom obviously drew heavily from American publications, and while the majority of the formal psychometric tests used were of American origin, later references to the influence of American clinical psychology on developments in Britain may not reflect real influence at the time. The direction of clinical psychology in the United States was driven by ideas of social utility from the 1940s, as illustrated by the massive support for clinical psychology training by the US Veterans Administration, with no parallel in Britain. The strong influence of psychoanalysis on American psychiatry, and hence clinical psychology, was largely absent in Britain. During the British process of professionalization, it is hard to find any record, or even awareness of, the American Psychological Association's 1947 Shakow Report, or the Boulder conference of 1949, that put forward the scientist practitioner model of training. The conclusion has to be drawn that the development and professionalization of clinical psychology in Britain was conducted differently from America.

The position by the late 1950s was that membership of the British Psychological Society was now open only to those with an approved psychology degree. The NHS now formally approved training for clinical psychologists, and laid down criteria for employment as clinical psychologists.

The professional separation between educational and clinical psychology within the BPS had been begun. While the academic roots of clinical psychology relied heavily on American sources, the function of clinical psychology within the British health care system, and the process of professionalization, was different. A distinct profession of clinical psychology now existed, but the primary role was not that of autonomous therapist.

Clinical psychology from 1960—psychologists as therapists

The single most significant transformation of the role of clinical psychologists was the inclusion of a therapeutic function from the 1960s. The original role as psychometrician was manifestly unattractive to new psychology graduates, and the old structure of single-handed hospital-based psychologists was also unable to retain psychologists in the NHS. From the earlier remedial work of educational psychologists, and the rehabilitative work of psychologists in a number of settings, there was a tradition of psychologists wanting to adopt a more direct therapeutic role.

This broadening of role was closely associated with government concern about conditions in both the large psychiatric hospitals and the then mental handicap hospitals. The numbers of psychiatric hospital inpatients in England had risen to the highest figure ever of 150,000 by 1955. Conditions within them remained very poor, and public concern about these conditions, and the scandals that were publicized, were factors that led the government to tackle the problem directly. There were two main consequences of this concern. The 1959 Mental Health Act liberalized the mental health law somewhat, and took the power of compulsory detention away from lay magistrates. Second, following the famous 'water tower' speech by Enoch Powell, then Minister of Health, in which he condemned the Victorian asylums as outdated, a dual programme of both replacing the asylums, and broadening the range of professional staff employed in the hospitals, began. This had a direct impact on the recruitment of clinical psychologists, and from the early 1960s, while new training courses were being established, there was a continuing unmet demand for clinical psychologists to work in the adult mental health field, and even more so in the then less popular field of mental handicap. These newly appointed psychologists often had an interest in the overall therapeutic milieu of the hospitals where they were working, and with their equally new social work and occupational therapy colleagues, contributed to the development of group work and meaningful occupation in both the older and newer hospitals.

The first attempts at explicitly psychological treatment were seen as being applications of learning theory, thereby appealing to the prestige of experimental psychology. One of the very first British published articles on behavioural treatment was written by Gwynne Jones, working at the Maudsley, in 1956. Early behavioural therapeutic work (including the ill-fated aversion therapy) was based on classical conditioning models. However, ideas derived from Bion and Foulkes' group analytic work, and more general group therapy ideas were also influential, and informed the interest in therapeutic communities. From the late 1960s operant conditioning-based therapies, such as token economy regimes, became more common. It is abundantly clear that the development of an explicit therapeutic role was taken up enthusiastically by most clinical psychologists, simply because of the evident massive underprovision of any psychological treatment in the NHS. This development cannot be explained simply by an appeal to Eysenckian rhetoric, or to the 1949 American 'Boulder' model of the scientist practitioner, or by seeing behaviour therapy as the sole justification for this change.

The tensions with psychiatrists created by the development of this therapeutic role led to the Department of Health setting up the Trethowan Committee in 1973 to review clinical psychology services in the NHS—the first NHS-commissioned report focusing on clinical psychology. The committee, with a membership mainly of doctors and clinical psychologists, reported formally in 1977. It viewed clinical psychology as an independent profession, and recommended the establishment of comprehensive multi-speciality psychology departments in each Health Authority area. Despite these recommendations, there were ongoing difficulties in the recruitment and funding of psychologists in the NHS during the 1980s, which led in turn to two linked reviews, the 1989 NHS-funded but independent Management Advisory Service (MAS) review of psychology services, and the government 1990 Manpower Planning Advisory Group review. Both of these considered clinical psychology as a resource for other professions, leading to the so-called consultancy model of service, with psychologists as skilled therapists and supervisors of other psychological therapists.

Continuing developments in theory and associated practice: towards a definition

After the initial impact of behaviourally informed therapies, other therapeutic modalities were successively introduced, including Kelly's Personal Construct theory, social skills training, Cognitive Behaviour Therapy (CBT), systemic family therapy, and integrative models such as Cognitive Analytic Therapy (CAT). Psychologists working with children have derived treatment approaches from attachment theory, and psychologists working with older adults have incorporated ideas derived from lifespan development. Increasing numbers of psychologists working in fields of general medicine, such as pain management, and coping effectiveness for people with traumatic spinal cord injuries, draw on methods informed by theories of information processing and by cognitive theories of stress and coping. Teasdale and Barnard's (1993) work on interacting cognitive systems illustrates the sophistication of recent fundamental research which has clinical implications, informed by new knowledge of brain–behaviour relationships.

Developments in therapeutic method have interacted with changes in practice. While the increasing numbers of psychologists working in adult mental health were initially mostly based in the large psychiatric hospitals, as those hospitals have steadily closed so the psychologists have shifted to become members of generic community mental health teams, and to work far more closely with colleagues in primary care settings. Services for people with learning difficulties, and many services for people with chronic physical conditions, are now based in community settings, shared with colleagues employed by social services departments or by voluntary agencies. The numbers of psychologists working in private practice, or employed by for-profit agencies providing, for example, secure services, have increased steadily. All these changes in demands and settings require changes in practice, a steady diversification of professional roles, and the development of working relationships with a wide range of other professions and groups.

It is possible to look at the changes in practice in clinical psychology over the past 50 years on a number of dimensions. Earlier service models assumed that psychological assessment was an adequate response to a diagnostically formulated individual case, usually seen within a specialist institutional setting after initial screening by a doctor. Service models would now see an initial psychological formulation as a first step to a problem-centred understanding of a person or family system, possibly self-referred and probably seen in an accessible community setting, with the psychologist now being an equal partner with other colleagues and probably supervising others to carry out psychologically informed interventions. The services would themselves be assertively targeting a variety of multiple systemic responses to biopsychosocial health need, in order to improve outcome and health gain in populations. The range of theoretical models of therapy and associated practice has increased beyond imagination compared to just 40 years ago.

A further factor affecting the form and function of any profession is the range of skills possessed by related professions. In the 1950s there was no other profession in a position to contribute to the development of a range of psychological therapies. Apart from very time-consuming psychoanalytic therapy, hardly available outside London anyway, the options for psychological therapies for adults were limited to group therapy and relatively unfocused supportive therapy. Counselling as a profession did not exist in Britain, despite the high standards of marital counselling conducted by the then Marriage Guidance Council, now known as Relate.

The continuing tension between cooperation and conflict across disciplines and professions, most obviously for psychologists with the powerful discipline and profession of medicine, continue to shape applied psychology practice to this day. The growth in related professions over the past 25 years, particularly of psychotherapists and professional counsellors, has created a degree of competition amongst the psychological professions in social welfare, health, and education. The picture is further complicated by the growth within the past 10 years in Britain of other branches of applied psychology, mostly counselling and health psychologists, but also forensic psychologists and clinical neuropsychologists.

What then emerges from these changes and competition as the distinctive role of the clinical psychologist? This chapter has demonstrated that the function of clinical psychologists in Britain has changed significantly over the past 60 years as a consequence of their knowledge base, their skills, the roles they occupy within a complex professionally diversified health and social care system, and not least by their substantial growth in numbers. The best prediction of their role in the future must therefore be that the profession will continue to face new challenges, and will only contribute positively if their knowledge and skills adapt to those challenges. What this means therefore is that any definition can only be transitional.

For now, however, we offer the following definition: A clinical psychologist is a psychologist who applies psychological theories and methods to the understanding, assessment, and treatment of primarily psychological disorders, and of the psychological consequences of physical conditions. He or she also contributes psychological competencies towards a systematic understanding of the quality and effectiveness of care, and facilitates others in applying psychological procedures.

Training and qualifications

Current training as a clinical psychologist builds on the foundations of initial study of psychology as an academic discipline, by developing trainees' competence in applying its methods and theories, in a range of settings, with a variety of client groups, with the aim of ameliorating difficulties and alleviating suffering. Essentially, the qualified clinical psychologist aims to apply the understanding and methods of psychology to effect change in people's lives, and to solve problems, specifically those that are presented in the sphere of health, well being, and illness. As such the clinical psychologist finds his or her professional roots from within a science-based discipline, but then uses the insights and methods of that parent academic discipline to try and bring about change in an uncertain and uncontrolled world, with unpredictable and challenging problems. Training involves developing the competencies to do this.

Underpinning clinical psychology training is a commitment to two different but equally important philosophies—that of the scientist practitioner and that of the reflective practitioner. Training therefore aims to develop the scientific skills of the graduate psychologist in practical application, but equally important is the development of the trainee's competence to work within an ethical and responsive framework. In other words, training is designed to equip psychologists with the ability to solve problems in the lives of service users, staff, and carers in health and social care settings by drawing on a science-based approach to their work, but also the ability and values to base their work on ethical and culturally sensitive reflection.

Looking first at the scientist practitioner model, in practice, clinical training aims to develop trainees' competence by using an iterative cycle of assessment, formulation, intervention, and evaluation with a variety of clinical problems. Hence clinical problems are approached systematically and the results of any assessment or intervention are used to improve the effectiveness of that intervention, or to improve the discipline's understanding and approach to similar problems in the future. Often this involves seeing individual clients or families whose difficulties involve psychological issues, and attempting to resolve these by following procedures suggested by psychological theories or models. For example, principles of selective reinforcement might be used to help an exhausted mother who is struggling with a 7-year-old child who refuses to sleep in her own bed, and who is finding it difficult to establish appropriate limits with her daughter. Treatment could be based on assessing what is happening within the family to maintain the child's inability to go to sleep without her mother, and trying to suggest ways of developing alternative behaviours at bed-time, possibly by introducing a schedule of reinforcement which encourages both the child's independence, and more appropriate limit-setting by her mother.

The scientist practitioner aspect of training also includes the ability to design and carry out innovative or original applied research, which is normally required as part of the doctoral level training. Hence the discipline aims to contribute to the knowledge base from which it has grown. Training in addition promotes the development of critical evaluation of published research, and encourages psychologists to play a key role in bringing evidence-based practice into routine clinical work, both within the profession and amongst other professional groups with whom psychologists work. Thus practice feeds and draws on research and theory that in turn influences practice.

Second, the reflective practitioner model in training aims to develop the trainee's capacity to reflect on their work to ensure that he or she works in an ethically aware and culturally sensitive way and in a way that allows for modification and development of theory and practice to fit individual circumstances. So in the example given above of the child with sleeping difficulties, the trainee psychologist also needs to be aware of what is expected of children with the family's cultural context, and not to impose his or her own values onto the family, while also holding the child's welfare as primary. Hence training also seeks to encourage certain values in trainees. These are based on the fundamental acknowledgement that all people have the same human value and the right to be treated as unique individuals. Clinical psychologists as a professional group aim to treat all people with dignity and respect, and to work collaboratively in partnership with them. Essentially they are committed to reducing psychological distress and enhancing and promoting psychological well-being through the systematic application of knowledge derived from psychological theory and evidence. Most trainees share such values, and have the opportunity during training to develop and consider these issues.

Clinical training in Britain

In Britain, all clinical psychology training is carried out within universities in partnership with the NHS. In 2004–5 there were 28 programmes offering training, all but one on a full-time basis, and all of them providing generic training (i.e. competence and transferable skills are developed across a range of clinical problems and settings). Entry to training requires the Graduate Basis for Registration (GBR) as defined by the BPS. All programmes are delivered at postgraduate level in accordance with the Framework for Higher Education Qualifications. The implication of this is that, when qualified, clinical psychologists should be able to make informed judgements on complex clinical and research problems, often in the absence of complete information, and will be able to communicate their ideas and conclusions clearly and effectively to specialist and non-specialist audiences. They should also be able to contribute to the creation and development of new knowledge and be able to continue to undertake applied research and development at an advanced level, and to be able to work autonomously using their own initiative in complex and unpredictable clinical situations. In Britain, successful candidates are eligible for Chartered status in the BPS. Chartered Psychologists agree to abide by the British Psychological Society Code of Conduct. In the near future (at the time of writing) it is probable probable that successful candidates will also be required to register as practitioners with the Health Professions Council.

Training itself normally involves an integrated programme of academic teaching, supervised clinical practice, private study, and research. The research aspect usually involves both small-scale, service-related research and a more substantial project concerning a specialist area that has clinical implications. Normally this programme of integrated training involves trainees spending around 2 days per week on academic study or teaching, and 3 days per week on clinical placements, gaining experience of clinical work under supervision, over a period of 3 years. Some programmes are organized on a 'block' system whereby trainees attend the University every 6 months or so for teaching for 3 or 4 weeks, followed by a longer stint gaining clinical competence under supervision, while others are organized on an integrated clinical/academic, weekly basis, as described earlier.

In the last few years, all clinical psychology training programmes have agreed to design their training around a competency-based model, and this is now required for accreditation and Chartering by the BPS. What this means is that, rather than specifying exactly what someone must spend time doing, with specific types of client, the emphasis is placed on the range of flexible skills and abilities that the trainee has the opportunity to develop. Hence within UK clinical training, all trainee psychologists should gain competence in working with:

- a wide breadth of clients—from acute to enduring, and from mild to severe (e.g. with a child with school refusal, and with an adult who has a serious and chronic health problem such as a spinal cord injury);
- problems ranging from those with mainly biological causation to those emanating mainly from psychosocial factors (e.g. from difficulties presented by an adult with Down's Syndrome to a woman suffering from severe stress reactions in response to being in an unexpected and traumatic road traffic accident);
- problems of coping / adaptation to adverse circumstances that are not themselves reversible by psychological intervention (e.g. coping with acquired physical disability, illness, or bereavement);
- clients from a range of backgrounds, which should reflect the demographic characteristics of the population (hence including people from ethnic minorities as well as the majority population, both genders,

and those with different sexual orientations, depending on the population served);

- clients with significant levels of challenging behaviour (e.g. work with excessively verbally abusive behaviour in an elderly nursing home resident);
- clients across a range of levels of intellectual functioning over a range of ages (including those with learning disability, and dementia);
- clients whose disability makes it difficult for them to communicate (e.g. a learning disabled adolescent with limited speech, who is finding it hard to deal with his developing sexuality);
- carers and families;
- social and contextual factors;
- teamwork, service delivery systems, and a variety of legislative and policy frameworks which impact on what services are provided (such as the Mental Health Act, National Service Frameworks, and Child Protection legislation).

Examples of work with this range of clients, problems, and contexts is given throughout this book.

Training programmes try to ensure that trainees can gain this wide variety of types of clinical experience in a diverse range of service contexts, including primary, secondary and tertiary care, as well as inpatient, outpatient, and community settings. Further, programmes liaise closely with local NHS services to allow trainees to experience work with different service delivery models, ranging from seeing clients for one-to-one therapy, to integrated inter-professional working, such as being part of a team all of whose members play a part in treatment, as might happen for instance in a unit for rehabilitation of brain-injured people. It is also important for trainees to become competent in the provision of staff training, supervision, and consultancy (such as providing advice about the best way to treat hearing voices in patients diagnosed with schizophrenia), as well as teamwork within multidisciplinary teams and specialist service systems. Ideally this includes experience of change and planning in service systems (as might be required for example when a group of learning disabled clients are moved from a small inpatient unit to a community-based service). Lastly, trainees should be able to work in more than one recognized model of formal psychological therapy (which can include psychodynamic, cognitive, systemic, or integrative approaches).

All of this means that, over the 3 years of training, trainees develop the ability to apply competencies in a wide range of settings, although they will not necessarily have experienced every type of problem that is likely to be presented to a clinical psychologist. The essential skill is one of flexibility, and the competence to call on psychological theory and evidence when approaching novel clinical problems. It is also recognized that the development of knowledge, skills, and competence is a life-long venture and that as professionals, clinical psychologists should be committed to a life-long learning agenda and continuous professional development which does not end when the 3 year initial training period is complete.

Another crucial component of training is personal and professional competence, which means that trainees are encouraged to develop an appropriate sense of themselves and ways of interacting as clinical psychologists, as well as effective methods of self-care. The competencies expected of trained practitioners in these areas are shown in Table 1.1. Training programmes have a variety of ways of encouraging the development of these competencies, particularly while trainees are working on clinical placements. Most programmes have recently developed ways of assessing trainees' competence to interact professionally with other staff and clients, and to act ethically both in clinical work and in the conduct of research. All programmes also offer support for trainees to develop self-care and awareness of the impact of distress upon them that is often encountered during routine clinical work. Some programmes fund confidential personal learning sessions for trainees, while others provide small groups run by an external facilitator, so that trainees can learn about themselves within a confidential small group setting,

What is training like?

The experience of training is often described as stressful and demanding, and it is certainly the case that the 3 years of training are very busy. Trainees are expected to take on a variety of new roles and responsibilities, including encountering human distress in a variety of forms, some of which means that trainees have to confront issues, such as mortality, abuse or trauma, which do not normally form part of many people's daily working lives. Some programmes require trainees to move to new clinical environments on a regular basis to ensure that they attain the required range of competencies, and this can be disruptive and unsettling. Some trainees find it hard to maintain as much contact as they might like with family or friends living elsewhere, and time is limited for socializing. The demands of the academic and research components of training mean that trainees face regular assessments and have to deliver doctoral quality work at the same time as meeting all the other demands. Most programmes cover a wide geographical area, so quite a lot of travelling is required over the 3 years.

It is not all negative however. Most trainees really enjoy the range of clinical work experienced and relish the opportunity to develop their clinical skills. The academic and research components are often fascinating and offer a

Table 1.1 Excerpt from Benchmark statements of competencies required of qualified clinical psychologists

Professional relationships

The award holder should be able to:

- participate effectively in inter-professional and multi-agency approaches to health and social care;
- recognize professional scope of practice and make referrals where appropriate;
- demonstrate understanding of consultancy models and the contribution of consultancy to practice;
- work with others to deliver effective health care;
- understand the impact of difference, diversity, and social inequalities on people's lives, and its implications for working practices;
- work effectively with users and carers to facilitate their involvement in service planning and delivery;
- maintain appropriate records and make accurate reports.

Personal and professional skills

The award holder should be able to:

- demonstrate the ability to deliver high quality patient/client-centred care both as a solo practitioner and as a member of multidisciplinary and multi-agency teams;
- practise in an anti-discriminatory, anti-oppressive manner;
- draw upon clinical psychology knowledge, theory, and skills in order to make professional judgements;
- demonstrate high levels of research skills and scholarship;
- work effectively at a high level of autonomy in complex and unpredictable situations, with awareness of the limits of own competence, and accepting accountability to relevant professional and service managers;
- demonstrate self-awareness and ability to work as a reflective practitioner;
- demonstrate a high level of communication skills in a style appropriate to specialist and non-specialist audiences;
- initiate and respond to change in a flexible manner, demonstrating transferable skills;
- understand the importance and role of continuing professional development and engage in self-directed learning that promotes professional development;
- manage the emotional and physical impact of their own practice;
- understand the importance and role of supervision and demonstrate its appropriate use;
- demonstrate self-management skills and independence of thought and action; and
- demonstrate culturally competent practice

chance to study and learn from others who are highly skilled and willing to pass on those skills. The requirement to complete a doctoral level dissertation provides a chance to develop competence in research methodology and to explore a topic in relative depth, as well as to contribute significantly to the knowledge base in the area. Very few psychologists ever find their jobs boring and most find it rewarding to able to contribute to a reduction in human suffering. Many also value the development of a professional identity and role within the Health Service.

What does a clinical psychologist do?

As will be seen throughout this book, clinical psychologists work in a wide range of settings with a variety of client groups. The core skills used in any professional activity are however likely to be the same.

- assessment
- formulation
- intervention
- evaluation and research
- communication

Assessment involves gaining an understanding of a person or situation, as well as of change and stability, and may also involve comparing the individual's performance or results with those of others. As indicated in the Clinical Psychology Benchmark statements (QAA, 2004), which provide a concise and nationally agreed statement of the core activities and competences of clinical psychologists, assessment procedures include:

- the development and use of psychometric tests (including an appreciation of the importance of sound psychometric properties of test instruments, such as reliability and validity);
- the application of systematic observation and measurement of behaviour in both daily life contexts and other settings (e.g. comparing interaction patterns between a child and his peers in a nursery, before and after an intervention designed to decrease his hostility towards other children);
- devising self-monitoring strategies for individual service-user, such as recording of daily activities or thoughts;
- the use of formal and informal interviews with clients, carers, and other professionals.

Carrying out a process of assessment almost always involves the ability to develop an effective alliance with clients or families, as well as the ability to choose and administer appropriate tests, or to carry out interviews. The clinical psychologist aims to make sense of the results of this assessment in the context of the individual, family, group, or organization. For example, a clinical psychologist might give a widely used assessment tool such as a depression inventory, and a standardized cognitive battery of tests when trying to understand the difficulties of an elderly man who is becoming increasingly withdrawn and non-communicative with his family, but when doing so will also seek to gain an understanding of his past and current family and personal circumstances. Psychologists may also devise and use one-off, individualized assessment procedures. So, for example, a psychologist working with a child with a specific but uncommon fear of butterflies might devise a scale around the fear-inducing characteristics of butterflies to assess the child's progress.

Formulation is a specific psychological process and is to be distinguished from diagnosis, which is a formal process normally carried out by medical colleagues to indicate the likely cause, treatment, and prognosis of a disorder. Formulation puts together and integrates information gained by assessment, and draws on psychological theory and data to provide a framework for describing a problem. Hence formulation provides a working hypothesis for how problems have developed and are maintained, and how they might be resolved. Different theories and models will call attention to different possible causal and maintaining factors of the problem, and will call on different types of supporting evidence. Whatever the model used, formulation is the key for intervention. As noted in the Benchmarks, this ability to 'access, review, critically evaluate, analyse, and synthesise data and knowledge from a psychological perspective is one that is distinct to psychologists'. Formulation is probably the most important and creative aspect of a clinical psychologist's work. Many examples of different formulations will be given throughout this volume.

The next step is the *intervention*, which usually involves using a psychological model or approach to facilitate change. It should be based on the formulation, although the formulation may change in the light of developments or new information gained during the intervention. So, for example, the formulation of the withdrawn elderly man noted earlier may be that he has become depressed as a result of growing isolation, as well as his belief that he no longer has any value as an older person, and that some form of CBT might be implemented to help him. If a psychodynamic model was considered to be more helpful in reaching the formulation, the intervention that might be chosen could be some of life review, allowing the man to gain a better understanding of his relationships and values. On the other hand, assessment might reveal some neuropsychological impairment such as dementia, in which case intervention might involve discussing the likely process and outcome of his disorder with him and with his relatives, as well as referring him on for other possible treatments or services. Any of these interventions are tests of the provisional hypotheses contained in the formulation and are subject to modification in the light of experience and new information

Interventions do not just involve individual clients, but could also include training of others, such as staff, relatives, and carers. An important role of clinical psychologist is often the provision of psychological knowledge though teaching, or the development of psychological skills through supervision and consultation. So, for example, the psychologist may have been asked to contribute to the treatment of a young woman with anorexia, but after assessment and formulation, might decide that the most appropriate form of intervention is to offer supervision to the dietician who had already made a good relationship with the client, and was eager to implement a psychologically based treatment programme. Likewise much work with children may most effectively be carried out by parents, although with help and directive guidance from the clinical psychologist.

Evaluation is a crucial and integral part of the clinical psychologist's work, which takes place both during and after intervention. Both the effectiveness of intervention, and any ongoing needs, may require evaluation, possibly by repeating measures used at the assessment stage, or maybe by devising new measures, such as satisfaction questionnaires, or by interviewing participants. A related but highly important activity is that of *research*. As stated in the Benchmarks 'research includes the on-going evaluation of assessment, formulation and intervention in relation to specific services provided. It also includes explorations of psychological processes and outcomes (basic research), the development and evaluation of specific psychological interventions (primary research) and the consolidation and evaluation of primary research (secondary research)'. Hence the clinical psychologist may go further than evaluating the effectiveness of specific interventions or services, to an investigation of the underlying psychological issues and how they operate, hence being able to contribute to the development of theory and new models for intervention.

Communication competence also plays a central part in all aspects of a clinical psychologists' work. This includes writing reports for service users and their families, and to professional staff such as doctors or community mental health teams. It is important that psychologists feel comfortable when communicating with others, both via direct face-to-face communication, and via all forms of electronic communication to individual clients. Equally important is the ability to teach and present information to families or carers, as well as to disseminate research findings through publication or through discussion.

When more senior, most clinical psychologists will at some point be asked to contribute to the running of services, and hence will need to develop managerial skills and the ability to represent clinical psychology beyond the confines of the discipline itself. Most clinical psychologists will also be asked to supervise others, especially trainee clinical psychologists, so it is important that psychologists have the ability to explain what they are doing and why, to a variety of audiences.

The environment within which clinical psychologists work

Any professional group working within a health and social care system should primarily be concerned about identifying the needs of the people they are likely to be asked to help. Historically the needs of individuals using health care services were defined primarily by their diagnosis. It is now accepted however that from a psychological point of view, a medical diagnosis does not necessarily define the problems an individual will face at any point in time. An excellent example of the implications of this shift in perspective is the way in which clinical psychologists working with those with psychotic conditions now focus on the presenting problems of those people, and see experiences such as delusions and hearing voices as exaggerations of mental variations to which we are all liable. This approach has been carefully argued by Richard Bentall, in his recent book *Madness Explained* (2003).

When clinical psychologists assessed most people following referral by another person, usually a doctor, they were protected from facing the whole range of problems in a local community that fell outside their area of competence. The way in which health care problems are successively 'filtered' as the person with them passes from one professional to another has been well described by Goldberg and Huxley. They point out that before a problem is ever presented for professional care, the person themselves will have tried to understand what is happening, in the light of their own knowledge and experience. If they cannot understand the problem on their own, they are next most likely to approach a friend, or maybe read a magazine article, or nowadays try the Internet. If they still cannot understand the problem and make it better, they may then approach their family doctor, who may treat the condition directly, possibly with input from a colleague within the local primary care team, or who may refer on to a specialist if it is apparent that specialist help is needed.

Clinical psychologists are now potentially faced directly with the whole range of levels of need illustrated by this sequence. This then raises an ethical dilemma, that of how best to respond to the person with a problem in front of them, and how best to design their practice and assign their time so that their skills are used most effectively to meet the needs of the local population. The latter option may suggest working with those at the earliest stage of a condition, in order to prevent further deterioration, or may indicate working with the most serious and complex problems. It may also suggest working in particular localities, where there are high levels of social deprivation, for example. Indices of social deprivation take account of differential levels of over-crowding, unemployment, and single-parent families, and are known to be associated with variations in need for psychological and social help.

Perhaps then the most important aspect of a clinical psychologist's working environment is the local pattern of population and individual need, relevant to their area of work. Precisely because clinical psychologists are a scarce and expensive resource, the way in which psychologists assign their resources to provide a service over the whole spectrum of need from primary and secondary prevention, through treatment and rehabilitation to possibly terminal care, and provide services to communities most in need, is now a major issue. Psychologists can themselves contribute to a better understanding of that need, by the use of systematic assessments of need.

A second aspect of a psychologist's environment is the local health and social care system. In Britain this will be determined mainly by the public NHS care system—both primary care and specialist care—and by local authority services, especially the local education, social care, and housing services. These are increasingly jointly planned and commissioned, and local service commissioners will also arrange the provision of some services from local independent or voluntary bodies, such as the provision of day services for people with a learning disability. While the NHS is run according to current government policies, the way in which these policies are applied locally varies substantially, according to local histories of, for example, the quality of a particular hospital or current financial pressures. For those in contact with a psychologist who have financial needs arising from unemployment, or disability, or family circumstances, welfare benefits are available, administered by a national agency. About 16% of total health expenditure in Britain is private, but the proportion of private expenditure in areas related to the work of clinical psychologists is considerably smaller.

There is now substantial variation in the way in which psychologists may be employed within the NHS. They may be employed directly by a Primary Care Trust, by a Care Trust—which is a formal partnership between local health and social care agencies—or by a provider Trust, which itself may be either a general medical Trust or a specialist mental health Trust. Within any one of these Trusts they may be employed within a distinct clinical psychology department, within a more inclusive psychological therapies service (inside which clinical psychologists and assistant psychologists are usually the largest group), within a generic therapists service, or directly within a single unit, such as a pain clinic, or a medium secure unit. However, whatever the exact management relationships, a psychologist will usually belong to a grouping of psychologists and will normally have access to senior colleagues for supervision. If the psychologist is employed by an independent healthcare company, or working privately as an independent practitioner, they may well have some links to other local psychologists.

In all these circumstances, the immediate colleagues of a psychologist are a major determinant of the support and satisfaction they receive in their work. The colleagues may be other psychologists, or may be other members of the multidisciplinary team of which they are a member, including social workers, nurses, occupational therapists, physiotherapists and teachers, as well as medical colleagues. Other colleagues will include a manager (the psychologist may of course be the manager of their own team), the person who is clinically supervising them (who may be a psychological therapist from another profession of origin), and often a trainee or assistant psychologist. The more the psychologist and their colleagues know and understand the resources available within their locality, and can work effectively with partner agencies and teams, the better they will help their clients.

The personal impact of being a clinical psychologist

The account of clinical psychology so far has distanced practice from the personal impact of that practice on the practitioner. Helping people in distress is socially valued, and there is personal satisfaction in seeing recovery and improvement in those with whom you work. Alongside those positive aspects of clinical work, being with, let alone working with, people who are themselves distressed, in pain, or disturbed is personally demanding. What then does it feel like to be a clinical psychologist, not just for a year or so, but for the duration of a career?

Being an effective clinician in any profession requires a number of attributes. The central skill expected from users of healthcare services is that they are competent to do their job. This implies both technical knowledge and possession of a set of skills. Those skills are usually assumed to include interpersonal and communication skills—a good 'bedside manner', a term still used even when a profession does not see people in bed! It is now recognized that knowledge, and the formal competencies required to treat people effectively, need regular updating to take account of new discoveries in both diagnosis (or problem formulation) and treatment. Another important attribute is the ability to manage the emotional and personal impact of this type of work, and that a key aspect of an effective clinician is the ability to sustain interest, commitment, and engagement.

The personal demands of being a member of one of the caring professions have been described over many years. Studies of doctors and nurses, the two largest identified professional groups in health care, have consistently shown that these medical professionals have a higher level of sickness and stress-related conditions than other members of the working population. Some of that sickness is directly related to the working environment of individual staff, such as high rates of low back pain in nurses and physiotherapists and others who regularly lift and move patients in the course of their work. Students in health care professions are also at risk, facing not only the usual challenges of their age-group as they leave home for the first time and meet the demands of academic study, but also facing the reality of their chosen profession, when inevitably some will realize that reality does not meet their expectations.

With the realization of those demands have come responses of a number of forms (Firth-Cozens and Payne, 1999). Encouraging early self-identification of stress is one primary preventive measure. Reduction of stress levels in the working environment can be achieved, perhaps by increasing autonomy and clarifying work role relationships. Sound general personal management practices such as regular appraisals and positive management of caseloads and workloads are obviously central. Setting up accessible workplace counselling schemes may also be helpful. An interesting idea is that of 'innovative coping', where groups of workers themselves devise strategies that are likely to work in their setting. This approach of course assumes that the workers have the discretion and authority to then implement those strategies.

Clinical psychologists are not immune from emotional pressures. Eysenck strongly advocated in 1949 that clinical psychologists should primarily be scientists and that clinical psychology should not involve a training in therapy, but that was before the major shift to a therapeutic role for the profession which developed from the 1960s. The selection procedures for clinical psychologists in Britain now mean that trainees are on average older than trainees in most health professions, and that virtually all trainees will have had some direct contact with those with health and social needs before selection, as demanded by the training courses. As recognized in the section about training, training courses increasingly recognize those demands, and typically offer a range of forms of support during training that may include a personal supervisor alongside clinical supervisors, 'buddy-systems' linking new with more experienced trainees, and opportunities for personal therapy.

More generally, a widening appreciation of the concept of reflective practice is helping clinical psychologists to acknowledge the demands of their work. This requires the ability to reflect self-awareness, honesty, and insight into one's own values, attitudes, and feelings. A special issue of Clinical Psychology (Cushway and Gatherer, 2003) was devoted to exploring the application of reflective practice ideas in clinical psychology. This offered many examples of how clinical psychologists feel about their work, including:

- coping for weeks—or months—with a concern for a young woman with a severe eating disorder who has a life-threateningly low body weight;
- being under pressure in a new job to demonstrate your own skills when disparaging remarks have been made about your predecessor;
- awareness that we may achieve vicarious healing through our patient's struggles;
- not wanting to hear problems presented to us that are so close to the problems we are ourselves grappling with;
- pleasure when an elderly patient returns home after many weeks in hospital;
- sharing the shock and confusion of a team when a long-term service user, known to most of the team, has unexpectedly taken his or her own life;
- the satisfaction of implementing a new care-planning scheme in a unit and seeing the interest of recently trained staff when implementation had initially been sabotaged by a senior staff member.

We are in a collaborative journey with users, and especially for psychologists working in the mental health field, challenging the 'them-and-us' barrier to forge a meaningful alliance between personal and professional expertise can in fact lead to a position of safe uncertainty, which is paradoxically more adaptive than a position of safe certainty supported by a supposed knowledge base. This position is well illustrated in the writings of Rufus May (2001), himself both a clinical psychologist and a service user. He sees psychology services, with their emphasis on understanding experience and collaborative approaches, as being well placed to meet this challenge. An important aspect of coming to terms with the demands of the job, and developing innovative coping methods that work for you, is therefore to see yourself as being subject to the same pressures as those who use your services. It also follows that, from the beginning of training, it is important to identify what feeds and sustains you as well as that which drains you.

Conclusion

It is hoped that this book will serve as an informative and helpful introduction to clinical psychology as it is practiced today, particularly in Britain. The book also aims to look to the future. Any discipline that holds as fundamental its responsiveness to human distress and well-being as does the profession of clinical psychology, must position the human qualities of ethical practice and sensitivity as its central core and this is likely to be unchanging. Nevertheless, the other key aspect of clinical psychology, its commitment to the scientist practitioner approach, means that the precise content and form of the profession will always be evolving, as evidence and theories change. Hence many of the activities and approaches described here have developed and grown since the first edition of this book, and the roles of psychologists and their working contexts have broadened and deepened, as could be seen by a successive reading of the first three editions of this book. It is immensely encouraging for us to have witnessed the evolution of the profession over this period and it will be fascinating to see how it develops in future years. We greatly hope that this book will contribute to the interest and enthusiasm of not only those who may be thinking about entering the profession but also to those who simply want to know a little more about it.

References

Bentall, R. (2003). *Madness Explained*. London: Penguin.

Cushway, D. and Gatherer, A. (2003). Reflective practice. *Clinical Psychology*, special issue, **27**, July.

Firth-Cozens, J. and Payne, R. (1999). *Stress in Health Professionals*. Chichester: Wiley.

May, R. (2001). Crossing the them and us barriers: An inside perspective on user involvement in clinical psychology. *Clinical Psychology*, **150**, 14–17.

Quality Assurance Agency, Clinical Psychology Benchmark Statements (2004). QAA www.qua.ac.uk/academicinfrastructure/benchmark/health/clinicalpsychology.asp.

Rose, N. (1999). *Governing the Soul*. London: Free Association Books.

Further reading

Butler, G. and McManus, F. (1998). *Psychology: A very short introduction*. Oxford: Oxford University Press.

Cheshire, K. and Pilgrim, D. (2004). *An Short Introduction to Clinical Psychology*. Sage: Newbury Park, CA.

Fleming, I. and Steen, L. (2004). *Supervision and Clinical Psychology*. Hove: Brunner-Routledge.

Hall, J.N., Llewelyn, S., and Lavender, T. (2002). A history of clinical psychology in Britain: Some impressions and reflections. *History and Philosophy of Psychology*, **4**, 32–48.

Knight, A. (2004). *How to Become a Clinical Psychologist*. Hove: Brunner-Routledge.

Chapter 2

Working in primary health care

John Cape and Yvonne Millar

Introduction

Today, many clinical psychologists can be found working within primary health care settings. This chapter concerns this development, and explores some of the issues raised by it. Health policy, in the United Kingdom and internationally, has increasingly emphasized the role of primary care and psychologists have recognized the importance of playing their part at this first point of contact in the healthcare system. Likewise, the potential of clinical psychology here has been recognized, and it seems highly likely that this trend will continue to grow in the coming years.

What is primary health care?

A distinction is commonly made between primary care, secondary care, and tertiary care services. Primary care services are those that people can access directly, without needing a referral from a professional in order to be seen in the service. Family doctors or general practitioners (GPs), health visitors, and sexual health clinics are all open-access primary heath care services where people can make an appointment to be seen directly. There are also primary care services outside health care, which people can contact directly, such as social services and community services. Secondary health care services such as hospital consultants and specialist mental health professionals cannot be contacted directly in Britain. Patients need to be referred by a health professional, usually the GP. Tertiary services are highly specialized services such as specialist cancer centres and adolescent inpatient units, which require a referral from a consultant or other secondary care service.

In the United Kingdom and most Western countries, primary health care normally refers to services based around the GP or family doctor and associated health professionals including practice nurses, health visitors, and district nurses, who provide open-access care for a very wide range of problems, and act as gatekeepers to other health services. These characteristics shape the role of psychologists working in primary health care. Like GPs they have to be generalists—able to respond to a range of problems. Like GPs they have to assess and determine whether to treat the problems themselves or to refer on to other services.

Primary health care is locally based and part of a local community. The family doctor, like the local minister and publican, is a key figure in stories and TV dramas of local community life. Modern primary health care is linked with a network of local community organizations. Links with local statutory social care services are essential in order to provide coherent health and social care, for example for people with dementia living at home and for older people with physical disabilities. Links with key local voluntary organizations ensure that primary health care can put people in touch with local befrienders, bereavement services, and other visiting and support services. Psychologists working in primary health care accordingly also link up with local community organizations. In recent years in the United Kingdom, the Sure Start early intervention initiative has led to a large number of psychologists working with local voluntary Sure Start organizations providing support to parents and young children, linked with local primary health care services. There is a significant overlap between psychology in primary health care and community psychology.

Because of the central role of primary health care as a gatekeeper to other services and its overview of the health care needs of its patients, health policy in the United Kingdom in recent years has given primary care an increasingly prominent role in the commissioning of other services. GPs and others in primary health care have been given responsibility for deciding how funding should be spent on secondary and tertiary health care services. This includes options to fund new services in primary care rather than referring to secondary care services. Psychologists in primary care can contribute to this commissioning role.

Problems presenting in primary health care

Primary health care deals with all ages from babies to very old people, for a huge range of health and human problems. People come asking for help for physical, psychological, and social problems and GPs, in their training, are encouraged to view all problems as having physical, psychological, and social dimensions. Problems range from self-limiting problems such as minor colds and minor anxieties to severe long-term life threatening problems such as severe heart disease and suicidal depression. Even when people are seen in a specialist outpatient service, they will also usually continue to see their GP for the same and other problems.

Multiple problems are common in primary health care with all varieties of complex interactions between different problems. For example, a man comes for a routine follow-up appointment with his GP to monitor diabetes, he has had longstanding marital problems the GP is aware of, he tells the GP on this occasion that he is depressed and also has had a chest infection for two weeks he cannot seem to throw off. What are the relationships between these different problems and what should the GP focus on in the 10-min consultation? Pragmatically the GP has to make decisions to focus on certain problems and ignore others, on the limited information available. Knowing the patient can and will return at a future date means the GP and patient will have a further opportunity to review and focus on other problems if needed. This characteristic way of working is shared by psychologists in primary health care, having to make choices of what to focus on in the context of greater time constraints than psychologists in secondary care. But, just as in the case of meeting the GP, it is easier for people to return and see the psychologist at a future date by virtue of the psychologist being based in primary health care.

The way people present problems in primary health care often differs from secondary care. People come feeling unwell, ill, with various physical, emotional, and social concerns, rather than with a specific focused problem. For example, a woman with a 6-month-old baby tells her GP she feels unwell, keeps getting bladder infections, has back pain, feels exhausted, her baby never seems to sleep, and that she is worried about the baby. Over a few appointments, the GP listens to her concerns, investigates her back pain and tests her urine for bladder infections, talks to her about being depressed and then refers her to a support group for women with postnatal depression run by a psychologist. By the time of the referral she has begun to talk about herself as having postnatal depression and this is what she tells the psychologist. Michael Balint (1964) described this process many years ago as people presenting with unorganized illness and the family doctor creating organized illness, implying there might have been alternative ways for the family doctor and patient to characterize and make sense of the patient's concerns. Primary health care shapes the ways that problems are described and classified. Sometimes the description and classification may be unhelpful as when patients' concerns are characterized as either physical problems (e.g. a 'real' pain from physical dysfunction) or psychological problems (an 'imaginary' pain for psychological reasons) rather than that all problems have physical, psychological, and social dimensions.

Because of these differences, diagnostic classification systems developed for secondary care are not always best suited to primary care. 'Mixed anxiety and depression' is the most common adult mental health problem in primary care, but does not appear in standard mental health diagnostic systems. Problems of 'major depressive disorder', 'panic disorder', 'generalized anxiety disorder' and other standard adult mental health diagnoses are certainly seen in primary care, but not as commonly as 'mixed anxiety and depression', which is not the same as some combination of the others. Expanded mental health classification systems for primary care have therefore been developed to better characterize problems in primary health care.

Most health problems are only seen in primary health care with a minority being referred on and seen in secondary health care. In the United Kingdom only about 10% of adults with mental health problems are seen in secondary care. Psychologists and counsellors working in primary health care see some others, but still the majority of people with mental health problems simply see their family doctor, health visitor, district nurse, or other core primary health care professional. The pyramid in Figure 2.1 represents everybody with a mental health problem. People in tier 1 are those who just see their GP, health visitor, or other core member of the primary health care team. As 90% of the population visit their GP at least once a year, there are only very few people who are not seen in tier 1. Tier 2 represents those seen by specialist staff such as psychologists and counsellors whose role is to support tier 1 staff in primary health care. Tier 3 and tier 4 are respectively secondary care mental health services and specialist tertiary services. This tiered model is the

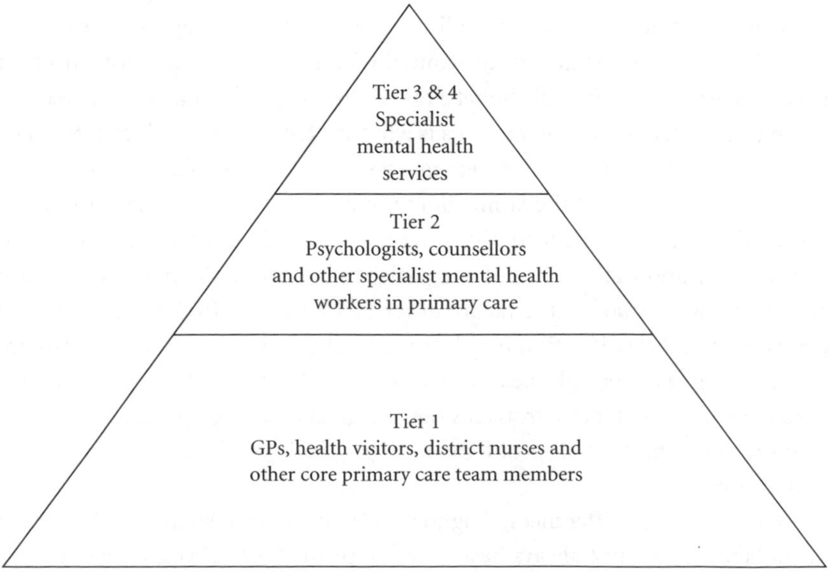

Fig. 2.1 Tiers of care for people with mental health problems.

standard way in the United Kingdom of describing different levels of child and adolescent mental health services starting from tier 1 (GP and health visitor) to tier 4 (e.g. specialist adolescent inpatient unit). It is also used increasingly to describe adult mental health services.

In an ideal world, one would expect tier 1 to comprise the common, less severe, less complex problems, with increasing levels of severity and complexity of problems as the levels increase to tier 4. This is in accordance with the 'stepped care' principle that people should receive the least intensive treatment first and, only when this has failed, be referred on for the next level (Bower and Gilbody, 2005). The reality is rather different. Many individuals and families with severe and complex problems are seen only in tier 1 and tier 2. They may perceive secondary mental health services negatively and refuse to attend or may consider them inaccessible in terms of location or in terms of expectation of keeping regular appointments. Or they may have received treatment previously in secondary mental health services, this has not been successful, and they have been discharged. In addition, many people with less severe and less complex problems may be seen in tier 3 and tier 4, because they are articulate and request referral or because their GP feels a special empathy for their problems and circumstances and wishes to make sure they get the 'best' treatment. These factors lead to white, educated, professional people being represented disproportionately in tier 3 psychological therapy services.

Primary care also sees a large number of people with longstanding, chronic health problems. In developed economies, an increasing proportion of health care relates to chronic diseases and conditions such as diabetes, arthritis, and coronary heart disease. Within mental health, schizophrenia, bipolar disorder (manic depression), and some forms of depression are chronic conditions, which may have periods of getting worse and better but are not 'cured'. Many people with chronic health problems will just be seen in primary health care except when they become acutely worse when they are admitted to hospital, while for others both primary care and secondary care are involved in 'shared care' of their condition. A developing role for psychologists in primary health care is in establishing and participating in programmes of care for people with all types of chronic conditions.

Organization and staffing of primary health care

In the United Kingdom and most Western countries, primary health care organization normally centres on a group practice of GPs, commonly in partnerships of 2–8 GPs. Whether the practice is just a single-handed GP or a group practice, a primary health care team supports the practice, a team that is larger or smaller depending on the size of the practice. In the United Kingdom, this team will comprise both staff employed by the group practice and staff who are employed by the local primary care trust or other local NHS body. Staff employed by the practice will include receptionists, secretaries, practice nurses, and a practice manager. Staff employed by the local NHS body will include health visitors (working primarily with mothers and young children) and district nurses (working primarily with older and housebound people). The health visitors and district nurses may be entirely based in the practice or may have office bases in separate health or community centres and cover more than one GP practice. In addition, there may be physiotherapists, podiatrists, welfare rights workers, social workers, stop smoking advisers, hospital doctors running outposted clinics, and a range of other staff who come occasionally to the practice and provide services to the practice's patients.

Clinical psychologists working in primary health care vary in the extent to which they integrate with the primary health care team. Some psychologists work, in effect, as attached staff to the primary health care team and are seen as key members of the primary health care team. This occurs especially where a psychologist spends several sessions (half-days) a week in a large group practice (as there are fewer clinical psychologists than GPs, it would be highly unusual for a full-time psychologist to only work with one GP practice). Some clinical psychologists will be relatively peripheral members of several primary health care teams, seeing patients in each for a session or two per week. Some clinical psychologists will work closely with certain primary health care team members and less with others. For example, clinical psychologists working with young children and families in primary care will have frequent contact with health visitors but less contact with GPs.

Clinical psychologists will usually not be the only specialist psychological or mental health staff working in primary health care. In the United Kingdom, many group practices have a counsellor or counselling psychologist working in the practice from anything from half a day to a few days a week. In some primary health care teams there may be attached community mental health nurses or other attached staff from community mental health teams. Also in England, since 2004, as a result of a government initiative, there are now graduate primary care mental health workers attached to many primary care mental health teams (Department of Health, 2003). These workers both see patients and help the practice and primary health care team with designing and monitoring systems of care for patients with mental health problems.

In Europe, Australia, and North America there may also be other mental health staff in addition to clinical psychologists. In the Netherlands there is a long tradition of social workers in primary care, while in the United States, a variety of mental health nurses, mental health social workers, and other mental health and behavioural trained staff may be employed. In Canada, some provinces have invested heavily in the provision of counsellors in primary care. In Australia, most of the funding of allied health professions under the Better Outcomes in Mental Health initiative has gone to psychologists.

Who do clinical psychologists see in primary health care?

Emotional, psychological, and behavioural problems are the most common problems seen. In adults these include depression, anxiety, panic, phobias, obsessive-compulsive problems, eating disorders, and problems in social, work, family, and intimate relationships. In very young children the most common problems seen by clinical psychologists are sleep, feeding and behavioural problems, while in older children anxiety and behavioural problems predominate. Clinical psychologists in primary health care see the full range of severity of mental health problems, but they generally refer people with more severe mental health problems, such as schizophrenia, on to secondary care mental health services.

Physical health problems such as diabetes, arthritis, and coronary heart disease are less commonly seen by clinical psychologists in British, European, and Australian primary health care, despite the important role that they could play in helping with these problems (see Chapter 12). This is more common in the United States, where clinical psychologists also frequently provide interventions for smoking and obesity, both major public health problems for primary health care.

In the United Kingdom, there are usually separate primary care psychology services for adults and for children, linking with adult or child and adolescent secondary care mental health services respectively. Occasionally there will also be a separate primary care psychology service for older people. Accordingly, it is rare in the United Kingdom for a clinical psychologist in primary health care to work with all age groups, other than that all psychologists often include other family members in a clients' treatment. Clinical psychologists working in primary health care in the United States are more likely to work across the age range.

Assessment and triage

Assessment and triage are where a psychologist meets with a client for the first time, finds out about their problems, and advises the client and primary care professionals about what best to do. The client may have been referred by their GP or other primary care professional or may, in some services, have referred themselves. At this initial meeting the psychologist asks about the current problems that concern the client, about problems in the past and about their family and life circumstances, but spends most of the time just listening. At the end the psychologist gives an opinion about the problems and about what, if anything, might help. Sometimes a second appointment may be needed to complete the assessment, but, with time being at a premium, this happens less frequently than in secondary care. Sometimes the psychologist may need to obtain information from other services between appointments, for example, when seeing children, from the child's school or nursery.

In the assessment the psychologist tries to create a climate where the client feels able to talk freely, both to obtain fuller information about the problems and to build a relationship where the client is more likely to trust the psychologist. As the assessment proceeds, the psychologist attempts to build an understanding—what are the key problems, their severity, what might have caused them, what might be maintaining them. Other chapters (see Chapters 3 and 4) describe the kinds of models of understanding or formulation of problems that are used by clinical psychologists. In primary care, the key understanding the psychologist attempts to obtain in the initial assessment is that which will inform the decision as to what, if anything, would best help. If early in the assessment it becomes clear that a secondary care or educational (school-based) or voluntary sector or some other service would best help the client, then collecting further information is not needed. The time is better spent in discussing with the client the reasons why a referral on might be in their best interest, and in helping them decide whether this is the option they want to take.

Triage, the process of deciding how and where, if at all, the client would best be helped, is thus a key role of clinical psychologists in primary health care. They need, from their assessment, to form an opinion as to whether the problems are likely to improve anyway without any intervention/treatment and as to whether there are treatments or other interventions that are likely to help. They also need information about the availability of treatments or other resources locally, including community resources that might help. One of the options that clinical psychologists will consider will be providing further advice, intervention, or treatment themselves, but this will be only one option.

In advising clients following assessment, primary care clinical psychologists are guided by the principles of minimal needed treatment ('stepped care') and informed choice. The principle of minimal needed treatment is that the least intensive treatment, with fewest disruptions to the person's life, should be tried first before more intensive and disruptive treatments, if it has a reasonable chance of success. Thus, a psychologist might suggest the client try a self-help approach first, and cognitive therapy later if it is not successful. The principle of informed choice is that clients are given full information about different options and are helped to choose.

Case Study

Mr Green was a 38-year-old single man referred by his GP after becoming anxious and depressed. Over a few months he had been feeling progressively more tired and losing enjoyment. Then one weekend he began feeling extremely anxious about his health, preoccupied with thoughts that he was dying, couldn't sleep, felt he couldn't cope, and stopped work. After a month being off work his GP prescribed antidepressants and 2 months later referred him to the clinical psychologist who attended the GP practice. By the time he saw the clinical psychologist 6 weeks later he was feeling less depressed and anxious and had arranged to return to work the following week. At assessment, he described a previous time when he had been depressed and off work for 2 months and was concerned about getting depressed again in the future. He also talked of his concerns about being single and past relationships not having worked out. The clinical psychologist discussed three options with him. First, a brief cognitive behavioural treatment at the GP practice looking at what happened when he got depressed and anxious and how he could prevent relapses. Second, a referral for group therapy where he could explore his difficulties with relationships. Third, to read self-help literature for depression and anxiety and to return in future if he felt depressed and anxious again, and be seen then for treatment. He selected to do some reading himself and see how he got on, which was also the minimal needed treatment as he was improving anyway.

Education and facilitation of self-help

Educating clients about the nature of problems and guiding them in self-help is a key role of clinical psychologists in primary health care. Although also used in secondary care as part of other treatments, in primary health care these are frequently the sole or initial intervention in a 'stepped care' approach, with more intensive treatment offered later if they do not help. Education and facilitation of self-help may involve a single meeting or a brief series of 2–4 meetings. Helping people to understand the problems that have given rise to concern and distress can enable them to feel less worried and anxious, and to feel they can deal with problems that previously have felt unbearable. This can be especially helpful for people with anxiety problems.

Case Study

Mr Ahmed, a Turkish speaking man, through an interpreter described panic attacks in which he felt he could not breathe and was frightened that he would collapse and die. The nature of panic attacks (see Chapter 4) is that the bodily effects of the panic attacks (e.g. tightness of chest, feeling dizzy) cause people to be frightened, which further exacerbates the panic. The clinical psychologist explained, through the interpreter, that blood pressure rises during a panic attack and therefore it was very unlikely that he would collapse as fainting is usually due to low blood pressure and insufficient oxygen reaching the brain. He also explained that breathing is automatic and will not stop if the chest muscles are tensed and tight. At the second appointment, Mr Ahmed reported fewer and less intense panic attacks and reported that when he had been feeling panicky he had said to himself that he would not stop breathing, he would not collapse, and would not die.

New ways of understanding problems can also suggest alternative and more successful ways of dealing with the problems. These alternatives were not apparent until the problems are understood in a different way.

Case Study

Mrs Smith made an appointment to see the psychologist at her local health centre at the suggestion of her health visitor. Her 2-year-old daughter would not settle to sleep at night. Whenever she or her partner left her daughter, the child would cry, so they would stay in her room to reassure her until she fell asleep and then tiptoe quietly out. But then she would wake, and they would have to return. Many times they gave up and brought her to their bed where she slept undisturbed. The psychologist explained that their attempts to deal with the problem, by staying in the room when their daughter cried, meant that she never got used to being on her own and to learn that this was nothing to be frightened about as her parents would reappear in the morning. With this new understanding of the problem, Mrs Smith was able to see a different more helpful way how she and her partner could respond to her daughter not settling at night—allowing her to cry, returning periodically to reassure her they were still there, but then leaving her on her own. At a visit 4 weeks later, Mrs Smith reported that they had carried this out, had found it initially hard to leave and to listen to their daughter crying, but over a few nights she settled and went to sleep more quickly. For the last 2 weeks she had not cried at all when they left and had gone to sleep after only a few minutes.

In this example, Mrs Smith was able herself to devise alternative more helpful ways of dealing with the problem, following the psychologist helping her to understand the problem in a different way. More commonly the psychologist contributes suggestions and different ways that the client might approach the problem and helps the client come up with a plan of action. In facilitating self-help, the psychologist's goal is for clients to learn alternative strategies of managing problems and to devise plans of action themselves. The brief intervention ends when the client has learned some alternative self-help approaches, rather than when they are 'better', although often there will be initial signs that the client's new approaches are helping.

Clinical psychologists frequently make use of a range of self-help books, leaflets, and other self-help materials to help people become more skilled at helping themselves. Some will be handouts which they or their colleagues have prepared themselves, while others will be commercially available books or materials. Such materials, read by clients between visits to the psychologist and/or after they have stopped seeing the psychologist, extend and reinforce their understanding and ways of dealing with their problems.

Education and facilitation of self-help is well suited to delivery in groups. Examples of groups led by clinical psychologists in primary health care are anxiety management groups, and parenting skills groups for parents who are having difficulty managing a range of behaviour problems of their children. In such groups, people obtain benefit from learning from each other in addition to learning from the input of the psychologist. Groups also help people to feel less isolated and alone with their problems.

Primary care psychologists also have a role in providing information and education about psychological issues to groups of people who might be at risk of developing psychological problems, and to the public as a whole in local communities. They may give talks to antenatal and post-natal groups about post-natal depression and how to improve parent–child bonding/attachment, or develop educational materials around suicide for young people, or work with local voluntary organizations on providing information to older people on loss and prevention of depression. Or they may advertise and run groups in community centres targeted at the general public on coping with stress or enhancing self-esteem. In these, the role of the psychologist is to prevent psychological problems and promote psychological health, complementing their usual role with people who already have psychological problems.

Brief psychological treatment

Much psychological treatment carried out by clinical psychologists in primary health care is brief, being abbreviated forms of psychological treatments developed and standard in secondary care (see Chapters 3 and 4). A brief Cognitive Behaviour Therapy (CBT) for adults in primary care is commonly 6–8 meetings, while in secondary care standard CBT is 16–20 meetings. In addition, while in secondary care appointments usually last 50–60 min and are weekly, in primary care they are more variable, from 15 to 60 min and from weekly to monthly. This is for two reasons. First, some problems in primary care are less severe and less complex and do not need the same length and intensity of treatment (Clark *et al.*, 1999). Second, the goals of treatment are more modest—to help people feel more optimistic about being able to deal with problems and/or to have made some progress in dealing with some problems. Once these goals have been achieved, clinical psychologists in primary health care are happy to leave their clients to continue on their own, with an open door to return in the future if needed. In secondary care the goals are commonly more ambitious—to help people substantially overcome problems and often also to help people deal with underlying characteristic ways of thinking or relating to others in order to reduce the possibility of further problems in future. In primary health care, these more ambitious goals are not routinely attempted, on the 'stepped care' principle that many people will make sufficient progress on their own after brief psychological treatment and not need more intensive psychological treatment.

Case Studies

Miss Cavendish was someone whose problem was sufficiently straightforward to be adequately helped in a brief, 6-session psychological treatment over the course of 4 months. She was referred by her GP for depression. She had retired a year previously from her job as school secretary of a primary school. Over the following year she had gradually felt lower and lower, had withdrawn from telephoning and seeing friends, and was now tearful and depressed and thinking of herself as 'useless'. In the first three meetings the clinical psychologist discussed with her the understandable disorientation she had experienced from being at the centre of the busy social world of work to being retired, and how her subsequent withdrawal from friends and thinking of herself as 'useless' had led to a vicious cycle, in which the less she did, the more 'useless' she thought herself to be and the more depressed she felt. They planned together steps she might take to make contact with friends again and ways she could recognize and challenge when she began to think of herself as 'useless'. Over three further meetings, at monthly intervals, she began seeing friends again, joined a ramblers group and went on a short outing with them, progressively thought of herself less as 'useless' and stopped feeling depressed. With her depression being recent, precipitated by the life event of her retirement, and with her being a resourceful person who had never been significantly depressed previously, this brief psychological treatment was sufficient to enable her to recover her previous good humour and zest for social life.

Benjamin, aged 11, had more complex problems but was seen in brief psychological treatment with limited goals. He was referred by his school for low mood and difficult behaviour. Together with his father, Kevin, Benjamin told the clinical psychologist that his mother had died two months previously. Prior to that, Benjamin had lived with his mother, sister, and grandmother. Benjamin had not been happy living with his grandmother, she had always been unkind to him, and after his mother's death, Social Services had decided that Benjamin could not continue to live with his grandmother, as her care of him was inadequate. Benjamin's parents had separated with considerable bad feeling nine years earlier, and Benjamin hardly knew his father. Nevertheless Kevin had offered to provide Benjamin with a home. Benjamin had therefore lost his mother and was separated from his sister, grandmother, and the house where he had always lived, and was living with a man he did not know, who had no experience of parenting. Over six sessions the clinical psychologist talked to Benjamin and Kevin about the huge adjustment they were both making. They looked together at household rules and parenting strategies to help Kevin find his feet as a father. The psychologist helped Kevin to engage with Benjamin's school and negotiated a plan of how to support Benjamin's better behaviour in school. Kevin wanted help to talk to his son about ordinary every day things and the more difficult topics surrounding the sad death of his mother and the neglectful childhood he had suffered. Having established that Kevin and Benjamin had found a way of communicating with each other, and that Benjamin's behaviour at school was improving and Kevin had more confidence to fulfil his role as a parent, the psychologist discussed how they could get in contact in future for further help if they did not continue to make progress on their own.

Standard and intermittent treatment

Like GPs, the work of clinical psychologists in primary health care is not all brief: a proportion also involves longer contact, some over many years, as in secondary care settings. They may see adult patients for a 16-session standard length CBT, or for 20-sessions of short-term psychodynamic psychotherapy (see Chapter 4). Other briefer approaches may have been tried first and, when unsuccessful, the clinical psychologist and client then agree to try longer psychological therapy. Or it might have been apparent at assessment that a briefer treatment would not help and a standard length psychological therapy was what the client and psychologist agreed at the outset. The standard psychological therapies carried out in primary care are no different from those carried out in secondary care, except that it may be more convenient for the client to attend at their local GP's surgery. It is also usually easier for the primary care psychologist to liaise with the GP about the client's treatment, which can be necessary when the GP is also prescribing medication such as antidepressants.

The other way that clinical psychologists see people over longer periods of time is when people choose to return. A key feature of primary care, as noted previously, is that it is easy for people to access. Clinical psychologists encourage patients to return if needed, this being one of the factors allowing psychological treatments to be briefer. This leads to a characteristic 'intermittent' treatment pattern in primary care, where people see the clinical psychologist for a period of time, then there is a gap, then they return for another meeting or series of meetings. Sometimes this pattern extends over many years. Such intermittent treatment is especially useful for people with chronic problems which can be ameliorated with psychological help and support, but which will not 'get better'. Intermittent treatment is also often the only kind of treatment possible for people who have difficulty, for various reasons, in engaging with and sticking with psychological treatment.

Case Study

Mr Brown had difficulty in engaging with treatment and was seen in intermittent treatment over several years. He was initially referred by his GP who was concerned about how angry he was, and about his telling the GP that he feared he might harm himself or somebody else. The GP had referred him to the community mental health team, but he did not attend his appointment and had then asked the crisis team to visit him at home, but he always arranged to be out or not answer the door. He agreed to see the clinical psychologist at his GP's practice, but did not attend his appointment. However, 2 months later he telephoned the clinical psychologist who spoke with him personally and arranged to see him the following week. He then came and described difficulties throughout his life, including depression and anger in the past 2 years, that he kept losing his temper, was worried that he might harm someone seriously and also thought about killing himself. He had a criminal past, including violent assaults, so knew what he was capable of. He had become more depressed and angry following the serious illness of an aunt, who was the one person throughout his life who he felt had been consistently concerned about him. His father had been mostly absent and his mother abusive. He felt humiliated by what he experienced as a child and was very distressed talking to the psychologist about this. The psychologist asked him how it felt to talk, and how he would find it hard to come back and talk further about how to deal with his difficulties. He said he thought it would be difficult and indeed did not return for his next appointment. However, 3 months later he got in contact again and a pattern developed of his attending once or twice, then stopping, then getting back in contact again some months later. Following the death of his aunt 4 years later, he made contact in a particularly distressed and agitated state, thinking of killing himself and frightened of killing others, and on this occasion attended five appointments before not coming again. He did not make further contact with the psychologist after this, but the GP, who continued to see him for treatment of asthma, reported that he was more settled, had less frequent violent and suicidal thoughts, and was living with a previous girlfriend and their son.

Throughout the years of intermittent treatment with Mr Brown, the psychologist and GP had many discussions about him. At times these were just brief half-minute updates, at times they were longer discussions occasionally including other members of the primary health care team also, and the practice link worker from the secondary care community mental health team. The psychologist also had access to the computer medical notes of Mr Brown's consultations with the GP, as she used the common computer note system at this GP practice.

Working in primary health care, clinical psychologists are very rarely the only professional seeing a client. The client is also seeing one or more of the GPs, and maybe the practice nurse and health visitor, or other member of the primary care team. Clinical psychologists in primary health care coordinate their input to clients with other members of the primary health care team, discussing with them or keeping track through the consultation notes of what each is doing. If there are issues that a client wishes to keep confidential, it is possible to do this, but in general there is a sharing of information between members of the primary health care team to provide the best help to a client.

Working with others

A major element of work in primary health care involves working with others. Rather than always working directly with clients themselves, the clinical psychologist works with others to help them provide better care to their clients. Clinical psychologists provide consultation and advice to GPs and other members of the primary health care team about patients they are concerned about, they give teaching and training to primary health care staff, they provide supervision of the work of some staff, and spend time in meetings and liaising with secondary care mental health staff.

Consultation and advice to GPs, health visitors, and other primary health care staff takes place in many forms. It can involve the GP or health visitor popping in to the psychologist's room when the door is open, a quick chat in the reception area, a telephone conversation, or a pre-arranged time to talk about a patient. The clinical psychologist, in whatever time is available, listens, asks questions to clarify the primary health care team member's concern and offers suggestions about how to better understand the patient, and what they might be able to do. To do this, the clinical psychologist needs not only to come to an understanding relatively quickly of the patient's difficulties, but also to have an understanding of the work and roles of the primary health care team member and what is and is not possible to do in that role. The best way for the GP or health visitor to address a patient's problems is not the same as the best way for the clinical psychologist to deal with the same problems. The GP and health visitor have different roles with patients, with distinct time constraints and different skills, and the clinical psychologist needs to think of what would work best for them.

Case Study

Dr Elliott approached the clinical psychologist about a man who was coming to see her twice a week on average with various concerns about his health, including worries about lumps, rashes, irritations, aches and pains, which he thought might signify serious illnesses. Dr Elliott would examine and reassure him, he would go away relieved, but then return a few days later, sometimes worried about the same symptom, sometimes by a new one. The clinical psychologist suggested to the GP that she arrange a regular weekly time to see the patient, tell him he should store up his worries and tell her then, and that he could not see her between these weekly appointments. The psychologist knew of research studies indicating such an approach in general practice could help similar patients for whom gaining reassurance by going to see the doctor for their symptoms relieves anxiety immediately, but they then feel that this is the only way to relieve the anxiety rather than finding other ways to tell themselves that there is nothing really to worry about. Dr Elliott arranged this with the patient and tagged the patient's computer notes so that the receptionists would know not to make an appointment with the patient outside this regular weekly time. Over the course of the following 6 months, Dr Elliott was able to decrease the frequency of regular appointments from weekly, to fortnightly, and then to monthly, and the patient reported feeling less anxious about his health.

As well as consultation and advice, clinical psychologists also provide clinical supervision to primary health care staff. The difference between consultation and supervision is that consultation is a one-off discussion, usually relatively informal, while supervision is a regular arrangement to discuss patients on a more formal basis. In Britain, clinical psychologists working with children often provide supervision to health visitors, particularly of their 'listening visits' to mothers with post-natal depression. These are visits made to mothers identified as depressed after administration of standardized post-natal depression questionnaires. The psychologist on a regular basis meets with the health visitors and listens to their accounts of their 'listening visits' and concerns about the mothers, and provides suggestions and advice. They also sometimes provide supervision to counsellors working in primary care and to graduate primary care mental health workers.

Teaching and training of primary health care staff by clinical psychologists usually takes place in one-off workshops or training days. Many primary care organizations set aside half-days or full days for staff training, to which clinical psychologists contribute. Training may be for GPs on using patient self-help materials in behavioural management of anxiety, for health visitors on working with mothers with post-natal depression, for district nurses on identifying and helping people who are housebound and depressed, and/or for receptionists on dealing with anxious and agitated patients. More extended teaching by psychologists includes training health visitors in listening skills for 'listening visits', training Sure Start home visitors in understanding mental health issues for parents and children, and training GPs in problem-solving therapy or in skills for brief CBT. Some clinical psychologists are involved in the formal training schemes for new GPs and family doctors. In the United Kingdom, this may involve meeting with a small group of GP registrars (doctors undertaking 3-year supervised experience towards qualifying as a GP), each of whom in turn presents a patient or situation which has caused them concern for discussion by others in the group and the psychologist.

In addition to working with primary care staff, clinical psychologists work with secondary care mental health staff, for example, liaising about referrals and about patients who are being seen both in primary and secondary care. They also advise and help secondary care mental health staff to understand how primary care works and what is happening locally.

In discussion with the local community mental health team, a clinical psychologist in primary care discovered the team was very irritated with a particular general practice for referring what were felt to be inappropriate patients and for failing to monitor patients on lithium (a medication for bipolar disorder or manic depression). The clinical psychologist was able to explain that the practice was going through a difficult time, with a senior GP ill and different temporary locum GPs. As a result, the community mental health team allocated a specific community nurse to liaise and work with the practice to improve joint care over this difficult period.

Developing systems of care

Clinical psychologists in primary health care, as they become more experienced, commonly take on roles working with general practices and primary care to develop improved systems of care. This may involve working with a single general practice to improve the system of care of that practice, or across several general practices, or with the wider community. Clinical psychologists may contribute to an initiative led by others or may take the lead themselves.

In one general practice, the clinical psychologist contributed to the development of a register to monitor the practice's adult patients with severe and enduring mental illness. A definition of such patients was agreed, and the practice computer records checked for patients who met the definition. The secondary care community mental health team's records were also checked. For each patient meeting the definition, information was added to the computer records as to whether they were being seen by the community mental health team and the name of the care coordinator for the patient. A recall system was then established, to ensure that a review appointment would be arranged for any patient on the register who had not been seen for 3 months. Further, it was agreed that the community mental health team would send the practice an updated list of the practice's patients under their care every 3 months.

Across another four practices, the clinical psychologist took the lead in establishing an enhanced care system for patients with depression using graduate primary care mental health workers. The clinical psychologist was aware of a growing body of research studies reporting that patients with depression in primary care are helped by having someone telephone or see them for a short period of time after they first see the GP for depression, supporting them with self-help strategies, and encouraging them to take antidepressants if prescribed. The psychologist obtained training materials for two graduate primary care mental health workers, recently recruited. Within the four practices, reminder systems were set up to prompt the GPs to refer newly identified patients with depression to the mental health workers. Under the supervision of the clinical psychologist, the workers contacted each patient and telephoned or met with him or her over five occasions.

In another initiative, a clinical psychologist facilitated the setting up of a self-help group for people with agoraphobia and related problems, working with a national self-help organization. There was no self-help group locally for people with agoraphobia and the psychologist felt her patients could be helped by such a group. It would need to be locally based given the nature of agoraphobia. Two of the clinical psychologist's patients with agoraphobia who had made good progress in part through, by chance, knowing each other and supporting each other's progress, expressed interest in helping others with such problems. The psychologist made contact with the national office and through them the two patients were helped to set up a local group.

Evaluation and research

Does the clinical psychologist in primary health care do any good? Are they helping the patients they see? Are patients with psychological problems receiving adequate care from their general practice? These are important questions that clinical psychologists attempt to answer through evaluation and audit of what they do and of the care provided by a practice, group of practices, or primary care staff.

In terms of their own clinical work, clinical psychologists in primary health care, in common with all clinical psychologists, receive regular clinical supervision from another psychologist or other professionals to oversee and help improve their work. In addition, they periodically audit and evaluate what they are doing and how effective this is. This may involve audiotaping a series of meetings with a patient and having another psychologist or trained person rate what they do against an established 'competency' scale. It may involve the psychologist's patients completing standard questionnaires of severity of their problems before and at the end of treatment, and comparing improvement to normative information. Or it might involve sending patients questionnaires as to what they found useful and not useful about seeing the psychologist.

Audit and evaluation of the care provided by a practice or primary care staff, carried out by clinical psychologists, might include checking how many mothers with post-natal depression are receiving the agreed number of 'listening visits' from their health visitor or checking how many parents of preschool children attending day nurseries, who have been identified by both parents and teachers as having behaviour problems at home and school, have been offered the opportunity to talk with a psychologist about their child's behaviour problems. When an evaluation indicates that care could be improved, the psychologist will discuss this with relevant staff.

An audit after 1 year of the recall and review system for patients on the practice's register of patients with severe and enduring mental illness, mentioned in the previous section, found that a number of patients were not reviewed as they did not come to the review appointment arranged. It was decided that when this happened in future, to discuss the patient at the 6-weekly practice mental health liaison meeting and arrange a home visit from the professional who best knew the patient. An audit the following year found that this had worked and that very few patients had not been reviewed as planned.

Some clinical psychologists in primary care contribute to research about problems in primary care, how the primary system at present works to help or hinder patients, and about how it could better help people. They may lead the research or assist in organizing or providing access to patients for research led by others. For example, one clinical psychologist led a project interviewing GPs to better understand why they refer some patients for psychological help and not other similar patients (Sigel and Leiper, 2004). Other psychologists treated patients in primary care using brief CBT for depression, as part of research comparing the effectiveness of brief counselling, brief CBT, and treatment as usual from the GP (Ward *et al.*, 2001).

Balancing roles—the individual patient and the population

A common dilemma for psychologists is how much time to spend seeing patients directly and how much time to spend in other work—working with others, developing systems, evaluation, and research—which may indirectly help patients. Within primary health care this dilemma is especially acute given the very large number of people with psychological problems. Is the psychologist's time better spent seeing a few more patients or in possibly helping a larger number of patients through working with other primary health care professionals, or developing systems of care? The psychologist's dilemma reflects a core dilemma of all modern primary health care, which attempts both to offer personal care to individual patients and care for a designated population of patients (the population of patients registered with the general practice and its local community). What should the balance be between responding to individual patients' health concerns and developing systems in the practice and with the local community to improve the health of the practice population and community as a whole? The challenge for clinical psychologists in primary health care, together with other primary care colleagues, is in bringing together a skilled highly personal approach to individuals' concerns with a population-based public health approach to the problems of a community.

References

Balint, M. (1964) *The Doctor, His Patient and the Illness*, 2nd edn. London: Pitman Medical.

Bower, P. and Gilbody, S. (2005) Stepped care in psychological therapies: access, effectiveness and efficiency. *British Journal of Psychiatry*, **186**, 11–17.

Clark, D.M., Salkovskis, P.M., Hackmann, A., Wells, A., Ludgate, J., and Gelder, M. (1999). Brief cognitive therapy for panic disorder: A randomized controlled trial. *Journal of Consulting and Clinical Psychology*, **67**, 583–9.

Department of Health (2003). *Fast-Forwarding Primary Care Mental Health—Graduate Primary Care Mental Health Workers*. London: Department of Health.

Sigel, P. and Leiper, R. (2004) GP views of their management and referral of psychological problems: A qualitative study. *Psychology and Psychotherapy: Theory, Research and Practice*, **77**, 279–95.

Ward, E., King, M., Lloyd, M., Bower, P., Sibbald, B., Farrelly, S. *et al.* (2000). Randomised controlled trial of non-directive counselling, cognitive-behaviour therapy, and usual general practitioner care for patients with depression. I: Clinical effectiveness. *British Medical Journal*, **321**, 1383–8.

Further reading

Berger, J. (1997). *A Fortunate Man: The Story of a Country Doctor*. New York: Vantage International.

Bower, P. and Gilbody, S. (2005). Managing common mental health disorders in primary care: Conceptual models and evidence base. *British Medical Journal*, **330**, 839–42.

Burton, M. (1998). *Psychotherapy, Counselling, and Primary Mental Health Care: Assessment for Brief or Longer-Term Treatment*. New York: Wiley.

Goldberg, D. and Huxley, P. (1992). *Common Mental Disorders: A Bio-social Model*. London: Routledge.

Frank, R.G., McDaniel, S.H., Bray, J.H., and Heldring, M. (2002). *Primary Care Psychology*. Washington, DC: American Psychological Association.

Chapter 3

Working with children and young people

Irene Sclare

Introduction

All clinical psychologists undertake training to work with children and young people before qualifying. Currently, approximately 600 clinical psychologists in Britain work with children and young people. Psychological work with this client group requires approaches and methodologies that are tailored to young people's developmental understanding and service needs. Clinical child psychologists work in a variety of child and family service settings, undertaking assessment, psychological therapy, work with parents, staff and carers, research and evaluation, and consultancy. They are trained to apply psychological theory and clinical skills to address complex childhood problems such as anorexia, child abuse, deliberate self harm, and youth crime, as well as to less troubling problems, such as bed-wetting, school refusal, and specific fears and phobias. Applying developmental theory and knowledge of the course of developmental disorders, psychologists also work with children with autism, Attention Deficit with Hyperactivity Disorder (ADHD), and chronic illnesses, such as diabetes or epilepsy.

In order to help reduce the impact of problems on children's lives and on their future well-being in adulthood, psychologists usually try to provide intervention as early as possible in a troubled or vulnerable child or young person's life, and to prevent the problems from recurring. They include parents in this work, teachers, and other professionals, to build families' capacity to manage their child's problems. They therefore draw on their clinical training in adult psychology, forensic mental health, and the psychology of systems as well as child and family mental health.

Psychological problems in childhood and adolescence

Although many children and young people experience significant difficulties in behaviour, feelings, or relationships at home or at school at some stage of their lives, troubled children and young people rarely refer themselves, and only a small proportion get referred for psychological help. Access to child psychologists is usually via teachers, GPs, or a social worker, and parental factors may drive the search for psychological help rather than the severity of the child's problem. Parents who seek psychological or psychiatric help for their child have been shown to be more anxious about the problems and perceive these as more worrying, than parents whose children have similar problems but who do not seek help. Some families may be reluctant to accept help from psychologists and from child and adolescent mental health services (CAMHS) because of perceived stigma and lack of awareness of services. CAMHS has traditionally been provided in clinics and hospitals, with some outreach work. In order to become more accessible to troubled children in need, parents and referrers, many child psychologists, and other CAMHS staff are increasingly working in schools, in multi-agency social service teams concerned with identifying troubled children, and in primary care alongside GPs and health visitors (see Chapter 2).

Prevalence and scope of children's psychological problems

Recent studies from a number of different countries, including the United Kingdom, have shown that between 10 and 20% of children and young people will have severe behavioural, emotional, or relationship problems during childhood that can be classified as *child mental health disorders* (Meltzer *et al.*, 2000). More children and young people develop mental health disorders in socially deprived areas and in communities affected by traumatic events. Children with severe problems are likely to have educational and learning problems, to underachieve, to truant and/or be involved in crime, and they may go on to have problems in adulthood. Problem severity is judged on the basis of the negative effect of the problem on the child and others, if the problem is very hard to manage, and/or has lasted a long time, if it occurs alongside other problems, or is not appropriate for the child's age.

An evaluation of the key influences on problem formation is an essential component of clinical psychology work. Cause and effect can however be hard to disentangle when assessing how to help resolve children's psychological problems. The context in which these problems occur can have a bearing on how the problems are dealt with, and also on the needs to be assessed. For example, children with disabilities have been found to be at increased risk of developing psychological problems. Parents of disabled children have been found to experience high levels of anxiety and depression and to have difficulties managing the child, especially as the child grows to adolescence.

The cause of the increased rate of problems in disabled children could be attributed to the child's neuro-developmental status, which makes it more likely that the child has difficult behaviour, and this creates parental stress. Some parents may be more vulnerable to anxiety and stress than others due to their own personal resources and lack of knowledge of the best way to handle the child's behaviour and needs, and may be less confident in handling the child's disabilities. The problems could also be attributed to the child's social and family context, such as financial pressures, social isolation, or lack of family support, all of which put the child and parent under stress.

Clinical psychologists see individual children and parents in order to work out a treatment plan uniquely tailored to the problem and the influences upon it. Intervention from psychologists can also be provided at a ward or service level, to improve the quality of care and their compliance with necessary treatment, thus hopefully protecting groups of vulnerable children and parents from stress. For example, many sick or disabled children spend stressful times in hospital, which can trigger the development of emotional or behaviour problems, or may fail to address existing problems. Eiser (1990) suggests that psychologists could help doctors and nurses to improve their communication skills with the child and family about the course of an illness or disabling condition, and treatment options, and could encourage the use of pain management techniques so that necessary medical procedures do not cause excess pain or distress. Other aspects of psychologists' work with sick or disabled children and their families will be discussed later in this chapter.

How do problems emerge?

As a means of planning how to change a referred problem, child clinical psychologists start by identifying factors that might have precipitated or triggered the development of the problem, the factors that are perpetuating or maintaining the problem, and protective factors that prevent a problem either developing or worsening (Carr, 1999). Psychologists need to bear in mind that certain groups of children are particularly vulnerable to developing severe and persistent psychological problems while others are more resilient. The reasons appear to be partly to do with genetic factors and are partly psychological in nature. Physical disability, chronic childhood illness, or brain damage, including epilepsy, autism, and ADHD, put children at greater risk of developing psychological problems, partly because of physical or neurological influences on their behaviour, and partly because of the parenting requirements and the impact on relationships. From temperament studies it has been shown that some children are more difficult to manage and are less rewarding for their parents from a very early age, and these children and parents may develop troubled interaction patterns.

Although certain events can trigger the onset of a problem, children can experience stress or loss but remain free of long-term psychological disorder if parents, or other key carers act as a buffer for upsetting experiences. Some parents, such as those who are harsh or inconsistent, highly anxious or depressed, and those with very poor communication skills may be less able to provide support, teach suitable coping strategies, or provide limits to acceptable behaviour. The school can also act as a buffer for vulnerable children by helping them achieve their potential, set clear limits to difficult behaviour, and facilitate friendships with peers.

Working with parents to resolve problems

Parents are legally responsible for providing adequate emotional and physical care for their children and for ensuring that a child feels valued and safe. They, rather than their children, have the responsibility, and usually the power, to change situations in which childhood problems occur. Parents set standards for their child's behaviour at home and at school, and act as role models for managing conflict, distress, and frustration. When psychologists work with children, it is essential that parents feel respected rather than blamed, and are helped to make changes that are in line with their own cultural values and norms. Changing patterns of behaviour that have been established between parents and their children can be challenging, and some parents will require intensive, multidisciplinary help to develop new parenting skills, especially if they themselves suffered abuse or neglect in childhood. Anxious children are quite likely to have anxious or troubled parents, who may create close but insecure relationships within the family, and poor models for managing fear or risk, perhaps because of their own world experiences or beliefs. Some very troubled parents and those with mental illness may need help in their own right from adult services.

Following the pioneering work of John Bowlby in studies of young separated children, the importance of the 'secure base' provided by parents, and the impact of the relationship between parent and child in the first few years of a child's life on later development are now more clearly understood. Attachment theory suggested that attachment to a caregiver is a biological drive in infants as a means of obtaining security and comfort under threat and as an anchor when exploring. The caregiver's pattern of responses helps the child to develop expectations about relationships. Many years of research in the field has established that several types of attachment relationship can be discerned in young children that have an impact on a child's self-estzeem, social behaviour, expectations of relationships, and their own capacity to parent. Although the majority of children develop 'secure' attachment relationships with their parents that help them to explore their environment and build relationships, other children develop an anxious or 'insecure' attachment pattern with their caregiver that is most evident on parting or reunion with the parent. Children may become inhibited and withdrawn under such conditions or show anxious and aggressive behaviour towards the parent. Ainsworth's classic study of toddlers described two types of insecure attachment, insecure-anxious avoidant, and insecure-anxious ambivalent, which develop as a consequence of parenting which is contradictory or insensitive to the child's immediate needs. A fourth insecure attachment pattern, 'disorganized attachment' has been identified in recent years, which appears to develop in young children whose parents are frightening and unpredictable. The child cannot therefore develop consistent behavioural responses that gain parents' approval. This pattern is indicative of very troubled and abusive parenting and has been found to correlate with social difficulties and emotional and behavioural problems in late childhood and adolescence. Clinical psychologists have developed interventions specifically to improve the quality of attachments between troubled parents and children and this is discussed in later sections of this chapter.

The nature of child mental health problems

Children and young people's problems are usually categorized as behavioural, emotional, or developmental, although in reality problems can occur in all three areas. Problems such as aggression, disobedience, and disruptive behaviour are the most frequently referred types of problem, and are more common in boys than girls at all ages. Behaviour problems often occur alongside school difficulties and particular parenting styles and troubled family relationships. If severe behaviour problems are left untreated, they can persist into adolescence, and children may develop attributions about their entitlement to be aggressive, with major effects on friendships, family relationships, and school achievements. Treatment generally involves helping parents and teachers to respond to the child consistently, after a thorough assessment of the child's behaviour and development and key influences of the problem, on child, parent, and school.

Case Study

James is a 12-year-old boy who has had a series of problems and difficulties at home and at school. He was an active and demanding toddler whose behaviour was hard to manage. At nursery he was often aggressive towards other children, particularly if they tried to share his toys. He found it hard to settle into school at the age of five, and needed close supervision from teaching staff in the playground, to prevent him from fighting with other children. He enjoyed football and did well in the school team but tended to react poorly to being told off in class. He became restless during lessons, often interrupting other children's work and was slow to learn to read and write. Inexperienced teachers found his behaviour challenging although if he was motivated he could be helpful and enthusiastic. His parents were loving but preoccupied by family problems. They were unable to handle him when he was angry and defiant and tended to give in to him. James moved to secondary school without having acquired age-appropriate reading skills and needed extra help from a specialist teacher to catch up with his classmates. He took to truanting from school whenever he found himself in conflict with teachers and began to hang around with older boys who encouraged him to join their gang. This greatly alarmed James' parents who were aware that he was likely to get into trouble with the police. Help provided include an assessment of James' learning abilities, help to improve the parents' skills in negotiating and managing conflict, individual work with James in clinic, frustration tolerance and self-esteem work, and school programmes to build his reading and attention skills.

Children and young people, like adults, can develop emotional difficulties such as anxiety and depression that affect their sense of self-worth, friendships, and learning capacity. Fears and worries can occur at all ages and stages as part of growing up and show up in various ways at home and school. However, these problems may be less easy to identify than disruptive behaviour. For example, young people can develop severe anxiety disorders such as obsessional-compulsive disorder (OCD) but are quite likely to hide their fears and rituals at school, to prevent being ridiculed by peers. Depression in childhood and adolescence can also get overlooked by parents or teachers until problems become entrenched, perhaps because of a lack of awareness. Young people who are depressed may make few demands on adults, will be quiet in class, and often only come to notice if a young person attempts suicide or school performance suddenly deteriorates. Childhood depression may arise as a consequence of long-standing family difficulties, major trauma, or as a result of bereavement. Symptoms are similar to those in adults, for example, hopelessness about the situation, suicidal thoughts, sleep and eating problems, social withdrawal, and lethargy. The problems will also impinge on learning and on peer relationships. Psychologists have played a significant part in developing effective methods of identifying depression and treating symptoms. New national (NICE) clinical guidelines have recently been published to ensure that depression is recognized by professionals, and effectively treated using Cognitive Behavioural Therapy (CBT) and other family approaches. Any risk of suicide and other self-harm such as cutting also needs to be carefully assessed. Some depressed young people present with difficult or challenging behaviour which masks their sadness, or despair, and their low self-worth, for example, young people from very troubled families who engage in destructive behaviour, substance misuse, criminal activity, or truancy. They may find it harder to reflect on their emotional problems than to act in anger but would benefit from help to boost their self-esteem and access to emotional support networks as well as anger management.

Case Study

Jane was a well-behaved and highly motivated child who enjoyed school and loved ballet and swimming, which were the centre of her life. Her mother was a professional dancer and Jane was encouraged to take up dancing and to succeed. She had one close friend at home who went to the same school and who also participated in ballet classes with her, but otherwise she interacted only minimally with the other children in her class. Jane was keen to do well in all of her work and took pride in her achievements. She was close to her grandmother who had been involved in her care since Jane's parents had separated when Jane was three and her older brother was six. Jane saw her father regularly but her parents continued to argue after the divorce. Jane believed that she was responsible for the rows between her parents, which intensified after her father met a new partner and remarried. Jane's grandmother then died following a short illness when Jane was 14, and she became noticeably withdrawn and sad, and reluctant to go to stay with her father. This coincided with Jane's best friend's departure to the United States with her own family. Jane's school performance deteriorated and she lost interest in her appearance. She failed a ballet examination, felt that she had let her parents down, and was reluctant to continue with dance lessons. She became reluctant to leave home in the mornings unless accompanied by the family dog. Her sleep was disturbed and she seemed tired and irritable after visits to her father's house. Her mother sought advice from the GP, who recommended psychological therapy for Jane and the parents. Treatment for Jane targeted her depressed and withdrawn behaviour, and her thoughts of self-blame. The psychologist worked with Jane and with her parents and teachers to improve relationships, and to develop an understanding of Jane's sense of bereavement and achievement needs.

Psychologists also assess and treat post-traumatic stress disorder (PTSD) in children and young people. PTSD is now recognized as a serious childhood emotional disorder, with far-reaching effects on a child's development and functioning unless treated. As with adults, childhood PTSD develops in some children or young people, after experiencing a traumatic or life threatening event, such as a road traffic accident or a violent attack on themselves or on a family member. PTSD, like childhood depression, may not be obvious to parents or carers especially if family members find it hard to deal with the traumatic events themselves. Children and adolescents with PTSD can experience intrusive thoughts about a traumatic event or accident, have heightened emotional reactions, sleep difficulties, and difficulties concentrating on schoolwork. Younger children may suffer from a sense of bewilderment, wrongly attribute the cause of the event, and problems may show up in their play or relationships. These may persist, requiring expert psychological help pitched at the right developmental level for the child. Cognitive behavioural approaches are generally recommended (see NICE Guidelines for PTSD, 2005). The work normally involves allowing the child to recall and process memories of the event, tackling symptoms such as nightmares, and addressing underlying ideas they may have developed following the event, for example, about their sense of responsibility for the events. It is usual to involve parents and siblings to help bring about changes. Recently, Yule and his colleagues have developed effective training packages for use by frontline professionals in war-torn countries with children traumatized by war or natural disaster (see www. childrenandwar.org.uk).

Young people with various types of eating disorders come to the attention of psychologists and other mental health staff in specialist teams. Anorexia is a severe and life threatening form of eating disorder, probably deriving from a complex interaction of psychological difficulties, and is more common amongst teenage girls than boys (see Chapter 7). Treatment usually requires specialist psychological skills, involving parents and other family members in the work as well as the affected young person. Because of the risk to life, care needs to be coordinated with medical colleagues, and some young people may require inpatient treatment if their condition deteriorates. Parents, teachers, and GPs need to be aware of the early signs of an eating disorder in young people and refer them for specialist help at an early stage in the formation of the problem.

The changing shape of the family

Rather than ignore important cultural and social change and maintain a stereotyped view of 'normal' family functioning, psychological services need to fit the realities of family life. Greater social mobility reduces extended family contact and diminishes family support networks, heightening the need for professional advice and community support. Very real inequalities of opportunity and income exist within urban populations and across Britain, especially for black and ethic minority children and young people. Lone mothers head the household in a large proportion of families in inner cities, placing major responsibility on the mother to attend to their children's needs, especially if the fathers are not in regular contact. Divorce is more common, and there has been a rise in the number of re-marriages to form step-families, challenging professional thinking about the role of parents in therapeutic work. More women have joined the workforce, often in less well-paid work than men. Yet the majority of women continue to bear the bulk of responsibility for childcare, and services need to take account of the time pressures and constraints when offering appointments. Shifts in the pattern of child clinical psychology service delivery, for example, working in GP surgeries, offering parenting courses for step-parents, or running evening clinics may help families access services, as will greater attention to cultural diversity.

How does information about the course of a child's development help the clinical psychologist make an assessment?

When a child is referred with a problem, epidemiological research data about developmental stages can guide assessment as to whether or not the problem is 'normal' or 'abnormal' for that child's age. Thus, a boy who is wetting the bed at the age of 8 years who is otherwise developing normally is judged to be more likely to need intervention than a child of 3 years because most boys of his age will have stopped bed-wetting before this. Social development also needs to be considered. An 8-year-old child is likely to feel different from his peers because of his bed-wetting and be aware of his family's reactions. Knowledge of child development also influences psychologists' approaches to assessment and therapy. When interviewing an 8-year-old who bed-wets, the psychologist will need to take account of the child feeling self-conscious and possibly feeling blamed in any discussion. Praise and reward from parents for success will be powerful techniques at this age, and he will be at the right age to benefit from the use of cognitive techniques and metaphors to help him play an active part in 'fighting' his bedwetting. Development is not unitary, and children's developmental progress occurs in several domains, with strengths and weaknesses. Teachers or parents may lack an awareness of a child's actual developmental needs in one or more area, and may inadvertently misread and label behaviour. A 7-year-old child referred, for example, because she is viewed as excessively shy, could in fact have speech and language developmental delays that undermine her capacity to communicate and her confidence.

It is also essential to assess a child or young person's cognitive developmental stage when evaluating what they recall and understand, for example, about a traumatic event and the reasons for it. Memory for events is age-related and affected by cognitive capacity. Young children do not recall information as easily as older children and need cues to help them recall events. They may not have acquired the capacity to verbalize thoughts and accurately judge the intentions of others. Interviewing young people about traumatic or shameful experiences in front of their parents influences their responses, because parents exert a powerful influence on children's ideas about right and wrong, at least until adolescence. Abusive parents may silence the child with threats, and children may seek to protect highly anxious parents by minimizing problems. Finally, it is important to remember that children of all ages and abilities have rights regarding consent to psychological assessment and treatment. In order to give informed consent, children need explanations about what a psychologist does and why they are meeting, at a level suited for their age and developmental stage.

Bringing a neuro-developmental perspective

A child seen as distractible, naughty, or unhappy could have suffered brain injury or have an underlying neurological disease that is affecting their behaviour and reactions. Making that evaluation requires a good working knowledge of normal emotional, cognitive, and physical developmental stages, the impact of trauma on a child's neuro-developmental functioning and the course of underlying brain pathology. Initial psychological assessment may lead to more detailed assessment methods alongside medical colleagues. Increasing numbers of clinical child psychologists now also undertake further studies in child neuropsychology to improve their assessment skills in these areas.

Developmental disorders with generally poor outcomes in adult life are autism and ADHD, both of which can be diagnosed under the age of 5 years. These disorders can involve marked difficulties in social relationships with peers and learning difficulties in school, and high levels of family stress. Clinical child psychologists often carry out complex assessments of such children's strengths and difficulties and help with diagnosis. Psychologists have also developed effective intervention packages to modify and shape social responsiveness and attention to tasks amongst children with ADHD and autism, using CBT (Happé, 1994). Additionally psychologists can help parents and teachers to set realistic learning objectives for the child and cope with any behaviour management problems. Working with such children requires clinical psychologists to be knowledgeable about social and cognitive developmental processes, in order to shed light on the nature of their impairments. For example, children usually develop the awareness of other peoples' perspectives or 'theory of mind' by the age of 5 or 6 years. Autistic children lack this ability, which causes them to have difficulty 'reading' the feelings and intentions of other people.

The effects of deprivation on children's development

Very adverse environmental conditions have a marked negative effect on young children's emotional and cognitive development. Classically these effects were observed in long-stay institutions in which there was an absence of emotional care and stimulation. Developmental recovery can occur only where warm, loving, and consistent care is made available. Severely dysfunctional family contexts can have similar negative effects on children's development, particularly if the parents are unpredictable and inconsistent in their approach and use extreme forms of punishment. Foster care can however help restore children's emotional and developmental well-being where parents are unable to look after their children, and is preferable to residential care.

New ways of helping children at risk

New government initiatives such as Surestart and Children's Centres in schools, concentrate on providing local child-care resources for vulnerable families in a locality at early stages in a child's life. Many of these young children are at risk of developmental and emotional difficulties because of their family and social circumstances. Surestart's aim is to help vulnerable parents to establish better relationships with young children, maximise the child's development and learning, and hopefully divert them from developing mental health problems in later childhood. Psychologists who work with very troubled families need to pay close attention to assessing whether children of all ages are at risk of harm, perhaps because there are concerns about the quality of parental care, or because the child has become involved in criminal activity, or because there is parental neglect. Recent child-care policies such as Every Child Matters (2004) spell out that it is essential for psychologists to work across all agencies with staff to help identify very vulnerable children and ensure that they are safe. This means being able to identify troubled attachment relationships, hostile and inconsistent styles of parenting, and violent and abusive family patterns that are known to have very harmful psychological effects on children. Children who have been beaten or sexually abused need intensive therapeutic help and carefully coordinated support to help them overcome the effects and an action plan to improve the family 'environment'. Reder *et al.* (2003) have set out frameworks for assessing abusive family relationships and attachment patterns, including parents' mental health and the child's strengths and difficulties, and the family's overall treatment needs.

If multi-agency professional help cannot change harmful or neglectful parenting, children and young people may need to be removed from the family, if there is evidence that their needs cannot be met at home. Psychologists may be involved in these assessments of children and parents, and in evaluating children's wishes and feelings about their future. These complex assessments are usually carried out by two or three professionals over a number of sessions with a child and parents, and involve court report writing.

Working with young people in substitute care

Some children who are looked after by the local authority and placed in foster families remain troubled and difficult to manage, despite the positive influences of new carers and a change of context. This is especially the case for children who have been sexually abused. Recent research showed that fostered children and young people are very likely to have serious child mental health disorders, but lack access to professional help. Very disturbed children who are removed from dysfunctional families and placed in foster care have a tendency to test adults' endurance and to find it hard to trust others. This in part could be due to the long history of difficulties in their original family, and to failures of the system to provide adequate and consistent substitute care. Child psychologists and other mental health staff are increasingly working with 'Looked After Children', and linking with the social work teams that are responsible for their care, in order to prevent placement breakdown, and further rejection and loss. Some of this work is based on attachment theory, helping improve the quality of the attachment between foster carer and young person (Golding, 2003). New treatment approaches developed in the United States such as Multi-dimensional Treatment Foster Care provide a 'wrap around' package of care for the whole 'system' of relationships. This includes psychological support and advice to foster carers based on social learning principles to help them manage and resolve challenging behaviour, psychological intervention for fostered children to help them with problem solving, social skills and anxiety management, and work with biological family members to help improve relationships with and management of the fostered child.

Settings in which psychologists work

National surveys of clinical child psychologists in Britain have shown there to be variation in the settings in which psychologists are based, although the majority are employed in the National Health Service (NHS). Child psychologists work in mental health NHS Trusts, in acute hospital Trusts, or in Primary Care Trusts depending on local arrangements, and in newer joint agency organizations such as health and social care Trusts. A few clinical child psychologists are employed within the voluntary sector or by Social Services departments, without formal links with child or adult mental health services. Over time, it is likely that inter-agency Children's Trusts will be set up to meet children and young people's educational, social, and psychological needs, blending the work of social services, community health, child mental health, GPs, and social services for children.

Many psychologists now specialize with particular types of age groups or problems, for example, adolescent mental health, preschool services such as nurseries and Surestart projects, children with disabilities, ADHD or autism, youth offending, or Looked After children. Others work as 'generalists' across age groups or problem types, either in multidisciplinary child mental health teams in clinics, or in community-based services. Some clinical psychologists work in specialist inpatient units providing 24-h care for children and teenagers with serious mental health problems, such as depression or psychosis.

Multidisciplinary teamwork

Across all child services, most psychologists are based in multidisciplinary teams in mental health, child health, or across agencies to provide a service to children and parents. Teams aid psychologists to work collaboratively with staff from other disciplines, and to adhere to agreed national clinical care standards. While skills and knowledge overlap, most psychologists in teams provide unique clinical psychology assessment work, undertake CBT and other psychological therapies, and help audit and evaluate new approaches and service user needs. Working in multidisciplinary teams can be rewarding and supportive, and allows for shared approaches and perspectives when dealing with complex and longstanding child and family difficulties. It also provides for in-service training and a forum for new ideas. However, problems can sometimes occur in teams, usually connected to unresolved conflicts about leadership and dominant models of treatment or resources.

Clinical child psychologists often work in partnership with the key adults who are involved in a child's life in the community, for example with teachers, parents, and school nurses, to create ways to solve that child's problem in the home setting and in class, rather than in the clinic. While this way of working is responsive to families and referrers, it can sometimes be difficult for front-line staff to draw in other more specialist services when these are needed, unless good links already exist. Some community clinical child psychology services find that multidisciplinary CAMHS teams overlap with theirs, and referrers can become confused about which service to involve.

Another way of working is for the clinical psychologist to be attached on a part-time or full-time basis to a service for children outside the mental health services, for example, in Looked After children's teams, youth offending teams, general paediatric services, and child development centres. This allows psychologists to work closely with social workers, teachers, or doctors to reach children and parents who have significant psychological needs but who may not access specialist child mental health services. A drawback can be that a psychologist employed in this way can become isolated from psychology and other mental health colleagues, and from access to supervision and support in handling very complex cases.

Organizing psychology services to respond to different levels of need

There have been important changes in recent years to the ways that health services for children and young people are delivered, to ensure better service coordination, and in line with child and family needs. All CAMHS are now expected to make sure that services are available for all levels of complexity. The new National Service Framework for Children's Services (2004) states that psychology and other CAMHS should become more accessible to children, young people, and families, by working in community settings as well as in specialist mental health clinics, and to develop more ways of meeting the needs of children and parents from culturally diverse backgrounds. Parents' and children's expectations of psychological treatment and responses to it will be taken more seriously, using questionnaires and verbal feedback from families about service plans and delivery. The rationale of organizing services according to level of child and family needs is that children's psychological needs can be addressed in a coherent way, with better access and earlier intervention, with specialized services being reserved for those most in need.

Ideally, CAMHS should match or fit the level of need created by the problem or problems, so that the most complex and severe problems receive the most specialist treatments in services, which are designed to offer longer-term psychological treatments, possibly involving two or more staff. Community based child and family services are designed to help treat moderate problems, and to support and train frontline workers such as teachers and health visitors to help treat mild problems, such as a fear of needles and injections, or a single behaviour problem which could be resolved with a relatively straightforward psychological input. Frontline staff skills and confidence in this work can be developed with psychological supervision and training.

The Parent Adviser Scheme in Bermondsey in South London, is a carefully evaluated service devised by clinical child psychologists, offering early intervention to parents of young children with mild to moderate child mental health problems in the community (Davis et al., 1997). Parent Advisers are not qualified psychologists but are frontline professional staff who have been trained in a model of parent counselling and problem solving skills that has been devised by clinical child psychologists. Staff trained as parent advisers are then offered regular supervision of this work. The approach has been shown to be effective in resolving a significant proportion of referred problems without the need for more specialist help, and also in building the skills and confidence of non-mental health staff such as health visitors to work with families. The model teaches skills in effective and respectful partnership working with parents and as such, could be applied to other child-care professionals' training.

The nature of work undertaken by clinical child psychologists

In this next section, examples will be given of the different sorts of activities which psychologists undertake to help referred children and their families, and the range of models or theories to explain how problems arise and to guide their thinking about intervention or treatment. When working with children and families, the psychologist needs to decide whom to involve in assessment and treatment, for example, the child, parents, brothers or sisters, or other key professionals. The process can be time-consuming given the range of variables and the different perspectives to be considered. It may lead to the setting up of training or consultation work with staff as well as, or instead of, direct clinical work with the family.

The assessment process

Tests of general intelligence are useful for ascertaining whether specific patterns of strengths and difficulties are present in a child or young person, and can aid in the diagnosis of developmental disorders such as ADHD. In recent years new tests have been devised which enable psychologists to assess specific cognitive abilities such as memory, attention, and distractibility. However psychometric assessment is no longer seen as the focus of psychological assessment work. Clinical psychology assessments of problems have broadened, to include a detailed appraisal of the nature of a problem, the effects on the child and family, the nature of family relationships, developmental factors, and the meaning the problem has for a child and family. Clinical psychology assessments appraise the child's problem in the social context, which involves evaluating family relationships, school factors, and peer group relationships and their contribution to the problems being experienced. This is achieved by discussion, observation, questionnaires, and reading reports. The aim is to collect information about the problem and the relationship with other aspects of the child's life, in order to chart the problem severity and the sorts of work needed to change the situation. Most parents want to know why a problem is occurring as well as what to do to change it. Similarly, the psychologist needs to determine what has helped create the problem or triggered it and what problem solving capacities exist to resolve it, within the child, the family, and the broader network.

Stages in the assessment process

First a detailed description is taken of the problem, as it exists at the present time, where and when it occurs and how long it has been in existence. Parents or teachers usually give a label to a problem they are concerned about, for example, 'aggressive and violent' or 'has a communication problem with her sister'. At this early stage in the assessment process it is helpful to get a set of behavioural descriptions for the problems, so that there is clarity about what actually occurs. The effects of the problem on the child are carefully noted, both the negatives and any positives. Any other characteristics of the child relevant to the problem would also be noted, such as their likes and dislikes, and their general developmental progress in other areas.

It is important to establish whether the problem occurs in all contexts or whether it is restricted to specific situations, so that an idea is obtained about how severe it is. In addition, the assessment needs to focus on links between the problem and the behaviour, and responses of others, and how the problem is influenced by other environmental factors. Is the problem being shaped by parental or sibling responses which are reinforcing the problem behaviour, such as attention? Is the child modelling others around him or her? Does the problem get triggered by an event or other stimulus? Is the physical environment not suited for a child with these needs?

The next step is to explore how everyone perceives the problem. This could include parents, brothers, and sisters, as well as the child giving their views about the nature of the problem and its severity. Family members can have differing perceptions of the behaviour that is causing concern and the reasons for it, some perhaps blaming one family member or attributing the problem to an event which occurred in the past. The referrer may have a different view from the parents as to what the problem is, and therefore what needs to change. There may be a general perception about the child as a 'bad lot' or 'an angel', which may prevent the family noticing adaptive or helpful aspects of the child. The child him- or herself may also feel worthless and perceive the situation as being beyond his or her control.

At a broader level of assessment, it is important to gauge the family members' feelings about the child and the problem, for example, whether the problem is creating intense anxiety or despair. In addition, family relationships need to be appraised, such as the quality of attachments in the family, family styles of communication and discipline, and whether the parents are in opposition to one another or able to solve problem together without conflict. This may be obvious from the interview or may need colleagues to assist, for example, by observing family interactions through a one-way screen. The psychologist will also wish to ascertain whether the parents are supported by friends or family and whether there are other stresses currently which affect coping, including the parents' own mental health, financial pressures, or harassment from neighbours. Some of this information can be obtained from checklists or self-report questionnaires. Historical information about past traumas or losses, changes in family circumstances, and how the parents and child have dealt with difficulties in the past is also needed. All of this information gathering can take two or three sessions and may require individual sessions as well as family interviews.

At the end of this assessment process, the psychologist should be ready to make a formulation about the problems and the salient factors associated with it, which will provide an explanation of the difficulties, what needs to happen to bring about change, and the approach to intervention. The psychologist, parent, and child then need to agree to the goals, the plan to solve the problem, and how changes will be monitored over time.

What sorts of treatment are carried out?

Advances in training, clinical practice, and research have widened the scope of interventions which clinical child psychologists now use. Effective child and family treatment approaches have now been established for problems such as OCD or social anxiety, or conduct problems, based on carefully researched protocols (Barrett and Ollendick, 2004). Target and Fonagy (1996) carried out a systematic review of treatment efficacy for childhood problems and concluded that both behavioural and non-behavioural approaches can be effective and have contributions to make. They note that there have been many more systematic studies of behavioural and cognitive behavioural treatments, which tend to be symptom focused, than of family therapy and individual psychoanalytic psychotherapy, which aim to treat associated difficulties within the family or child. In practice, many psychologists integrate ideas and techniques from several theoretical approaches, as in the case of Barbara (see the following paragraphs). A behavioural approach was used in the assessment and intervention work with a mother and young child, although attention was also given to the parents' cognitions, attachment relationships, and current family interactions.

Case Study

Barbara was the younger of two daughters and was a lively 3-year-old who ate very little food and had great difficulty sitting at table to eat her meals. Her mother, Christine, was desperate to change the mealtime problems as she was going back to work soon. Mealtimes were fraught and the parents disagreed about how best to get Barbara to sit and eat. Barbara's father felt that Christine was too lenient and that she had given in to Barbara.

Christine found it wrong to chastise children as she herself was given harsh discipline by her parents when she was a child. She could not break the pattern of feeding Barbara on the floor while she played because of her worry about Barbara's low food intake. Barbara was born prematurely and there were medical concerns about her growth and development in her first year of life.

The psychologist met Barbara and Christine at the office, and Christine described the problems in detail. The psychologist sought to create a relationship of respect and trust with both Barbara and her mother and at all times tried to validate Christine as worthy and resourceful. Christine was asked for some information about the family and any other stresses they were facing just then, and she described their worries about financial matters, which had led her to plan to return to work, which she was dreading. The psychologist checked details of Barbara's general development at present and learned that there were no current medical concerns, but that Christine still felt watchful and protective. The psychologist also asked about the child's relationships with other adults and children, and about her general temperament, for example, whether Barbara was usually easy or difficult to manage, happy or unhappy. She observed Barbara with Christine during the session, noting the close and affectionate way in which they communicated and played together in the room, yet that Barbara would not put the toys away despite being asked to do so repeatedly.

With the parents' agreement the psychologist then went to observe a mealtime at the family home, noting the context in which the meal took place and the patterns of behaviour and responses between the mother and the two children. She next began to collect further information to assess the problem in a wider context. In order to determine what Barbara's diet actually comprised, Christine agreed to record everything that Barbara ate over a period of 7 days in the form of a daily inventory of her food intake, including snacks such as sweets and crisps. She was also encouraged to visit the health visitor at the local baby clinic to have Barbara's weight and height measured and compared with other children of her age. In addition, Christine completed a standardized questionnaire to elicit measures of the level of stress and anxiety she experienced as a parent. The scores from the questionnaire showed that Christine had very high levels of anxiety and felt stressed in her role as a parent. The diary showed that the little girl was eating small snacks during the day but rarely ate what her mother gave her at mealtimes. Despite Christine's worries, Barbara's height and weight were within normal limits for her age.

The psychologist then shared her hypothesis about Barbara's eating problems with Christine, suggesting that Barbara had learnt that it was worthwhile screaming as her mother then let her eat on the floor while playing. She suggested that Christine gave in to Barbara when she would not eat, because she believed that it was of prime importance that she should not be a harsh parent because of her own past experiences and should be especially protective towards Barbara because of her early developmental problems. They discussed the report from the health visitor about Barbara's weight and the evidence that Barbara had grown in health and strength since babyhood and was now more resilient. In addition they discussed ways of being firm and fair without being harsh or cruel. The psychologist described the approach she thought might help to set new conditions by using rewards to shape sitting at table. She suggested that Christine should decide what Barbara needed to eat at table before being allowed to play. If she ate, Christine would praise her and let her play with a favourite toy. If she screamed, Christine would not cajole her but instead would ignore her and eat her own meal quietly. Christine was also encouraged to cut out snacks so that Barbara had an appetite at mealtimes, and was asked to set up the dining area differently so that the toys were less accessible. Christine agreed to try the approach, and with the psychologist drew up a programme describing what actions were to be taken and how Barbara would be rewarded. They arranged that Barbara's father would be briefed about the new plan and asked to offer support along the lines set out. Christine was given a diary to record whether the child sat and ate or ran to play, and whether she resorted to feeding Barbara, or managed to ignore her.

Christine and the psychologist agreed to remain in touch by telephone during the next week, and to meet the following week for a review. Christine returned to the health visitor so that Barbara's weight could be monitored under the new mealtime regime. As progress was maintained, a review was held a fortnight later, during which time they discussed Christine's feelings about the changes and her desire to continue to set limits and not let her daughter determine the routines at home, while remaining a loving parent. As well as diary reports of Barbara's increased food intake, evidence of change came from the scores in the parenting stress measure. When repeated at the end of treatment, the measures indicated that Christine felt less stressed and perceived herself as better able to cope. This was backed up in further discussion about the return to work, the effects on both children, and her relationship with Barbara's father.

Types of treatment approaches used with children and families

This example involved assessing and changing 'here and now' behaviour patterns, and the responses of a mother to her child, with associated factors being tackled indirectly. Few problems can however be defined or solved without addressing other aspects of the child and family situation and the home environment, especially if there are chronic problems associated with the referred problem such as overcrowding or maternal depression. If these obstacles are present, the psychological work would need to shift to other aspects which are open to change, and which can facilitate change in the child's behaviour. In practice, most psychologists tackle referred problems eclectically, by addressing the child and his or her social context at several levels. The choice of treatment approach will be influenced by the resources that are available to the psychologist and the level of their expertise. Barbara's problem, for example, could be addressed in a number of ways, depending on the conceptual framework applied to the situation, including behaviour modification, CBT, family systems therapy, or psychodynamic psychotherapy. Some health visitors also carry out psychological treatment with parents and young children with feeding problems using behavioural or counselling approaches in the home or clinic.

Behaviour therapy

Behaviour modification or behaviour therapy was developed by applying social learning theories and principles to children's problems. Behaviour therapy aims to reduce undesirable behaviour and teach positive sequences of behaviour which fit the child's age and stage. It relies on using systematic rewards for desired behaviour, and stopping those for unacceptable behaviour. After a very detailed analysis of behaviour and responses, parents are taught new ways of responding to their child's behaviour. This involves shaping new and more appropriate behaviours by altering the reinforcement used, and thus altering the problem patterns of interaction. The context in which problems occur is also changed to make it more rewarding to a child. Behaviour therapy is a particularly useful approach for resolving problem behaviour where parents are motivated to change their responses to their child and to reward children systematically. It is especially helpful in work with young children and parents.

Cognitive therapy

Cognitive therapy focuses on tracking and changing perceptions and beliefs about self and others in order to alter feelings and behaviour. The model was developed with adults and has been adapted for use with young people, especially effectively with anxious and depressed adolescents and those with a range of other disorders, including early onset psychosis. Cognitive therapy is based on the theory that an individual's psychological problems derive from specific habitual errors in thinking and interpreting events under stress, and underlying beliefs and assumptions about the world. Cognitive therapy involves identifying and testing out a person's perceptions of reality to challenge their assumptions about their situation. Using this approach involves exploring thoughts and feelings as they relate to actions and experiences. Cognitive therapy can help children to master their fears, and to challenge their negative expectations of people and situations. Cognitive techniques are frequently used with young children who are impulsive or distractible to help them to anticipate and control their behaviour, alongside behavioural interventions. However, it is less suited for younger children under the age of 8 years, because they have not yet developed sufficient cognitive skills needed to identify and evaluate their own and others' thoughts and feelings.

Cognitive Behaviour Therapy

Many psychologists use CBT with children and families, which integrates both cognitive and behavioural elements, and aims to develop new problem solving strategies. This model acknowledges the importance of children's thoughts and feelings in the origin and maintenance of problems, and emphasizes the role of parents and peers in problem solving. The approach draws on social learning and behavioural management alongside cognitive techniques. The therapist will work as 'coach' with the child and also draw the parents in to help the child to carry out agreed behavioural assignments, or work directly with a young person. Kendall (1991) describes relevant clinical programmes for a range of childhood problems, including the treatment of hyperactive children, oppositional behaviour, and PTSD. CBT can be carried out directly with the referred child, individually or in groups, for example, teaching fearful children to face rather than avoid frightening situations and to use cognitive strategies to solve problems and adapt.

Family therapy

Family therapy has had an influence on the practice of many clinical child psychologists. The family is conceptualized as a system of mutually influencing relationships, in which change in one relationship affects other relationships. In line with systems theories, the approach connects a child's problems with other family members' behaviour and perceptions. This model also gives a framework for analysing family relationships and patterns of interaction.

Systemic therapy encourages consideration of family transitions and the influence of culture and context on problem definition and resolution. In recent years, the emphasis has moved to a concern with developing narratives that address family difficulties collaboratively with family members, and exploring beliefs and ideas about change. Systemic ideas have also been applied to understanding the network of professional helping agencies that become involved with a family when a child is seen as having a problem.

Behavioural family therapy incorporates skills teaching, collaborative problem solving, group support, marital therapy, and family relationship change. Webster Stratton and Herbert (1993) describe an integrated behavioural family therapy treatment approach for children with severe disruptive and defiant behaviour difficulties. The treatment programme has been thoroughly evaluated and has been found to be effective with children aged 3–8 years. The package of intervention begins after careful assessment and interviews. The parents are the focus of the therapy, rather than the child, and they are seen in groups in community settings. Psychologists trained in this approach generate discussion amongst the group on specific topics such as rewards and punishments. Alternative behaviours are modelled by the therapist or via specially prepared videos. Although it is intended as parent training, it is collaborative in its approach and offers help at several levels, to address current patterns of behaviour between parent and child, family interactions, and the child's developmental needs.

Psychodynamic approaches

Some psychologists apply psychoanalytic models to their understanding and their work with children, seen individually or in groups. This approach can incorporate play and art therapy techniques. The aim is to allow a safe place for a child to explore strong confused or conflicted feelings, and is particularly useful in cases of abuse. Parents may also receive psychoanalytically based help to address mental health problems that affect parenting, for example, difficulties in attachment relationships. Community services such as Newpin pioneered group interventions based on psychoanalytical principles with isolated and depressed young mothers in inner city areas. Mothers who completed a set of therapy sessions were trained to befriend other mothers who were new to the service thus increasing social support within the local community. The service was shown to be very effective, although evaluation studies failed to demonstrate an influence on the mothers' parenting skills.

Consultation work with staff

Few psychologists spend all of their time working directly with referred children. Most psychologists also work with other professionals who work with children, such as social workers or teachers. The primary aim of this consultative work is to help deliver psychological care indirectly to children or young people who might not access help directly. By consulting about problems, psychologists help other professionals to devise new ways of responding to the needs of children or parents. Psychological ideas can be passed on to staff who are involved with vulnerable children, to enhance their skills and confidence and to reduce the likelihood that outside help will be needed in future. The psychological input can take the form of discussion of difficult cases, training, setting clear work objectives for complex cases, and supervision of their psychological work with children or families. Consultation can also focus on aspects of work with children that cause staff stress and anxiety, and thus should help staff to recognize emotional strains and conflicts inherent in work with troubled children. Research studies have demonstrated that organizational factors such as the nature of shift work and the degree of autonomy in decision making influence the way that staff interact with children in residential care, especially the amount of communication and play they initiate. Consultation therefore needs to be carefully negotiated with staff managers to ensure that the organization supports the psychological input and is willing to consider new ways to address any identified work stresses.

Psychologists usually build up consultation links in two major ways. First, they may involve themselves with staff who work with children known to be at risk of developing psychological problems due to family circumstance, social factors, or their special developmental problems, or a combination of all three. Obvious workplaces therefore are nurseries, hospital wards, and residential care facilities. Second, consultation may evolve as a result of team or service links with a particular agency or staff group who refer children with problems to the psychologist and who might wish to change their work practices.

A group of physiotherapists worked together in a community child health service in an inner-city catchment area. Their main tasks were to provide home based treatments for disabled young children, and to ensure good communication with other professionals involved with the families. The physiotherapists were members of the local Child Development Team for children with physical and learning disabilities, as were the clinical child psychologist, the speech therapist, two community paediatricians, and an occupational therapist. The psychologist received referrals from all team members to assess and treat disabled children who had emotional or behaviour problems as well as their families.

After receiving four consecutive referrals from the physiotherapy staff concerning children with muscular dystrophy who had problems dealing with the impact of this degenerative neuro-muscular condition on their quality of life, the psychologist offered to meet the physiotherapists to discuss alternative ways of helping the staff to help these children and their families. It emerged that the physiotherapists were unsure about whether or not to discuss emotional aspects of the disease and as a result tended to avoid talking about feelings. If a parent of a child with muscular dystrophy seemed distressed, or if a child seemed lethargic, they would refer the family to the psychologist for help. One of the physiotherapists had however also tried to counsel a mother and child with muscular dystrophy at home. The mother became very distressed once she talked about her feelings and the physiotherapist felt she had done more harm than good.

Careful discussion with the physiotherapy group revealed that the majority wanted to communicate with parents and children about their feelings and felt that it would be beneficial to integrate their practical work with a psychological approach. However, they felt wary of changing their role, and wanted to practice basic counselling skills as a group. The psychologist agreed to provide some teaching on communicating with distressed parents and children and then met the staff on a regular basis to consult about effective ways of working with specific families. This arrangement was ratified by the senior physiotherapist on behalf of her staff, with a review session built in after 3 months.

As the group sessions continued, the staff shared some of their own distressed feelings about working with disabled and dying children and about feeling helpless to change the children's condition radically. The sessions allowed staff to set more realistic yet meaningful objectives for their work with the children and to improve the quality of the emotional support provided. The physiotherapists also reviewed their caseloads and planned to devote more time for home-based sessions specifically with children with deteriorating physical conditions, and their parents, to ensure that they discussed emotional issues with the family and offered additional support. The psychologist also agreed to help run a group for parents of the sick children who sought more support and wanted to discuss the stresses they faced and ways in which they could support one another.

Summary

This chapter has described some of the contributions that clinical psychologists are currently making to the psychological well-being of children and young people and the families who care for them. It has outlined three major aspects of clinical child psychology work—the problems children experience, the ways that services are structured to meet their needs, and the sorts of work that clinical child psychologists undertake. Children's problems arise and are maintained in the context of relationships with significant others, primarily their parents. Social and environmental factors have an influence on both the problems and solutions. This means that psychological assessment and intervention needs to be wide ranging in order to be useful and relevant. There is some variation in the way that problems are conceptualized by psychologists, and an outline has been given of the types of treatment approaches. Continued efforts are needed to evaluate their effectiveness and appropriateness. Psychologists working with children and young people usually work with parents as well as directly with children and families. All approaches adopted need to respect parents and to support their endeavours to respond to their children. Finally, consultation and staff support are also important ways of improving children's care and examples have been outlined here.

References

Barrett, P. and Ollendick, T.H. (2004). *Handbook of Interventions that Work with Children and Adolescents. Prevention and Treatment.* Chichester: T Wiley.

Carr, A. (1999) *The Handbook of Child and Adolescent Clinical Psychology. A Contextual Approach.* London: Routledge.

Davis, H., Spurr, P., Cox, A., Lynch, M., Von Roenne, A., and Hahn, K. (1997). A Description and Evaluation of a Community Child Mental Health Service. *Clinical Child Psychology and Psychiatry*, vol 2, 221–238.

Eiser C. (1990). *Chronic Childhood Disease. An Introduction to Psychological Theory and Research.* Cambridge: Cambridge University Press.

Golding, K. (2003). Helping Foster carers, Helping Children: using attachment theory to guide practice. *Adoption and Fostering*, **27**(2), 25–37.

Happé F. (1994). *Autism: An Introduction to Psychological Theory*. London: UCL Press.

Kendall P.C. (Ed.) (1991). *Child and Adolescent Therapy Cognitive-Behavioral Procedures*. New York: Guilford Press.

Meltzer, H., Gatward, R., Goodman, R., and Ford, T., (2000). *Mental Health of Children and Adolescents in Great Britain*. London. The Stationery Office.

NICE (2005). *NICE guidelines for Post Traumatic Stress Disorder (PTSD): the management of PTSD in adults and children in primary and secondary care*. London, National Institute for Clinical Excellence.

Reder P., Duncan, S., and Lucey C. (eds). (2003). *Studies in the Assessment of Parenting*. Hove and New York: Brunner-Routledge.

Target M. and Fonagy P. (1996). The psychological treatment of child and adolescent disorders. In A. Roth and P. Fonagy (eds.) *What Works for Whom? A Critical Review of Psychotherapy Research*. New York: Guilford Press.

Webster Stratton C. and Herbert M. (1993). *Troubled Families: Problem Children*. Chichester: Wiley Press.

Further reading

Carr, A. (2000). *Family Therapy, Concepts, Process and Practice*. Chichester: Wiley.

Copley, B. and Farryman, B. (1987). Therapeutic Work with Children and Young People. London: Robert Royce.

Davis, H., Day, C., and Bidmead, C. (2002). *Working in Partnership with Parents: The Parent Adviser Model*. London. The Psychological Corporation.

Dowling, E. and Osborne, E. (1994). *The Family and the School. A Joint Systems Approach to Problems with Children*, 2nd edn. London: Routledge.

Edwards, M. and Davis, H. (1997) *Counselling Children with Chronic Medical Conditions*. Leicester: BPS Books.

Frude, N. (1990). *Understanding Family Problems. A Psychological Approach*. Chichester: Wiley.

Herbert, M. (1991). *Clinical Child Psychology Social Learning, Development and Behaviour*. Chichester: Wiley.

Meadows S. (1993) *The Child as Thinker. The Development and Acquisition of Cognition in Childhood*. London: Routledge Press.

Stallard, P. (2002). *Think Good—Feel Good. A Cognitive Behaviour Therapy Work Book*. Chichester: Wiley.

Steele, H. (2002) State of the Art: Attachment. *The Psychologist*, **15**(10), 518–22.

Trowell J. and Bower M. (1995). *The Emotional Needs of Children and their Families. Using Psychoanalytic Ideas in the Community*. London: Routledge.

Chapter 4

Working with adults of working age

Sue Llewelyn

Introduction

Psychological distress has always been widespread amongst at least a proportion of adults of working age in many societies, both currently and in the past, and there has always been a range of ways of trying to respond to it. Most distress is never presented for professional help but is dealt with by family, friends, and communities, for better or for worse. Clinical psychology represents just one source of help for adults who are depressed, anxious, or who have major relationship problems. Within clinical psychology there are a range of models which inform interventions for those disorders. This chapter outlines some of the main types of difficulty often presented, and will describe the range of treatments available to reduce distress. Throughout the chapter there is reference to the competencies which clinical psychologists aim to call upon in all areas of their work and which are used specifically when working with adults. The importance of theory and research on effectiveness in this area will also be demonstrated whenever possible. Some of the most serious types of distress in adults such as psychosis or eating disorders are referred to in other chapters of this volume and are not covered here. Some of the disorders and treatments are also featured in primary care settings and so some of the topics raised in this chapter parallel those that have been covered in Chapter 2.

Setting of clinical work

In the early days of clinical psychology, many psychologists working with adults with mental health difficulties saw their clients only in inpatient or outpatient psychiatric settings. Hence patients were normally referred just for assessment of personality or cognitive functioning, in order to assist in the delivery of psychiatric (mostly medication-based) treatments. Gradually clinical psychologists became more involved in treatment, but until the early

1970s most adult mental health psychologists still worked almost entirely in psychiatric settings, with patients referred by psychiatrists. Now that most mental health services are provided in community or primary care settings, only a very small minority of patients with problems such as depression, anxiety, or obsessive- compulsive disorders (OCDs) will be referred by psychologists and seen as inpatients. General Practitioners (GPs) or multidisciplinary teams will refer the majority. Hence most people will be attended to and treated in community mental health or primary care services, or will attend the clinical psychology service connected to and located in a particular geographic area. Some are still treated in clinics or outpatient departments, while others may be treated in their own homes. Some patients may also been seen privately in their psychologists' own offices and still others may be seen by a service provided by another organization, such as in a student counselling service or with the occupational health department of a large employer.

Common psychological difficulties

The range of difficulties presented to psychologists is considerable. The most commonly occurring emotional problem is probably depression, which although usually first treated pharmacologically, is present along with anxiety in most people making up most adult mental health psychologists' case load. Often referred to as the 'common cold of psychiatry', depression ranges from persistent low mood, to major and debilitating despair, hopelessness, loss of motivation, lack of purpose in life, appetite, enjoyment, or desire to live. The cognitive model of depression (see below) describes it as having no hope in oneself, the future, or the world (other people, activities, or anything). Often depression can be seen to be triggered by loss, or when an external event seems to provide evidence to support someone's beliefs (in cognitive terms their schemas) concerning their lack of self-worth, or to undermine their self-esteem. For example, Tanya, a young student whose parents had separated when she was young and who had never found it easy to make friends, but who nonetheless had done well at school, became seriously depressed when she first went to university and had to cope with increased academic pressures together with severe homesickness.

Other common forms of distress include various manifestations of anxiety including phobias, panic, social anxiety, generalized anxiety disorder (GAD), OCD, post-traumatic stress disorder (PTSD), and health anxiety. Here a person is prevented from enjoyment or even lacks the ability to function effectively in life because of fears of negative consequences. The person usually does have a sense that the fear is out of all proportion, but is nonetheless unable to reassure themselves or reason away their fears, and hence reduce their anxiety. Frequently the well-intended and helpful actions or sympathy of others paradoxically reinforces the anxiety, so that the anxious person never tests out their fear of the dreaded consequences.

Case Study

Mira, a 40-year-old mother of two children, developed a fear of going shopping in the city centre after feeling faint one day in a busy supermarket. Thereafter, she avoided going into big shops and before long started avoiding smaller shops too for fear of making a fool of herself in public. She asked her children to run all the errands for her and soon became virtually housebound. Many people suffering from anxiety avoid exposure to the feared situation and hence never learn that the anticipated catastrophe either would not happen, or that even if it does (for example for Mira that she did indeed faint in a supermarket), the consequences would not be not as dreadful as they fear (in Mira's case, it is likely that people would actually probably be sympathetic if she fainted and would try to help rather than laugh at her).

Other mental health difficulties include addictions (Chapter 8), eating disorders (Chapter 7), psychosexual difficulties, interpersonal problems such as loneliness or relationship difficulties, psychosomatic problems, and personality disorders. This last group are increasingly often presented to clinical psychologists, especially the type known as Borderline Personality Disorder. Such people may have a repeated pattern of difficulties in settling in relationships, may swing chaotically between jobs, partners and life-styles, and may have harmed themselves or attempted suicide. They may also report a feeling of chronic emptiness, and meaninglessness, alternating with a sense of importance or 'special-ness'. Although it is still a somewhat controversial label, there do appear to be a substantial number of people who turn to clinical psychologists for help whose difficulties seem to be longstanding, distressing, and connected in some way to their personal orientation to the world. Some people labelled as 'personality disorder' may have had a history of childhood sexual abuse (CSA), while others may have had some involvement with the legal system. In the past such people were often seen as untreatable by psychiatrists, and indeed it is hard to see how they fit into a medical, illness model of mental distress, whose symptoms should be most appropriately treated by medication. With background knowledge of personality and social development, clinical psychologists may be well placed to offer some way of resolving the distress experienced.

Classification of mental health problems

There are two main classification systems used in the UK to categorize and hence to indicate what form of treatment may be appropriate. The International Classification of Disease (ICD-11) is used mostly in Europe, but is probably less popular than the revised Diagnostic and Statistical Manual (DSM-IV), which originated in the United States and is widely used there and elsewhere. In DSM-IV, a major distinction is made between Axis 1 disorders such as anxiety and depression, which are seen as 'illnesses' and Axis 2, which are seen as 'characterological'. It is possible for someone to have disorders on both axes, or on one but not the other. It is generally assumed that Axis 1 disorders (such as anxiety) are more easily treated than Axis 2 (such as personality disorder) and this is supported by evidence. In practice many people who consult clinical psychologists experience a variety of forms of distress and are not easily classified into one category or another.

In this chapter, this possibly rather traditional, individualistic method of classifying and treating distress has been followed, since this is still the predominant approach used by most UK clinical psychologists working with adult mental health problems. In opposition to this, many other clinical psychologists have questioned the value of using what is essentially a psychiatric, medically oriented system to describe human unhappiness, especially in light of the widespread nature of distress in our society and its undisputed links to social problems such as unemployment and poverty. Nevertheless the health care system in which clinical psychologists operate does require some form of classification for both record keeping and communication between different professional groups. For that reason, and for ease of description, this system has therefore been used here. It is important to bear in mind the limitations of such an approach.

The competent clinical psychologist

The competencies used by clinical psychologists working with adults of working age with mental health difficulties are broadly the same as those used by clinical psychologists in other settings, namely the use of assessment, formulation, intervention, evaluation, and communication in an iterative cycle, informed by and informing the scientific knowledge base, and calling on reflective awareness together with the need for ethical and culturally sensitive practice. Each of these competences will be considered in turn as it applies to this client group.

Assessment

On first meeting a client, most clinical psychologists will start by assessing their needs in psychological terms so as to reach an understanding of what an appropriate treatment response should be. Normally the psychologist will ask the client for their own view of the difficulty, and for some background details, including the history of the problem, the context of the problem, key relationships, details of employment etc. Most psychologists will also want to ask about significant life events and some will ask about early family experiences, any prior experience of therapy, and about the client's self-assessment. According to the model used, the psychologist will pay particular attention to the ways in which clients describe themselves and their difficulties, and will try to see if there is a pattern in their responses. For example a cognitive therapist may ask for specific examples of how a client describes his experiences, and may try to uncover some of his negative assumptions, while a more psycho-dynamically oriented psychologist may pay attention to the client's way of seeking to relate personally to the psychologist. A family therapist will see the client together with significant family members.

The purpose of any first interview is to establish a working alliance, to explore the presenting difficulties so that some sort of understanding can develop, and to assess the client's motivation and ability to work psychologically. Many clinical psychologists will also ask clients to complete some form of psychometric assessment, either at the end of the first meeting, or in fact prior to this, so that the client brings the completed forms to the first session. The point of this is both to inform the psychologist and also to permit comparison with scores obtained before and after treatment. A frequently used psychometric assessment is the Beck Depression Inventory (BDI), which measures a range of symptoms that can quickly and reasonably reliably indicate the severity of depression. Other frequently used measures for assessing adults with mental health difficulties include the Beck Anxiety Scale, the General Health Questionnaire (GHQ) and the Robson Self-esteem questionnaire. Many departments of clinical psychology will collate a series of measures for administration to all new clients, which can also be used in departmental audit. Increasingly widespread is the CORE system, which includes a range of well-validated and reliable tests for a range of symptoms (Evans *et al.* 2002). Clients may also be invited to self-monitor, or keep a diary, so that they and the psychologist can gain an increased understanding of when and why difficulties may arise.

Although assessment invariably takes place at the start of treatment, it is in fact an ongoing process that occurs throughout treatment as the psychologist seeks to ensure that the treatment is having the desired effect. Some theoretical approaches also suggest that formal assessment should take place over several sessions so that enough information can be obtained to produce a reasonably comprehensive formulation. As new ideas or information emerges during treatment, it is often necessary to re-assess the difficulty, and reformulate. For example, someone who presents with depression may reveal after several sessions of treatment that they have experienced traumatic sexual abuse as a child, which will undoubtedly need further exploration, will probably modify the formulation, and will suggest changes to the treatment offered.

An important source of information, which is considered during the assessment, is the client's ability and wish to engage in treatment. Besides being an important indicator of the likely success of the intervention, the client's views of what they want from treatment has to be assessed carefully for the psychologist to be sure that the client is fully consenting to the intervention. For this reason part of the assessment phase normally also involves the psychologist in describing the likely course of treatment, and giving an indication of what can be expected in terms of time needed, and the likely outcome.

Formulation

As noted in Chapter 1, formulation is the key skill for clinical psychologists working with adults, as with all other client groups. Normally formulation is carried out in collaboration with the client, and aims to make sense, for both client and psychologist, of the presenting difficulty. Some approaches, notably the cognitive, provide well-worked-out models of many of the commonly presenting mental health problems which can act as convenient templates for understanding many of the difficulties. Nonetheless, all clients differ, and the clinical psychologist's critical and creative skills are needed for adapting the formulation to the individual case. Normally attention is paid to the background, predisposing factors which provide the setting, or sensitizing context, for the problem to develop. In most cases this is found to be some adverse childhood experience or learning, which sets up a readiness to develop symptoms when triggered by some internal or external factor. For example, many people who develop phobic disorders will have had at least one parent who was anxious and who tended to encourage cautious responses to animals, heights, closed spaces, and so forth. Likewise many people suffering from health anxiety may have experienced significant instances of sickness in their families, together with a familial tendency to interpret any symptomatology as serious.

Other issues normally included in the formulation include an account of how physiological, behavioural, cognitive, and affective reactions interact in maintaining the ongoing dysfunctional symptoms. Some models of treatment such as Cognitive Behaviour Therapy (CBT) provide a diagrammatic representation of the problem, which can be shown to the client and which displays visually the links between previous experience, the formation of dysfunctional assumptions or behaviours, how they were triggered by critical incidents, how this led to the negative automatic thoughts or imagery, and how this then led to the mental health problem. This in turn is demonstrated as being maintained by an interlinked set of behaviours (such as avoidance or checking of bodily sensations); physical reactions (such as increased arousal); cognitions (such as rumination or focussing on body changes); and affect (such as anxiety or depression). Cognitive Analytic therapists will also provide a written reformulation of the client's difficulties, which is a short, sympathetically written prose account of when and why the client's problems arose, and how the client's symptoms are often a dysfunctional attempt to resolve problems, but instead trap the client into perpetuating the problem. A psychodynamic formulation will not normally be presented to the client, but will likewise represent the psychologist's provisional understanding of the conflicts experienced by the client, in terms of unresolved or unexpressed wishes or fears, with the symptoms conceptualized as symbolic manifestations of conflict.

Treatment

Just as the formulation should follow logically from information gained during the assessment, so the formulation in turn should drive the treatment. Research into effective treatments for mental heath problems has meant that much more is becoming known about what works for whom, although most clinical psychologists agree that there is still a huge amount that is not yet known. Nonetheless, effective therapeutic interventions are now being described in considerable detail in treatment manuals, and guidance is provided by government or national bodies such as NICE regarding the most promising treatment to use given a specific diagnosis. There is still scope for clinical judgement, since no one approach has been shown to be effective for all clients and all problems. Whatever model is taken, however, effective clinical psychology treatment works best when it is based on a model, which is used to guide intervention and which can in turn lead to modification of the model in the light of experience.

Duration and mode of treatment varies, according to the presenting problem and the nature of the therapy provided. Most clients with the type of difficulty described in this chapter are seen on a one-to-one basis, for between 6 and 20 weeks, although some may be treated with their families. People with a personality disorder, or a range of complex problems (often with both Axis 1 and Axis 2 disorders, as well as social and economic difficulties) may be seen for a considerably longer period. In the United Kingdom, the Department of Health Treatment Choice Guideline (2001) has suggested that fewer than eight sessions are unlikely to be helpful except in the case of simple phobias or panic.

Evaluation

As noted in Chapter 1, the assessment–formulation–intervention–evaluation cycle guides all therapeutic input, so that evaluation of the effects of treatment should be monitored both during and at termination of treatment. Where the clinical psychologist has administered psychometric assessments, or some individually derived measure prior to treatment, it is normal practice to repeat the measure on termination, as well as to ask for qualitative reports of improvement. Many departments of clinical psychology ask clients to send back measures such as those included in the CORE battery, after the therapy has concluded, and sometimes some months later to check on maintenance of gains. Client satisfaction studies are also used by many services to assess their effectiveness in meeting client need and to modify existing services.

Communication

Almost all psychological work carried out with adults with mental health problems requires communication with the wider network around the client. This may involve simply a referring doctor, or the community mental health team. Sometimes the referred adult may be only one of a number of family members in contact with services. For example, a parent suffering from depression may also have a child receiving help from a family service, and the child may be in contact with education as well as clinical services. The family may be in receipt of help from the probation service and have input from social services in connection with a child protection concern. The adult may also be having educational support for literacy problems. In situations such as these the clinical psychologist is likely to be involved in protracted communication across health, social, and education services, and any therapeutic input will only provide a small element of the response to the presenting difficulties. A key skill is therefore that of communication and the ability to present psychological reports in ways that make sense to the wider care network as well as to the clients themselves.

Models: Cognitive Behaviour Therapy and Cognitive Therapy

The most prominent treatment model in UK clinical psychology for adults is probably CBT, now often developed to emphasize primarily the cognitive component, and known as Cognitive Therapy (CT). The predominance of these models for working with adults with mental health problems is partly the reasonably solid evidence base for treatment (Roth and Fonagy, 1996) but also because of the ready applicability of cognitive models, which provide a clear framework for intervention and evaluation (Clark and

Fairburn, 1997; Wells, 1997). Although many other professional groups also use CBT and CT, and although clinical psychologists also use other models, CBT and CT are most closely associated with clinical psychology, and all training courses aim to provide training to at least a basic level of competency in use of the model. The basic assumption of CBT and CT approaches is that emotional problems are best understood and resolved by addressing the meanings, beliefs, or cognitions the person holds about themselves and their difficulties. An additional important assumption is that many mental health difficulties have developed via maladaptive learning, and that solutions to them may also be understood and learned. A good therapeutic relationship is seen as an important framework for treatment, but not as being therapeutic in and of itself.

Essentially, treatment involves a careful assessment and specification of how problems arose and how faulty cognitions, or inappropriately learned behaviours, may be maintaining the problem. This is followed by joint examination of the cognitions or inappropriately learned behaviours, and the development, through homework and experimentation, of alternative, healthier ways of thinking and behaving. A central feature of both CBT and CT is that of collaboration, with an emphasis on problem solving in the present, rather than trying to reach an understanding of the past or to make profound personality changes in the client. Normally treatment opens by taking a careful history of the client's symptoms, beliefs, and current and earlier life circumstances, which then leads to formulation and recasting symptoms in terms of the model, which is then shared with the client (known as socialization to the model). This is followed by a series of negotiated challenges to the client's current ways of thinking and acting, through discussion (often via Socratic questioning, during which clients are invited to examine the rational basis and evidence for and against their beliefs) or by practical experimentation, a key aspect of which is approaching the feared object or situation. So for example a person with a fear of spiders is encouraged to approach and touch a live spider (possibly after graded exposure to pictures of spiders and picking up containers with spiders safely inside), since evidence suggests that only through learning and understanding that no actual harm will come of this, will the person unlearn his or her irrational fears. Gradually the client is encouraged to revise his or her inappropriate strategies and to develop new less restrictive understandings and behaviours. Provision is also made for maintaining therapeutic gains after the end of therapy, by anticipating future challenges and planning for ways of coping with them. Hence therapists may provide a 'blueprint' of therapeutic principles for the client to use after termination, as a way of preventing relapse.

A small range of models for specific types of mental health problem, and associated treatments, are described in the next section.

Treatment examples: CBT and CT for panic, anxiety, OCD, and depression

(i) Panic disorder This is experienced as sudden onset of intense fear, associated with feelings such as dizziness, nausea, and palpitations, often occurring 'out of the blue'. Sufferers may fear that they are having a heart attack or going mad. The cognitive model of panic proposes that individuals who experience panic do so because they have a relatively enduring tendency to misinterpret bodily sensations in a catastrophic fashion; hence normal sensations of anxiety are seen as indications of an immediate impending disaster. Therapy normally involves identifying the catastrophic interpretations, generating alternative, non-catastrophic interpretations and testing out the validity of these by discussion and experimentation.

Case Study

George, a 30-year-old mechanic, experienced a series of terrifying panic attacks while on holiday in Spain. Convinced he was suffering a cardiac arrest, he sought admission to a Spanish hospital, only to be discharged almost immediately. On returning home, he experienced further attacks, particularly of hyperventilation, each attack leading to a trip to the emergency department, where he was assessed and discharged as essentially healthy. Only partially reassured, George took time off work and became progressively more anxious about himself, avoiding exercise or travel. Prescription of sedatives did not appear to help and he was eventually referred for psychological help. Therapy involved exploring George's beliefs with him, and then carrying out simple experiments in which he was encouraged to test out and challenge his belief that a period of hyperventilation would inevitably lead to a heart attack. George and his therapist also discussed, and successfully revised, some of his beliefs about safety and danger, which they were able to trace back to warnings from George's father who had always been terrified of travel. George was eventually able to modify his assumptions about danger and to take a more measured view of his health and the riskiness of travel.

(ii) Social anxiety According to the cognitive model, this is assumed to result from a strong desire to convey a particular or favourable impression of oneself to others, and insecurity about one's ability to do so. When faced by a social situation, the person fears that other people will notice his or her anxiety symptoms, such as sweating, shaking, speaking quickly, or blushing, and that he or she will make a fool of himself or herself, leading to rejection and ostracism. Self-focussing, combined with a range of behaviours adopted to cope with the situation, leads to a vicious cycle in which the anxious person feels as if they were the centre of attention, which leads to higher levels of anxiety and increased self-consciousness.

Case Study

When Pamela went to the school gates to collect her son from the playground, she felt sure others would notice her anxiety, find fault with her, and reject both her and her son. Focussing on how she thought she must appear to others, she became convinced that the other mothers were all watching her and noticing her hands and legs shaking, which led her to stand apart from them and to concentrate on controlling her fear. As a consequence she did not respond when other people looked towards her. Feeling out of control, Pamela had a vivid image of herself shaking uncontrollably and others nudging each other and laughing. As a way of coping, Pamela leaned against the school gates, looked at the ground and took deep breaths, thus calming herself. Although this worked in the short term, it did not challenge her belief that other people were watching her critically. As soon as her son appeared from school, Pamela would flee back into the safety of home, although once home she regularly found herself conducting an agonising 'post-mortem' of the playground ordeal.

This pattern was repeated day after day until eventually Pamela, feeling very depressed and wretched, went to see her GP. After a period of counselling which did not appear to help, Pamela was referred for CBT. Treatment involved at first, reviewing episodes of Pamela's social anxiety and how her beliefs were maintaining the problem, and then encouraging Pamela to shift away from an internal focus, by asking her to concentrate on external features, such as the clothes other mothers were wearing. Pamela was also encouraged to reduce her 'safety behaviour' (see later in this chapter) of leaning on the gate and looking at the ground, but rather to check out if other people were looking mockingly at her. To her surprise she realised the other mothers were not doing so, and as she moved a bit closer, one or two smiled at her. In addition the therapist explained how the 'post-mortem' simply made things worse, and should be abandoned. In time Pamela's social anxiety diminished, and she eventually struck up a friendship with one of the other mothers. One approach sometimes used with people with social anxiety (although not with Pamela) is to use videotape to demonstrate to people that, contrary to their fears, their physical symptoms of anxiety are only minimally visible to others, if at all.

(iii) Obsessive-compulsive disorders These are characterized by distressing thoughts, impulses or images (obsessions), and stereotyped, ritualistic behaviours (compulsions), which the person knows are excessive but feels powerless to control. Often, but not always, the two are linked as the compulsions may follow the obsessions as a way of trying to control or neutralize the obsessions. Typical obsessions include impulses to harm loved ones or carry out obscene acts, or may include repeated thoughts, in the absence of evidence, that one might have inadvertently have done harm to another, such as knocking over a cyclist while driving to work. Compulsions include strong urges to prevent harm, such as carrying out extensive washing, decontamination or cleaning rituals, checking potentially risky items such as electrical switches, or counting and naming objects. Some people with an obsession about being a danger to cyclists might repeatedly drive back and forth along a particular stretch of road in an attempt to reassure themselves that no cyclist was lying injured by the roadside. One key feature of compulsive behaviour is that the client often feels an excessive sense of responsibility for negative events or consequences, while a common aspect of compulsions is the client's assumption of thought–action fusion, that is, that if one thinks of doing something, one will automatically carry it out. Both these features of OCD can be addressed effectively through CBT.

Case Study

Ed had occasional thoughts of behaving aggressively towards his baby son (which most parents probably experience sometime or other when babies do not stop crying). Being horrified by this thought, and believing that the fact he had experienced this thought meant that he actually wanted to harm his son, and would be sure to do so, Ed started avoiding contact with his son, attempted to suppress such thoughts, and made himself carry out a ritual of repeating his family's names in a particular order as a way of cancelling out the 'bad' thoughts. To his distress, these thoughts appeared to increase in frequency, and Ed then had to develop other routines and rituals to try and control his belief that to think a thing, automatically means one will perform it. Gradually this pattern generalized to other aspects of Ed's life and he became unable to go to work, eventually being hospitalized, as he simultaneously became more and more depressed. As part of his treatment, Ed was helped by his clinical psychologist to carry out a small survey of acquaintances, which led him to discover that many parents feel anger towards crying babies, and might even imagine acting violently, but that most of these thoughts are fleeting and do not indicate that the person is about to act upon these thoughts.

Treatment of compulsive behaviour is not easy, as it requires clients to take what is to them a huge risk in reducing or abandoning rituals that they believe are preventing significant harm. Nonetheless some evidence exists for the effectiveness of treatments known as response prevention, in which the client is supported to expose themselves to something which they believe has been 'contaminated', without carrying out their compulsions (Salkovskis and Kirk, 1997). Having a good therapeutic relationship between therapist and client is crucial, so that a client such as Ed can tolerate the anxiety caused when asked to relinquish rituals, and hence to learn that feared consequences to do not arise.

(iv) Depression A range of research studies has shown that CBT and CT are effective in reducing depression. For many people a course of antidepressant medication may be both simpler and more convenient, and indeed most patients are initially treated medically. Some patients are however reluctant to take antidepressants, and for others, pharmacological treatment is insufficient. Some studies have suggested that a combination of CBT and antidepressant medication is the most effective long-term approach (Williams, 1992).

Case Study

Tanya in the example introduced earlier, showed a number of typical features of depression. Sitting alone in her student accommodation following the return of an essay which had received some criticism, she ruminated on her apparent academic failure, and concluded she was unworthy of her University place. She compared herself negatively with the other students around her who appeared to have more friends, be wittier and more attractive, and to be doing well in their studies. She remembered asking a friend to return a phone call, who had failed to do so, and concluded that she had no friends. She had a vivid image of herself failing her end of term exams and returning to her home where her mother would be angry about the money and time wasted. This led to an acute pang of longing for home, where she felt that at least she could hide from further failure. When she phoned home, her mother who had recently established a new relationship explained that it would not be convenient if she came home just then. At that point, Tanya felt overwhelmed with a sense of hopelessness, and took an overdose of painkillers. After brief treatment in hospital, she was referred for therapy from the clinical psychologist attached to the student counselling service. In addition she was prescribed antidepressant medication, although some concerns remained about the possibility of her taking a further overdose, if provided with the means to do so.

After carrying out an assessment of Tanya's distress, and bearing in mind the possible future suicide risk, the psychologist introduced Tanya to the cognitive approach, with the aim of helping her to see how she was making a number of thinking errors such as overgeneralization, catastrophising, and exaggerating the negative, which then contributed to her feelings of despair and hopelessness. In addition it became clear that Tanya, feeling bad about herself, had cut back on a number of activities which had previously given her pleasure, such as playing badminton and telephoning old school friends. As a first step, Tanya was encouraged to keep a diary of her moods and thoughts, and was asked to bring this to the subsequent session. For example, her records provided a good example of how an incident where a fellow student apparently ignored her, led her to conclude that she was friendless and that no one liked her. The psychologist helped her to generate alternative explanations for the fellow student 's behaviour, for example that he was preoccupied or that he had not even seen her due to his short sightedness. They then looked at Tanya's belief that this incident meant that she would never be able to make friends. Tanya realized how she was systematically ignoring other evidence, for example that other friends had recently invited her over for coffee and old school friends had been telephoning her. It became clear that Tanya had established a long-standing almost automatic pattern of responding to events with self-blame, which appeared to be linked to beliefs about her self-worth, such as 'I am worthless'. Using the cognitive model, the psychologist drew up a formulation for Tanya, which presented a possible understanding of her depression. Predisposing factors, such as her parents' marital problems and lack of time and attention available for her, led her to develop assumptions that only if she succeeded academically would she be worth anything. On receipt of slightly negative academic feedback, and in the context of apparent rebuffs from both fellow students and her mother, her core belief in her worthlessness was triggered.

Therapy was carried out over several months during which time Tanya was encouraged to challenge her automatic negative thoughts and to re-establish activities which gave her a sense of mastery and pleasure. Other issues emerged over the course of therapy such as her sense of vulnerability and low self-esteem, and Tanya was helped to see how she was judging herself more harshly than she judged others, and was failing to reach a balanced view of her skills, attributes, and relationships.

Recent developments

Cognitive therapy has developed enormously since its early application to depression, and now there are effective models and treatment approaches proposed for most mental health difficulties. More attention has been paid to process issues and how the therapist–client relationship may affect outcome. The work of Salkovskis (1996) on 'safety behaviours' for example, has increased understanding of how some attempts by therapists (and families) to address symptoms, such as providing reassurance to someone with panic disorder or health anxiety, are in fact counterproductive, and distract from the need to face the feared object or thought. Aspects of clients' experience, such as imagery, are also now being included in cognitive treatments. For example in treatment of post-traumatic stress disorder, and of eating disorder, images which are assumed to be stored pre-cognitively, and are less easily available for rational examination, are addressed and modified. For further detail of this development in the treatment of eating disorders, see Chapter 7.

Psychodynamic therapy

Another model used by a substantial minority of clinical psychologists working with adult mental health clients is the psychodynamic, although only a very small number will provide classical psychoanalysis. Hence clients may be seen weekly and are unlikely to be asked to use a couch or to recount dreams. The psychologist will normally aim to gain an understanding of the dynamics that underpin the symptoms, and to resolve them by helping the client obtain insight or understanding of the conflicts, which have led to the symptoms (Coren, 2001). For example a man presenting with repeated urges to harm himself might be encouraged to explore his feelings of self-disgust and where they came from, as well as possible angry feelings towards others. Another key component of psychodynamic approaches is the use of transference and counter-transference whereby the client's relationship with the therapist is analysed and discussed. For example the client may report feeling increasingly anxious to please the therapist and may bring in an expensive gift. The psychologist will seek to understand this as a strategy possibly developed earlier in life as a response to feeling unworthy and will help the client to explore the fragility of their self-esteem, with the aim of increasing acceptance of the self. Therapists will also encourage clients to stay in touch with painful or challenging emotions, in order to try and understand their origins, and hence to more fully address and accept feelings such as loss, grief, or anger.

Eclectic and integrative approaches

In practice, high proportions of practising clinical psychologists draw upon a number of different models to inform their therapeutic work, according to the apparent need of the individual client. While using a broadly cognitive approach, for instance, some psychologists will also seek to make use of transference understandings of the client's distress and will seek to encourage an understanding of childhood dynamics as well as to encourage clients to address problems directly. For example, a woman who had experienced childhood sexual abuse and who found it hard to trust people, especially men, might be encouraged to take a series of small steps towards developing friendships with colleagues, while at the same time being encouraged to retell her story of trauma, and to re-learn, with the psychologist, that it is possible to be vulnerable and emotionally intimate with another person without being harmed.

While many psychologists work eclectically without developing any particular underlying integrative model, specific approaches such as Cognitive Analytic Therapy (CAT) have developed, which aim to draw upon the strengths of both cognitive and psychodynamic approaches (Ryle and Kerr, 2002). CAT is a time-limited focussed approach which aims to help people to shift their distress in significant ways in a relatively short time, and to give clients tools, or ways of thinking, which will enable them to avoid dysfunctional patterns of relating to themselves and others.

Case Study

Navin, herself a psychiatric nurse, was admitted to a psychiatric hospital following a manic episode in which she went on a spending spree and ordered expensive gifts for her children, followed by a brief psychotic episode, and then by a long period of deep depression. Stabilized by medication, she expressed a wish to learn more about what triggered her reaction and to address various areas of her life that she felt were dysfunctional and was referred for CAT. After four sessions of assessment, during which Navin's psychologist asked her about her early and current relationships, and heard about her ways of responding to herself and others, the psychologist drew up a reformulation of her difficulties. These were understood as being Navin's best, although unfortunately damaging way of coping with childhood trauma. It emerged that Navin had been sexually assaulted as a child, but had never told anyone, fearing the consequences threatened by her abuser. While growing up, she had then experienced a number of violent and abusive relationships with men, but had always felt she deserved this. When she met her current husband, a kind man from a different cultural and ethnic background, she found it hard to accept his wish for physical intimacy, and started behaving in progressively more challenging ways, as if to provoke what she feared would happen sooner or later, that is, he would reject or abuse her. In addition, she worked long hours at her job and frequently felt extremely stressed leading to angry and tearful outbursts at home.

Navin and her psychologist then worked out how she appeared to be following a number of procedures, or patterns of feeling, thinking, and behaving which trapped her into feeling bad about herself and distancing others. For example, believing she was essentially worthless, Navin would strive to please others, working long shifts, never considering her own needs, and then become exhausted, and eventually resentful, at which point she would lash out, express anger, or on the occasion of her admission to hospital, overspend wildly. Next, she would feel enormously guilty, and conclude from her own behaviour that she was indeed worthless and bad. She would then start to make up for this and strive to please others again, leading to exhaustion, hence perpetuating the cycle. The psychologist helped her first to recognize these patterns and then to develop alternatives, both by looking at Navin's account of what happened with other people, but also looking at the therapeutic relationship itself, in which Navin soon reproduced the relationship pattern of wanting to please and also of fearing closeness. With the help of her psychologist, Navin began to develop alternative ways of responding, which she was able slowly to generalize outside therapy, such that she eventually felt able to return to work and to develop a warmer relationship with her husband.

Family and group therapy

While most clinical psychologists work with clients on a one-to-one basis, some psychologists also work as family or group therapists. Evidence suggests that group work can be just as effective as individual work, and for some types of problem, may offer additional therapeutic benefits, such as the sense of not being the only one with a problem, and enhanced self-esteem, which can be gained from helping others. A number of residential units provide group therapeutic treatment for personality disordered patients, in which groups may be run daily, during which patients are invited to explore their dysfunctional patterns of relationships in great depth. Out-patient group approaches may be used for a range of problems, including those presented by phobic clients or discharged psychiatric patients. Important components of treatment include a sense of cohesion, interpersonal learning, and shared experiences.

Marital or family therapy may also be provided by clinical psychologists working in secondary services for cases when it seems most appropriate to see clients in the context where the problem has arisen. This is most obviously true when the difficulty is primarily between the couple, for example sexual problems, or relationship difficulties. Some innovative work has been carried out by Vetere and Cooper (2001) in which some forms of family violence are addressed psychologically, in an attempt to develop alternative ways of communicating and relating between family members. The model applied here is systemic, in which problems are thought to be best understood and addressed in relation to the system (or family) as a whole. Hence for example a woman's fear of leaving her house may be understood as a way of calling attention to a dysfunctional marital relationship, rather than being a problem with the woman herself.

Teamwork and training

Mental health services, particularly for more complex cases, are almost always delivered by teams. Hence one important role for clinical psychologists is contributing to, and in some instances managing teams of fellow professionals. The psychologist's understanding of group dynamics can help both themselves and their teams to make sense of and hopefully reduce some of the negative effects of groups, such as the tendency to stereotype others outside the group, to develop inter-group rivalry, and for the contribution of junior members to be given less attention than those of senior members, irrespective of their merit. Team leadership is an important role for more experienced psychologists, as is management and supervision.

The formulation skills of psychologists are also crucial, as psychologists may be able to propose a way of understanding and working with a particular client's difficulties, which, because it draws upon a wide variety of therapeutic approaches and an overall grasp of normal human functioning, may permit the development of innovative and effective interventions. Hence the assessment and treatment of complex cases is increasingly being seen as the core task of clinical psychologists working in secondary care settings, although delivery of treatment may be carried out in collaboration with the wider mental health team.

Psychotherapy (defined in a way that includes all the models described in this chapter) has recently been listed in the UK National Service Framework for Mental Health (2004) as one of a range of effective treatments for mental health problems, and is therefore now being seen as a basic component of mental health care, not an option. It is also included in relevant NICE guidelines, for example, on anxiety disorders (NICE 2004). Psychotherapy is not however the prerogative of psychologists: many other professional groups also claim competence to deliver psychological care. What follows from this is not only that clinical psychologists need to be good team players as well as effective individual therapists, but also that they need to be able to demonstrate their unique contribution to the delivery of care, and as such to ensure that they contribute psychological research skills and evidence-based practice to a multidisciplinary health service. It is likely that the clinical psychologist in any given team has a relatively high level of research training, and is thus well equipped to contribute a research-based perspective to the team, as well as to carry out service related research projects when appropriate. It is this, as well as competence in the delivery of psychotherapy, which provides the unique contribution of the profession.

A further consequence of the emphasis on team working is that an additional role for clinical psychologists is that of a trainer or supervisor, since a wide range of staff groups such as nurses, occupational therapists, and doctors are employed to deliver services using psychological concepts and therapies, but most will probably not have had as much grounding in these approaches as have clinical psychologists. CBT in particular has been taught by clinical psychologists to a variety of mental health care staff, allowing greater numbers of patients to receive appropriate treatment than would be possible without such skills-sharing. Competence in dissemination is therefore recognized as crucial, and many training course include some input on the skills of teaching and supervision. Training for new psychologists is also needed, with the majority of qualified psychologists working in adult mental health now being expected to take on supervision of new trainees two years after qualification.

Policy and organization of services

Given that services are now mostly organized on a care-group, not on a professional- group basis, many clinical psychologists working with adults of working age will be managerially accountable to a member of another professional group, although they may still be professionally accountable to and clinically supervised by a qualified clinical psychologist. This brings both challenges and opportunities, since psychologists working in multidisciplinary settings need to be clear and firm about their particular professional contribution, but can also have a greater impact than they would be able to have if working alone. In the past there was a degree of friction with psychiatry, since many clinical psychologists resented working apparently under the wing of the medical profession. This seems to be less a prominent theme now, but conflicts with other members of multidisciplinary teams sometimes remain and this can cause some discomfort and loss of professional confidence.

Other organizational issues that can be challenging include the high level of demand for services, and the limited resources that are available. Most clinical psychology services for adults have long waiting lists, which cause distress both to psychologists and obviously to the clients. A number of initiatives have been attempted to reduce waiting times, such as opt-in systems, triaging, and the provision of self-help material, but it is likely that waiting lists will remain a major difficulty for many adult mental health services for many years to come.

One further challenge is the need to ensure that services are equally available and accessible to all sectors of the community. Research from the UK Office for National Statistics suggests that members of black and ethnic minority communities are significantly less likely to receive psychological therapy than members of white communities, and where services are provided, there may be issues around ensuring the appropriateness of services offered, and the need for cultural sensitivity. For example, it is known that suicide risk is higher amongst young Asian women than their white counterparts, and some studies have linked this to conflicts around arranged marriages and intergenerational conflict. Addressing issues such as these requires both theoretical sophistication in adapting treatment formats (e.g. by using translators) and personal sensitivity to cultural variation.

Effectiveness, research, and ethical practice

Much research evidence exists that testifies to the effectiveness of psychological work with adults of working age, and this evidence is used by most clinicians as a starting point for their interventions with their clients. The bulk of research studies has been carried out within CBT and CT, and has demonstrated the helpfulness of these therapies for many conditions. A number of studies have however also shown that other approaches can be equally effective (Roth and Fonagy, 1996; Lambert and Ogles, 2004). There is no conclusive evidence regarding which therapy is the most effective for the majority of conditions, although the evidence base for CT and CBT is more extensive, and evidence for approaches such as psychodynamic is harder to establish. This means that in practice, most psychologists do make use of the CBT approach, although individual clinicians still hold the professional responsibility of deciding which approach is best suited for their individual client.

Overall the present emphasis on evidence-based practice, and the publication of guidelines on treatment approaches (such as those by NICE), has been welcomed by the majority of clinical psychologists who have been actively involved either in contributing to research into treatment effectiveness, or as consumers of published research. It is undoubtedly the case that the rapid growth in the profession of clinical psychology is in part due to the success of the profession in being able to demonstrate its clinical effectiveness, through well-publicized research and outcome studies, and in its promotion of evidence-based models of a range of disorders. The development of qualitative approaches has further enriched the research input provided by psychologists, especially where it contributes a greater understanding of the service user perspective.

Nevertheless, the assumption that clinical work with adults can ever be genuinely based on evidence has been disputed. For example, although the growing use of manualized treatments based on treatment models developed from efficacy studies have been welcomed by some, others have claimed they undermine the individual responsiveness of clinicians to the unique presentation of their clients, as well as being largely irrelevant to most clients who in fact often have a complex mixture of social, cultural, and psychological problems. Supporters of critical psychology, for example, suggest that the use of a quasi-medical, individualistic model by clinical psychologists diverts attention away from social and cultural issues that are in fact more important drivers of psychological distress than individual psychopathology. One helpful response to this has been the development of practice-based evidence which tries to link the work of practitioners with that of researchers in a more productive cycle, by taking into account the context of many clinical problems which can include violence, poverty, deprivation, and a host of interconnected difficulties.

Whatever stance is taken, most clinical psychologists working with adults do subscribe to the scientifically oriented competency model, which specifies the iterative cycle of assessment, formulation, intervention, and evaluation. In parallel with this, most psychologists are fully aware of the need to practice with sensitive awareness of ethical issues and to reflect on their own practice. Experience of working in this speciality is both negative and positive, in that many of the problems presented can seem to be close to home: there can be few psychologists who have never themselves experienced anxiety, depression, or difficulties in relationships, and some will be survivors of childhood trauma or abuse. This requires the ability to be aware of one's own sensitivities and relationship patterns, and not to impose them onto the client. Such awareness contributes to both the rewarding-ness of work within this speciality, and some of the difficulties. Again, many of the clients seen will be similar in age and background to clinical psychologists, heightening the need for self-awareness and maintenance of appropriate boundaries

Overall, working with adults is fascinating and stimulating, and can allow psychologists to gain privileged access to an enormous range of human experience. It is hugely rewarding to help someone find a way out of the distress and destructiveness of anxiety or depression, or to overcome the effects of childhood abuse or trauma. Equally rewarding is the opportunity to contribute to services by encouraging effective teamwork, establishing research projects to improve services or treatments, or to contribute to the professional development of others through teaching and supervision. As in all areas of work, there can be conflicts and doubts, but for many, working with adults can be a stimulating and challenging professional career choice.

References

Clark, D.M. and Fairburn, C. (1997). *Science and Practice of Cognitive Behaviour Therapy.* Oxford: Oxford University Press.

Coren, A. (2001). *Short-Term Psychotherapy: A Psychodynamic approach.* London: Palgrave.

Department of Health (2001). *Treatment Choice in Psychological Therapies and Counselling,* London.

Department of Health (2004). *Organising and Delivering Psychological Therapies,* London.

Evans, C., Connell, J., Barkham, M., Margison, F., McCrath, G., Mellor-Clark, J., and Audin, K. (2002). Towards a standardised brief outcome measure: psychometric properties and utility of the CORE-OM. *British Journal of Psychiatry,* **180**, 51–60.

Lambert, M. and Ogles, B. (2004). The effectiveness of psychotherapy. In M. Lambert, (ed.) *Bergin and Garfield's Handbook of Psychotherapy and Behaviour Change,* 5th edn. New York: Wiley.

NICE (2004). Clinical Guideline 22: *Anxiety Management.* Department of Health, London.

Roth, A. and Fonagy, P. (1996). *What Works for Whom?* New York: Guilford Press.

Ryle, and Kerr, I. (2002). *Cognitive Analytic Therapy.* Chichester, Sussex: Wiley.

Salkovskis, P. (1996). *Frontiers of Cognitive Therapy.* New York: Guilford Press.

Salkovskis, P. and Kirk, J. (1997). Obsessive-compulsive disorder. In D.M. Clarke and C. Fairburn (eds.), *Science and Practice of Cognitive Behaviour Therapy.* Oxford: Oxford University Press.

Vetere, A. and Cooper, J. (2001). Working systemically with family violence: Risk, responsibility and collaboration. *Journal of Family Therapy,* **23**, 378–96.

Williams J. M. G (1992). *The Psychological Treatment of Depression.* London: Routledge.

Wells A. (1997). *Cognitive Therapy of Anxiety Disorders.* Chichester, Sussex: Wiley.

Further reading

Bennett-Levy, J., Butler, G., Fennell, M., Hackmann, A., Mueller, M., and Westbrook, D. (2004). *The Oxford Guide to Behavioural Experiments.* Oxford: Oxford University Press.

Butler, G. and Hope, T. (1997). *Managing your Mind.* Oxford: Oxford University Press.

Chapter 5

Working with people who have severe mental health problems

John McGovern

Introduction

It is an exciting time to work in this field of clinical psychology practice, since there have been many important research and treatment developments in the past 20 years for individuals with serious mental health problems. The issues are broad ranging. Conditions attracting the psychiatric diagnoses of schizophrenia, schizoaffective disorder, delusional disorder, and manic depression do not affect just an individual. These problems also impact on families, and families can therefore play an important rehabilitative role in delaying relapse, apart from having their own needs. They too may require appropriate care and interventions to cope with the exceptional circumstances they face. Many individuals experiencing severe and enduring mental health problems are affected not only by distressing symptoms, but may also experience stigma, restrictions in their social functioning, and difficulty in accessing employment. Surveys of the views of both service users and relatives show that these quality of life issues take priority over the management of symptoms.

Being confused and overwhelmed is an experience not unique to those using services, but is also shared by the providers of services. While much progress has been made in this field over the past 15 years, there remain many unresolved questions which emphasize the need for an ongoing synthesis between practice and research findings. The roles and responsibilities of a clinical psychologist working in this field therefore include the conduct and dissemination of research, as well as training and consultancy. Clinical psychologists additionally have a vital role to play in assisting colleagues from other disciplines to grapple with their differing professional identities and range of theoretical positions, to produce a joined-up, effective, accessible service for users.

What are severe and enduring mental health problems?

The task of defining severe and enduring mental health problems, or severe mental illness, (commonly referred to as SMI) is far from simple. Local differences in definition mean that senile dementia may be defined as a severe and enduring mental illness in one area of the country, and excluded in a neighbouring area. In practice there are a number of ways of defining this population in relation to the work of clinical psychologists:

- by diagnostic groups
- by the course of the condition
- by the levels of impairment they experience and their range of needs

Diagnostic groups

Traditionally the majority of this population will be individuals with diagnoses of schizophrenia or related conditions. Their group of symptoms, or symptom profile, will usually include positive symptoms (phenomena additional to normal experience) such as hallucinations, delusions, and disorganized speech. Their profile may also include negative symptoms (the absence of normal phenomena) covering apathy, poverty of speech, and a flattening of emotional responses. They may also display more general symptoms such as anxiety and lowered mood.

A smaller proportion of those considered to have SMI will experience severe mood disorders, often called manic depression or bipolar disorder. In manic depression the individual experiences marked episodes of mood swings from severe depression to mania to normality. In mania they may also experience a decreased need for sleep, a disruption to their daily biological rhythm, and show inflated self-esteem or grandiosity.

Others may not have a formal psychiatric diagnosis, but may more appropriately be described as 'vulnerable adults' who require long-term care. This grouping covers young adults with serious head injury, adults with a moderate degree of learning disability, and those with behavioural problems.

Lastly, the diagnostic category of personality disorder has also been targeted by recent guidance from NIMHE (2003) with their publication 'Personality Disorders—No Longer a Diagnosis of Exclusion'. Professionals from all disciplines are now asked to offer individuals with personality problems a comprehensive bio-psychosocial service, rather than labelling these individuals 'as not medically ill' and refusing to treat them on this basis. This chapter, however, does not focus on personality disorder.

The course of the condition

The main reason that these mixed groups of conditions are considered as severe mental illnesses is due to their long-term course, their treatment-resistant nature and their severe impact on social and occupational functioning. The course of schizophrenia has traditionally been described as varied: one-third having one episode only, and two-thirds having repeated episodes leading to a chronic condition. The premise that relapse begets relapse is also very applicable to manic depression, where 93% of this population have relapses, usually increasing in frequency throughout their lifetime. This condition is generally less feared and stigmatized than schizophrenia due to its fluctuating nature, with periods of normality allowing higher occupational functioning. It also has been linked with artistic creativity in line with the famous individuals affected by the condition, such as the comedian and writer Spike Milligan.

The range of impairments

In contrast to many of the adults with psychological problems described in Chapter 4, the levels of impairment in social functioning can be very high in individuals with severe and enduring mental health problems. Care may have to be provided in hospital settings, hospital hostels, or other forms of supported accommodation. In the acute phase of illness a person's condition can be so severe that they are considered at serious risk of harming themselves or others. Some may then be admitted on a compulsory basis to an acute psychiatric ward under the Mental Health Act. A small minority of individuals admitted this way might have committed violent and aggressive acts. They may therefore find themselves admitted to a psychiatric intensive care unit (PICU) or to one of a range of secure inpatient services, depending on the assessed level of risk of violence or absconding (see chapter 10 on working with offenders).

The multi-function acute admission ward of today is very different to its predecessor before the 1970s, when most accommodation for adults with severe and enduring mental illness was provided in large psychiatric hospitals built during the nineteenth century. With the closure of these large hospitals, not only in Britain but in Europe and North America, acute psychiatric admission ward have now to cater for a very mixed population and a wide range of complex demands. They face severe challenges in creating a positive therapeutic environment or delivering treatments other than medication and clinical management.

Against this background, many of the individuals treated there have repeated admissions, earning them the title of revolving door patients or the 'new long stay'. Longer periods of stay are often related to a lack of positive alternatives, such as respite centres, or to a shortage of places in community-based rehabilitation units or supported accommodation for individuals who are homeless, or who are unable to cope with independent living. Accordingly, increasingly the main focus of service provision is now to prevent hospital admission and to minimize the adverse effects of institutionalization by maintaining skills and independence. To achieve these aims there is increased funding for early intervention services for those with psychoses (as soon as the probability of a severe condition is recognized), for improved day services, for assertive outreach services (to maintain contact with those who would otherwise lose contact with services), and for teams focusing on providing crisis intervention and linked home treatment services.

Their range of needs

Given the above descriptions it is clear that individuals with severe and enduring mental health illness have a complex range of levels of needs. For some, their positive symptoms may be so severe that they are unable to function in the community and therefore some stabilization of their mental state will be a priority need, particularly where this relates to some area of risk. This will normally take the form of adjustments in their medication, which can be upsetting and may create psychological barriers about the benefits of this approach. If substance misuse has been an associated factor, they may be suffering physical or psychological withdrawal symptoms, and need some assistance to have a greater degree of control over their substance misuse. These immediate presenting problems may be compounded by the trauma of their first acute episode and their first compulsory admission. Those with repeat admissions may have increased feelings of hopelessness at finding themselves back in hospital despite their efforts. Others may be relieved at getting away from adverse living conditions and may be fearful of having to return to the community.

A second group of individuals, whose level of risk and symptoms are less severe, are likely to be living in some form of supported accommodation in the community or in their own home with frequent visits from an assertive outreach or home treatment team. Their social functioning and quality of life may be greatly affected by either their positive symptoms, such as a fear of being persecuted leading to social isolation, or their negative symptoms, such as apathy leading to restricted opportunities to benefit from social interaction. Some of this group may have fallen through the care net, particularly those with both substance misuse and chronic severe and enduring mental illness, who make up a substantial proportion of the homeless.

A third group of individuals may be living independently in the community either on their own, or with their partner or relatives. While their needs for day-to-day support may be minimal, the fear of relapse may still be a significant area of concern, so they need to be visited frequently by a member of a community mental health team or support worker, who will monitor their mental health and help them to structure their daytime activities. Even though they may be able to live independently, the majority of these will find it difficult to find work and sustain employment, and so are caught in a poverty trap. Individuals in this third group who have greater contact with their family then create a range of needs related to the functioning of the family unit as a whole. Services are often aware of the best ways of helping families to cope with these exceptional circumstances and how to support each other, and can help families cope with the roller-coaster ride of emotions that may be experienced when caring for their relative.

Reconceptualizing the problem and the response

Redefining severe and enduring mental illness

The language so far used has referred to the conventional diagnostic categories of Western psychiatry. It is useful to remember that these diagnostic categories only emerged in the last 100 years or so. Accumulating evidence is now questioning their validity, challenging the premises that underpin these discrete categories, and suggesting that these conditions are actually not qualitatively different from the experiences of the general public. The full details of this analysis are contained in Richard Bentall's (2003) *Madness Explained*, and in a paper on the evidence supporting a continuum model of psychopathology (McGovern and Turkington, 2001). A brief summary of this model suggests that we are approaching a paradigm shift in how we conceptualize serious and enduring mental illness.

Central to the original nineteenth century concept of schizophrenia by Emil Kraepelin as 'dementia praecox' was the idea that it is a deteriorating chronic condition, so that services for this group were traditionally based on a 'service-for-life' model. Long-term follow-up research has however produced growing evidence of considerable numbers of individuals diagnosed with schizophrenia who have had positive long-term outcomes. Cluster analysis of the symptoms of groups of psychiatric patients, containing both individuals with neurotic problems (anxiety, obsessions, and depression) and psychotic problems (schizophrenia and schizo-affective disorders) shows that the majority of individuals fall into a cluster containing both neurotic and psychotic symptoms, rather than in two discrete diagnostic groups. Numerous questionnaire studies have also confirmed high rates of co-morbid anxiety, depression, mania, substance misuse, and personality disorders in those with a diagnosis of schizophrenia. However, the most compelling evidence of a continuum of psychopathology, ranging from the general population under stress, through to the disintegration of a sense of self-characteristic of severe schizophrenia, stems from the successful impact on treatment-resistant schizophrenia of cognitive behavioural approaches (CBT), adapted from previous work with neurotic disorders. This is discussed in more detail later.

The above points on the recognition of late-recovery phenomena in the course of schizophrenia, an increasing awareness of problems with the validity of the term schizophrenia, the positive findings achieved by talking therapies, as well as the growth of the voice of consumer power through charities and voluntary organizations, all suggest a very different landscape in which clinical psychologists play an increasingly important role. In a recent radio broadcast Robin Murray, one of the worlds leading psychiatrists with expertise in schizophrenia biological research, stated that he no longer employed the term schizophrenia because of the problems of validity highlighted earlier.

Mental health services are therefore revisiting their model of delivery, to counteract the possibility that current services are inadvertently maintaining mental illness. The growth in the service user and carer movement and associated organized charities, and their level of influence on policy, has moved social exclusion up the agenda. Researches from these charities and professional colleagues have shown that consumers of services do not view symptoms as their most important area of need. Added to these changes is the optimistic philosophy generated by the Recovery movement.

A Recovery philosophy—transcending symptom focused approaches

The fact that social exclusion has been given such emphasis reflects the increasing influence of the experiences and views of service users and carers at a national and international level. Pioneers in this approach are services in New Zealand and four states in the United States who have adopted a user-led Recovery philosophy as the basis for their mental health service provision. There are signs that similar moves are underway in the United Kingdom, with the publication by the National Institute of Mental Health in England (NIMHE) of their report 'Guiding Statement on Recovery' (2005).

The main premise of this service-user led philosophy is that individuals are encouraged to transcend their symptoms and use self-management approaches to improve their quality of life and access important social roles. Concepts of hope, empowerment, personal meaning of the psychotic experience, and spiritual understanding, all play a central role. Proponents of this approach draw mainly on literature on users' personal accounts of recovery. They also cite evidence stemming from long-term studies showing that a substantial proportion of individuals with an original diagnosis of schizophrenia are symptom- and medication-free at follow up, after between 15 and 35 years.

One of the leading proponents of the recovery approach is clinical psychologist Rachel Perkins who, together with her nursing colleague Julie Repper, has gathered this evidence together in *Social Inclusion and Recovery* (2003). One of the key points made by the authors, echoing the views of service users, is that service providers typically use a deficits model where their main focus is on the resistant nature of symptoms, and the consequent lifelong dependence of service users on medication and support from mental health professionals. In contrast the Recovery model proposes that people should take a major role in managing their own health, and lead a normal life despite symptoms, rather than being dependent on the care offered by professionals to maintain them and stop them from getting worse. Figure 5.1 shows an example of a how a service user compared a maintenance approach to service delivery, contrasted to a Recovery approach.

This optimistic Recovery philosophy is a very exciting development, although research on this approach is in its infancy. Clinical psychologists may then begin to pose questions about their own practice such as, is current practice biased towards a deficit approach? Do we know as much about positive emotions or qualities, such as happiness and resilience, as we do about

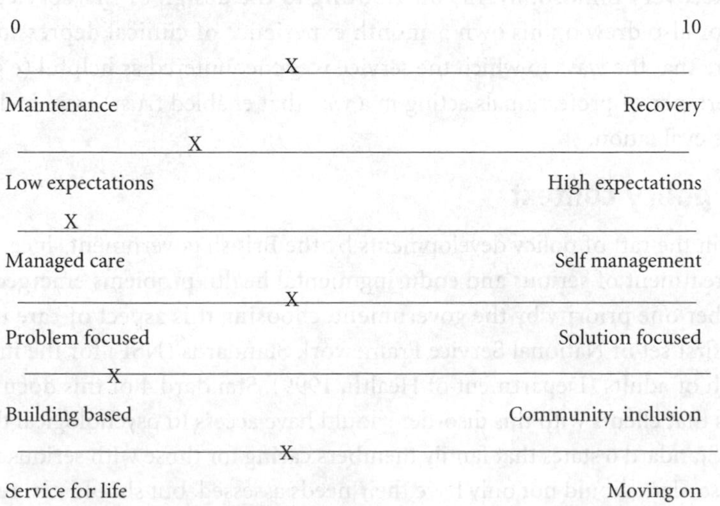

Fig. 5.1 Maintenance versus recovery approach.

thoughts and feelings around the distressing emotions of sadness, fear, guilt, and anger? Growing numbers are investigating ideas from the field of positive psychology in response to these questions, generating new forms of clinical interventions. These ensure that a person's strengths are incorporated into needs-led individual formulations. Psychologists can then also use well-established psychological models, such as learned helplessness, denial, and models of coping with loss based on attachment theory, to better understand the experience of service users in their interactions with services. Whereas an approach dependent on a medical diagnosis might categorize a person's refusal to accept they are ill as a psychotic symptom ('lack of insight' in DSM IV-R), an adjunct individual formulation approach might take into account the losses a person has experienced as a result of the diagnosis, to posit that the distressing nature of this has caused the person to adopt a position of denial. Such an approach is an adaptive life preserving phenomenon when present in cancer sufferers, and this may equally apply to people with serious mental illness.

Against this background, Rufus May has recently revealed that prior to qualifying as a clinical psychologist he was diagnosed with schizophrenia, and spent time as an inpatient. As a champion of the Recovery approach, he is currently using his psychological knowledge and training to find innovative ways of facilitating the recovery of service users, by involving them in planning and delivering training to mental health professionals. The author of this chapter is currently working in a low secure forensic service and drawing on his research training to evaluate with colleagues a service based on the Recovery philosophy. In contributing to the design of this service, the author also drew on his own 5-month experience of clinical depression, to ensure that the ways in which the service was encountered as helpful (e.g. the importance of professionals acting in a way that enabled trust) were included in the evaluation.

The policy context

Within the raft of policy developments by the British government since 1997, the treatment of serious and enduring mental health problems emerged as a number one priority by the government, choosing this aspect of care in the very first set of National Service Framework Standards (NSF) for the mental health of adults (Department of Health, 1999). Standard 4 of this document states that clients with this disorder should have access to psychological therapies. Standard 6 states that family members caring for those with serious mental disorders should not only have their needs assessed, but should *also* receive a package of care to meet those needs. This government recognition of the value of psychological approaches with individuals with severe and enduring mental health problems was change indeed, following the struggle of pioneers—psychologists, psychiatrists, and nurse therapists—for 30 years to legitimize the value of talking treatments with families and individuals. Further recognition of the value of psychological therapies for people with severe mental health problems was indicated by their inclusion in implementation guidelines for 50 new Early Intervention and Assertive Outreach services proposed by the NHS plan (Department of Health, 2000).

Against this background, more multidisciplinary professionals are being trained in psychological and psychosocial approaches for serious and enduring mental health problems. Psychological interventions are clearly no longer the unique preserve of clinical psychologists. A large part of the multidisciplinary training has been delivered by psychosocial intervention (PSI) courses, usually 1 year in length, where professionals are taught aspects of case management, family intervention, and cognitive behavioural therapy for psychoses. The main rationale for these short courses is a Stress Vulnerability Model, which assumes that individuals with a biological vulnerability become unwell in a context of increasing stress, so the task of the mental health professional is to help individuals and their families manage stress.

Alongside the clinical recommendations of the NSF, the government has also developed policies to address exclusion from normal roles and community provision experienced by individuals with serious and enduring mental health problems. The 2004 report by the Office of the Deputy Prime Minister on 'Mental Health and Social Exclusion' examined what could be done to reduce the vicious cycle of social exclusion affecting adults with mental health problems, leading to withdrawal and rejection from society, unemployment, debt, homelessness, and loss of social roles, leading to further worsening of mental health problems. The report identifies five main reasons for social exclusion: stigma and discrimination, low expectations from mental health professionals, lack of clear responsibility for promoting vocational and social outcomes for adults with mental health problems, lack of ongoing support to enable them to work (poverty trap of benefit system), and barriers to engaging in the community. A programme of concerted action is proposed, with a sustained programme to challenge negative attitudes, promote awareness of people's rights, and increase employment opportunities through supported employment schemes.

The reason for the government's concern is illustrated by some statistics. Only 24% of adults with long-term mental health problems are in work (the lowest employment rate for any of the main groups of disabled people);

a person with schizophrenia can expect to live for 10 years less than someone in the general population; mental health problems are estimated to cost over £77 billion a year through the cost of care, economic losses, and premature death; more adults with mental health problems claim sickness and disability benefits than the total number of unemployed people in the United Kingdom claiming Job Seekers' allowance. In contrast, employment rates of over 50% among people with severe mental health problems have been achieved in the United States by Individual and Placement Support Programmes, suggesting considerable potential for improvement on this area of social exclusion.

From the above analysis it is clear that there has been a considerable shift in government policy towards people with severe mental health problems over the last 30 years. The previous reliance on medication, associated with a dominant medical model, initially evolved to a recognition of the crucial importance of environmental and life events in the course of severe and enduring mental illness, and of talking treatments based on stress vulnerability or cognitive behavioural theory. The main focus of these approaches was however on managing symptoms and reducing the frequency of relapses. The recent emphasis placed on social exclusion therefore reflects an important further shift to a holistic view of individuals with severe and enduring mental illness, where the quality of life of individuals and their relatives is the main target of interventions, and where services support individuals to take primary responsibility for managing their life and their illness. This evolution in policy is reflected in Figure 5.2. The reference to 'the illusion of service delivery' is to emphasize the danger that any policy may be simply a label or a rhetoric that does not reflect what happens in practice. Services should not simply re-badge themselves as Recovery services without real change in practice.

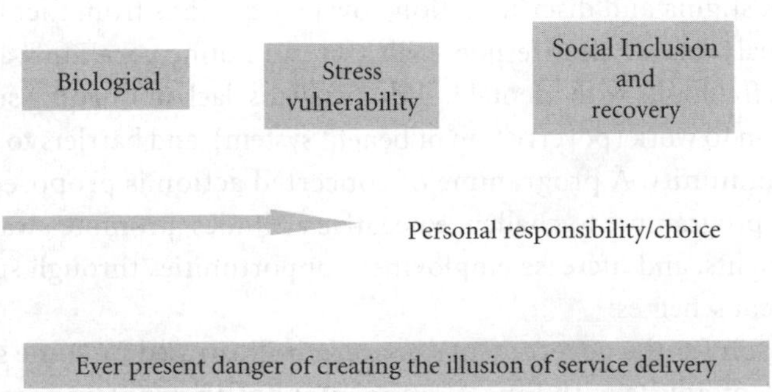

Fig. 5.2 Political and philosophical change underpinning service delivery.

The expanding pattern of services and roles for clinical psychologists

Historically psychologists initially became involved in a range of services for people with severe and enduring mental illness, often called generically 'psychiatric rehabilitation', with the implication of 'facilitating the return of the individual to their optimum level of functioning'. From the 1960s, however, the initial optimism of behavioural therapy with these people was blunted, as psychologists endeavoured to produce gains in reducing positive symptoms of schizophrenia to parallel those achieved with simple and complex phobias. Attention then moved to focusing on changing the environment around the individual with schizophrenia (for example token economies and behavioural family interventions) as a more hopeful way of producing change. From the 1970s token economy approaches, based on the principles of operant learning, became widespread, where patients were systematically rewarded for increased interactions and activity.

Individualized behavioural techniques, and a range of opportunities to exercise a wider range of daily living and social skills, characterized these hospital-based rehabilitation wards, acting in part as half-way houses for institutionalized individuals prior to their resettlement in the community. With the closure of the asylums the role of these units evolved to skills training, risk management, and relapse prevention for the 'new long stay'. A crucial role of psychologists in these settings was to assess individuals' needs (Baker and Hall, 1994), but these were often determined in terms of what services the unit had available. Today, rehabilitation functions are delivered by hostels or wards in the community, staffed by multidisciplinary teams providing 24 h care, and equipped with a range of domestic equipment, often together with a garden area. Proponents of the Recovery philosophy however argue against continuing psychiatric rehabilitation as a model, stating that it involves 'doing things to people' rather than helping people do things for themselves.

In the present policy and conceptual climate, with its emphasis on community care, social inclusion, and recovery, clinical psychologists who are interested in severe and enduring mental illness have the opportunity of working in an expanding range of teams. Those working in Early Intervention teams will typically be involved with individuals aged between 18 and 30 in their first episode of care, and will need to be familiar with psychological approaches for adolescents, as well as research such as that emanating from the Early Psychosis Prevention and Intervention Centre in Australia (McGorry *et al.*, 1996). This suggests that the initial period of approximately 2 years is critical to the illness course, if the psychosis remains untreated. During this period well-designed preventative health education material is valuable, as is assisting individuals to gain appropriate social and employment skills.

Clinical psychologists working in Assertive Outreach teams will be working very closely with other multidisciplinary team members to support a small caseload of individual with complex needs and usually chaotic lifestyles. A key target of these teams is to remain engaged with clients, and to create a level of ongoing consistent support so that the individual remains stable enough to avoid the need for hospital admissions. Given the relatively low turnover of clients receiving these services (approximately 80% of case loads are stable) there is an opportunity for long-term work on assisting the individual to create a better quality of life and tackle social inclusion, requiring flexibility of role, and a capacity to assist in practical ways, not exclusively as therapists. Knowledge of substance misuse and its interactive effects with severe and enduring mental illness is essential.

Most clinical psychologists working in the community have until very recently been employed in Community Mental Health Teams (CMHTs), which, with the movement away from hospital provision, are often viewed as the 'cornerstone of care'. Two separate factors are now changing this function. The development of Primary Care Trusts and the provision of services for mild- to moderate- mental health difficulties at the primary care level are progressively shifting these services away from the CMHT. With the steady development of the Early Intervention and Assertive Outreach teams already mentioned, significant subgroups of those with severe mental health problems are also being shifted away from the CMHT. CMHTs nationally are consequently experiencing a change of function, and are reacting in different ways to these changes. Clinical psychologists in these teams therefore have to consider how they can make the biggest impact on the service as a whole through one-to-one sessions, group approaches, consultancy, supervision, and training of colleagues from other disciplines.

A number of post-qualification courses now exist to train those from a range of disciplines in psychological therapies for this client group. Someone who has completed further training in cognitive behavioural approaches to psychoses (often taken as a 2-year day release Masters course) may acquire more specific skills than those possessed by a newly qualified clinical psychologist who has only received core training coverage of this area. The author of this chapter has been involved in the design and delivery of an innovative Manchester University MSc and postgraduate diploma course, offering rigorous training for multidisciplinary professionals in family and individual CBT for psychosis. This obviously leads to situations where clinical psychologists work closely with professionals from other disciplines who have attended these courses in psychological approaches. This may challenge the historical differential rates of pay for different professions, as reflected in the Agenda for Change modernisation of NHS pay scales, where rewards are based on training and skills rather than by the profession of origin by itself.

Specific interventions with severe and enduring mental health problems

An essential first step in planning any intervention is to try and understand each person's strengths, difficulties, and treatment needs in terms of an individual formulation, drawing on psychological general and clinical theories, rather than simply relying on an assigned discrete psychiatric diagnosis. In this formulation, individual early experience will be considered to determine whether the individual has dispositional psychological vulnerabilities derived from their childhood experience as well as biological vulnerabilities inherent to stress vulnerability models.

The development of behavioural family interventions for people with severe and enduring mental health problems

The evolution from behavioural approaches to cognitive-behavioural approaches, in line with research on information processing and the mediating role of thoughts, has generated one of the most important therapeutic advances for this group of people in the last 20 years. Psychological treatments have been developed using a broad range of cognitive behavioural approaches covering coping strategies, normalization, focusing, belief modification, and schema-focused work addressing rigid beliefs, some of which may stem from early experience. Despite continued use of medication, the majority of individuals with schizophrenia continue to experience residual positive symptoms (e.g. hallucinations, delusions), and studies using CBT approaches have produced significant symptom reductions. Non-specific therapeutic factors are important too, since reductions in pretreatment symptoms have also been achieved by befriending and supportive counselling alone. In today's climate of quality assurance there is an increasing demand for evidence-based practice, and comprehensive reviews of the evidence on psychological intervention for psychoses have now been published (Turkington *et al.*, 2004; Pilling *et al.*, 2002).

An important subgroup of interventions that have emerged from the 1970s with a robust evidence base are behavioural family interventions. The theory which underpinned these interventions was that ambiguous, highly emotional, and overcompensating social environments undermined the stability of the individual with schizophrenia. This in turn led to an increased frequency of relapse, greater burden on the family, and greater indirect and direct health service costs. A key measure used in this work was the categorization of families, or home environments, as high expressed emotion (HEE) on the basis of comments related to criticism, hostility, and over-involvement made during audiotaped semi-structured interviews with the family. A number of clinical psychologists and psychiatrists in the United Kingdom and United States then developed a range of family interventions that consisted of alliance building with relatives, educating families about schizophrenia, decreasing stress in family environment, enhancing problem solving in relatives, decreasing expressions of anger and guilt, maintaining reasonable expectations for patients' performance, achieving changes in relatives' behaviour and belief systems, and increasing patient independence using a graded approach to achieving goals. In Britain guidelines have been produced on the current level of evidence of different treatments for schizophrenia (NICE, 2002) and CBT approaches for both family intervention and individual interventions are both accorded the highest level of evidence.

The author's own orientation in this area has been the needs-led formulation approach developed in Manchester by Nick Tarrier and Christine Barrowclough. Given the severity of the condition it is expected that the family will be under severe stress. The rationale for this approach is that family members have expert knowledge on the day-to-day experience of the individual with schizophrenia, and have an important long-term role in helping their relative cope with their mental health problem and so reduce that stress. The most consistent finding for cognitive behavioural family interventions for schizophrenia, usually delivered over at least a nine-month period, is that they result in a significant delay in relapse compared to treatment as usual. It has also been found that there are increases in medication adherence, social functioning, and a reduction in relatives' burden.

Two other conditions have been addressed with these methods. Psychological approaches for bipolar disorder or manic depression have been relatively neglected compared to the number of controlled studies of psychological approaches for depression and schizophrenia. Both individual and family cognitive behavioural family intervention for bipolar disorder can result in reductions in relapse. Second, a major challenge are individuals who are labelled 'dual diagnosis', a term used to describe individuals who meet criteria for a diagnosis of both a severe and enduring mental health problem and a substance misuse disorder. The prevalence of substance misuse in schizophrenia in the United States is estimated to be approximately 40–50%. In general the picture on interventions with severe mental illness and coexisting substance misuse is not so encouraging (see Chapter 8), but a randomized control trial which examined an integrated psychological approach for individuals with schizophrenia and coexisting substance misuse, and their families, led to improvements in global functioning and symptom reductions at 18-month follow up (Barrowclough *et al.*, 2001).

Closing the research–training–practice gaps—Brian: an example of cognitive behavioural family and individual intervention

The following example illustrates a cognitive behavioural family intervention, supplemented by additional individual work, with an individual with schizophrenia and coexisting substance misuse. It draws on a range of methods, and is influenced by the needs-based individualized formulation approach of Tarrier and Barrowclough noted above, and the work of Gillian Haddock and Jan Moring, all of which also inform the content of the multidisciplinary training courses at Manchester University.

An important feature of this type of work is the process of gaining a picture of each family member's perspective. This involves both informal and formal assessment measures. Formal measures completed with family members include a Relatives Assessment Interview (RAI) which is a semi-structured interview looking at the impact of relatives' illness. The Knowledge about Schizophrenia Interview (KASI) questionnaire examines existing beliefs about schizophrenia and substance misuse. Other standard measures used might include the Positive and Negative Symptoms Scale (PANSS) that also covers general psychopathology, and the Social Functioning Scale. Scales covering the expression of anger (such as the Novaco Anger Scale) and the level of distress in relatives (such as the short version of the General Health Questionnaire—GHQ-12) could also be used.

Another distinctive feature is the use of co-therapists. Prior to the first meeting with a family the clinical psychologist and other therapist—often the care-coordinator or a CPN—discuss their respective roles in delivering the family intervention. The more experienced practitioner, who should have undergone family intervention skills training and who may have had specialist placements under supervision, will take the role as lead therapist. The co-therapist should have at least some grounding in family interventions for schizophrenia. The co-therapist role involves supporting the lead therapist in their structuring and delivery of the session, taking notes during the session, and observing the non-verbal behaviour of those present. The co-therapist can also conduct one-to-one assessments with family members.

Case Study

Brian was aged 32 and had a 13-year-old history of severe and enduring mental illness, during which time he had 12 admissions to the acute ward at his local district hospital. Between admissions he had lived in a range of flats and friends' houses, as well as periods at the family home with his mother Jean, aged 56, and father Phil, aged 60. His latest admission followed a complaint from his parents' neighbours who reported that he had been throwing furniture and household objects from his bedroom window. When the neighbour called at the house Brian lunged at him and accused him of 'bugging the house'. Brian was reportedly drunk at the time, as well as being under the influence of amphetamines. When Brian was visited shortly afterwards by a psychiatrist and social worker he was sectioned and admitted with the assistance of the police to a locked psychiatric acute admission ward.

During a 4-week period on the acute ward, where his medication was reviewed and he received counselling about his drug use, Brian was referred to the Community Mental Health Team (CMHT). While still retaining psychotic symptoms of delusions and hallucinations his mental state was reportedly much improved. As he had coped well with extended leave from the ward, the ward team held a Care Programme Approach discharge meeting, attended by the community psychiatric nurse who took over the care coordinator role, and by the CMHT clinical psychologist. Part of Brian's referral to the community mental health team was for cognitive behavioural family and individual interventions. There was concern about the ability of Brian's parents to care for him in the family home, as Brian's father Phil had a heart attack 2 years previously. Brian and his parents agreed that Brian would be discharged to his parents' home and that they would receive family and individual cognitive behavioural therapy sessions at home.

The initial session took place with Brian and his parents at home. The clinical psychologist was accompanied by the case coordinator who had agreed to act as co-therapist. The aim of this session was to explain what the intervention would entail, explain why it might be helpful, and to determine whether the family was willing to give it a try. The therapists explained that there was no evidence that families were to blame for the illness, but on the contrary there was considerable evidence that families have a crucial role to play in the rehabilitation of their relative. They then explained that before starting the intervention it was crucial that the therapists learn from the family's expert knowledge, and gain an accurate picture of the areas they might work on. The first step therefore would be to meet individually with each family member to obtain his or her perspective. Then there would be a feedback session where the therapists would agree together with the family a draft list of areas it might be beneficial to work on. The lead therapist explained that the intervention would involve meeting weekly or fortnightly and that the intervention might last nine months with frequent reviews to check on its value. The family agreed to give the intervention a try.

Prior to the initial meeting the clinical psychologist had a meeting with the care-coordinator CPN, who had started a postgraduate module in family intervention (but had unfortunately withdrawn from the course due to staff shortages) to discuss their respective roles in delivering the family intervention. During the initial meeting with the family, Phil had responded positively a number of times to remarks made by the co-therapist. As it was agreed there was a natural alliance there, the co-therapist conducted the one-to-one assessment with Phil, and the lead therapist agreed to conduct the one-to-one assessment with Jean and Brian. Informal interviewing of each family member supplemented by the informal and formal assessment measures already mentioned, together gave a comprehensive picture of the family's experience of the illness, current functioning, and beliefs and attitudes. Both parents commented on the RAI that it was the first time any professional had asked in any detail how the experience of Brian becoming ill had affected them.

Both Phil and Jean had previously consulted the Internet and obtained some information from library books, and pamphlets they had been given by ward staff. They appeared to have a relatively good grasp on heritability and positive symptoms, but were less clear on negative symptoms. Brian said that the psychiatrist had told him that he had a chemical imbalance in the brain and this was responsible for his ideas about being bugged. Brian partly suspected that his psychiatrist was in on the conspiracy through Home Office connections, and believed that if he stopped taking drugs and drank less that these ideas would disappear. Phil and Jean shared these views and they were both unsure about the value of Brian taking any prescribed drugs.

The main area of distress for both parents was Brian's illegal drug use and his occasional violent outbursts when he frequently smashed objects or made verbal threats. Brian had punched Phil twice when Brian was 21 and in a later episode when he was 23. Both parents were concerned at what would happen to Brian in the longer term when they were not around to care for him. Jean also revealed that she resented the fact that she had not been able to pursue her career as a retail manager because of the time she had taken off to look after Brian. Both believed that if Brian could develop a more structured day and some interests it might distract him from his difficulties. Both parents had spent a considerable amount of energy trying to persuade Brian to give up his drug use. Phil in particular saw Brian as being unable to control his addiction, and being tormented by strange experiences. Phil's strategy was therefore to compensate Brian with cigarettes and money. Brian was then spending increasing amounts of time away from the house drinking at the local pub. Jean, in contrast, was disappointed with Phil for being too soft with Brian, even putting up with violent outbursts from him. She therefore coped by trying to be strict with Brian, letting him know what she thought of his indulgences and unacceptable behaviour. Brian himself was most distressed by his arguments with his parents, about being treated 'like a kid', and by his lack of money. The voices and the bugging also distressed him although at times he admitted he found it quite exciting. He was also unhappy about his life and commented that it was 'going nowhere'.

It was clear that both Jean and Phil cared enormously for Brian. They both had previously lived very active social lives, and the fact that they had remained involved and were willing to share the family home with Brian showed considerable staying power. Brian himself had been in his 3rd year of an electrical engineering degree when he had his first episode, and had continued his interest in computers. He had been a keen swimmer and cyclist as well as someone who was renowned for his sense of humour and had many friends.

The feedback session started with the lead therapist explaining that a useful approach to identify potential areas to work on was to organize the information gathered into strengths, understanding of illness, ways of coping, areas of distress, and areas of dissatisfaction. The elements of the formulation already outlined were then fed back to the family. Particular care was taken to emphasize the existing strengths of the family to cope with the exceptional levels of stress they had experienced. Specific instances of these, which had emerged in the interviews, were fed back to the family. For example, the lead therapist who had interviewed Phil had talked about Phil's knowledge of Brian's fears on bugging and how Phil was keen not to pretend to Brian he shared these ideas or to make a joke of them. These examples of existing strengths were fed back to not only praise the family's efforts but also to give a very clear and important signal to the family that their views had been listened to and taken seriously. Throughout this session the lead therapist acknowledged Brian's efforts in taking part in the session.

During the discussion of the formulation the following list of areas to work on emerged:

1 Understanding the illness and interaction of symptoms with substance use. While Phil and Jean seemed very knowledgeable about the positive symptoms, it was agreed it might be helpful to discuss negative symptoms and anger a bit more, and that it would be beneficial to explore the possible benefits of medication.

2 Examining how to help the family cope with stresses arising from changes in Brian's condition linked to a worsening of symptoms or an interaction with substance misuse. Secondary to this were the arguments and stress experienced by all family members, which were linked to different family members having different views on how best to cope.

3 Breaking the cycle of repeated relapses and hospital admissions. All family members rated this as a huge concern and commented that it sometimes preoccupied them. They were therefore keen to pursue further the idea of the 'staying well' plan introduced to them by the therapist.

4 Responding to Brian's fear that his life was going nowhere, with a family effort to help Brian increase his independence and have enjoyable ways to structure his day and move forward in his life.

5 Looking at Brian's long-term future and exploring a range of possibilities to help him achieve what he wanted.

The lead therapist explained that it would be useful if they could take a flexible approach to sessions and the timing of different areas on the development list. While there would be some occasions when everybody would attend sessions, there would be others where two or one family member would meet with both, or one of the therapists. The lead therapist also discussed the value of ground rules, so that they should all try to talk in a constructive manner and try to avoid interrupting one another. The session concluded with the family being asked to discuss possible areas for development during the week as a 'between session task'.

The following is a summary of how the areas for development list were worked through over a 9-month period.

Understanding the illness and substance misuse

Four sessions were conducted to build an alliance with Phil, Jean, and Brian. Three of these were with Phil and Jean, being joined by Brian (who was receiving individual CBT) joining them for the fourth family intervention session. The sessions were also designed to increase the family's knowledge of negative symptoms, anger and medication, and to explore the issue of substance misuse, and whether this was hindering them in understanding that Brian was also suffering from a severe and enduring mental illness. To achieve this, the family was provided with clear information about the difference in duration, course, presentation, and outcome in a diagnosis of drug-induced psychoses and a diagnosis of schizophrenia. This information was delivered in a discussion format, with frequent reference to points family members had made on the adapted KASI. The discussion culminated in a view that, provided side effects were monitored, there may be more benefits than costs to Brian trying a period of sustained medication compliance. This latter discussion also helped the family understand how the picture on medication was complicated by the presence of negative symptoms and how these affected a person's motivation.

The decision to only see Phil and Jean for the initial sessions stemmed from observations of severe criticism of Brian by both Phil and Jean during the one-to-one sessions. The therapists agreed that allowing them to discuss their feelings openly during these initial education sessions on understanding the illness would be helpful. Brian was asked to attend the fourth session and he was asked to tell his parents about his perspective on becoming unwell. Following this session, Jean had made empathic comments about what Brian had been through. While still difficult, there were signs that an alliance was being built up with the family and that therapists and family were operating more as a team.

The lead therapist also fed back that Brian had warmed to the individual CBT work and particularly the motivational interview component. While he was continuing to drink and take amphetamines, he had also expressed some fears about damage he may have done himself with long-term amphetamine use. It seemed that he had shifted his position somewhat, with an increasing recognition that there were negative aspects to amphetamine and excessive alcohol use. Brian had also commented that he had found the joint discussion and information on symptoms he was experiencing quite useful. As he also spoke positively about linking stressful events and exacerbation in symptoms to substance use, it was felt that the work could move to look at helping the family cope with stress.

Coping with stress related to symptoms, substance misuse, and family arguments

The alliance built with the family then allowed the therapists to tackle some of the more distressing incidents. Family members and therapists spent some time reviewing how stress could be defined, how it could be identified, and how the family could monitor its occurrence. All three were asked to monitor stress between sessions by recording any episodes where there was a significant change in their mood. All family members then discussed incidents from these diaries in sessions, and ways of coping were considered. They came to realize that by taking a step back, and checking out the evidence or alternative explanations, they could prevent their mood from escalating. On other occasions a problem solving approach could be used. This approach was particularly useful in helping both Jean and Brian discover what coping strategies worked best with which problem, rather than the 'you're too soft, you're too strict' entrenched positions revealed by the assessment. This in itself had a huge impact on the family's stress levels as it reduced dramatically the frequency of Phil and Jean's arguments over how to respond to Brian's behaviour. All family members were also taught emotion-focused coping through relaxation and distraction. These were particularly useful for Jean and Phil when they were confronted by evidence of Brian spending all his money on amphetamines, especially as they were trying very hard not to 'police' his behaviour.

With a marked improvement in the family's emotional climate, the intervention then moved on to look at Brian's fear that his life was going nowhere, and Phil and Jean's concern to help Brian increase his independence and have enjoyable and meaningful ways to structure his day. A constructive approach to goal setting was taken, so that Brian's inactivity was not viewed as a deficit, but instead the question was asked: what level of purpose and activity would a 32-year-old man without schizophrenia be enjoying? In line with this approach, each family member was asked to complete a form covering Brian's Strengths, Problems, and Needs. Brian's strengths were then used to start working on a graded approach towards achieving his needs. An example of this was Brian's interest in computers. In consultation with the family, a home task was set up where Brian would visit the local college to gain information on computer courses. In the session when this was discussed, Brian mentioned that he might experience some difficulty remembering to get up on time as well as going into the college on his own. It was agreed that Brian would give Jean permission to prompt him about getting up and that Phil would accompany Brian to the college.

Staying well

A key concern of the family, particularly in the light of the progress achieved, was a fear of relapse. The therapists therefore worked with the family to complete a 'staying well' plan. Each family member's views on any changes in Brian's thinking, feeling, and behaviour were to be collated. With Brian's help in particular these signs were arranged into three stages of severity: stage one—very early signs; stage two—increasing frequency and severity of signs; and stage three—the signs linked with a full-blown illness. For each of these stages appropriate actions were agreed with the family involving early appointments, revisiting stress management techniques, changes in medication, and if necessary hospital admission. Interestingly the discussion of Brian's previous admission resulted in Brian completing an advanced directive saying he would want to be given medication in hospital if his symptoms reached the acute stage. This decision was based on the previous admission where Brian now recognized that his refusal to take medication had considerably lengthened his stay.

Individual therapy

In tandem with Brian's family intervention sessions, he also continued individual CBT sessions with the clinical psychologist. The motivational interview work of the initial sessions was threaded throughout all subsequent CBT sessions. The areas covered in these included normalization, where a continuum model stretching from normality to neurosis through to disintegrated psychoses was explored. This also involved examining the crucial role of stressful life events in moving individuals along the continuum. The therapist and Brian then explored the relevance of this model to Brian's life. He was able to see that his increased drug use at the age of 18, following the break up of a 4-year relationship with his then girlfriend, and his subsequent sacking from his job, may have had some role in his first episode at the age of 19. He was also able to see how his sophisticated knowledge of electronic signalling devices might have some role in the formation of his delusion. He was helped to make these links to the cognitive model and his understanding of how the initial thoughts we have are not facts but rather are interpretations, which colour our feelings and affect our behaviour.

Brian also found it helpful to look at how behavioural and cognitive avoidance may have led to vicious circles of thoughts, feelings, and behaviours maintaining his beliefs. Particularly helpful were the techniques of modifying his initial automatic thoughts by generating alternative explanations, using behavioural experiments to reality test. Thus signals from the 'Main Frame' telling him not to trust the neighbours since they were after his secret electronic powers were examined to determine to what extent they could be due to auditory hallucinations against a background of stress and amphetamine use.

These techniques were supplemented with behavioural techniques, particularly for Brian's problems with anger, where he learned to identify and manage his anger using additional behavioural approaches of muscle relaxation and time out. The exploration of psychological models of normal grieving after loss, and of the mechanism of denial of unpleasant experiences or information, are also emerging as important aspects of work to further understand mental illness. All of these approaches were used in conjunction with a comprehensive individual formulation covering early experience, critical incidents, and current thoughts, feelings, and behaviours.

Clinical psychology in relation to severe mental illness

The extended case example, and the other issues covered in the chapter, gives a taste of the work of clinical psychologists in this field. They also illustrate approaches to redefining severe mental illness, and the interactions between evidence and current policy that have led to the increasing recognition of the value of 'talking treatments' with this group. An important theme of the chapter is the implications of a Recovery model, and the avoidance of a deficit model of working where too much emphasis is placed on the reductions of symptoms. Instead, important areas like meaningful day activity, equipping individuals to deal with stigma, and facilitating individuals to be fully included in society then become meaningful targets for the profession. The reflections on positive psychology and the opportunity for clinical psychologists to optimize their application of general psychological knowledge gained from the general population, for instance psychological models of grief and denial, are particularly relevant here.

There remain many challenges for psychologists working with the severely mentally ill. One of these is the growing multidisciplinary recognition of the need to offer interventions to individuals with personality problems. This may well be the next area for development for those working with serious mental health problems. The author is reminded of the words of Professor Steven Hayes at a recent conference: 'As a science we are only 90 years old: there is much to discover'.

References

Baker, R.D. and Hall, J.N. (1994). A review of the applications of the REHAB assessment system. *Behavioural and Cognitive Psychotherapy*, **22**, 211–31.

Barrowclough, C., Haddock, G., Tarrier, N., Lewis, S., Moring, J., O'Brien, R., Schofield, N., and McGovern, J. (2001). Randomised controlled trial of Motivational Interviewing, Cognitive Behavioural Therapy and Family Intervention for patients with Co-morbid Schizophrenia and Substance Use Disorders. *American Journal of Psychiatry*, **158**, 1706–13.

Bentall, R.P. (2003). *Madness Explained: Psychosis and Human Nature*. London: Penguin Books.

Department of Health (1999). *National Service Framework for Mental Health for Adults of Working Age*. London: Department of Health.

Department of Health (2000). *The National Health Service Plan*. London: Department of Health.

Harrison, G., Hooper, K., Craig, T. *et al.* (2001). Recovery from Psychotic Illness: a 15 and 25 year international follow up study. *British Journal of Psychiatry*, **178**, 506–17.

McGorry, P.D., Edwards, J., Mihalopoulos, C., Harrigan, S.M., and Jackson, H.J. (1996). EPPIC: An Evolving System of Early Detection and Optimal Management. *Schizophrenia Bulletin*, **22**, 2, 305–25.

McGovern, J. and Turkington, D. (2001). Seeing the Wood from the Trees: A continuum model of psychopathology advocating cognitive behaviour therapy for psychoses. *Journal of Clinical Psychology and Psychotherapy*, **8**, 149–75.

National Institute for Clinical Excellence (2002). *Schizophrenia: Core Interventions in the Treatment and Management of Schizophrenia in Primary and Secondary Care*. London: NICE.

National Institute of Mental Health England (2001). *Journey to Recovery*. London: NIMHE.

National Institute of Mental Health England (2003). *Personality Disorder—No Longer a Diagnosis of Exclusion*. London: NIMHE

National Institute of Mental Health England (2005). *Guiding Statement on Recovery*. London: NIMHE.

Office of the Deputy Prime Minister (2004). *Mental Health and Social Exclusion*. London: Office of the Deputy Prime Minister.

Pilling, S, Bebbington. P., Kuipers, E., Garety, P., Geddes, J. *et al.* (2002). Psychological treatments in Schizophrenia: I. Meta-Analysis of family intervention and cognitive behavioural therapy. *Psychological Medicine*, **32**, 763–82.

Turkington, D., Dudley, R., Warman, D.M., and Beck A.T. (2004). Cognitive-Behavioural Therapy for Schizophrenia: A Review. *Journal of Psychiatric Practice*, **10**, 5–16.

Turner, D. (2001) Wild Geese: Recovery in NSF. Kingston upon Thames, Rethink (formerly National Schizophrenia Fellowship).

Further reading

Barrowclough, C. and Tarrier, N. (1992). *Families of Schizophrenic Patients*: Cognitive *Behavioral Intervention*. London: Chapman and Hall.

Bentall, R.P. (2003). *Madness Explained: Psychosis and Human Nature*. London: Penguin Books.

Morrison, A.P., Renton, J.C., Dunn, H., Williams, S., and Bentall, R.P. (2004). *Cognitive Therapy for Psychoses: A Formulation Based Approach*. Hove, UK: Brunner Routledge.

National Institute for Clinical Excellence (2002). Schizophrenia: Core Interventions in the Treatment and Management of Schizophrenia in Primary and Secondary Care. London: NICE.

Repper, J. and Perkins, R. (2003). *Social Inclusion and Recovery*. London: Balliere Tindall.

Chapter 6

Working with older people

Jane Fossey

. . . For age is opportunity no less
Than youth itself, though in another dress
And as the evening twilight fades away
The sky is filled with stars invisible by day.
Morituri Salutamus Longfellow

Introduction

An interest in and perspective on lifespan development is essential for anyone working with older adults. How people have adapted through the phases of their lives and in the context of their cultural history often makes assessment and intervention with older people a rewarding experience. Inevitably the clinical psychologist is also faced with issues of personal reflection and development as they lead their own lives towards their own old age, and so need to be mindful of how this contributes to the work they do. They also need to be aware of their own preconceptions. The principles and practices of therapeutic work with adults certainly apply, and can be adapted for an older client group quite easily. However, ageist attitudes have continued to abound in society, many of which go unnoticed or are taken as fact. Samuel Johnson noted in the eighteenth century that *there is a wicked inclination in most people to suppose an old man decayed in his intellect. If a young or middle-aged man, when leaving a company, does not recollect where he laid his hat, it is nothing: but if the same inattention is discovered in an old man, people will shrug their shoulders and say 'his memory is going'*. The broad impact of similar attitudes is evidenced today in *The Times* newspaper, which has invented an anti-ageist column '*Not Dead Yet*' to challenge in a humorous way the many negative remarks made about people as they age in our society.

To guard against age discrimination in the current provision of health and social care services, the development of a specialty working specifically with those over the retirement age of 65 has recently grown up and flourished.

Whether the age at which individuals qualify for this specialist service increases in coming years will be interesting to see. Changing demography and future plans to increase the retirement age of workers largely due to financial pressures on pension provision will no doubt impact on the provision of services in the future. Changing attitudes of what constitutes 'old age' and the skills and abilities of people reaching their sixties and seventies also probably mean that, in future, the age of 65 years will no longer be a meaningful marker for service differentiation.

The age of 65 years used as a cut-off for service eligibility is however currently a practical way of protecting people's rights against institutional ageist practice, thus providing access to psychological care for needs which might be overlooked or put down to being 'all part of growing older'. It enables specific developments in psychological assessment and intervention skills related to our knowledge of the normal psychological processes of ageing, and the sociocultural context of ageing such as relinquishing old roles and developing new ones (for example, alteration in work role from worker to volunteer, change in family status from parent to grandparent, changes in structure and choice of ways to spend time). In addition, as people age, they become more prone to physical illness and may be faced with altered roles, either of caregiver to frailer partners or friends, or care recipient themselves, all of which has an impact on psychological well-being. They may also experience an increased number of life events perceived as stressful, and increased losses which need addressing in the context of their ability to cope with change developed through the years. Using psychological theory and skills in developing effective practice for these transitions does require specialist understanding and consideration. A specialist service also enables modification of practices developed in other specialist areas to more fully meet the needs of an older client.

A growing population—a growing specialty

Approximately 18% of the UK population are over age 65 years, this figure varying between localities around the country from 35% to 12%. The number of older people is growing, with the oldest age groups being the fastest growing proportionally, such that the number of people over 90 is predicted to double in the next 30 years. The British Government recognized the need to address the health needs of older people specifically in publishing the National Service Framework (NSF) for Older People (2001), showing awareness of the disproportionate need for access to services and a requirement for guidelines to root out age discrimination in order to ensure accessibility to services.

A similar demographic trend is evident in Australia which will have an increase from 12% to 18% of people aged over 65 in its population by 2021. This trend is also mirrored in the United States where the population of people aged 65 to 84 is currently increasing, and is expected to grow by 73% between 2010 and 2030, when the baby boom generation starts to reach the age of 65.

In most areas of the United States, Britain, and Australia, older peoples' services also extend to younger people who have specific conditions more commonly associated with advancing age, for example dementia, where the onset is earlier than 65years. Currently, expertise around dementia is primarily based in older adult or neurology services, although it is recognized that those who are younger do have different needs from those in their seventies, eighties, or nineties, and where possible, separate subspecialties are developed within existing older adult services to try to meet this need.

In the United Kingdom, PSIGE, the national special interest group for Clinical Psychology in relation to older adults was developed to promote this work, and it has grown successfully over the years. The first conference in Oxford in 1980 attracted a handful of attendees, the interest strengthening over the last 20 years, as evidenced by attendance of around 300 delegates at the conference in 2004. The need for increasing numbers of psychologists to specialize in working with older people is well recognized, not least because of the growing number of the population who are over 65 years old.

Extent of need

Although 40% of the NHS budget and 50% of Social Care budget in Britain is used for the care of older people, they are traditionally underrepresented in mental health practice despite having similar prevalence rates for psychological problems compared with younger adults, and higher rates of physical ill health which have psychological sequelae that may benefit from treatment. In the British Psychological Society Briefing Paper 5 on Purchasing Clinical Psychology Services for Older People and their Families (2004), it is noted that '*In a typical district service with a total population of 250,000 there will be*
45,000 over the age of 65
4,500–6,750 will have depression of which 1,500 will be severely depressed
6,000 will have anxiety related disorders
2,250 will have dementia
2,000 will be living with consequence of stroke of whom up to 100 will be experiencing mood disorders and 700 will need to adjust to permanent cognitive deficits'.

Prevalence rates for depression are at least twice as high among older people with a chronic physical illness or dementia, who have had a stroke, who are socially isolated, or who live in residential and nursing home accommodation.

Barriers to accessing services may come from both care providers and older people themselves. In identifying difficulties, depressive symptoms may not readily be reported or can be thought to be a normal part of ageing or ill health. The erroneous belief persists that older people find it hard to change and have a rigid style of thinking which is not amenable to therapy. Services may make it difficult for someone with reduced mobility or access to transport to attend an appointment. For older people themselves a reluctance to seek help may result from the stigma they associate with 'mental illness', or because of limited understanding of how psychological intervention can help people adjust to changing circumstances or life transitions, or simply because of an acceptance that unhappiness, stress, or low mood is an inevitable part of the physical ageing process. The reality in fact is that older people with mental health problems can and do benefit from psychological assessment and therapy.

What's so special about the specialty?

The work of a clinical psychologist with older people is extremely varied, in terms of the kinds of difficulties with which clients present, the interventions which are used, and the settings in which the psychologists work, including clients' own homes, residential and nursing homes, GP clinics, day care, voluntary agencies, and wards in mental health, community, and general hospital settings. Trainees on placement often comment on the variety of work and the opportunities to work at different levels within the health and social care system, applying psychology in its broadest sense.

A key feature in any of this is team work, to an extent that may not be the case in some other specialities. Often clients' complexity of need necessitates that psychologists work as part of a wider social, mental, and/or physical health team to contribute towards a part of the total package of care. The need for this both on an interprofessional and interagency basis was highlighted in the United Kingdom's 'Forget Me Not' report (Audit Commission 2002) which states 'agencies should collaborate to provide specialist multidisciplinary teams for older people . . . provide advice, support and training to the staff of residential and nursing homes . . . make every effort to provide a continuing care agreement . . . and develop clear agreed goals for older people with mental health problems'.

Other crucial members of the 'team' may also be members of the older person's family or wider support network. A guiding principle needs to be to establish the client's needs and what they hope to gain from any contact with a psychology service. The need to maintain their independence, dignity, and respect as far as possible, as with any other adult, goes without saying. However, many people who come to psychology services have been encouraged by family or other care agencies to attend, and so it is also crucial to consult with the person about the relevance of involving these other individuals in any work that is undertaken, either in terms of assessment of the difficulties or engagement in elements of intervention. It is important at this point to try to gain express consent from individuals about who can be consulted and what information they can be party to, since from time to time ethical dilemmas can arise for the practitioner, most commonly around sharing information and confidentiality. At times too, it becomes evident that it is more helpful to work with the couple or the family system than with an individual.

It often is not the nature of the problems that arise for older adults which make the difference to the therapeutic activity which takes place. For, by and large, they are just the same as anybody else. What may be helpful to consider are the factors and processes in the assessment and intervention relationship which may need to be modified in order to achieve the same aims. Knight (2004) identifies the differences in working with older adults as being around:

1 The *context* in which clients are seen. Differences may exist in physical terms, of seeing people in nursing homes or in their own home environment rather than a clinic setting, which influences the information available to the psychologist (for example being able to see pictures of family members, notice socioeconomic information, and gain indirect information about their ability to look after themselves) and also in the establishment of rapport at an early stage.

2 An awareness of *cohort effects* in terms of language usage, social and historical knowledge, and attitudes. This requires us to consider what cultural influences there are on people's understanding of their problems and how they might be understood from the client's point of view, rather than our current practice viewpoint. Additionally, we need to consider whether, for example, psychometric test norms developed 20 years ago for 80-year olds are appropriate *now* for people who are 80, but were 60 at the time the norms were first published. Psychologists also need to be aware of how they are influenced by their own age cohort experience and its influence on the therapeutic interaction. This is perhaps particularly true in intergenerational family work where the therapist may feel more closely allied with members of their own age cohort.

3 *Maturation* over an adult lifespan can be used positively in therapy to help an older client identify positive changes and ways to deal with current difficulties by rediscovering old coping skills. By identifying their successful selves on previous occasions they may then be able to view their situation more positively and used well-learned skills in a new situation. There may also be times when people identify unhelpful patterns which they seem to repeat. Identifying these, and possibilities for 'doing things differently' can be very rewarding.

4 *Normal cognitive changes* associated with ageing also need consideration when planning assessment and therapy sessions. Broadly speaking, selective attention gets poorer with age so it is harder to screen out irrelevant information, and working memory span reduces, so the amount that may be covered in a session may be slightly less than one might plan with younger people.

5 Specific challenges—*illness and disability*—require realistic planning of therapeutic goals. These will vary from person to person, but it is worth attending to the impact that an increased frequency of negative events can have. Limitations on the person's own likely lifespan or enduring cognitive ability to resolve issues may also limit the amount of time available to engage in therapeutic work.

In practical terms, the influence of the factors above mean that assessment is often complex and challenging requiring a range of factors to be taken into account. The length of treatment may tend to be longer, because less material is covered per session than with younger people because of slower processing with ageing, cohort differences, the often chronic nature of problems, multiplicity of problems and possible effects of medication, as well as possible impairments of hearing or vision which can influence participation in a session. Some reports suggest that older people have more difficulty with thinking abstractly about problems, for example identifying negative automatic thoughts during cognitive therapy, and hence modifications may need to be made to younger adult protocols. Several examples of this will be discussed later. It is also worth considering the use of educational handouts or tapes to back up some of the therapy ideas, being careful to word materials simply, and also to think about using larger font size of print and contrast colouring in order to make these accessible for people with visual and/or auditory impairments.

Range of roles for clinical psychologists

Clinical psychologists working with older adults engage in work directly with individual clients but also provide advice, consultation, and training to colleagues and organizations. The types of difficulties they might advise on generally result from an interaction between physical, social, and psychological factors, and although there is usually a primary focus on one of these aspects, they are rarely, if ever, treated in isolation from a more holistic viewpoint.

Direct work with clients with problems with a psychological focus

Depression is one of the most frequent and serious challenges of ageing and comes in many forms and to varying degrees of severity. It is often linked to feelings of low self-esteem and a sense of loss of control over circumstances or a person's own abilities. Anxiety, either generalized or specific, is also a common presenting problem, frequently related to health issues, or to a loss of confidence which has developed through changing circumstances or roles. In recent years, the range of therapeutic models for treatment of older people has been increasing and the evidence base for effectiveness has begun to grow. The most common approaches used in treatment are outlined below, though the exclusion of other therapies from this chapter does not mean that they are never practised with older people.

Cognitive Behaviour Therapy

In the United Kingdom there has been much recent activity in developing the use of CBT with older adults, paying attention to modifications to make its use more effective, and to encourage the active participation of the client in therapy (Laidlaw *et al.*, 2003). There is good current evidence for its effectiveness for the treatment of depression, anxiety, and in reducing somatic preoccupation. As with the work with younger adults, it is a directive, structured, and time-limited approach which focuses on the role of cognitive processes in the maintenance of difficulties. The acknowledgement of the developing therapeutic relationship seems crucial as part of this, and there is a need to be flexible in the way that 'homework tasks' and the recording of information, which is routine in therapy with younger adults, is discussed and delivered within the therapeutic relationship. Specific protocols for particular groups of clients are also starting to be developed and evaluated, for example with depressed family caregivers of people with dementia (Charlesworth, 2001; Marriott *et al.*, 2000). These interventions make use of ideas from interpersonal therapy and also aspects of psycho-educational approaches to facilitate carers' understanding about dementia, alongside a therapeutic framework which helps carers consider the way they think themselves, in order to help reduce their depression and increase positive coping responses to genuinely very challenging circumstances.

Interpersonal Therapy

The growing evidence base for the effective use of IPT (Interpersonal Therapy) with older people as a maintenance treatment preventing the recurrence of depression has encouraged an increasing number of practitioners to obtain training in this model of therapy (Reynolds *et al.* 1999). It is a short-term, focused, manual-based therapy designed to be implemented by health care professionals, and is not the specific remit of psychologists alone. The focus of therapy is on interpersonal conflicts rather than intra-psychic ones and it deals with present issues rather than those of the distant past. It seems well suited to depressed older people, and can directly address issues of loneliness and isolation. The methods do not require clients to have a high level of education or psychological mindedness as there is a strong psycho-educational component. A formulation is developed between therapist and client based on the history and detailed knowledge of patient's social network, which links the onset of the depression with difficulties in one of four focus areas: transition (retirement, change in marital status, becoming a carer); bereavement; conflict with significant others; and deficits or long-standing difficulty in making and sustaining relationships. The focus on interpersonal relationships and re-establishing patterns of activity can be extremely useful for people who find it more difficult to accept a CBT perspective and wish to be introspective about their own thoughts and assumptions.

Systemic approaches

Systemic work clearly recognizes that family or system dynamics are central in mental distress. Often clinicians working with older people already work with clients' families to a lesser or greater degree, and a systemic understanding of issues can be helpful. It is not uncommon for clients in their eighties to be part of a five-level intergenerational family, and experience one of their roles as a great- great- grandparent. Being part of any intergenerational group can give rise to difficulties at times of change, as each member adopts a new or changing role. The emphasis in systemic work is on exploring meaning, changing patterns and beliefs, and understanding how problems arise at transitional points in people's lives. The skills of therapy are transferable to (and from) work with any mental health difficulty, and the crucial requirement for undertaking this work is that members of the significant family or social system are willing to be seen together. The information obtained is therefore different from times when individuals are seen separately. The range of systemic approaches includes structural family therapy looking at family organization, boundaries and alliances; life cycle approaches; solution focused therapy; and narrative therapy. All involve specific skills in questioning and reframing situations with the family group. Systemic approaches may consist of a formal, structured clinic setting involving a team approach, or the framework may be used to aid individual therapists' and clients' understanding of their difficulties.

Cognitive Analytic Therapy

This time-limited therapy has its roots in the combination of CBT and psychoanalytic psychotherapy and in particular Object Relations theories which emphasize the internalized relationships between the child and the caregivers (objects). The basis of future social interaction is formed by internalized relationships (rather than the individuals themselves), whereby expectations from those relationships are realized or frustrated. Meetings between client and therapist are highly collaborative, with time early in treatment being given to gathering history, background, and context, and the identification of recurring patterns of belief, expectation, and behaviour. The collaborative nature of Cognitive Analytic Therapy (CAT) can be useful for older people who are not particularly psychologically minded, and the time taken to listen and understand a client's life story can enable the client to feel empowered within the therapeutic relationship. It is often a treatment most suitable for those who have 'personality difficulties' or who have had loose contact with services in the past, but have had little benefit from drug and psychological treatments. There is also developing work using this therapy to understand transference relationships in dementia care, both between the person with dementia and the family carer, and also between formal care providers and family carers. The role of caring engenders strong emotions in all who engage in it, and CAT can provide a useful framework for self-reflection and insight into reactions which can be valuable to the carer and thus to the client.

Reminiscence and life review

The potential for reminiscence based work to have a positive effect on the quality of life and well-being of individuals was recognized in the 1960s. It is perhaps the one therapy used by clinical psychologists which was developed specifically for older people and which is based on a theory of ageing, that is, Erik Erikson's psychodynamic theory of life stages. For many years it was seen as a single activity, in which groups of people were asked to share memories or ideas stimulated by themes from newspapers, photographs, and other prompt sources, although it was often difficult to predict exactly how such activity would affect an individual. Life Review is regarded as more structured than reminiscence and is generally carried out as a one-to-one activity between a client and therapist, in which more private reminiscences are shared. The aims of therapy are described as being to resolve past conflicts and promote ego integrity. Although this work continues, reminiscence activities now tend to be seen as having a variety of purposes, and are based on client needs. These may be for communication between clients, or between clients and staff, emotional and social stimulation, or a way of using cognitive skills and promoting a sense of self-identity. There is also some evidence for Life Review as being effective in the treatment of late-life depression (Bohlmeijer *et al.*, 2003) and that group Reminiscence can also be effective, although no more so than other treatments (Watt and Cappeliez, 2000). Working in this way may help clients recall memories and re-evaluate negative recollections in a constructive way and can be a helpful therapeutic resource in clinical practice. Whichever therapeutic framework is chosen with an older person, the need for flexibility of approach and respect for their life experience is essential.

Case Study

Alan was a 75-year-old man who had had contact with mental health and prison services for over 50 years, and was referred to the psychology service following an in-patient admission because of paranoid ideas, violent behaviour, and over-use of alcohol, which had meant he was a risk to himself and his neighbours. As part of a package of support for his discharge from hospital, which included housing services, social work, occupational therapy, and community nursing, clinical psychological support was provided to help him with compliance with medication and anger management. His lengthy negative history with mental health services made it difficult to build up trust initially. Sessions at his home helped him to feel more comfortable than attending a clinic and gave the therapist insight into his interests and hobbies and gain a more rounded picture of him as an individual.

Initially Alan was only prepared to discuss his feelings of anxiety about leaving his flat and concerns that he might be ridiculed by his neighbours. The therapist started by working on a concrete plan to overcome Alan's fear of going out to the local shop, and used some basic CBT principles, and also, with Alan's consent, collaborated with his care worker to support this, since Alan had no close family to assist him in going out. Therapy jargon needed to be avoided at all costs, since Alan already felt vulnerable and disempowered, and the term 'Cognitive Therapy' was of little value to him in trying to explain what the treatment approach was about. Plain language about his way of thinking and his physical experiences enabled him to understand and use techniques to control his fears. Written information about therapy helped him to consider issues between sessions, since his anxiety in sessions made it difficult for him to concentrate on what was being said. He found that using a structured diary to record his experience was unhelpful, and so refused to use one, partly because it awakened memories of school which had been a negative experience for him. He chose instead to write a verse about some of the information he was given, since this was something he enjoyed, demonstrating very clearly that he had assimilated the essence of the discussions.

We are but as our thoughts
From this there's no escape
Though we may build an image false
Which poses, grows or imitates

For by our thoughts we do create
Our inner self and present state
So the choice is ours to make
What sort of thoughts we entertain
Some uplift, enlighten and set free
Others enslave, corrupt or degrade
Though we are free at any age
To change our life and start again
So it's never too late
For we are what our thoughts create.

As trust grew in the therapist, Alan was able to disclose that he also heard voices telling him to harm himself and other people, which he found very distressing. He talked about the way he had managed these symptoms over many years, largely through the use of alcohol, aggressive actions, and self-harm. Alan had never understood what the voices were, and found it difficult to accept he was unwell, but because he felt his skills had been recognized early in therapy and he was valued, he was prepared to collaborate further with the therapist to increase his understanding and develop new and less destructive ways of coping when the voices occurred.

Direct work with clients with problems resulting from cognitive impairments

Most clinical psychologists specializing in the area of older people work with people with cognitive impairments. Most commonly this is with people with dementia, stroke, or Parkinson's disease, although depending on the local service structure, people with any of these conditions may be seen by clinical psychologists working within separate services. In general, work with people with dementia is undertaken in dedicated mental health services, whilst people who have had a stroke or have Parkinson's disease are seen through physical disability services. In dementia services, clinical psychologists normally carry out assessment and therapeutic interventions with the persons themselves, or work with family caregivers, either in relation to improving direct care practices with the recipient of care, or in relation to the caregivers' own psychological well-being in their role.

Neuropsychological assessment

In the early years of development of work with older people, neuropsychological assessment was one of the key activities of the clinical psychologist. The proportion of time now spent engaged in formal psychometric assessment has reduced, and has been given over to therapeutic interventions, but since the recognition of the importance of early diagnosis of dementia and the possible use of 'anti-dementia drugs' (anti-cholinesterase inhibitors) there has been a clear role for psychologists to play in differential diagnosis. In addition, knowledge of the strengths and weaknesses of a person's cognitive abilities assists the planning of rehabilitation, and support in communication skills. Assessment can also help carers to understand changes in behaviour and abilities, and how best to help. For the individuals themselves, an early diagnosis can be useful in helping them plan for their future. Australian policy is somewhat further ahead than in Britain, with the NSW Committee on Ageing report 'Taking Charge. Making Decisions for Later Life', which gives clear guidance on advance directives (wishes expressed by the person regarding their future treatment), enduring power of attorney and guardianship issues. The disclosure of diagnosis is certainly a difficult topic, and the practices currently used borrow many of the features of good psychological practice which clinicians in oncology services have developed over the last 20 years.

Psychological therapy with individuals with dementia

Towards the mid-1990s, our understanding that individuals who have dementia also experience emotional reactions which are not necessarily blunted by the cognitive difficulties they experience, has led to the development of some psychotherapy services tailored specifically for their needs. Pre- and post-diagnostic counselling services are now linked to many memory clinics. In addition, psychotherapy groups in which people can explore the impact of their diagnosis on their own sense of identity and on their changing relationships have been found to help reduce anxiety and depression. Individual treatment of CBT for anxiety conditions has also been possible with some individuals, when care is taken to simplify the information and to provide records of the therapy sessions, in order to help overcome difficulties with introspection and memory deficits which might be present. Other therapeutic approaches such as life review and CAT have also been modified and used, as detailed earlier in this chapter, to positive effect. The interest of psychologists in working collaboratively and creatively with people in the early stages of dementia to help them maintain self-esteem and self-identity, despite cognitive decline, is growing.

Rehabilitation

Cognitive rehabilitation for people with early dementia has also been recognized as important and possible. Often associated with memory clinics, group training in self-management memory strategies and the use of external memory aids have been shown to be helpful for a proportion of people. A key to this is that although sessions may take place in groups and be mutually supportive, the elements of the intervention which are adapted from experimental psychology (for example spaced retrieval via recall in gradually increasing intervals, errorless learning, building on preserved procedural memory, structured practice of specific skills, and goal setting to maintain activities of daily living) are individually tailored to each person's own needs and goals. Another effective type of rehabilitation has been developed in Australia which focuses on maintaining skills of daily living. This consists of 6–8 week programmes of community dementia care in which people are supported to live at home and improve their diet, use of medication, communication, and practical household management, rather than to move into residential facilities.

Validation Therapy

This was developed for use with people generally over the age of 80 years, and with those with a more progressed state of dementia who show signs of disorientation. The approach focuses on understanding and sharing the reality of the experience of the client, and responding to that in order to meet the psychological needs being expressed. For example, Edna, an 84-year-old lady on a continuing care ward repeatedly said 'I must go and make my children's tea' at around 4 PM each day, and would make some vigorous efforts to leave the building. No amount of reminding her that her children were in their fifties and sixties themselves and could make their own tea, or well-meant attempts to get her to sit down and wait for her own tea, had any effect. By taking account of the importance that care-giving had had for Edna throughout her life, and through discussions with the psychologist about her fears that she would be letting her family down, it was possible for nurses on the ward to develop ways of including Edna in care-giving activities during the day, and to provide a positive sense of achievement which reduced the frequency of her distress.

Treatment for family caregivers

Help for disabled older people is mainly provided by family members, many of whom are over the age of 65 themselves. There are many adverse consequences to the role of a caregiver including high levels of depression, anxiety, and feelings of anger, as well as grief for lost opportunities and changes in a loved one's abilities. The persistent nature of the role also impacts upon the individuals involved, and the complex challenges which arise in the changing relationship and responsibilities which each person encounters, often necessitating the relinquishing of old roles and development of new ones. The NSF for older people highlights the need to assess carers' needs separately when considering which services might be helpful. Psychological interventions for caregivers have been developed to include individual counselling and therapy, professionally led psycho-educational groups and peer-led support groups. Psycho-educational interventions typically include education about the illness, problem-solving, skills training to manage specific problems, and the provision of information about legal rights and financial entitlements. Sessions of cognitive therapy for individuals that involve education about dementia, identification of assumptions and beliefs about the care recipient and their needs, stress management, and positive coping strategies have also been shown to be effective (Marriott *et al.*, 2000). It is known that prolonged depression in caregivers can exacerbate the symptoms of dementia in the person being cared for, and leads to a greater demand on services, including earlier institutionalization. Providing effective support for carers therefore has a benefit for them as individuals and for the person they look after.

Direct work with clients with problems with a physical focus

Clinical psychologists also may be involved in helping people to adjust to physical changes associated with ageing. To illustrate the issues of working in this area just two examples will be given. *Sleep disorders* are a common presenting problem, with older people tending to experience more severe insomnia, especially as many pharmacological treatments have a high rate of iatrogenic effects. Older people also often report their sleep as less satisfying, and sometimes this is exacerbated through worry about lack of sleep, itself leading to reduced sleep. Therapeutic interventions include: stimulus control—teaching people to associate the bed and bedroom with rapid onset of sleep by stopping activities which would keep them awake (e.g. watching TV whilst in bed); sleep restriction so that people do not spend an excessive amount of time lying in bed; sleep education on what is usual and what changes normally occur in our need for sleep with increasing age; appropriate 'sleep hygiene' activities and routines which will positively promote sleep; and cognitive restructuring to identify and change faulty assumptions and worries about the effects of a reduced time asleep. Relaxation training is also used as an adjunct to the methods described and some people have found it very helpful, although the research evidence for its effectiveness is less convincing than for the other methods.

The treatment and rehabilitation of people who have had a *stroke* has been largely conceptualized in physical terms because so many of the sequelae such as hemiplegia and dysphagia are obvious or visible. However, the subtle problems which arise such as disorders of memory, visual perception, problem solving, and changes in personality are areas for involvement of the clinical psychologist. Mood disorders, particularly depression, are unfortunately often thought to be a natural response to a major life event such as stroke, with the prevalence being between 30 and 50%. Hence it is commonly under-diagnosed and under-treated either medically or psychologically, despite evidence of the effective use of medication and CBT in improving mood.

Team work is often key in medical settings where the focus is strongly on rehabilitation which is concerned with enabling people with a short- or long-term disability to obtain the greatest degree of independence possible. Clinical psychologists working with older adults with such disabilities are often asked to be involved in a variety of ways and across very different settings, for example working alongside physiotherapists running clinics to reduce the risk of clients falling. The aim would be to develop motivation, effective goal setting, and self-confidence in those with limited mobility. Other rehabilitation interventions might be to encourage confidence building and skill development to go out and use public transport again following a stroke or an episode of related depression. Often intervention concerns maintaining or regaining skills for activities of daily living and social interaction, and may involve collaboration with occupational or language therapists as well as the client and their family.

In the United Kingdom, a recent development has been involvement in intermediate care services which have been developed to 'bridge the gap between acute hospital and primary and community care' (NSF for Older People, DoH, 2001). The need for greater community-based services for older adults, particularly the need to prevent admission to hospital 'for want of community-based services that would better meet their needs' has been acknowledged. Psychologists are therefore becoming involved in advising both general hospital staff about issues of capacity to return home, which may arise for people with mental health difficulties who have been treated for physical problems, and advising home care staff about communication skills and treatment plans once people have been able to return home. The collaborative nature of the initiative between health and social services is also in line with the promotion of integrated services in preventing unnecessary hospital admission, and the promotion of independent living. This is a welcome step in recognizing the holistic nature of healthcare.

Indirect clinical work

The provision of advice and consultation to paid carers and other professionals is an effective way of providing psychological knowledge and passing on skills to non-psychologists. Advice to multidisciplinary team members aimed at enhancing their work with specific areas of practice can be carried out through formal and informal supervision sessions. As monitoring of standards in residential and nursing homes has increased, psychologists have been asked to provide systemic consultation about care practices both at an individual level of care, and when looking at the organization of practice at a wider level, thereby helping staff recognize the psychological impact of their work. Much of the work of psychologists in residential and nursing home care is directed at understanding the needs of clients with limited communication skills, which may result from dementia, stroke, or other neurodegenerative condition, and who may show behaviours perceived by some care staff and visitors as difficult to understand or cope with. Examples of such behaviours include repetitively shouting or walking about the home, inappropriate urinating or unwanted sexual advances. Understanding and formulating behaviour seen as challenging by staff usually makes use of the model of person-centred care developed by Kitwood (1997) in which the impact of the individual's previous lifestyle, personality, physical health, degree of neurological impairment, as well as their current social and interpersonal environment are all understood as contributing to the behaviour. All behaviour is hence seen as a meaningful action which communicates the person's need in some way. The aim of such work is to help maintain each person's sense of well-being and personal worth despite their physical and social losses.

While much of the work can be done through care staff, there are also times when direct assessment and intervention with the individual is indicated in order to arrive at an accurate formulation of the difficulties. For example, an elderly married woman repetitively calling for help from her husband who is not present, may be expressing a feeling of vulnerability, fear, and a need to feel that somebody familiar is taking care of her. If so, she may benefit from reassurance and comfort from staff, while a factual response about the whereabouts of her husband is not sufficient to meet her needs. However, it could also be that she misses her husband greatly, and that asking her husband to provide an audio- or video-tape of conversation can provide comfort and security at times when he is not available (known as simulated presence therapy). Clear information from staff about his likely visiting times, and opportunities to phone him may also meet this particular need. Each person and situation is unique, and careful assessment can enable the response to be appropriately tailored to each different person's situation.

Interventions can often be very simple. For example environmental changes such as providing clear signage in the building to help residents find their way around, and ensuring that there are regular and accessible activities in which they can participate with support as required from care staff, can reduce a sense of boredom and provide occupation. Likewise, providing familiar objects from home can enhance a sense of identity and belonging. Altering or being flexible with the care routine to ensure that environment and timings meet the needs of the person can reduce much of the behaviour which is seen as difficult.

Helping care staff to understand residents by getting to know their personal history and taking heed of their preferences can also reduce staff members' anxiety that someone is behaving oddly or is at some kind of risk if they are not complying with the usual routines in a home. For example, Mr. Jones was always an early riser because he worked as a baker prior to his retirement, such that he normally got up around 4 AM. The nursing home routine of staying in bed until 8 AM was unfamiliar to him and so he continued to get up at 4 AM and walk around. The staff felt concerned that he might annoy other residents or damage himself or the property if he was up early, and spent some frustrating mornings trying to persuade him to return to bed. Once they realized that this was his lifelong routine, they were able to adapt their practice and invite Mr. Jones to join them for an early cup of tea in the office, and engage him in activities, thereby ensuring both that he was enjoyably occupied and that those who stayed in bed until later were not disturbed.

Many staff have had little training in psychological approaches when they begin care work and find it very helpful to be given a framework for understanding their roles which goes beyond that of being task oriented. Helping care staff to engage in reflective practice can also be helpful in identifying ways that they interact with clients which may inadvertently contribute to difficulties. Figure 6.1 illustrates how a negative cycle of communication at an individual level might be maintained (or easily changed) using a CBT framework.

Such a diagram might be used to discuss a particular resident with care staff team, and may help staff to understand both the resident's behaviour and distress, and their own role in either maintaining the behaviour, or in potentially helping to modify it in the resident's interests.

Teaching and training

Clinical psychologists are often formally involved in training by contributing to the continuing professional development of their psychology colleagues, and colleagues from other professions, and on an informal basis through discussion about individual clients or organizations with whom they are working. This provides opportunities to share psychological knowledge and to develop the use of skills more widely, particularly when ongoing supervision and support is made available. Skills transfer has often been seen as a useful way of working, given that the number of psychologists is still relatively small and the demand for services is high. This is particularly important in long-term care settings, such as residential and nursing homes. A few decades ago

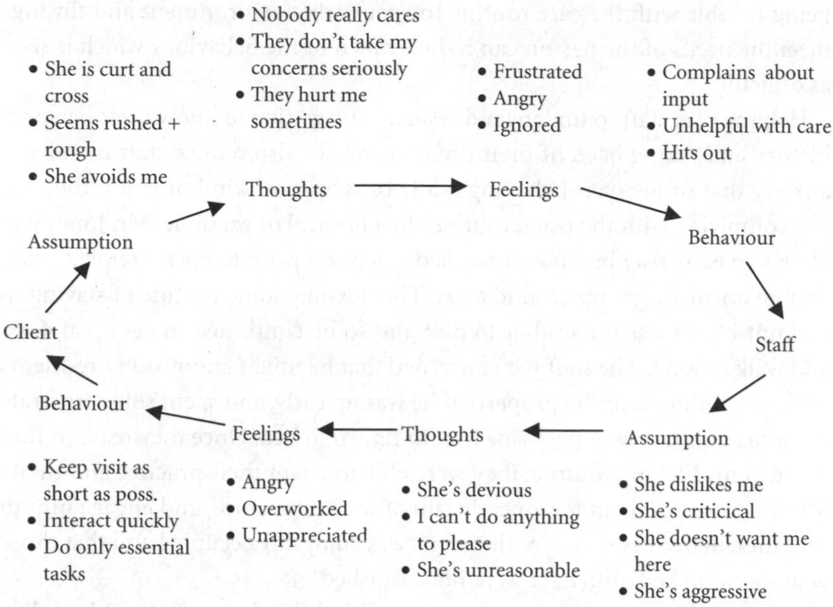

Fig. 6.1 Negative cycles of communication (from Ogland-Hand and Florsheim, 2002).

there was recognition from surveys in the United States that nursing assistants with little or no training were providing up to 90% of the direct care for people living in these facilities. A key to developing training in practice was a shift in societal attitudes about care provision moving from a custodial and medicalized one, to a more therapeutic, rehabilitative model, in which the emotional, personal, and interpersonal aspects of people's experience were acknowledged, and seen as influencing care. Alongside this attitudinal change were policy changes in the United States, Canada, and Britain towards community care, aimed at enabling people to receive treatment and stay in their own homes as long as possible. Consequently the people receiving care in institutional facilities were often those with the most complex health needs and greatest disability.

Clinical psychologists have been influential in developing training interventions for staff in such facilities, with a number of aims. Most commonly the objective is to increase staffs' knowledge, and to change beliefs and attitudes towards older people and mental illnesses such as dementia and depression. Another aim is to enable staff to implement new skills or care practices such as the reduction of physical or chemical restraint, and the development of person-centred care principles and practice by, for example, the use of information about a person's life history, which can inform choice and preference for people who have difficulty with current communication. The psychological impact of the physical environment has also been a feature of both training and recommendations for intervention to help to improve care.

There is a paucity of good evaluation of the effectiveness of such training programmes, most of which to date have been conducted in the United States. The evidence that there is suggests that although knowledge of attendees increases following training courses, the implementation of new practice is much harder to achieve and even harder to sustain. The sociocultural environment of many care homes makes staff behaviour change difficult. There is therefore a need to incorporate training work at an organizational level, in order to foster rehabilitative and creative vision within the environment, and at a systems level to ensure that there is opportunity to facilitate practice of skills disseminated in teaching sessions.

Research

Some clinical psychologists working with older people may be involved in fundamental research developing theoretical and practical applications for use in client care, while others may be involved in action research to evaluate the services in which they work, as well as advising and collaborating with colleagues. It would be naive to think that psychological interventions are only ever positive, and may not be neutral, unhelpful, or even harmful in some circumstances, or that what works with one group of individuals will be automatically useful with another. It has been important for example to look at whether mixed-age or cohort-specific groups are more helpful in treating older people with alcohol problems. Although evidence continues to be rather mixed, there seems to be an indication that cohort-specific groups may be more helpful in developing peer bonds and support, and that this is useful in ensuring the most effective use of resources. It is therefore important that as psychologists we maintain an inquisitive stance when assessing what we do. The effectiveness of many interventions is ideally assessed through the use of randomized control trials (RCTs), a methodology which is however often difficult to utilize for psychological interventions, since it is difficult to develop adequate control conditions and to ensure that assessors are 'blind' to clients' research status. It is therefore important to carefully evaluate psychological work by a range of methods to increase the range of information available on effectiveness.

Conclusion

Work with older people has grown as a distinctive specialty for a number of reasons. For the individual psychologist there may be a need to confront one's own ageing as part of one's work, but other reasons may include the richness of using a lifespan perspective which recognizes the many historical experiences and skills of the client group. Also relevant is the knowledge base of changes associated with ageing, social and behavioural gerontology, the frequent interaction of mental and physical symptoms and sensory impairments, the need to adapt adult treatment models to meet older clients' needs, the need to master specific assessment procedures and treatment approaches, the requirement to work within age-segregated services, and last but not least the desire to combat frequent societal negative attitudes towards this age group. The prevalence of work through other carers, and the necessity of involving family and the wider network in many activities is also a specialist skill, which brings many satisfactions. Older people themselves contribute a wealth of skill to the assessment and therapy setting; having made it this far they have been doing something right for a very long time! Our task is therefore to help them identify and acknowledge those skills again to deal with the events which are currently facing them, and to ensure that the process of ageing is as dignified and satisfying as possible.

References

Audit Commission (2002). Forget Me Not Report: Developing Service for Older People. London, Audit Commission.

British Psychological Society (2004). *On Purchasing Clinical Psychology Services for Older People, their Families and other Carers (DCP briefing paper 5)*. Leicester: British Psychological Society.

Bohlmeijer, E., Smit, F., and Cuipers, L. (2003). Effects of reminiscence and life review on late life depression. A meta-analysis. *International Journal of Geriatric Psychiatry*, **18**, 1088–94.

Charlesworth, G. (2001). Reflections on using cognitive behaviour therapy with depressed family caregivers of people with dementia. *PSIGE Newsletter* **78** 26–30.

Department of Health (2001). *National Service Framework for Older People*, London.

Erikson, E.H. (1980). Identity and the Life Cycle, 2nd edn. New York: Norton.

Kitwood, T. (1997). *Dementia Reconsidered: The Person Comes First*. Buckingham: Open University Press.

Knight, B.G. (2004). *Psychotherapy with the Older Adult*. London: Sage.

Laidlaw, K., Thompson, L.W., Dick-Siskin, L., and Gallagher-Thompson, D. (2003). *Cognitive Behaviour Therapy with Older People*. Chichester: Wiley.

Ogland-Hand, S.M. and Florsheim, M. (2002) Family work in a long term care setting. In: Norris, M.P., Molinari, V., and Ogland-Hand, S.M. (Eds) *Emerging Trends in Psychological Practice in Long-term Care*. New York, Haworth Press.

Marriott, A., Donaldson, C., Tarrier, N., and Burns A. (2000). Effectiveness of cognitive behavioural family intervention in reducing the burden of care in caregivers of patients with Alzheimer's Disease. *British Journal of Psychiatry*, **176**, 557–62.

NSW Committee on Ageing (1999). Taking Charge. Making Decisions for Later Life, Sydney NSW Committee on Ageing.

Reynolds, C., Frank, E., Parel, J., and Imber, J., Corner, C., Miller, M., Muzumbar, S., Houck, P., Dew, M., Stack, J., Pollock, B., and Kupfer, D. (1999). Nortriptylene and interpersonal psychotherapy as maintenance therapies for recurrent depression. *Journal of American Medical Association*, **281(1)**, 39–45.

Watt, L. and Cappeliez, P. (2000). Integrative and instrumental reminiscence therapies for depression in older adults: interventions strategies and treatment effectiveness. *Aging and Mental Health*, **4**, 166–77.

Further reading

Duffy, M. (ed.) (1999). Handbook of Counselling and Psychotherapy with Older Adults. New York: Wiley.

Hepple, J., Pearce, J., and Wilkinson, P. (eds.) (2002). Psychological Therapies with Older People: Developing treatments for effective practice. New York: Brunner- Routeledge Hove.

Marshall, M. (ed.) (2005). *Perspectives on Rehabilitation and Dementia.* London: Jessica Kingsley.

Woods, R.T. (ed.) (1999). *Psychological Problems of Ageing, Assessment, Treatment and Care.* Chichester: Wiley.

Chapter 7

Working with eating disorders

Hannah Turner

It's not about food, it's about me

Introduction

Although public awareness of eating disorders has increased considerably in recent years, many myths continue to surround these often severely debilitating disorders. Commonly misconstrued as 'a diet that got out of hand', the concept of an eating disorder can leave many feeling frustrated and perplexed, as they struggle to understand what appears to be an extraordinary state of obsession with eating, weight, and shape. However, beneath these worries there often lies a story of insecurity, anxiety, and fear. No one just wakes up one morning with an eating disorder—rather these are complex illnesses that develop over time and often as a result of multiple influences. The range of causative factors can be diverse and may include genetic and physical factors, personality traits, family dynamics, relationship problems, and adverse life events. People with eating disorders often experience intense underlying feelings of inferiority and worthlessness, and commonly believe they are undeserving of the good things in life. Plagued with guilt at the thought of considering their own basic human needs, they face the daily task of juggling these desires with the belief that they must fulfil others' needs if they are to be loved and accepted by those around them. The pervasive nature of an eating disorder means it invariably has a profound impact on sufferers' lives, including their education, employment, and social relationships, as well as on the lives of partners, families, and friends.

Working in this field can be challenging, frustrating, and rewarding. Challenging, because a range of issues need to be untangled; frustrating, because you can't make people change; and rewarding, because when they do, you share in the development of a life less constrained by food and enhanced by freedom and choice. Working with people with eating disorders is concerned with much more than behavioural change; most centrally, it's about engaging with people. Through developing a therapeutic relationship based on openness, honesty, and trust, a clinical psychologist can offer support as the process of exploration, understanding, and acceptance begins, getting to grips with questions such as why and how it developed, and what keeps it going. Through treatment, the psychologist can also offer a non-judgemental space in which change can be contemplated and steps taken towards recovery. Throughout this process it is important to be mindful that responsibility for change remains with individuals; our role being to empower those with whom we work to take control of their lives and their recovery.

Definitions and key features

There are two diagnostic systems used in this field; the Diagnostic and Statistical Manual (DSM) developed by the American Psychiatric Association, and the International Classification of Diseases system (ICD) overseen by the World Health Organization. In recent years, recognition that patients often move between diagnoses has fuelled debates regarding the clinical utility of the current diagnostic system, and it is likely that further revisions will be made in the future. However, present diagnostic groups and their key characteristics are described in the succeeding sections.

Anorexia nervosa

Behaviourally, anorexia nervosa is characterized by extreme dietary restriction, such that individuals maintain their body weight at least 15% below that expected for age and height (body mass index (BMI) = <17.5; BMI = kgs/m^2). Weight loss is commonly achieved through avoidance of 'fatty foods' and dietary intake is often rigid and limited in the type and range of foods eaten. A subgroup of patients will also engage in other weight loss behaviours, such as driven exercise, self-induced vomiting, and laxative misuse. Amenorrhoea is present in post-menarcheal females and both men and women may report loss of sex drive. From a cognitive perspective, patients often experience intense feelings of fatness, as well as extreme fears concerning loss of control over eating and weight gain. These patients also tend to evaluate themselves almost exclusively in terms of their weight, shape, and ability to control food, for example, 'if I gain weight it means I'm worthless/a bad person' and 'if I lose weight it makes me feel more in control—it makes me a better person'. For others, their lack of self-worth means they feel totally unworthy of food; not eating constituting a form of self-punishment for being the person they are.

Although eating disorders invariably start with a reduction in food intake, the path into this behaviour can be varied. For some natural bodily changes that accompany puberty or a negative weight/shape related comment from another may lead to a conscious decision to diet. For others, an episode of physical illness with associated weight loss, such as glandular fever, may lead to more intentional dietary restriction. Commonly occurring in the context of low self-worth, positive feedback in the form of attention from others initially serves to reinforce dieting behaviour and further weight loss. Patients with anorexia nervosa sometimes report a physiological 'buzz', as well as a sense of euphoria at being in control of their weight. For others it brings feelings of success and a fleeting sense of superiority at achieving something few in the general population can accomplish.

As the illness develops, so food takes a place of central importance, permeating all areas of life through its dominance in thoughts, feelings, and actions. Behaviours around food become increasingly rigid and deceptive, and the range of acceptable foods slowly diminishes. Cognitive rumination about weight and shape becomes all consuming and an increasing amount of time is given to thinking about food, the persistent dilemma about what to eat and what not to eat, meaning that for many 'not eating' becomes easier than eating. As time passes general functioning become increasingly impaired, interest in other areas of life fades, and day-to-day routine becomes characterized by social withdrawal and isolation, reinforced over time by the fear that no one will understand.

It is widely recognized that individuals with anorexia nervosa tend to be perfectionists; imposing extremely high standards upon themselves in a varicty of life domains, such as academic achievement. They are also likely to present with obsessive-compulsive personality traits, often evident in a variety of rigid, ritualistic behaviours, such as obsessive tidiness and order at home. Those with anorexia nervosa may have difficulty recognizing their needs and emotions in day-to-day situations; emotions such as anger may be difficult to tolerate and express, and an avoidant style of coping may predominate in everyday life.

Bulimia nervosa

Bulimia nervosa is characterized by two key features; firstly, recurrent episodes of binge eating, during which an objectively large amount of food is consumed with associated loss of control; and secondly, compensatory behaviours aimed towards the avoidance of weight gain. These may include self-induced vomiting, misuse of laxatives or diuretics, excessive exercise, dietary restriction or, in the case of those with diabetes, insulin misuse. As with anorexia nervosa, those with bulimia nervosa tend to evaluate themselves almost exclusively on the basis of weight, shape, and ability to control food, and a proportion will have a history of anorexia nervosa.

Although most people with bulimia nervosa tend to fall within the normal weight range, the illness is characterized by an initial period of dieting. However, the extreme nature of this invariably leads to episodes of binge eating. Plagued by fears of weight gain, many begin to use compensatory behaviours, such as self-induced vomiting, in an attempt to 'undo the damage' caused by bingeing and over time a vicious cycle of dietary restriction, bingeing, and purging develops. This cycle of behaviour invariably has a detrimental impact on other areas of functioning, such as work and social relationships, and it can have significant financial implications, leading some to steal money or food from others. People with bulimia nervosa tend to 'value' their symptoms less, compared to those with anorexia nervosa and often binge and purge in secret. Feeling too guilty and ashamed of their condition to ask for help, many often live with their disorder for years before seeking treatment.

Evidence suggests that a significant proportion of people with bulimia nervosa have difficulty regulating their emotions, and for many, bingeing may serve as a form of emotional regulation, a means of reducing the intensity of emotions when they become intolerable. Many also have impulse control problems and a history of interpersonal difficulties. A subgroup will also present with co-morbid depression and/or borderline personality disorder, and many of these will engage in a range of self-destructive behaviours, such as cutting, overdosing, and substance misuse, the dominant behaviour changing over time.

Atypical eating disorders

Over the past few years it has become increasingly recognized that a large number of people presenting for treatment in the community do not fall neatly into the two diagnostic categories described. Described as 'atypical' or 'eating disorder not otherwise specified' (EDNOS), this group of patients have, to date, been largely ignored in research circles and thus their key features remain poorly described. However a number of subgroups have been suggested. For example, a proportion present with all the key features of bulimia nervosa but fail to fulfil the diagnostic criteria relating to frequency of occurrence of behavioural symptoms. Others may present with all the diagnostic features of anorexia nervosa but (in the case of women) may continue to menstruate at a BMI of 17.5 or below. It has also been documented that a subgroup with anorexia nervosa are aware that they are underweight, don't experience feelings of fatness and are embarrassed by their skeletal frames, yet feel unable to give up their apparent addiction to weight loss.

Perhaps the most well recognized subgroup is patients with binge-eating disorder (BED) who present with all the characteristic features of bulimia nervosa but do not engage in compensatory behaviours. Consequently, this clinical group can be significantly overweight or obese. Other key characteristics include eating much more rapidly than normal, eating until feeling uncomfortably full, eating large amounts of food when not feeling physically hungry, and feeling disgusted with oneself or very guilty after overeating.

The issue of history and culture

Anorexia nervosa has a relatively long history dating back to 1873 when Lasegue published his seminal paper on 'anorexic hysterique', a condition in which patients presented with amenorrhoea, weight loss, and restlessness. Although many of these symptoms are still recognized today, key presenting features have been shown to vary with time and place. Initially viewed as a 'Western' syndrome, there is now growing evidence that anorexia nervosa can be found in diverse cultural settings, including Asia, South America, and Africa, although the exact incidence and prevalence remains unknown. The detail of the clinical picture also remains unclear; for example, clinical accounts indicating that symptoms of weight phobia and body image disturbance are absent in those presenting with sustained low body weight in non-Western countries have led some to suggest that the 'weight phobia' associated with anorexia nervosa may be culture specific.

By comparison, bulimia nervosa has much younger roots. Although an increasing number of case reports of bulimia nervosa type syndromes were published in the 1960s, this cluster of symptoms were initially viewed within the context of anorexia nervosa. It is the psychiatrist, Gerald Russell, who is widely regarded as responsible for the identification of the modern day syndrome. In 1979 he published a case series of 30 patients presenting with what he described as 'bulimia nervosa', the key features of which remain central to the present diagnostic criteria. It is most commonly seen in young females living in Western society. However, in the United Kingdom, Muslim Asian women have been identified as a particularly 'at risk' group. Further detail regarding the history and culture of eating disorders can be found in Fairburn and Brownell (2002).

How common are eating disorders?

About 1 in 250 females and 1 in 2000 males will experience anorexia nervosa, most often in adolescence and young adulthood. About five times that number will suffer from bulimia nervosa (NICE, 2004). In community studies, prevalence rates of bulimia nervosa have been estimated between 0.5% and 1.0% in young women. Anorexia nervosa is less common, with prevalence estimated at

0.3% in young women (Hoek and van Hoeken, 2003). The prevalence of EDNOS remains unclear, although reports suggest it is the most common presentation seen in clinical practice.

Who is at risk of developing an eating disorder?

A number of risk factors have been identified. Some are general factors, such as being female and living in Western society, while others are more specific, reflecting adverse early experiences such as childhood sexual abuse or parental neglect. A number of risk factors have been identified for bulimia nervosa, including early menarche and childhood obesity, while a number of premorbid traits, such as perfectionism, have been associated with the development of anorexia nervosa. A more detailed summary can be found in a review by Fairburn and Harrison (2003).

Eating disorders across the lifespan

Although typically associated with the young adult population, eating disorders can present in varying forms across the lifespan, from young children to older adults. Although bulimia nervosa is rare in children under 14 years of age, when it does present the clinical picture tends to be the same as that found with older people. In contrast, although the psychological features associated with early onset anorexia nervosa mirror those seen in adults, children and younger adults may also present with stunted growth or delayed puberty, and it is often parents or teachers who raise initial concerns. For some, their illness may be an attempt to arrest developments associated with puberty, while for others it may constitute a means of negotiating developmental tasks associated with adolescence, such as separating from parents and developing an increasingly independent identify.

A number of other types of childhood eating disturbance have also been described in the literature, the most common being food avoidance emotional disorder (FAED) and selective eating (Lask and Bryant-Waugh, 2000). FAED is recognized as an emotional disorder in which food avoidance constitutes the key presenting feature. Children with FAED have a history of faddy eating and food restriction but fail to meet the criteria for anorexia nervosa. In contrast, selective eating is a term applied to those who eat only a very limited range of foods, typically five or six different foods such as certain biscuits and a particular brand of crisps. Although this group do not tend to cause concern in relation to physical health, as they get older they often experience difficulties in relation to social situations where they might be faced with having to eat foods that are outside their limited range, for example, birthday parties. Although a large percentage eventually grow out of selective eating, this disorder can become increasingly problematic for those in whom it persists into adulthood.

In relation to later stages of life, eating disorders among middle aged and older adults are not always recognized and therefore may go untreated. For those in their forties and fifties, life events such as divorce, bereavement, grown children leaving home, and physical signs of aging, may leave some feeling that life is increasingly out of control. For them, an eating disorder may serve to engender a sense of control over life and/or represent an attempt to slow down realities of ageing. For older adults, underlying factors are also likely to relate to life circumstances. Social burden and financial strain, as well as the physical and cognitive abilities required to prepare a meal may all contribute to decreased food intake among this group. Eating disorders for older people may also serve as a protest against living conditions (e.g. in a nursing home), an attempt to get attention from family members, or reflect a lack of enthusiasm for life.

Setting for clinical work

Before describing how clinical psychologists might work within this field it is important to outline the clinical context, which has changed rapidly over a relatively short period of time. Until the last few decades of the twentieth century, anorexia nervosa was primarily managed by physicians, with treatment principally consisting of bed rest and re-feeding on medical wards. This was followed by the development of specialist units in which supportive nursing formed the cornerstone of treatment. Predominantly led by psychiatry, treatment programmes were primarily based on behavioural principles, whereby weight gain was rewarded with additional activities, such as walks, visitors, or home leave. Inpatient units have since moved towards a more holistic treatment ethos, with programmes aiming to address underlying psychological issues, as well as eating disorder behaviours and physical health.

The past two decades have also seen a significant increase in the number of people treated on an outpatient basis, and treatment is now commonly delivered in a range of settings, including primary care, community mental health teams, and specialist community eating disorder services. Services are also moving towards developing more intensive day care programmes, aimed towards those who would otherwise require inpatient admission.

The role of the clinical psychologist

The range of skills clinical psychologists can bring to an eating disorders team was summarized in the British Psychological Society document Service

Table 7.1 Skills clinical psychologists can bring to a specialist eating disorders teams.

Training in a range of psychological interventions
Theoretical training in and an understanding of multi-factorial causations and treatment packages which have taken account of this
A philosophy of collaborative care between therapist and patient
A professional culture and training committed to scientific and evidence-based practice
Training and skills in service evaluation and research

Guidelines for People with Eating Disorders (Bell *et al.*, 2001). These are summarized in Table 7.1.

Although eating disorders have serious medical consequences, psychological interventions remain at the core of treatment options for the majority, as recently highlighted in the NICE guidelines (NICE, 2004), which recommend that a specific type of Cognitive Behavioural Therapy (CBT-BN (bulimia nervosa)—Fairburn *et al.*, 1993) be considered as a first line intervention for bulimia nervosa, with an adapted version (CBT-BED) recommended for BED. Clinical psychologists have a central role to play in the implementation and evaluation of evidence-based treatment. Hence clinical psychologists work in all of the settings described previously. For some, their focus may be concerned with delivery and evaluation of individual outpatient therapy, while others may be more involved in setting up day services, or providing individual and group therapies in an inpatient setting. Clinical psychologists may also provide consultation and supervision to other professionals, including nursing staff, GPs, and other mental health professionals working in the community. Senior clinical psychologists are also likely to be involved in service planning and development, and may well fulfil the role of service and clinical lead.

Additional knowledge and skills

Although medical responsibility for patients invariably remains with medical practitioners, clinical psychologists should have a basic understanding of the physical complications associated with eating disorders (Birmingham and Beumont, 2004), as well as a working knowledge of other physical health conditions that sometimes present in the context of eating disorders, such as chronic fatigue syndrome and type I diabetes mellitus. This can be invaluable when liaising with medical colleagues, although it is important to be clear about the boundaries of expertise. Given that a shared understanding is essential if a cohesive package of care is to be delivered, it is imperative that clinical psychologists draw upon their communication skills to articulate and communicate a clear and logical psychological formulation to all involved.

The complex picture often seen in clinical practice means it is not uncommon for professionals within and between teams to be divided in their clinical opinion, and such differences need to be contained and addressed if treatment is to stand a chance of success. Given that clinical psychologists working in eating disorders often form part of a multidisciplinary team, it is also essential that time is taken to develop an understanding of how other colleagues work—this not only facilitates development of comprehensive packages of care, but also provides a multitude of opportunities for further learning.

Clinical assessment and formulation

A large proportion of people with eating difficulties feel ashamed of their symptoms and many are ambivalent about seeking treatment. Hence, assessment forms a crucial part of the treatment process. Taking a supportive and non-judgemental stance, one of the initial key aims is to understand the patient as a person with a unique experience, rather than as an 'anorexic' or 'bulimic'. Through engendering a sense of being listened to and heard, the foundations for a trusting therapeutic relationship are laid, and the process of understanding can begin. This reflects the second overarching aim of assessment, which is to work towards developing a shared understanding, set within the patient's developmental history, which, as the cornerstone of treatment, can be revised in the light of new information.

Areas for assessment

Assessment should cover psychological, social, and physical needs, as well as assessment of risk to self and others. Assessment should also aim to clarify what has prompted the patient to seek treatment at this time, as well as their expectations, fears, and wishes for therapy. From this should emerge a comprehensive personal history in which themes, patterns, and current life situations can be understood, including the development of self-identity, and the individual's personal style in areas such as coping, emotional expression, and communication. The development and course of the eating disorder should also be covered, including any history of dieting and/or eating disorders within the family. It is useful to note any previous treatment episodes and their perceived usefulness at the time. This process can be facilitated by various tools, including lifelines and genograms. It can also be useful to ask patients to complete a functional analysis of their eating disorder and associated behaviours. It is perhaps without doubt that an eating disorder initially develops as a 'solution', and it is imperative that these functions are understood. Examples of the wide range of functional roles an eating disorder can fulfil are shown in Figure 7.1.

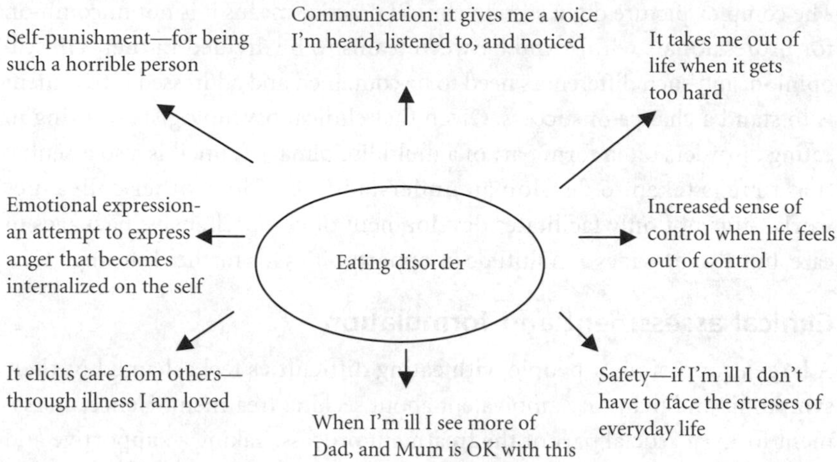

Fig. 7.1 The possible functional roles of an eating disorder.

Assessment should also cover the individual's general mental state, as well as associated personality traits, such as obsessionality, perfectionism, and impulsivity. The history and presence of other self-destructive behaviours should be noted, alongside a review of occupational status, social functioning, and impact on partners and relatives. Although the assessment of physical risk will involve liaison with medical colleagues, information relating to height and weight, menstrual status, blood potassium level, and other physical diagnoses, such as diabetes, should all be obtained.

Other assessments tools

Alongside conducting a clinical interview, clinical psychologists can draw upon a wide range of self-report questionnaires. Examples of questionnaires to assess specific aspects of psychopathology include the Eating Disorder Belief Questionnaire (Cooper *et al.*, 1997) while others constitute more generic measures of underlying psychopathology, for example, the Young Schema Questionnaire (Young, 1998). Semi-structured interviews, such as the Eating Disorder Examination (Fairburn and Cooper, 1993) can be useful when a detailed clinical picture is required. Other tools include food diaries and thought records, which constitute potentially useful ways of collecting detailed information relating to thoughts, feelings, and behaviours.

Approaches to treatment

The last decade has seen a steady increase in the range of psychological therapies developed and applied to the treatment of eating disorders. While early models and their deriving treatments focused on specific disorders, a number of recent theories have adopted a 'transdiagnostic' approach, aiming to account for the wide variety in eating disorder presentation. Some of the key interventions are outlined here.

Working with individuals

Motivation and readiness to change

Given that a large proportion of those presenting for treatment are likely to be uncertain about change, a significant amount of time and energy has been directed towards exploring the concept of motivation to change. While research initially focused on understanding and measuring the concept, more recently attention has been given to investigating the possible benefits of employing motivational strategies as a first step in treatment. Such techniques are likely to include asking patients to consider pros and cons of current behaviours, as well as encouraging them to consider how life might look if they continue with their behaviours over the coming days, weeks, or months. However, recognition that motivation to change is likely to vary over time has fuelled an ongoing debate as to the usefulness of motivational interventions in this field. The debate aside, from a clinical perspective it is essential that the patient has an opportunity to consider the costs and benefits associated with change, particularly at the beginning of treatment, and later if required.

Cognitive Behavioural Therapy

Until the mid 1990s, the psychological treatment of eating disorders was dominated by CBT, a treatment primarily based on a maintenance model that aims to account for the processes that serve to maintain eating disordered behaviours in the 'here and now', as opposed to providing a framework for understanding their development. CBT represents the most extensively researched and validated psychological therapy for bulimia nervosa and much of this early work is based on treatment derived from Fairburn's maintenance model of bulimia nervosa (for further detail see Fairburn *et al.*, 1993).

Case Study

Emily was a 23-year-old trainee accountant who lived with her partner. At assessment she described being obsessed with food. She tried to restrict her intake to 700 calories a day through avoiding 'high' fat foods, but this led to episodes of uncontrolled binge eating during which she would consume large amounts of food. Driven by an intense fear of weight gain, Emily routinely made herself sick, sometimes 3–4 times a day. She reported that this repetitive cycle left her feeling emotionally and physically drained; her mood and self-esteem were low and her behaviours were beginning to have a negative impact on her social relationships. Emily reported feeling fat and disgusting most days, commenting that if only she were thinner she would feel better about herself and life would be okay. Drawing upon Fairburn's model, it was hypothesized that Emily evaluated her self-worth almost exclusively on the basis of her weight and shape—providing an immediate measure of personal strengths and weaknesses. Coloured by perfectionism, Emily adopted dietary rules that reflected dysfunctional styles of reasoning as well as disturbances in information processing—such as dichotomous thinking, over-generalization and errors of attribution (e.g. foods can only be 'good' or 'bad'; 'I must restrict my intake to 700 calories a day'; 'if I gain weight my partner might leave me'). Emily's dietary rules were unattainable and increased her vulnerability to bingeing in two ways: firstly, they made her feel hungry, a powerful physiological trigger; and secondly, the beliefs she held about food meant that even minor transgressions were viewed as catastrophic and grounds for abandoning the rule and bingeing. Such transgressions not only promoted further concern about weight and shape, but also left Emily feeling increasingly negative about herself.

During the initial stage of treatment, the therapist worked collaboratively with Emily to develop the above formulation. Motivation issues were addressed and Emily was encouraged to challenge her dysfunctional beliefs about food, eating, and weight by drawing on psycho-educational material and behavioral experiments. The overall aim of this was to reduce dietary restriction, normalize intake, and reduce associated anxiety. The therapist supported Emily through meeting with her at least weekly, and she gradually began to feel more in control of her eating; she was able to reduce her bingeing and vomiting, and increase the variety and quantity of foods she could eat. Emily also learnt that these changes did not lead her to gain weight uncontrollably. Following this, treatment moved on to address triggers for residual bingeing, which were often interpersonal in nature, as well as Emily's concerns about weight and shape. Through exploring these areas, Emily was then able to begin to develop alternative coping strategies, as well as challenge the central importance of weight and shape. In the final stage of treatment Emily was encouraged to practice the techniques learned, her concerns about ending treatment were discussed, and a relapse prevention plan was agreed upon.

Schema focused Cognitive Behavioural Therapy

It has now become clear that early models and their derived therapies, although useful, only help a proportion of people. Outcome studies suggest that at best only 50% of those who receive CBT are likely to be free from their symptoms at follow-up, 20% can expect to continue with a full diagnosis, while the remaining 30% will experience episodes of relapse or will continue with a sub-clinical form (NICE, 2004). Consequently, researchers developed broader CBT models including the schema level. Rather than focusing exclusively on the present, schema focused cognitive behavioural models (SFCBT) attempt to develop an understanding of the role of past experiences, detailing the underlying role played by unconditional core beliefs, as well as affective and somatic states. A schema is a mental structure, which develops in childhood and serves as a template for processing later experiences—like a lens shaped by previous experience that colours subsequent interpretations, emotions, and behaviours. Schemas are thought to be rich in meaning and are held in multiple modalities including emotional, verbal, tactile, and visual forms. For example, Waller's model suggests that while restrictive behaviours serve as a means of primary avoidance, that is, avoiding the negative affect being triggered in the first place, bulimic behaviours are hypothesized to achieve secondary avoidance through reducing the experience of the affect once it has been triggered (Waller *et al.*, in press). Other self-destructive behaviours, such as self-harm and alcohol misuse, may have a similar function of emotional blocking, whereby the behaviour serves to reduce the intensity of negative affect experienced. It is thought that specific behaviours are influenced by experiences across the lifespan, such as parental modelling, as well as factors such as speed and duration of effect.

Case Study

Helen was a 19-year-old student presenting with a history of anorexia and self-harm. She had received previous treatment as an adolescent, but had been re-referred following an episode of increased dietary restriction. This was triggered by attendance at course lectures on child protection issues. In her past, Helen was subject to physical and sexual abuse from her uncle from the age of 6 to 11. During this time she was repeatedly told that this was her fault, and she was left feeling dirty, ashamed, and deserving of punishment. As a result of her early experiences, Helen developed a belief that she was 'a horrible person' who was 'unlovable', and deserving of punishment. Aged 11, she began to scratch her arms and this soon led to cutting; physical pain being easier to tolerate than emotional pain. Aged 13, Helen began to restrict her food intake. Not only did this serve as a more constant means of avoiding her emotions, but she also believed that weight loss would make her a better person—a person deserving of love and respect. Lectures on child protection and men showing an interest in her both served to trigger Helen's core schema that the world was a dangerous place, and that she was dirty and unlovable. She felt fat and repulsive, her heart raced and her hands felt sticky and clammy. Helen dealt with her 'inner state' through a range of schema processes, including avoidance (starvation), deflection (cutting), and compliance (seeking punishment through having sex with men she didn't know). Although perceived as the only coping strategies she knew in the short term, these processes all served to maintain her core negative beliefs as well as her presenting behaviours.

The importance of developing a clear formulation in which the patient can understand that their experiences make sense within their developmental history is a pivotal component of treatment. This process is important as it assists individuals in beginning to reattribute events externally, thereby reducing their belief that negative events are caused by factors internal to them. Careful consideration should always be given as to when it might be most appropriate to use SFCBT. This treatment is probably most appropriate for those presenting with factors that might otherwise reduce the success of conventional CBT, such as very poor self-esteem, a history of trauma, and co-morbid personality disorders.

Interpersonal psychotherapy

Interpersonal psychotherapy (IPT) is a time limited, goal focused treatment that targets interpersonal problems. Used as a comparative treatment in trials of CBT-BN, this therapy has been shown to be equally effective as CBT-BN in reducing core eating disorder symptoms at long-term follow-up, making it a viable alternative for the treatment of bulimia nervosa and binge eating disorder. Its effectiveness for anorexia nervosa remains unknown. Within an IPT framework, it is assumed that eating disorders develop in a social and interpersonal context, the maintenance of the disorder and response to treatment all being influenced by interpersonal relationships between the patient and those around them. The primary aim of treatment is to alter the problematic interpersonal patterns and life situations in which the eating disorder is developed and maintained. This is achieved through the resolution of problems within four possible domains outlined in Table 7.2.

Treatment consists of three distinct time-limited phases. During the initial phase an eating disorder diagnosis is made and the patient is assigned a 'sick role', the aim of which is to relieve them of meeting others' needs rather than their own, and facilitating their cooperation in the process of recovery. An interpersonal inventory, which includes a review of the patient's past/current close relationships and social functioning, is conducted along with a chronological timeline of significant life events, changes in mood and self-esteem, interpersonal relationships, and eating disorder symptoms. The therapist then makes connections between life experiences and the eating disorder symptoms, the aim being to link the eating disorder with one of the four interpersonal domains. Although patients may fit into several problem areas, the

Table 7.2 IPT problem areas and descriptions

Problem area	Description
Grief	Complicated bereavement following the loss of a loved one
Interpersonal deficits	A history of social impoverishment and inadequate interpersonal relationships
Interpersonal role disputes	Conflicts with a significant other: partner, another family member, co-worker, or close friend
Role transition	Economic or family change: the beginning or end of a career, a move, promotion, retirement, or diagnosis of a medical illness

time-limited nature of treatment means that one, or at most two, problem areas must be agreed as the focus for treatment.

The intermediate phase of treatment then focuses on the identified area, the therapist drawing on a range of treatment strategies specific to that problem area. For example, in grief, the goal is to facilitate mourning and help the patient find new activities and relationships to substitute for the loss. During the final stage of treatment, the patient is encouraged to describe specific changes in their eating behaviours. Termination issues are addressed and plans for maintaining progress in the identified problem areas are drawn together. Patients are also encouraged to identify early warning signs of symptom relapse and create an action plan they can draw upon if required. The focus of treatment remains on the interpersonal context of the patient's life, rather than the eating disorder and its related behaviours and cognitions.

Dialectical behaviour therapy

Alongside SFCBT, other therapies have been developed specifically for use with patients presenting with an eating disorder together with other problem behaviours, such as self-harm and substance misuse. These patients are more likely to have a history of emotional instability and a high percentage will have a diagnosis of borderline personality disorder (BPD), commonly being referred to as 'multi-impulsive'. Given that treatment of this group using conventional CBT is often unsatisfactory, researchers have begun to investigate the effectiveness of other therapies.

Dialectical behaviour therapy (DBT) was initially developed for use with people with BPD and recurrent self-harm. Based on the 'biosocial model', BPD is viewed as arising from a possible biological tendency towards emotionality shaped by early invalidating environments (Linehan, 1993).

DBT is an intensive treatment typically lasting a year and comprising individual therapy, skills training, telephone contact for skills training, and a weekly consultation group for staff running the programme. The overall aim is to validate the experience of patients and encourage them to become more skilled in managing feelings, behaviours, and relationships. During therapy, detailed chain analyses are completed when exploring the antecedents and consequences of difficult feelings and actions. The skills are taught in a weekly group and are organized into modules: mindfulness, interpersonal effectiveness, distress tolerance, and emotional regulation. In some cases, patients may also contact their therapist by telephone between sessions, usually in response to a crisis, the aim being to 'coach' patients in the use of skills to survive distressing crises. Preliminary findings suggest DBT may constitute a useful intervention for the subgroup of patients who present with an eating disorder and co-morbid BPD, particularly those with more impulsive and affect-driven presentations, and further studies are warranted.

Other treatment developments

Cognitive Analytic Therapy

Although only two studies evaluating the use of Cognitive Analytic Therapy (CAT) in the treatment of eating disorders have been conducted to date, results suggest that this intervention may be of use in the treatment of anorexia nervosa. Combining elements of CBT with theories from the psychodynamic school of thought, CAT aims to enhance self-efficacy and self-reflection, and to generate change (Ryle and Kerr, 2002). This is achieved through identifying problem behaviours (e.g. anorexia); reciprocal roles, in which the self and others take polar opposites (e.g. abusive/abused), and procedural patterns (emotions, cognitions, and behaviours) arising from the reciprocal roles and serving to keep the individual stuck. CAT is divided into three main processes, reformulation of problematic interpersonal and behavioural patterns, recognition of these patterns, and then, through recognition in day-to-day life, revision of these patterns. Treatment is focused and time-limited, usually lasting 16–24 sessions. The aim of the reformulation stage is to facilitate understanding of current problems in the context of early experiences. The therapist takes a detailed history of early life experiences and the development of current difficulties, and the patient completes the Psychotherapy File, a questionnaire that lists commonly occurring problematic procedures. The patient is then invited to consider their current situation and list patterns of thoughts, feelings, and behaviours that may be serving to keep them stuck. As part of this process two or three target problems are identified as the focus for therapy, and once agreed, the procedures that maintain them are described and understood in the context of early experiences. A reformulation letter describing target problems, problem procedures, and reciprocal role relationships is written to the patient. In it, clear links between past and present are made, and predictions are made as to how procedures and reciprocal roles might play out in therapy and elsewhere. Goals for change are suggested and the letter ends with a summary of target problems and associated procedures. The patient is given a draft copy of the letter and encouraged to suggest changes. The reciprocal roles and procedures are drawn out diagrammatically, and this 'map' is used in subsequent sessions to understand instances when procedures are enacted either in therapy or in day-to-day life.

The second stage of treatment focuses on encouraging patients to recognize when they are re-enacting their procedures. It is through this process of reformulation and recognition that a therapeutic alliance is formed, and this forms the vehicle through which the therapist and patient work together to develop ways of revising problematic relationship patterns and procedures, a process that can draw upon a range of therapeutic techniques. Expression of emotion is encouraged and the patient is also encouraged to experiment with new behaviours. The process of ending, which can be distressing and challenging for many, especially those with abandoning relationship patterns, is an important component of treatment, and discussion of this begins at least four sessions from the end. The aim is for the patient to acknowledge both the good and bad aspects of therapy and the therapist, and to accept the treatment experience as having been 'good enough'. Good-bye letters are written, which review progress, predict potential difficulties and identify further work, and these are exchanged.

Working with families

In the last 10–15 years the evidence base for the effectiveness of family therapy in the treatment of adolescent anorexia nervosa has steadily increased, paralleling a shift in focus within the systemic field. Historically anorexia nervosa was viewed in the context of dysfunctional family interactions; however, recent writings have emphasized the importance of understanding how the family environment changes in its attempts to cope with the arrival of a chronic illness; a process that invariably culminates in the illness taking centre stage. Family therapy is therefore now less concerned with untangling causal dynamics, focusing instead on supporting families to generate solutions that will help them negotiate the transitional stages inherent in normal family life, enabling them to play an active role in supporting recovery. A small number of services have also developed multiple-family therapy day programmes, during which a number of families are treated together. Although clinical effectiveness has yet to be determined, positive service user feedback suggests this represents a promising line of treatment. There is also anecdotal evidence to suggest that systemic therapy may constitute a useful intervention in the treatment of adults with eating disorders, and as such this forms another avenue for further research.

Treatment of atypical eating disorders

With the exception of BED, no clinical trials have been conducted on those presenting with EDNOS. Thus it is currently recommended that therapists treat these patients following the principles suggested for the eating disorder that the eating problem most closely resembles. Modified versions of CBT, IPT, and DBT have all been developed for use with those presenting with BED, and thus it is recommended that these interventions be used where appropriate (NICE, 2004).

Group interventions

Clinical psychologists are often involved in providing group interventions, whether in outpatient, inpatient, or day patient settings, including self-help for those with bulimia nervosa and those focusing on motivational issues, DBT skills, and support for carers and relatives. When running any type of group it is important that clinical psychologists draw upon their knowledge of group dynamics to manage the group setting and facilitate progress.

Working in an inpatient setting

Intense interpersonal dynamics, competition between patients, and high levels of emotion, can all make the inpatient setting a difficult place to be for both patients and staff. Many clinical psychologists work part-time on an inpatient unit, and key roles may include providing advice on implementing psychological interventions or behavioural programmes, and providing individual therapy for patients. They may also be involved in providing supervision and support to unit staff responsible for the day-to-day care, such as health care assistants. This can take the form of group sessions, the aim being to support staff through helping them understand team dynamics as well as their own reactions towards patients on the unit. The potential for staff splitting, for example where one staff member may be erroneously informed by a patient that another member of staff has made a particular decision, makes team time an essential part of any inpatient service.

Supervision and teamwork issues

As in many areas of mental health, working in eating disorders can be anxiety provoking and draining, and thus a space for regular clinical supervision should be available. Clinical psychologists are also often involved in providing supervision for others and they can play a useful role in mapping team issues, which can help team members understand the potentially destructive dynamics that can be enacted in eating disorder teams, which can mirror those seen in the families of the patients treated.

Ethical issues

Anorexia nervosa has the highest mortality rate of any psychiatric illness and although a proportion of those avoiding treatment can be engaged through a genuine alliance, there remains a minority of patients who refuse to engage in treatment despite their physical health becoming seriously endangered. For this group, it may be necessary to consider compulsory treatment under the Mental Health Act. While some authors argue that compulsory treatment forms a breach of autonomy and human rights, others remind us that for some patients this forms a necessary and essential part of recovery. For those locked deep in their illness compulsory treatment can be viewed as an act of compassion, in which professionals realize the seriousness of the situation and are willing to offer the intensive support required to help patients increase their energy intake and manage anxieties associated with this process. In some cases compulsory treatment can be met with a sense of relief by patients and their families, who temporarily hand over responsibility to health care professionals.

Audit and research

The training clinical psychologists receive in research methods means that as a profession we are well placed to address recent government initiatives, such as the drive towards clinical governance and the implementation and evaluation of evidence-based practice. Evaluation of treatments in the eating disorders is likely to be concerned with behavioural and cognitive change. This may involve monitoring of weight restoration and weight controlling behaviours, as well as change in relation to the central importance of eating, weight, and shape. Given the multiple functions of eating disorder behaviours, it can be useful to assess change in relation to broader areas, such as general psychosocial functioning (including work and interpersonal relationships) as well as mood, self-esteem and coping style, and other self-destructive behaviours. A wide range of tools, both self-report and semi-structured interview-based, can be used to assess change over time. Service evaluation initiatives may also focus on service user feedback. Alongside audit focused tasks, clinical psychologists can also play a role in advancing treatments for eating disorders; given that psychological interventions lie at the core of treatment options, this is viewed by many as a crucial role not to be sidelined by the various demands placed upon our time.

Conclusions

The past 20 years have seen significant developments in the psychological treatment of eating disorders. Consequently, the role for clinical psychologists continues to develop and expand.

For those interested a specialist placement provides a good opportunity to find out more, however the learning curve on entering the field can still be steep; skills relating to risk management need to be honed and issues touching a range of topics must be carefully considered. This chapter aims to convey a sense of what eating disorders are about, and give a flavour of the variety of tasks in which clinical psychologists working in this area might be involved. Along with our multidisciplinary colleagues we have a key role to play in advancing treatment and knowledge, and although often challenging, eating disorders can be a richly rewarding and varied field within which to work.

References

Bell, L., Claire, L., and Thorn, E. (2001). *Service Guidelines for People with Eating Disorders.* The British Psychological Society, Division of Clinical Psychology, Occasional Paper No. 3.

Birmingham, C.L. and Beumont, P.J.V. (2004). *Medical Management of Eating Disorders: A Practical Handbook for Healthcare.* Cambridge University Press.

Cooper, M.J., Cohen-Tovee, E., Todd, G., Wells, A., and Tovee, M. (1997). A questionnaire to assess assumptions and beliefs in eating disorders: Preliminary findings. *Behaviour Research and Therapy*, **35**, 381–8.

Fairburn, C.G. and Cooper, Z. (1993). The Eating Disorder Examination, 12th ed. In C.G. Fairburn and G.T. Wilson (eds.), *Binge Eating: Nature, Assessment and Treatment*, pp.317–360. New York: Guildford Press.

Fairburn, C.G. and Harrison, P.J. (2003). Eating Disorders. *The Lancet*, **361**, 407–16.

Fairburn, C.G., Marcus, M., and Wilson, G.T. (1993). Cognitive-behavioral Therapy for Binge Eating and Bulimia Nervosa: A Comprehensive Treatment Manual. In C.G. Fairburn and G.T. Wilson (eds.), *Binge Eating: Nature, Assessment and Treatment* (pp. 361–404). New York: Guildford Press.

Hoek, H.W. and van Hoeken, D. (2003). Review of the prevalence and incidence of eating disorders. *International Journal of Eating Disorders*, **34**, 383–96.

Lask, B. and Bryant-Waugh, R. (2000). *Childhood Onset Anorexia Nervosa and Related Eating Disorders* 2nd edn. UK: Psychology Press.

Linehan, M.M. (1993). *Cognitive-Behavioural Treatment for Borderline Personality Disorder: The Dialectics of Effective Treatment.* New York: Guildford.

Nice (2004). Eating disorders: Core interventions in the treatment and management of anorexia nervosa, bulimia nervosa and related eating disorders. *National clinical practice guideline.* Number CG9. London: The British Psychological Society and Gaskell.

Ryle, A. and Kerr, I.B. (2002). *Introducing Cognitive Analytic Therapy: Principles and Practice.* Chichester: John Wiley and Sons.

Waller, G., Kennerley, H., and Ohanian, V. (in press). Schema-focused cognitive behaviour therapy with eating disorders. L.P. Riso, P.T. du Toit, and J.E. Young (eds), *Cognitive Schemas and Core Beliefs in Psychiatric Disorders: A Scientist-Practitioner Guide.* New York: American Psychological Association.

Young, J.E. (1998). Young Schema Questionnaire—Short Form. New York: Cognitive Therapy Centre. (Available at http://www.schematherapy.com).

Further reading

Palmer (2000). *Helping People with Eating Disorders: A Clinical Guide to Assessment and Treatment.* London: Wiley.

Treasure, J., Schmidt, U., and van Furth, E. (2003). *Handbook of Eating Disorders*, 2nd edn. London: Wiley.

Fairburn, C.G. and Brownell, K.D. (eds.) (2002). *Eating Disorders and Obesity: A Comprehensive Handbook*, 2nd edn. New York: Guilford Press.

Chapter 8

Working with addictions

Shamil Wanigaratne, Kirsty Ashby, and Alison Jones

Introduction

In recent years there has been growing interest amongst clinical psychologists in working with those who experience a variety of addictions. This chapter outlines the role of psychologists within addiction services and the nature of the individuals they work with. Our current conceptualization of the term 'addiction' includes any human behaviour that has become excessive, with the individual's control over it impaired, which is damaging to the individual and society. Addiction has been described as the single most pervasive public and mental health problem of our time. The word 'addiction' is derived from the Latin verb addicere meaning 'to devote; to give oneself over' and implies impaired control. Behaviours that are commonly considered addictions include gambling, smoking, drug misuse, alcohol use, excessive sex, and eating disorders. Smoking can be considered the most damaging addiction with regard to the disease burden worldwide. Health, social, and economic consequences of excessive alcohol consumption are also a major burden. The recent public debate over the introduction of a new gambling bill (2004) in the United Kingdom raised all the issues about addiction and how a behaviour that can be pleasurable to a majority of people could become problematic and seriously damaging to some.

Orford (1985) identified similarities across the range of addictive behaviours that include: (a) the process of their development (b) predictable stages of change, and (c) process of reinstatement of previous levels of behaviour following periods of abstinence or control. Within this chapter we focus predominantly on substance abuse such as drugs and alcohol; however, as Orford suggests, many of the theories and models can be applied to a variety of addictive behaviours.

In recent decades psychology as a discipline has undoubtedly made the greatest single contribution to the field of addiction and substance misuse. It has led the move towards changing the key conceptualization within the field from a disease-oriented approach to a holistic biopsychosocial model. Major contributions by psychologists span the areas of treatment, prevention, training, research, and policy development. Considering the impact that psychology has had in the field at large, in the United Kingdom at least, relatively few clinical psychologists appear as yet to have made the choice of working in this field. The potential for contribution of clinical psychology to the field of addiction both within the National Health Service (NHS) and without is however immense. It is clear that we are no way near reaching this. We hope that this chapter will contribute in some way towards rectifying this, since working in this area can be both challenging and rewarding. The 2002 Department of Health document 'Models of Care' and the UK national strategic framework for treatment of alcohol and drug use has placed strong emphasis on the importance of psychological care for substance misusers. It provides a great opportunity for clinical psychologists to be at the centre of treatment provision for this client group.

Settings and services

It is highly likely that most clinical psychologists in all specialities will regularly come across clients who use substances, or have some form of addictive problem, which contributes towards their psychological difficulties. Co-morbidity, or dual diagnosis, is very common. This chapter, however, primarily considers services for, and work with clients who decide, or for whom it is decided, that the addictive problem is the major area of concern.

Most services for people with addictions are offered on a multi-professional basis, where clinical psychologists contribute as members of integrated teams. A variety of facilities and approaches are normally provided by services, depending on the needs of individual clients, the specific locality, and the range of common presenting and accompanying problems. Clinical psychologists may have input at any stages of a client's contact with the service, depending on local configuration of services. Settings include dedicated clinics, programmes based in out- and inpatient hospital wards or units, and community based facilities. The services provided by a large London NHS Trust is given here as a case example.

Case Study

The Addictions Division of the South London and Maudsley NHS Trust is one of the largest conglomerations of substance misuse services in the country. It serves seven London boroughs, comprising 16 different services including inpatient units, community services, and special services such as the Drug Treatment and Testing Order Service (DTTO). The clinical psychology service in the Division of Addiction is centrally coordinated and is provided by a team of 30 psychologists working according to service level agreements. Inpatient wards, staffed by a variety of professionals, run detoxification and rehabilitation programmes which involve assisting the client or patient in withdrawing safely from their primary drug of dependence using pharmacological and psychosocial interventions. The programme's aims are to provide a secure environment offering psychological and care relapse prevention techniques and strategies that are intended to assist patients in abstaining when they return to society outside the programme. Most patients have a keyworker (who is unlikely to be a psychologist) and are given support for any problems related to housing and benefits. Their stay can last for 10 days to 28 days depending on the patient's needs. A clinical psychologist working on these units would work with patients providing one-to-one sessions, group work, and neuropsychological assessment if required. The referrals to the inpatient units come from a number of sources including General Practitioners (GPs), psychiatrists, voluntary sector agencies, community alcohol and drug teams, and psychiatric services to name a few.

There are also a number of borough-specific community services that clients may be referred to. Again these referrals come from a number of sources, as well as self-referral. Here the client is assessed by their keyworker and referred for psychological intervention, such as one-to-one and group sessions if deemed appropriate.

Specialist settings such as DTTO provide treatment and support for offenders who have drug use problems. Probation Officers are employed here, and make the initial contact with the client, referring them to clinical psychology for one-to-one and group sessions, if this is suitable. Clients may then receive one of a number of possible psychological treatment approaches, together with input from other team members as needed.

Up until recently there have been few specialist services for children and young people with substance misuse problems in the UK. However, many addiction services are beginning to recognize the need for such intervention and services are now being set up to provide treatment for this client group. An example of this is within the South London and Maudsley NHS Trust, where a cannabis service for young people is in the process of being developed. The aim of this project is to provide psychological intervention to young cannabis misusers.

In all these settings, clinical psychologists work with a range of clients including adults and adolescents, across both genders and different ethnic backgrounds. The diverse nature of the clients means that it is essential to address factors that may coexist alongside the substance misuse. Mental health issues are also common amongst those who misuse substances and therefore need to be taken into consideration.

Epidemiology and scope

The magnitude of problems resulting from addictive behaviours far outweighs other areas in terms of concerns to the NHS and others. Substance misuse cuts across virtually every key area of NHS targets, including accidents, cancers, cardiac problems, sexual health, suicide, and mental well-being. It is estimated that 100,000 people each year die prematurely of tobacco-related diseases in the United Kingdom. Treatment of smoking-related diseases cost the NHS an estimated £1500 million each year (Parrot et al., 1998). In England and Wales, 25% of all hospital bed occupancy is said to be due to alcohol related problems. The yearly social cost of alcohol use is estimated to be £12 billion.

The prevalence rates of addiction problems are difficult to establish. The best estimates we have in the United Kingdom for substance misuse are derived from combining data from various sources such as national household surveys, psychiatric surveys, and research reports. Use and dependence varies according to age, sex, and ethnicity. Farrell *et al.*, (2003) report the following estimates for tobacco, alcohol, and drugs:

Tobacco: Amongst adults, 30% aged 16–74 reports current smoking while 23% class themselves as ex-regular smokers although 47% of the UK population reports never smoking regularly. Men are more likely than women to smoke heavily (11% versus 7%). The 20–24 year age group reports the highest rate of smoking (44%).

Alcohol: Of the UK population, 48% reports drinking more than twice a week, 21% of men and 12% of women report drinking four or more times a week and 2% of the population reports drinking more than six drinks per drinking session on a daily basis.

Drugs: The most commonly used illicit drug in the United Kingdom is cannabis with 25% reporting using it at some point in their life. Amphetamine comes second with 7% reporting ever using it. Ecstasy, cocaine, and LSD use were reported by 4% of respondents while less than 1% reported that they had used crack cocaine, heroin, or non-prescribed methadone. There are clear indications that drug use is increasing among the UK population; in 1993, 5% reported using any drug in the past year, this figure had risen to 12% in 2000. Young men appear to make the most significant contribution to this increase.

Multiple use: There appears to be a strong association between smoking, drinking, and drug taking. In all age bands and in both sexes, smokers were twice as likely to have used drugs compared to non-smokers. Similarly, those with high scores on alcohol dependence measures are much more likely to be dependent on one or more illicit drugs.

Links with psychiatric conditions: There is a consistent body of evidence that relate nicotine, alcohol and drug dependence, and psychiatric disorder. The estimates for prevalence rates in the United Kingdom for drug and alcohol problems and psychiatric disorder (dual diagnosis) range from 13 to 30%. The association appears to be even stronger with personality disorders.

Case Study

Anna is a 19-year-old woman who was referred to the Psychology Team by her keyworker in the Community Alcohol Team. Anna had been drinking excessively since the age of 14 and when drunk she would end up in situations which put her health and safety at enormous risk. Although the keyworker had some success in supporting Anna and had been able to suggest several harm reduction strategies, she was still in a cycle of bingeing on alcohol, getting into trouble, and then feeling unhappy and remorseful. After assessment it became clear that Anna's binge drinking was usually triggered by memories of sexual abuse she had experienced as a young child. She drank to deal with the intolerable emotional consequences of these experiences, which she had never shared before. Psychological formulation allowed Anna to see how her alcohol use had become functional in dealing with these traumatic memories, and intervention was aimed at helping her find alternative ways of coping with her past.

The role of the clinical psychologist

The role of the clinical psychologist in addiction services can be extremely varied. Many psychologists are involved in providing assessment, psychological interventions, consultation, supervision, teaching, research, and also management. Working in an evidence-based manner enables the clinical psychologist to deliver treatments that as far as possible have scientific support for their effectiveness. Since clinical psychologists use research to inform their clinical work, it is essential that they also contribute to the evidence base.

Teamwork is important too, as clinical psychologists working in the field of addictions are usually linked with a team. Although some work with other psychologists, most are placed in multidisciplinary settings alongside doctors, nurses, social workers, occupational therapists, and drug workers with varied backgrounds and training. This multidisciplinary approach is often seen to be more effective as it is holistic, and ensures that different team members address many of the client's needs, using their own profession-specific skills.

Assessment

Within most addiction settings, clinical psychologists obtain their first information about a new client from a referrer via a standardized referral form, which allows the psychologist to assess the likely needs and suitability for treatment of specific clients before their initial meeting. This procedure provides the psychologist with a basic understanding of the client including their physical and psychological history. On initial assessment, the clinical psychologist normally conducts an extensive interview as well as completing a standard assessment and outcome evaluation measure, which then allows them to produce a formulation from which a treatment plan will be devised.

Stimulant users and cannabis users form the bulk of substance misuse-only referrals to psychology services. In general, alcohol and opiate users are seen primarily by other members of the multidisciplinary team and are referred to psychology services only if there are specific psychological problems. Normally, referrals to psychologists for these groups are made for assessment and help with psychological problems such as depression, anxiety disorders, post-traumatic stress disorder, obsessive-compulsive disorders, personality disorders, and psychosis that coexist with their substance misuse problems. Sometimes clients make specific requests to talk to a skilled therapist about childhood traumas such as childhood sexual abuse and these individuals are often referred to the psychologists.

Treatment

The treatment plan for the individual client will vary greatly depending on the settings in which they present themselves as well as their immediate problems. A brief intervention approach may be used on short-stay units with the aim of a further referral to psychology services in the community. The psychological work in community and inpatient settings normally consists of one-to-one and group work, providing the most suitable intervention for the client's needs. If the presenting problem is purely a substance misusing one, then the interventions would be based on Motivational Interviewing, relapse prevention (strategies to maintain change), and Cognitive Behavioural Therapy (CBT) (focusing on assumption and beliefs that contribute to substance misuse). Explanations of these approaches is given later in this chapter. Choice between these interventions is based on the nature of the problem or the particular combination of problems, the evidence for effectiveness of a particular approach, and the theoretical orientation of the psychologist. For example, CBT would be the treatment of choice for depression and anxiety disorders, while a post-traumatic disorder might be treated with some form of exposure therapy. Individuals with personality problems may be offered CBT, psychodynamic therapy, or dialectical behaviour therapy (DBT) depending on the nature of the problem, the setting, and the skills and orientation of the psychologist.

Consultation, supervision, and training

In most settings in the NHS, including addiction services, the demand for psychological work far outstrips resources in terms of the available expertise of highly trained professionals. Increasingly, working through other professionals and frontline workers via consultation and supervision is becoming a key role for psychologists. In many addiction services, keyworkers and other professionals consult the psychologist on problems they are experiencing in managing their clients. In brief individual consultations or in group meetings, psychologists offer advice to the colleague on assessment and management of cases from a psychological perspective. Often these discussions take place on an ongoing basis and the psychologist shares clinical responsibility for the client. The consultation model, that is, working through other workers, enables psychological care to be provided to a greater number of individuals compared to the traditional referral model. Sometimes a combination of working models offer the best solution; for example the psychologist would see a client for a one-off assessment, and through a detailed report and ongoing consultation, would provide support for another colleague to carry out the psychological intervention.

Clinical supervision is a more formal and regular mode of operating the consultation model outlined above. In practice, there will be a formal agreement or a supervision arrangement with individuals or a group of individuals in terms of the format for supervision and the frequency of meetings. The meetings are normally used to discuss clinical cases within the principle of reflective practice. This usually involves providing constructive feedback on the supervisee's work as well as a supportive environment to discuss difficulties. Often supervision covers both a quality assurance agenda and serves a teaching and training function.

Audit, quality assurance, evaluation, and research

Audit and service evaluation are often seen as areas where clinical psychologists can make a significant contribution. Audit is essential for all services, in order to ensure that services are functioning at an effective level and delivering high quality of care. Ideally, audit should evaluate the clinical outcomes of the care being delivered, as well as completing checks that all levels of the service are performing correctly, from administration to the delivery of clinical interventions. Continuous service improvement is the general aim of audit activity, and with their research and evaluation skills, psychologists in each team and area can contribute directly or indirectly to this process. Many psychologists working in addiction services have been able to contribute in this way, as shown in this example.

Case Study

The psychologists in an addictions team were asked to carry out an audit to evaluate the effectiveness of the DTTO programme, because the programme, as it stood, was under threat following rapid expansion to accommodate government targets. The aim of the audit was to examine client retention and any reduction in client offending and drug use. The evaluation was carried out over a 1-year period, assessing all clients at the beginning of their treatment and at 3-monthly follow-up intervals. The results showed that there was a 45% retention rate, as well as a significant reduction in the rates of offending and drug use (offending = reduction of 72%; drug use = reduction of 56%). These results were then compared with available data on other programmes in the country, which indicated that this DTTO programme's outcomes were significantly superior. These findings were then used to strengthen the case to retain elements of the programme, which was under threat.

Apart from responding to requests for service evaluation and audit, each member of the psychology team is often also involved with specific research programmes, and is supported to do this with access to resources and time. For instance, the research portfolio of the London-based department described in the example above includes projects ranging from neuropsychological investigations of clients with disorders linked to substance misuse, to the utility of computerized self-assessment in routine assessments, to an evaluation of CBT with stimulant and cannabis users, to an evaluation of dialectical behaviour therapy with substance misusing clients who have also been diagnosed with a personality disorder. Psychologists are generally expected to take the lead in research activity, and to support, supervise, and encourage other members of the multidisciplinary team to conduct research.

Strategic planning, management, and service development

Most senior psychologists play a significant role in the management of the services where they work. For example in the London-based service described above, senior psychologists contribute to strategic planning, service development, and the management of the Addiction Division, which is the umbrella structure within the local Trust. The head of clinical psychology for the Addictions Division and senior psychologists may also meet with commissioners who purchase services and local (borough) Drug Action Teams who set priorities regarding specific service developments within a local area. The needs and priorities for substance misuse services may vary significantly depending on the demographics of an area. Psychologists should be well equipped to lead certain service developments such as services for stimulant users, cannabis users, and continuing care (after-care) for substance users. Psychologists' involvement at a strategic and service planning level therefore makes a significant contribution to the development of these services.

Multidisciplinary work

Lastly, clinical psychologists can contribute to teamwork and effective multidisciplinary functioning. For example, in the London-based service described above, multidisciplinary review meetings are usually held on a weekly basis with the agenda of reviewing clients who are currently attending the service. These meetings provide a supportive arena for staff to receive advice and feedback on continuing work with what can be a very demanding client group. Multidisciplinary teams in addictions can consist of doctors and psychiatrists, nurses, occupational therapists, psychologists, social workers, and probation officers. It is expected that psychologists make a unique contribution towards the cases discussed at these meetings from a psychological perspective both in terms of understanding and in terms of potential interventions.

A typical week of a psychologist

During a typical week, a clinical psychologist working in the addictions field is likely to spend only a third of their time on assessment and treatment. The rest of their time may be spent engaged in the other activities noted earlier. It is expected that one or two sessions a week be also spent on continuing professional development activities.

Psychological interventions in addictions

Having reviewed the settings in which clinical psychologists work and their likely roles, this chapter now considers in some detail the interventions that a psychologist might use with this client group. Before this, however, it is necessary to provide a brief over-view of psychological theories of addiction, which inform the interventions normally used.

There is no shortage of explanations of the nature of addiction. There is however general consensus that addiction is a biopsychosocial phenomenon. Although theories and models of causation and maintenance have been developed in each of the constituent disciplines of the biopsychosocial model, it is often difficult to separate the psychological from the biological and social. Nevertheless, these can be separately defined as:

- Biological (Bio): Physical sensations/changes within the body (e.g. withdrawal).
- Psychological (Psycho): Thoughts and feelings (e.g. 'drinking will make me feel better').
- Social relationships: Environmental stimuli and situations (e.g. meeting drug-using friends).

It must also be emphasized that there is in general considerable overlap between psychological, biological, and social spheres, and many professional disciplines will therefore be involved in delivering treatment, simultaneously or separately.

Psychological theories and models that attempt to explain the cause and maintenance of addictions can be grouped into three categories:

- Learning theory-based and cognitive models
- Psychodynamic theories
- Transtheoretical models

Learning theory-based and cognitive models

Learning theory-based models have been developed from classical and operant conditioning and social learning paradigms to explain addictive behaviour as over-learned habits that can be analysed and modified in the same way as any other habits. Taking substance misuse as an example, the development of addiction can be seen as a continuum from experimentation and recreational use of substances, such as ecstasy, amphetamines and cannabis, through to problematic use and dependence. The continual, excessive use and loss of control over the severity and frequency of drug use, marks the passing over of the threshold into dependence. Addiction is seen as a maladaptive coping mechanism that has led to negative consequences. Theories based on classical conditioning have been used to explain the acquisition of an addiction and the phenomenon of craving, which is central to the concept of addiction. Environmental stimuli associated with drug taking such as drug paraphernalia can come to exert conditioned effects in their own right, and these effects may be involved in the phenomenon of drug craving, for example when observing tin foil and needles. This theory has led to the development of cue exposure as a treatment of addiction, which aims to break down the conditioned drug effects that are thought to contribute to the behavioural pattern of drug seeking that characterizes an addiction (Drummond, 2001). Treatment uses the classical conditioning principle of extinction, and is built on the premise that repeated, non-reinforced exposure to drug cues (e.g. the sight of a syringe) will diminish any conditioned drug effects.

Operant conditioning paradigms have also been used to explain the nature of addiction. An addictive behaviour or a drug is seen as a reinforcer in the conditioning process in much the same way as food or sex. Drugs of abuse can serve as both positive and negative reinforcers. For example, when a drug alleviates the symptoms of withdrawal, it is acting as a negative reinforcer, and when a drug induces a state of euphoria, it is acting as a positive reinforcer. Complex reinforcement schedules and processes have been put forward to explain a range of addictive behaviours. Drive Reduction Theory, based on classical and operant conditioning, has been the dominant explanatory model in the psychology of addiction for more than 40 years. Currently, positive reinforcement explanations are favoured over negative enforcement explanations, such as the avoidance of withdrawal distress.

Social learning perspectives have led to interventions such as relapse prevention work, which aims to increase a person's awareness of, and ability to cope effectively with the relapse process, and his or her own history in relation to this, for example by examining the patterns of their previous relapses and coping strategies. Relapse prevention requires the development of specific coping strategies to deal with high-risk situations, such as social skills training, and more global coping strategies to address issues of lifestyle imbalance and covert antecedents of relapse. A good relapse prevention programme equips the person with a sense of preparedness and confidence, similar to that of someone who has undergone 'fire drill' training. For example, a client referred in the early stages in their addiction must be advised of the possibility of lapses occurring during the recovery process. A lapse is defined as a 'one-off' or brief return to misuse, whereas a relapse is defined as a more serious loss of control.

The cognitive model of addiction describes addictive behaviours as arising out of interplay between layers or levels of beliefs. An individual's core beliefs, or core schemas, are activated by a critical incident, which gives rise to anticipatory beliefs related to addiction, which in turn give rise to cravings. An example might be when an abstinent alcohol misuser who after a major argument with his spouse, believes that one drink will make him feel better, but who subsequently continues into a relapse. Cravings then activate permissive beliefs to indulge in the addiction, which subsequently leads to the addictive behaviour. Therapies developed from the cognitive model will be described in more detail later in the chapter.

Psychodynamic models

The psychodynamic approach to addictions covers a range of viewpoints or schools of thought, from the psychoanalytical school and analytical psychotherapy to transactional analysis. A recent formulation, encapsulating much of the previous theory, suggests that the main cause of the addiction syndrome is the unconscious need to entertain and enact various kinds of homosexual and perverse fantasies, and at the same time to avoid taking responsibility for them. The new, and perhaps most salient, aspect of this theory is the link between addiction and past traumatic experiences. This theory brings up to date the psychodynamic perspective with an accumulating mass of evidence from other perspectives in psychology, neurochemistry, and neurology linking substance misuse and personality disorders as aspects of a post-traumatic syndrome.

In the United States some other theories have focused on self-deficits, and introduced the concept of motivation for substance misuse as self-medication. The self-medication theory has had considerable influence particularly in the area of dual diagnosis, that is, substance dependence and mental illness.

In treatment settings, psychodynamic concepts continue to have a large influence, and are based on the idea that the client could achieve abstinence through the therapeutic relationship with a drug worker. Counselling is, however, often carried out by people with little or no training in psychodynamic therapy, and without much acknowledgement of the underlying psychodynamic processes. Likewise the humanistic perspective has no specific theory or model for addictions and it could be argued that this approach may not facilitate change in addicted individuals. Unfortunately, therapeutic work that makes use of psychodynamic processes such as transference, counter-transference, projection, and projective identification, often takes place without the supervision and theoretical framework such work requires. This lack of framework or clarity may account for much of the 'stuckness' (i.e. counselling continuing for a long time with no change in the patient's condition) that is seen in some psychological work in addiction treatment settings, which arguably is damaging to both the patient and the counsellor. A more pragmatic psychodynamic school is now emerging in Britain, which is having an impact in clinical settings. The work of Martin Weegmann, a clinical psychologist, is notable in this area (e.g. Weegmann and Cohen, 2002; Weegmann and Reading, 2004).

Transtheoretical models

The phenomenon of motivation is now central to our understanding of addiction and how addiction can develop and could be overcome (Miller and Rollnick, 2002). The Stages of Change model (Prochaska and DiClemente, 1996) was developed from evidence from smoking cessation studies to explain the process of how people change. The central concept is that behaviour change takes place in discrete stages:

- The 'pre-contemplation' stage is the period before the individual recognizes the need to change
- The 'contemplation' stage is when a person recognizes that he/she has a problem and considers doing something about it. An individual could remain at this stage indefinitely
- A 'decision' or 'preparation' stage precedes the 'action' stage
- In the action stage the individual attempts to change behaviour
- Success in changing the behaviour leads to a 'maintenance' stage; failure to maintain change leads to a 'relapse' stage.

In the light of research evidence, the model itself has undergone a number of changes. The early version of the model was progressive, whereby individuals were seen to go through the stages in a linear manner. However, a spiral is now thought to be a better representation of the change process. While the model has received much criticism, its influence has been immense. It has led to the development of the counselling approach known as Motivational Interviewing (Miller and Rollnick, 2002), which has had a huge impact in the field of addiction and beyond. It has also influenced treatment matching or targeted interventions for individuals at different stages of change.

Finally, a psychological model of addiction formulated by Orford (1985) views addictions as excessive behaviours, and addicted individuals as having an excessive appetite. This model seeks to explain key aspects of the process of addiction, such as:

- How an individual takes up an addictive behaviour
- How personal inclinations or factors within the individual may contribute to making the behaviour excessive
- The breakdown of restraint
- The development of strong attachment to the behaviour
- Internal conflict
- Decision making
- Self-control

This integrative model looks at evidence from the biopsychosocial fields to explain the phenomenon of addiction, and points to ways that individuals may be helped to overcome their problems. It thus enables addictions to be viewed as potentially arising out of any behaviour, such as substance use, gambling, or sexual behaviour.

Intervention in addiction

In the previous section the chapter looked at a range of theories in addictions. The following section will consider how a number of different models of intervention can be applied by clinical psychologists.

Matching and stepped care approaches

New conceptualizations and models for planning interventions for addiction problems have emerged in recent years. The matching hypothesis and stepped care approach have been particularly useful in developing the model of intervention that underpins service provision. The matching hypothesis is schematically presented as a spectrum of intervention responses in Figure 8.1.

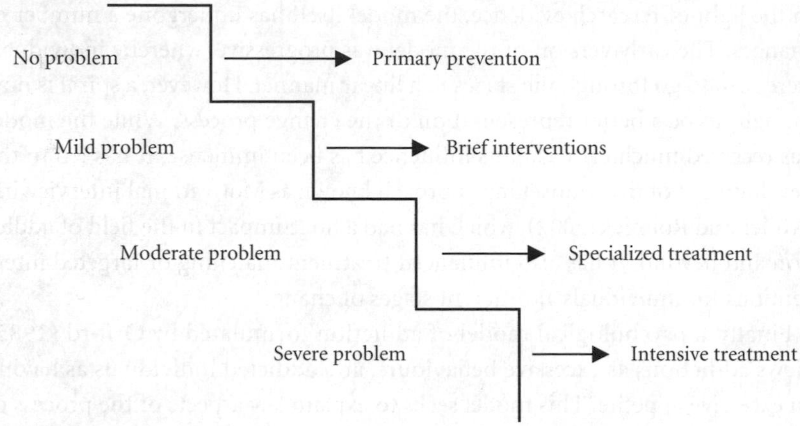

Fig. 8.1 Matching hypotheis model for interventions for addictions.

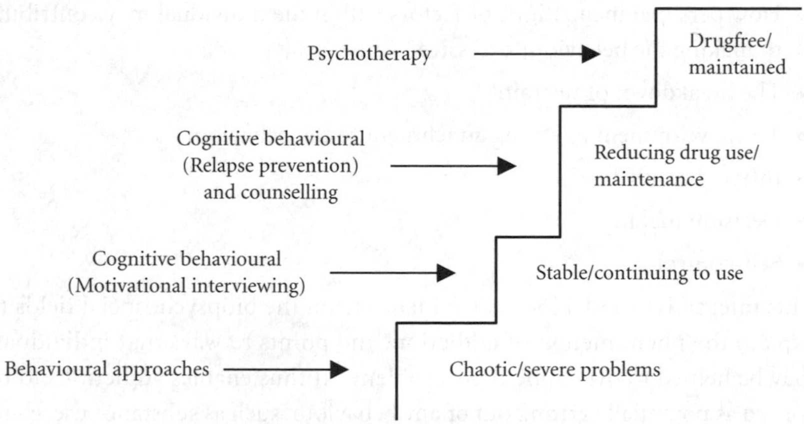

Fig. 8.2 Stepped care model for treatment of substance misuse problems.

A stepped care model for treatment of substance misuse problems (Wanigaratne and Keaney, 2002) is schematically presented in Figure 8.2. The steps in the model could also be seen as overlapping with the Stages of Change model described earlier. Although appearing to be obvious, simple and logical, in fact targeting treatment approaches in the above fashion is as yet far from common practice in addiction treatment settings, probably because psychodynamic approaches have traditionally underpinned psychosocial interventions in many treatment settings, and they are not clearly compatible with this approach. Nevertheless, the stepped care approach allows for an individual care plan to be devised, depending on the individual's level of need, and is therefore a valuable and important model to use given the range of clients that present themselves to addiction services. Many clients have a number of issues to address and factors affecting their treatment, thus requiring different levels of interventions. Interventions based on this model provide the client with a pattern of treatment tailored to their individual needs rather than those that are generalized to all clients. This model can lead to treating patients more cost- and time-effectively, as it enables the clinician to make a decision about the number of sessions required rather than being dictated to by a prescribed treatment programme.

Psychosocial interventions

These have been found to be the most successful addiction treatment. Raistrick and Tober (2003) suggest three reasons for this:

- They improve outcomes of pharmacological treatments
- They work better than doing nothing
- Survey data show that help-seekers want such interventions

Psychosocial treatments are planned uniquely for individuals. The first step is to encourage a shift in the individual's motivation. This can then be followed by a plan for behavioural change and finally the modification of the social context in order to achieve the treatment goal.

Motivational interviewing

An example of an intervention to initiate change is motivational dialogue. This intervention uses specific psychotherapeutic strategies and methods to diminish resistance, resolve ambivalence, develop discrepancy, and trigger behaviour change. In Motivational Interviewing the therapist asks particular open questions to elicit certain kinds of discussion, and will then reflect on particular elements, drawing out how the client defines their substance misuse, their concerns, and goals. The main skills a therapist uses are open-ended questions, selective reflective listening, and affirmation. The main underlying principle is for the patients to recognize and persuade themselves that attempting change is the best action to take, and that this will be beneficial to them. An example of this intervention is a therapist discussing with a client a visit she is making to her young daughter who is living with her ex-husband. They discuss the client's feelings of frustration and loss at no longer living with her family and how much she misses them. The therapist steers the conversation to talk about what led to the breakdown in the marriage, which was due to her high drug use. The client states how she would like to be with her family and reunite this bond. The therapist elicits a clear intention to achieve abstinence to demonstrate her love and desire to be with her family.

The client's goals and aims for the future become predominant and clear in her mind.

This approach is also shown in another example:

Steven was a 28-year-old crack cocaine user spending all his available money on drugs. After leaving school he commenced a flourishing career in advertising, but then began to experience mental health problems in his early twenties. He had to give up work and found himself isolated and bored. At this time, he began using crack. He presented to substance misuse services on the suggestion of his community mental health worker. At his first appointment he was adamant that he did not want to change his drug use. Using the principles of Motivational Interviewing, the psychologist listened to Steven's reflections about his situation, allowing him to draw up his own list of advantages and disadvantages of crack use. It became clear to Steven that the disadvantages, which included his home being used as a crack den, having no money for himself, losing interest and not caring for himself, the negative impact on his mental health, not having a girlfriend, isolation from his family, and little chance of getting back to work, outweighed the advantages of his use. At this point Steven began to contemplate the possibility of change. This enabled him to progress in his treatment to work on the next stage of change.

The outcome of this stage of treatment depends on a number of variables, which relate to the characteristics of the client and the extent of their substance misuse, and to the characteristics of the therapist and their skills in this setting. For example, a consistent finding is that individuals who are socially or psychologically unstable do less well, whatever the treatment.

Cognitive–behavioural approaches

These approaches tend to take a somewhat didactic approach. Techniques include advantages–disadvantages analysis (guiding the client through the process of listing and re-evaluating the advantages and disadvantages of substance misuse), and identifying and modifying drug-related beliefs (where the clinician assists the client by raising awareness of their beliefs, encouraging them to monitor their beliefs and automatic thoughts, leading in turn to the client gaining understanding of their drug use). Another useful intervention is the downward arrowing technique, which involves the therapist questioning the client's catastrophic thoughts in order to guide them to a more rational level of thinking. A common technique also used within addiction services is a daily thought record, a form completed by the client to record their emotions and thoughts associated with drug use, which encourages them to think objectively about the behaviour and its consequences. The aim of this approach is to focus on the client's behaviour, and to evaluate triggers and high-risk situations. One example of this is the use of 'drugs diaries' to identify behavioural patterns and automatic thoughts. This intervention focuses on cravings, and then on developing different coping mechanisms for clients, for example, distraction techniques and flashcards.

Network approaches

Community or network approaches focus on the need to change environmental support. The main principles are to recruit community and social network resources to create a supportive environment and diminish contacts with users, and reduce dependence. For example, services may recommend drop-in community services that substance misusers can attend, and gain support from key workers. Clinical psychologists may work with social workers and others to seek to reduce the likelihood of relapse when clients return to their communities, by encouraging the development of links with people who are not users, or with other non-drug using communities.

Fellowship approaches

Examples of these approaches are the groups run by Alcoholics Anonymous (AA) and Narcotics Anonymous. The main aim of such groups is to create a support network of addicts or recovering addicts who are able to share their experiences with each other, and to provide strength and hope for each other. Members are focused on becoming abstinent, and giving spiritual and behavioural support for problem resolution. AA Meetings are held all over the world and there is no fee for membership. The approach is based on 12 steps, which take the recovered alcoholic through their own story of their problem drinking, describing the sobriety they have found and inviting newcomers to the fellowship. Clinical psychologists may refer clients to such groups in some areas.

Neuropsychology in addiction

In addition to working therapeutically, another key and specialized role for clinical psychologists working in the field of addictions is to carry out neurological assessments. Neurocognitive deficits are commonly found in those who misuse substances. A recent review concluded that 50–80% of individuals with alcohol disorders experience moderate to severe neurocognitive impairment. Substances of misuse such as tobacco, cannabis, opiates, benzodiazepines, stimulants, and substances such as ecstasy all produce different patterns of cognitive deficits in users. The extents of the deficits are dependent on the particular substance as well as factors such as pattern of use, quantity and frequency, chronicity, age, and gender.

At a clinical level, clinical psychologists are often the only professional in the multidisciplinary team who have the skills and the competence to carry out neuropsychological assessments of substance misusing clients. These assessments, particularly in alcohol treatment settings, become a crucial part of clinical decision making. Neuropsychological assessments have become important for diagnosing conditions such as Wernicke-Korsakoff Syndrome, which is a brain disorder involving loss of specific brain functions. Symptoms may include vision changes, unsteady, uncoordinated walking, loss of memory, profound inability to form new memories, confabulation (elaborating or making up facts or stories), and hallucinations. Neuropsychological assessments assist in making decisions about the appropriateness of proposed therapeutic programmes, or future care and placement of individuals. Thus a clinical psychologist becomes a central member of a substance misuse clinical team, particularly when dealing with alcohol problems.

Conclusions

This chapter has highlighted the importance of psychological input within addiction services. We have discussed the role of clinical psychologists and the settings that they may work within. We have given an explanation of the theories of addiction and how they have informed the interventions undertaken. We have briefly covered research and audit and the importance of neuropsychological assessment. Within the addiction field, psychologists have had a great impact. The recognition of the importance of addictions is reflected through the activities of the membership of the British Psychological Society's Faculty of Addictions, which supports psychologists working in the area in a number of ways, including having regular academic meetings, study days, seminars, and conferences. It also regularly produces guidelines on important issues such as training, outcome measurement, and evidence for effectiveness of treatment. The Faculty of Addictions plays a role at the national level as an advisory body on issues relating to psychology and addictions and has input to or made comments on national policy documents, for example, Models of Care for Drug Users. It now has a permanent representative in the clinical team of the National Treatment Agency of the Department of Health advising on and developing national policy.

As one of many specialist areas that clinical psychologists can work in, we believe that addiction is an area that is both challenging and rewarding. Most clinical training courses include teaching on substance misuse and addiction psychology in their core curriculum, as the knowledge and skills needed to deal with these problems are a necessary prerequisite to work in most areas of clinical practice. Most courses offer elective specialist placements in addictions, and some competency-based courses offer trainees an addiction placement as a general adult placement. We hope that in this chapter we have succeeded in encouraging an interest in the field, as well as contributing to the awareness of addiction issues in all those who may be considering entering clinical psychology as an applied profession.

References

Drummond, D.C. (2001). Theories of drug craving, ancient and modern. *Addiction*, **96**, 33–46.

Farrell, M., Singleton, N., and Marshall, E.J. (2003). Epidemiology of tobacco, alcohol and drug use. *Psychiatry*, **2** (12), 5–8.

Harris, A. and Wanigaratne, S.D. (1995). Counselling and Clinical Psychology in HIV and AIDS. In A. Miller (ed.), *Medical Management of HIV and AIDS*. Berlin: Springer-Verlag.

Marlatt, G.A. and Gordon, J.R. (1985). *Addictive Behaviours: Readings on etiology, prevention and treatment*. Washington, DC: American Psychological Association.

Miller, W.R. and Rollnick, S. (2002). *Motivational Interviewing: Preparing people for change*, 2nd edn. New York: Guilford press.

Orford, J. (1985). *Excessive Appetites: A psychological review of addictions*. Chichester: Wiley.

Parrott, S., Godfrey, C., Raw, M., West, R., and McNeill, A. (1998). Guidance for commissioners on the cost-effectiveness of smoking cessation interventions. *Thorax*, **53**, 510–38.

Prochaska J.O. and DiClemente C.C. (1996). Towards a comprehensive model of change. In W.R. Miller and N. Heather. (eds.), *Treating Addictive Behaviours*, 2nd edn. New York: Plenum.

Raistrick, D. and Tober, G. (2003). Psychological Interventions. *Psychiatry*, **3**(1), 36–9.

Wanigaratne, S. and Keaney, F. (2002). Psychodynamic aspects of relapse prevention in the treatment of addictive behaviours. In M. Weegmann and R. Cohen (eds.), *The Psychodynamics of Addiction*. London and Philadelphia, PA: Whurr Publishers.

Weegmann, M. and Cohen, R. (2002). *The Psychodynamics of Addiction*. London, Whurr.

Weegmann, M. and Reading, B. (2004). *Group Psychotherapy and Addictions*. London, Whurr.

Further reading

Beck, A. Wright, F. Newman, C., and Liese, B (1993). *Cognitive Therapy of Substance Abuse*. New York: Guildford Press.

McMurran, M. (1994). *The Psychology of Addiction*. East Sussex: Taylor and Francis.

National Treatment Agency for Substance Misuse (2002). *Models of care for treatment of drug misusers: Framework for developing local systems of effective drug misuse treatment in England*. London: Department of Health.

Teesson, M., Degenhardt, L., and Hall, W. (2002). *Addictions*. East Sussex: Taylor and Francis.

Wanigaratne, S., Wallace, W., Pullin, J., Keaney, F., and Farmer, R. (1990). *Relapse Prevention for Addictive Behaviours*. Oxford: Blackwell Scientific Publications.

Chapter 9

Working with people with intellectual impairments

Chris Cullen and Helen Combes

Case Study

Mr A has cerebral palsy. He uses a wheelchair and it is very difficult to understand him because his speech is indistinct. Care staff have to help him with his activities of daily living, including taking him to the toilet. It seemed to staff at the day service that Mr A was upset. He would hit members of staff, even those he trusted, when he was taken to the toilet. They asked for help to manage his behaviour. His sister had suggested that they should seek help from a psychologist, because his family had also noticed that his demeanour had changed. When first meeting Mr A, the psychologist thought that he looked sad. He would cry, particularly when his sister and carers talked about how worried they were about him. When he was moved from his wheelchair into an ordinary chair he became more animated and would laugh and talk more. When asked where he wanted to sit he always pointed to an ordinary chair, rather than his wheelchair. It was clear that he wanted to be able to participate in the meeting. Mr A had apparently become more upset since his mother had died. During this time he appeared to be suggesting that he had been hit at the day service; he had returned home bruised and was saying 'hit me' when his family examined him.

The psychologist began working with Mr A. She engaged him in conversation by sitting together doing jigsaws, and drinking tea. Mr A pointed to the pictures in the jigsaw and the psychologist asked questions about the picture. He smiled and nodded. Over 3 weeks she noticed that he often chose the same picture of a family group. While looking at the picture Mr A became tearful. She asked if he would like her to meet his family. He nodded. This was the start of a relationship between the psychologist and the Mr A's family.

The purpose of relating this example is to introduce the notion that an important part of the role of a clinical psychologist is to form a relationship with the person, and to understand the context in which they live their lives. This has to be done as an essential part of the psychological approach. It is a matter to which we will return later in the chapter.

What is an intellectual impairment?

We have chosen to use the term 'intellectual impairment' rather than the British term 'learning disability' or the American term 'mental retardation'. We have done this because, while terminologies do change over time, it seems to us that the notion of an impairment of intellect better captures the essence with which we are concerned. 'Intellectual impairment' is the term used in Australia and New Zealand. For the past few years there has been a debate in the United States on how to change their outmoded terminology, and in the United Kingdom many clinicians and academics now prefer to use the term 'intellectual disability' or 'intellectual impairment'. One of the major international professional bodies has also changed its name to the International Association for the Scientific Study of Intellectual Disabilities.

In its International Classification of Functioning (ICF), the World Health Organization has emphasised the influence of contextual factors—that is personal and environmental factors—on impairments. These factors interrelate with physiological and bodily functions and influence the extent to which people can participate in activities. The ICF also highlights how impairment can be construed in different ways and how this can facilitate or hinder people's opportunities to execute tasks. The WHO defines impairment as 'difficulties in bodily function or structure such as a significant deviation or loss'. Seeing, hearing, thinking, and remembering are defined as bodily functions. To consider an extreme example, someone with severe levels of impairment can function very well if he or she has high levels of support. Professor Stephen Hawking, who has motor neurone disease, has specially designed mobility and voice production aids in order to ameliorate his physical impairments.

This framework highlights the complexity associated with working with people with intellectual impairments. Until recently, learning disability (or intellectual impairment) was defined categorically as a deficit in intellectual ability (intelligence) associated with at least two other impairments in functioning, such as social skills, adaptive behaviour, and so on. This new approach highlights the changing nature of disability; people will move in and out of services as their lives, physical well-being and social circumstances change. For example, one of our clients was referred because he was having outbursts of temper at a day centre. By talking to him it became clear that he felt devalued at not having a job for which he would receive a weekly wage. After a good deal of negotiation he was found a job, and the outbursts ceased. He is now a valued member of a workforce tending Local Authority gardens. He no longer attends a day centre for people with intellectual impairments. To what extent does it now make sense to think of him as a 'client' needing a service?

For the purpose of this chapter, we will acknowledge the changing nature of disability, recognizing that there will be times when people will need the support of specialist services, and that there will be times when people do not. A case example might be a woman who has lived independently throughout her life. On the birth of her child she may—because of her intellectual limitations—find it more difficult to cope with her child; she may have little social support to help her look after the baby. If statutory agencies draw our attention to this woman then it is possible that she would receive the help of our services at that point in her life. Our intervention would be time-limited and focused on a specific area of her development. As her child develops and grows, she may no longer need the help of our service. If that woman had a network of support she may never have needed the help of specialist services. However, the worst case—but fairly common—scenario is that the child would be taken into care because she was not offered psychological and other support.

While acknowledging the changing impact of impairment, we do recognize that there are people with complex conditions which mean that they and their families may frequently need the support of specialist community services. In view of these complexities, it is important to understand the reasons that someone may have a difficulty in learning.

Consider some developmental issues. For example, one would not expect a child who has not yet started to count, or who cannot tell which is bigger or smaller, to be able to understand the complexities of money. This may be because the child is too young rather than because he or she has an intellectual impairment. In defining intellectual disability, therefore, we have to take into account that the person is unable to do something which most others in their age group can do. However, there is a growing body of evidence that people who would previously have been categorized as having an intellectual impairment actually have a physical problem—such as cerebral palsy, juvenile Parkinson's disease, or hearing impairments—which have obscured an understanding of their intellectual abilities. Commenting on the importance of his speech synthesizer, Stephen Hawking says on his website 'One's voice is very important. If you have a slurred voice, people are likely to treat you as mentally deficient (*sic*).' Genetic research is also beginning to highlight distinct syndromes, which are associated with developmental differences—such as Down syndrome, Rett Syndrome, and William's Syndrome (Howlin and Udwin, 2002). The distinct developmental profiles, complexity of health conditions, and behavioural phenotypes associated with these syndromes are now better recognized, and should allow us to avoid putting everyone with intellectual impairments in one 'catch-all' category.

Many services, however, continue to place people in traditional learning disabilities' settings, from which they may feel estranged and separate. In consequence, the extent to which most people with intellectual impairments are able to exert control and make choices about their lives is dramatically limited.

Current thinking on service options

In 2001 the government published its White Paper 'Valuing People'. This proposed fundamental shifts in how services work with, and respond to, people with intellectual impairments. It highlights, the need for service providers to change their emphasis to prevention, health promotion, and improving participation by removing the social and psychological barriers to providing health and social care to people with learning disabilities. In essence, Valuing People has focused on a number of areas for service and community development. One is that services should provide person-centred care, which strives to achieve the 'seven accomplishments' of service provision. These are having a presence in one's community; achieving competence so far as one is able; being able to choose amongst options in most areas of life; having individuality valued; being given status and respect; having continuity throughout the transitions of life; and having supportive and meaningful relationships. Services should be providing care which is shaped and responsive to an individual's needs, rather than to the needs of the service.

All person-centred approaches share some common elements. They all require a facilitator to establish the context for person-centred planning, who helps the learning impaired person to put their plan into place. The facilitator should also ensure that the key people in the person's life and community are included, such as family, friends, and neighbours (Turnbull and Rutherford Turnbull, III, 1999). The plan may additionally include people from services who are important to the person. There should be a planning meeting which is relaxed and inclusive, and it should encourage relationships and the sharing of ideas where differences are explored and accepted. The meeting should identify a range of themes and ideas, and establish an overall aim and plan (based on these emergent themes). A person-centred approach should draw on a variety of techniques to enable the persons to express themselves (Combes *et al.*, 2004). Once the goals are identified, the circle of support considers who else needs to help, and will then be invited to future meetings. This is a constantly evolving process which emphasizes the wishes of the focus person.

A typical response to this directive has been to facilitate staff training in person-centred planning. Although the topic is clear, the extent to which person-centred planning actually improves the lives of people with intellectual impairments is not yet established. There is little research evidence available to date which demonstrates that people are being involved in making decisions about their lives (Heller *et al.*, 2000) or that there have yet been demonstrable differences in how services are delivered. This is especially the case for people with multiple impairments, and it is very challenging to think of how they might be enabled to make decisions about their lives.

Traditionally the structure of support within the United Kingdom for people with intellectual impairments has primarily been through state provision. The refocus on community provision reorientates people to obtain support from their families and local communities. Such social networks are believed to have a positive effect on psychological well-being. This makes it important that we understand that there is a role for clinical psychology, not only in helping people to gain control and autonomy in their lives, but also in supporting change in service models.

The role of the clinical psychologist

Most clinical psychologists are employed in a multidisciplinary context where a number of different professionals work with people with intellectual impairments and their families. There will be a wide range of such people including teachers, social workers, psychiatrists, community and specialist nurses, speech and language therapists, occupational therapists, and support workers. There are two interrelated ways in which psychologists may work. Firstly psychologists will apply findings from research to their work and help to develop services by feeding back findings from both published resources and their clinical work into service development. Secondly, they will use their skills to apply psychological ideas in their own clinical practice at both an individual and a societal level.

The different roles may include:

- Assessment of the person's current situation, and through this producing a clinical formulation which guides psychological and other interventions—many psychologists working in a learning disability field base these assessments on a functional analysis—which we will describe in more detail later.
- Providing therapy which has been derived from the assessment and formulation—this therapy may be based on cognitive behavioural, systemic or psychotherapeutic principles (Beail, 1998).
- Using skills and theoretical knowledge to influence and change the social context. A clear example of this has been research into alternatives to institutional care, many of the contributors to which have been clinical psychologists.

We will return to these roles below, but first we need to re-emphasize a point we made at the beginning of the chapter.

Establishing a relationship

As we suggested earlier, an integral part of helping a person with intellectual impairments is establishing a therapeutic relationship (Kohlenberg and Tsai, 1991). It is important to develop a relationship both with the person who has been referred, and also with their families and other professional colleagues. When establishing a relationship with a person with an intellectual impairment—particularly where there are language and motor impairments—it is important to think about how we ordinarily develop relationships and how to be creative in using different ways to develop meaningful relationships. This process can often be helped by listening and responding to the needs of the client's carers.

A focus on the therapeutic context is of paramount importance in situations where communication is difficult. This context requires the psychologist to be sensitive, caring, and responsive to clients if they are to facilitate meaningful change in people's lives. For example, some people may be constrained by wheelchairs, which place them at a different height in conversation. Many clients have few opportunities to access private spaces to express themselves. It can be surprisingly difficult to find a quiet and private room in a busy Local Authority day centre. Many a time, a confidential conversation between psychologist and client is interrupted by a member of the day centre staff, or other clients, entering the room to get some keys, a book, or just to find out what is going on.

Thinking about how a room is arranged is an essential part of any psychotherapeutic context. The environment itself can constrain effective communication—for example, if there is a lot of noise it is both hard to hear and to concentrate. Colours and pictures may distract some people; for other people they can make the environment feel welcoming and relaxing. It is therefore, important to carefully consider the kind of context which will best facilitate communication.

Assessing the needs of the person and their family

Assessment is generally considered to be one of the key roles of the psychologist. There are many different purposes for which we may be asked to provide assessments. It might be important to know what diagnosis a person has. For example, do they have an autistic spectrum disorder? Knowing this can open doors to appropriate services. However, these can also be a downside to using psychological assessments to label a person. Consider the person living happily in supported accommodation meant for people with learning disabilities. An intelligence test reveals him to have an IQ of around 80—many services would then expect him to move out of the learning disability service.

Assessment is an integral part of therapy; we need to know what changes are being achieved. Sometimes assessments are required for legal purposes, to assess whether the person has the ability to give consent; to manage their own finances; to understand court processes; and so on. An important role for assessment is also to inform action. We need to find out enough about the person to help to develop an individual plan. It is not sensible to initiate an initial assessment without having a good reason (Cullen and Dickens, 1990). A clinical psychologist may need to assess people with intellectual impairments in many different ways; they may be asked to complete assessments ranging from questions about capacity, to an estimation of parenting ability. This assessment may be requested from colleagues who are concerned about making decisions on someone's behalf, from social workers who may have to make decisions about adult and child protection, or from the courts about the capacity to make legal decisions and to give evidence. This requires the psychologist to think very clearly about the need for the assessment and for whom the information is being provided. This balancing of personal rights and the idea of doing no harm to the person is one which clinical psychologists are confronted with almost every day in their work, particularly when it is hard for the persons to express their own needs.

Many people are referred to psychological services because they challenge the people who work for them and the services that help them. The two authors of this chapter use functional analysis as their assessment tool. This is a flexible technique which endeavours to find the reasons for challenging behaviour and to provide clear information to provide interventions (Oliver and Head, 1993). Psychologists using a functional analysis will complete a semi-structured interview with people in a variety of contexts. These interviews will be held where possible with the person themselves, their family members, and people from the referring agency. Psychologists may also complete observations across a variety of settings. The types of observations will vary according to the difficulties the person is experiencing, but may consist of time sampling, fixed interval or fixed ratio observations over events (specific tasks) or durations (length of time). It is important that the clinician is clear about the types of observations they have completed because how the data is collected will influence how it can be interpreted. Once these observations and interviews are completed the psychologist will formulate the problem, that is, present their best judgement of what the problem is and how things might change. This may consist of advice around contextual change, specific psychotherapeutic intervention (such as anger management, psychotherapy, or Cognitive Behavioural Therapy), or skills development. Observations will take place again after the intervention to see whether there has been any behavioural change.

Our functional assessment process can also use norm-referenced tests as well as clinical observations and interviews. The advantage of the former is that it can focus attention on a particular skill or deficit relative to a particular population, which can then be used to recommend how to intervene. Such procedures can highlight individual differences in cognitive understanding, emotional understanding, and skills development. The disadvantage of these assessments is that they do not always offer ecological or face validity; consequently they are not sufficient alone to aid and inform formulation. It is important to gather this information through getting to know the services one is working in, observing the clients in different contexts and talking with the persons themselves, their families, and their carers, and developing a functional analysis which will take into account a variety of factors which influence behaviour.

Consider the case of neuropsychological assessments. We do not know the exact prevalence of neurological problems in the population of people with known intellectual impairments, but it is likely to be substantial. Finding out the nature of an individual's specific strengths and needs in the form of a neurological assessment may have psychological benefits by enabling the person (and others) to understand their difficulties differently and offer some evidence for specific individually-oriented support.

Case Study

Miss H was referred to the clinical psychology department when she was 18. Her family were worried about her because she seemed to be crying more frequently. Her friend had died earlier that year, and it had been thought that her distress was part of her grieving. However, she also reported being generally 'unwell' and her family doctor had been puzzled by her symptoms and had ordered a CT scan. The CT scan at that time had shown some neurological damage which appeared to be consistent with early onset dementia.

The psychologist could not find any literature on people of 18 having a dementing condition. The neurologist was unwilling to make a formal diagnosis at this stage, given Miss H's age. Her parents wanted to know what the likely long-term prognosis was so that they could give her all the support that she needed. There was little published information available. Miss H wanted to remain at college and to be supported in getting there, but had been sent home on a few occasions because she had been incontinent. A multidisciplinary meeting had failed to get the family any appropriate social care support because of the lack of evidence for women of her age having dementia.

The psychologist was asked if a formal assessment would help to shed any light on the situation. At first the psychologist tried to complete the short form of the Weschler Intelligence Scale, but Miss H started to cry and said she did not want to continue with it. The family and Miss H completed the Down syndrome Dementia Rating Scale independently. This assessment suggested signs of early onset dementia, but some of the difficulties seen at this stage may have been related to depression. However, when Miss H wrote a letter—to express her thoughts and feelings—the therapist noticed that the text was only half formed and she located it only across one side of the paper. She was asked to draw a rabbit and she drew just half of it over to the left hand side. Her mother remembered that she often turned her plate around when eating and that she had recently removed her clothes from the drawer to put them on the shelves. Miss H said that this was so that she could find her clothes. The neurologist confirmed that this visual neglect was likely to be because of early onset dementia, and, in the light of information from this assessment and the family's observation, formally diagnosed dementia of the Alzheimer Type (Down syndrome related). From the assessment it was clearly evident that Miss H should be cared for at home and not disorientated further by changing college or being admitted to hospital. As a result of this work, services were able to apply for funding for a support worker to enable Miss Hayes to continue at college. As she became more disoriented, this worker was able to support her at home. Her condition did not improve and she died when aged 21, supported by her family, the paid carers, community nursing, and the palliative care nurses.

A number of ethical issues were raised during this time. It was clear whenever Miss H did not want to be assessed, because she looked tired and would say 'no'. However, she did want to be able to carry on doing the things she enjoyed. This placed her at risk, unless she had someone to support her at college and when out shopping, tasks she had previously done independently. The psychometric assessment was in fact stopped very early on in the relationship because of the distress it caused. Her parents played a video to the psychologist which showed their daughter participating in a play. It was clear that there had been significant changes in her abilities over a relatively short period of time. Her parents had other children with disabilities to care for and needed help to maintain her quality of life. The ethical dilemma concerning whether or not to assess her needs psychometrically was considerable, but it was always clear that Miss H and her family wanted to make sense of what was happening and to be helped in living with her illness. The psychologist did not make a diagnosis, but did provide information to help other people to make their decisions, which in turn enabled additional services to come in and help to care for Miss H at home. Consistent and reflective observation and supervision enabled the psychologist and colleagues to change their interventions in response to her current abilities. The nurses, physiotherapists, and occupational therapists helped to provide environmental adaptations, such as wheelchairs and beds, which enabled Miss H to continue to participate in the things that she enjoyed whenever she was able to.

A useful addition to formal assessments is to take a comprehensive history, or lifeline, from the person and their family. This can help to identify when and how particular skills and difficulties developed. Lifelines can also highlight when things that have previously been acceptable have become a problem. They may show, for example, that a young boy has rarely played relationally with others, but that this has only become a problem since he has started to attend school.

Understanding the person's cognitive abilities is important. On one occasion a man was referred to the psychology department for an assessment of his sexual awareness and his capacity to have a sexual relationship. The issue was that he was having sex with another man who had said that he was not consenting to this relationship. The staff group considered the referred client to be a 'perpetrator' and believed that he understood that he was abusing the other person. In a meeting it was asserted that the client believed that the other person 'belonged' to him. The psychologist asked how the staff knew if he would be able to understand right from wrong, and could comprehend the concept of ownership. She asked whether, for example, he would be able to separate fruit from vegetables. Care staff replied that he would not be able to make such discriminations. Other simple discriminations were tried out, and it quickly became clear that the general view was that the client's intellectual level was such that the staff thought it highly unlikely that he would be able to understand many concrete discriminations, let alone abstract ones such as 'right–wrong'. When the psychologist met with the client and carried out some relatively basic testing, it was confirmed that he was indeed operating at a relatively unsophisticated level. Moral reasoning—an abstract concept—is a cognitive skill which emerges later in development than categorising objects. If he was not able to do relatively simple tasks, then this demonstrates that he would need the support of others when making more complex moral decisions. With this in mind, and with his agreement, he was moved into an environment with more staff to support him.

The psychologist and therapy

To some extent the role of being a therapist is always entailed in developing a relationship and in assessing and evaluating people's needs. It is sometimes hard to see these processes as distinct categories from therapy. There may however be times when assessment and formulation lead the psychologist to offer a specific psychotherapeutic or cognitive behavioural intervention (Kroese *et al.*, 1997). If the person has low self-esteem and considers that they are not 'worthy', then cognitive-behavioural therapy may help to challenge these beliefs and improve their self-esteem. However, if the person who has been referred has a profound learning disability and does not communicate verbally, but the psychologist feels that he or she would benefit from an intense and meaningful therapeutic relationship, then they may see how the person responds to intensive interaction. Intensive interaction is designed to help people who may be socially isolated, and as a consequence who participate in a range of self-stimulatory behaviours, for example self-injury, rocking etc. It is a technique which has been developed for people with severe intellectual disabilities and complex needs. The aim of intensive interaction is to develop the individual's communicative or interaction skills by attending to them and mirroring their movements and vocalizations. The therapist will observe the person and respond in synchrony to their vocalizations and movements, facilitating the communicative and relational environment, and supporting the person to communicate, respond, and interact, by adapting their own voice, gaze, or body language in synchrony with the person with learning impairment (Nind and Hewett, 2001). In all such therapeutic intervention, the psychologist will still be 'testing' or piloting an intervention, by ensuring through feedback and reflection that it is helping rather than harming the person.

Case Study

A young woman was referred to the psychology department because she was hurting herself by hitting her head against the floor. Miss S was blind in one eye and had a severe loss of vision in the other. She would rub her eye, causing a lesion to the side of her head near her eye, and signalled that the television was too loud by shouting. In addition she would not tolerate people near her and would push them away. Her father said that the hitting action had started when she used to pat a silver whisk against the side of her face. He thought that she liked the shimmering near her eye. After spending a great deal of time observing her in the home, and completing a functional analysis, the psychologist concluded that she had little personal control over her environment and recommended that she should receive a day service from a charity specializing in people with sensory impairments who would help her develop her sensory experiences. The staff began to get to know Miss S by sitting near her and mirroring her movements. Later she would take their hands and they would rock together. Over time the team enabled her to learn to control specially adapted switches on her radio and television. Through intensive interaction she learnt to tolerate new people and would rock with them on her mat. Throughout this time, her level or self-injury was recorded, and evidence showed that her self-injury reduced substantially. Following the removal of a tooth from her jaw, it stopped completely for a 3-month period. Miss S continued to hurt herself when she was unwell or during times of transition, particularly when she was being supported by someone she did not know, but the frequency and severity of her self-injury overall has substantially reduced.

The complexity of some therapeutic work can be shown in the following example:

Case Study

Miss J lived in a nursing care home and was referred because she was refusing to eat; the psychiatrist asked the psychologist to provide a cognitive-behavioural intervention for anorexia nervosa. Miss J had been admitted to hospital because her weight had fallen to a dangerously low level, and she was being fed through a naso-gastric tube. At the first meeting she told the psychologist that she did not like where she lived and had stopped eating so that she would be able to go home to live with her parents. This appeared to have been based on earlier experiences; when Miss J had stopped eating in the past, her parents would become extremely worried about her health and take her home to look after. After conversations with her and her family, it emerged that Miss J had ulcers and suffered from indigestion, particularly after heavy meals. Repeated requests for her to be given small and manageable meals (of food that she liked) had not been met. If the care home had prepared curry, then that is what she would be given. She was however happy to eat smaller light meals. In addition to this, during the meeting with the psychologist, Miss J had a couple of seizures. Because she was in an electric wheelchair, it was hard to manoeuvre her out of situations: something which she wanted. Through spending time with her, the psychologist noticed she became animated and laughed when there were three to four people with her, but that if there were more, she would become quieter and looked away. After asking her some questions it became apparent that she had stopped liking her care home when it had been extended: there were now twelve people living with her when previously there had been six. She would repeatedly say that people did not understand. It was also apparent that to some degree she was right—the organisation of the care home no longer enabled her individual needs to be attended to. It was also clear that she enjoyed telling stories about her life, and the therapeutic context enabled her to develop this very important role. In the psychology sessions the need to be understood would overwhelm her and she would cry for long periods of time. It was hard to leave her crying, but distracting her and challenging her belief that people did not understand her seemed disrespectful to the intensity of her feelings. It seemed to be important to listen to what she had to say and to help her to find a place for her to live where she was happy.

A general framework for interventions

We have referred to the importance of considering the whole context in both assessment and therapeutic interventions. A useful framework for doing this is to adopt the following four component approach (Donnellan *et al.*, 1988). For a successful contextualist psychological intervention, each of the components must be present:

- *Identify a reactive strategy*. This involves helping the client, or those around the client, to find ways of ameliorating the problem in the here-and-now. Sometimes the person's psychological difficulties can be ignored while seeking longer-term solutions, but sometimes there is a need to identify ways of coping with a difficult situation. If the person were hitting themselves, for example, then this might involve active holding procedures. If the person is finding great difficulty interacting with others, then a suitable reactive strategy might be to enable them to have some private time on their own. Whatever reactive strategy is chosen, it should be one which is acceptable to the person, does not compromise their dignity, and is as neutral as possible (so as not to be something which the person would be actively seeking). The only purpose of a reactive strategy is to acknowledge the difficulty and to help the person to cope with their current distress.

Once suitable reactive strategies are identified, and the person and others are safe and protected, then proactive strategies will need to be put into place. There are three elements to these.

- *Environmental considerations.* It is essential, as we have discussed above, to understand the person's current environmental situation. Quite often this in itself may be creating the problem. Someone who is uncomfortable in large groups may react violently to a busy day centre. Someone who is in constant pain from an earache or toothache may be trying to deal with the pain by slapping the side of their head. Someone who is asked to do tasks which are far too difficult for them may behave badly in order to avoid such requests, or to escape from the demand situation. Someone who is being abused at home may react in sexually inappropriate ways at school. There are a multitude of environmental factors which we know will affect behaviour, and it is essential, as part of any psychological intervention, to be able to identify environments which are unhelpful, and to identify those environments which are likely to support more adaptive behaviour. In recent years there has been a very encouraging increase in the use of cognitive based therapies, notably Cognitive Behaviour Therapy (cf. Kroese *et al.*, 1997) with people with intellectual impairments, and this adds to the 'richness' of our approaches.
- *Constructional alternatives.* It is always worth asking the question 'if the person were not engaged in this problematic behaviour what might they be doing'? It is always essential to consider what appropriate ways of thinking, feeling, and behaving a person ought to be helped to acquire as part of the solution to their psychological problems. The person with profound disabilities who is hitting himself may be trying to tell us that he is unhappy with his current situation. What alternative ways of conveying his feelings should we help him to acquire? Someone who is withdrawn and isolated may need to learn how to interact with people. A person who behaves in socially unconventional ways which create offence to others may need to learn about the rules of appropriate social behaviour.

Both environmental considerations and teaching constructional alternatives are ways of addressing difficult behaviour in the long term. They are not designed to have an immediate impact on the referred behaviour in a reactive way (see above), but are meant to move us away from dealing with behaviour in isolation. However, the fourth element in this framework is also often needed.

- *Direct psychological treatment.* Sometimes there will be a need to introduce specific psychological treatments aimed at the person's current distress. It is outside the scope of this chapter to go into this in more detail, but there are procedures which deal directly with challenging behaviour (Ball *et al.*, 2004). The aim in direct treatment is to deal with psychological distress in order to allow the environmental considerations and constructional approaches to replace the difficulties with more adaptive and long-term alternatives.

Our argument is that sound contextualist approaches should have all four elements present, in varying degrees, according to the individual case.

Systems and structures

So far we have described aspects of the psychologist's role that involve one-to-one contact with clients and their families. However, there are broader aspects to psychologists' work. One of these involves the need for psychological skills to be transferred to direct care staff which can sometimes involve challenging existing ways of doing things. Psychologists often work more with people who have direct contact with clients rather than with clients themselves. In this case our role is to give staff the space to reflect on their practice and to identify alternative ways of doing things. Psychologists can help staff to develop and reflect upon their core helping skills, and can encourage services to provide contexts for staff to improve their practice (Reid *et al.*, 1989). However, we know from recent research into staff perceptions of their role that their view of clients, and their relationship with them, has to be taken into account in sophisticated ways (Jones and Hastings, 2003; Whittington and Burns, 2005).

Many psychologists have become directly involved in attempts to influence wider social attitudes. Notable here is the movement to enable people to achieve more socially valued roles in society, influenced by the writings and teachings of the American social theorist Wolf Wolfensburger, who argues that many people in society are placed in devalued roles, and that this devaluation becomes exaggerated as people are placed in services which are in themselves devalued. He goes on to argue that the ultimate aim of social role valorization is to place people from devalued groups into contexts or situations which are highly valued and prized within their society. This approach has had an impact upon government thinking, notably in the White Paper 'Valuing People' (DoH, 2001).

Research

Most clinical psychologists have begun to develop research skills through their clinical training. These skills are highly valued within the health service. One way in which psychologists can help people is to share their research skills with people with learning disabilities, and there is a growing body of literature on emancipatory research paradigms (Barnes *et al.*, 2002). By sharing research skills, psychologists can help both individuals and services to draw attention to the wishes and needs of people with learning disabilities. A case study illustrates this.

Case Study

Following a therapy group addressing the issue of friendships, the participants started to discuss research. They thought they would like to learn how to do research themselves. A regular time and date to meet was set and a local community service allowed the use of their premises for the group in the evening. The group covered a broad range of subjects, including ethics and how to ask research questions. They addressed basic aspects of research appreciation, such as how to tell if numbers are bigger. They tried changing environments and situations to see if this changed how people behaved. They tried asking one another questions in different ways and thought about how the questions made them feel. The group came to realize that research skills can give the power to change things and to challenge people. They also understood that this could help them to tell the stories of people with learning disabilities and to share them with others. All members of the research group have been involved in teaching to professionals in a number of different contexts. They have also advised on the teaching of a nurse training course. The group has helped them to feel more confident, both in asking questions, and also in presenting themselves to other people. The group is currently trying to draw up an ethics proposal to evaluate the service which they attend. They hope that this might help to bring in additional funding to their project.

Outcomes

Assessing and evaluating the extent to which psychology has helped people and made a difference to their lives is an essential element of the reflective and scientist–practitioner model. So what has happened over time with the people we have mentioned in this chapter? The extent to which our assessment, formulations, and interventions have made a difference to each person's life has been variable.

Case Study

Mr A continued to be aggressive on particular days at the day service. A trusting relationship with a regular keyworker did help him when he was at the day service, and this enabled us to get a better picture of what was happening in his life. The anger was often associated with throat and urinary infections—which the GP felt were connected. After many months of trying to get specialists to see him, we were able to take him to a consultant who told his family that he would probably be in a great deal of pain whenever his bladder was full. His condition was such that to empty the bladder it had to go into spasm. Mr A was frightened of going to the hospital and asked the psychologist to support him and his family. This visit highlighted the immense barriers there still are in the physical environment (moving from a wheelchair to an examination couch), and in the communicative environment (explaining prognosis and medication), for people with impairments accessing specialist health care. The family remain concerned about his condition, but were relieved that his condition was now being investigated.

Miss H died last year. She continued to participate in things that she enjoyed throughout her life. Her parents felt supported by services, and are glad that they enabled her to remain involved in family life.

Miss S continues to go to the day service and enjoys relaxing at home. She does still hurt herself, but not as often. Her father is pleased with seeing her continue to learn and become more involved in things. He would like her to have more opportunities.

Miss J continues to live in the large group home. She had a person-centred planning meeting where she continued to tell us that people do not understand her. The psychological service continues to support her, but the service has not been able to respond to her wish to move. She is currently looking for a human rights lawyer to help her to achieve her wish to move to a smaller unit with people to understand her health and psychological needs.

References

Ball, T., Bush, A., and Emerson, E. (2004). *Clinical Practice Guidelines: Psychological Interventions for Severely Challenging Behaviours Shown by People with Learning Disabilities*. Leicester: British Psychological Society.

Barnes, C., Oliver, M., and Barton, L. (2002). *Disability Studies Today*. Oxford: Blackwell.

Beail, N. (1998) Psychoanalytic psychotherapy with men with intellectual disabilities: A preliminary outcome study. *British Journal of Medical Psychology*, **71**, 1–11.

Combes, H.A., Hardy, G., and Buchan, L. (2004). Using Q-methodology to involve people with intellectual disability in evaluating person-centred planning. *Journal of Applied Research in Intellectual Disabilities*, **17**, 1–11.

Cullen, C. and Dickens, P. (1990). People with mental handicaps. In D.F. Peck and C.M. Shapiro (eds.), *Measuring Human Problems*, pp. 303–16. London: Wiley.

Department of Health (2001). Valuing People: A new strategy for learning disability for the 21 Century, London.

Donnellan, A.M., La Vigna, G.W., Negri-Shoultz, N., and Fassbender, L.L. (1988). *Progress Without Punishment: Affective Approaches for Learners with Behaviour Problems*. New York: Teachers College Press.

Heller, T., Miller, A.B., Hsieh, K., and Sterns, T. (2000). Later-life planning: promoting knowledge of options and choice-making. *Mental Retardation*, **38**, 395–406.

Howlin, P. and Udwin, U. (2002). *Outcomes in Neurodevelopmental and Genetic Disorders*. Cambridge: Cambridge University Press.

Jones, C. and Hastings, R.P. (2003). Staff reactions to self-injurious behaviours in learning disability services: Attributions, emotional responses and helping. *British Journal of Clinical Psychology*, **42**, 189–203.

Kohlenberg, R.J. and Tsai, M. (1991). *Functional Analytic Psychotherapy: Creating Intense and Curative Therapeutic Relationships*. London: Plenum Press.

Kroese, B.S., Dagnan, D., and Loumidis, K. (eds.) (1997). *Cognitive Behaviour Therapy for People with Learning Disabilities*. London: Routledge.

Lovett, H. (1996). *Learning to Listen*. Baltimore, MD: Paul Brookes Publishing.

Nind, M. and Hewett, D. (2001). *A Practical Guide to Intensive Interaction. Kidderminster*. Avon: BILD publications.

Oliver, C. and Head, D. (1993). *Self-injurious behaviour: Functional analysis and intervention.* In R.S.P. Jones and C.B. Eayrs. *Challenging Behaviour and Intellectual Disability: A Psychological Perspective.* Avon: BILD publications.

Reid, D.H., Parsons, M.B., and Green, C.W. (1989). *Staff Management in Human Services.* Springfield, IL: Charles C. Thomas.

Turnbull, A.P. and Rutherford Turnbull III, H. (1999) Group action planning as a strategy for providing comprehensive family support. In L. Kernkoegel, R.L. Koegel and G. Dunlop. *Positive Behavioural Support.* Baltimore: Paul Brookes.

Wittington, A. and Burns, J. (2005). The dilemmas of residential care staff working with the challenging behaviour of people with learning disabilities. *British Journal of Clinical Psychology*, **44**, 59–76.

Wolfensberger, W. (2000). A brief overview of Social Role Valorization. *Mental Retardation*, **38**, 105–23.

Further reading

Jacobson, J.W., Foxx, R.M., and Mulick, J.A. (eds.). (2005). *Controversial Therapies for Developmental Disabilities: Fad, Fashion, and Science in Professional Practice.* London: Lawrence Erlbaum Associates.

Koegel, L.K., Koegel, R.L., and Dunlap, G. (1996). *Positive Behavioural Support. Including People with Difficult Behavior in the Community.* Baltimore, MD: Paul H. Brookes.

Matson, J.L. and Mulick, J.A. (eds.). (1991). *Handbook of Mental Retardation*, 2nd edn. New York: Plenum Press.

Repp, C. and Singh, N.N. (eds.). (1990). *Prospectus on the use of Nonaversive and Aversive Interventions for Persons with Developmental Disabilities.* Sycamore, IL. Sycamore Publishing Co.

Chapter 10

Working in forensic mental health settings

Richard Barker and Chris Moore

Introduction—The broad context

Case Study

A 22-year-old male attacked a female passer-by as she walked down by a river on a late summer's evening. The attack appeared arbitrary in nature with the victim stating that the attacker had been murmuring to himself as she had approached him. She sustained injuries to her hands and arms, but was able to escape by jumping into the river. She was rescued by a passer-by on the other side of the river and the attacker ran away. Later that night a man fitting the description she provided was arrested in the centre of town when he had been seen on CCTV wandering down the main road.

On questioning, he was uncommunicative, stating only 'they were going to kill me'. He was identified by fingerprint and discovered to have a history of substance abuse, petty theft, and sporadic involvement with psychiatric services as an outpatient. A review by a police surgeon concluded that he was suffering from a mental illness and after further assessment he was transferred for assessment to the intensive care unit of the local Regional Secure Unit under the Mental Health Act (1983).

The above fictitious example approximates a typical admission into a medium secure hospital. This chapter examines the wide range of roles provided by a clinical psychologist working within a forensic mental health setting. It examines the broad context in which clinical psychologists come into contact with forensic patients and forensic settings, as well as looking at a few examples of the kind of problems that such work is likely to bring. The chapter looks at recent advances in working with offending behaviour and how such work fits into the overall therapeutic milieu of clinical psychology. It explores the range of consultancy roles that such a specialist position brings as well as examining some of the ethical and process issues, and looks to future developments in policy, procedure, and the career in general.

Historically, psychologists concerned with offending and antisocial behaviours have been employed within the penal system and in health settings where violent or disruptive behaviours are prevalent. In the mid- to late 1800s, reform of the prison system, meant that not only was there a greater emphasis on prison being used as a deterrent to offending, but also more weight was starting to be placed on the rehabilitation of offenders. This was most probably brought about by the dawning realization that punishment alone was inefficient at reducing reoffending. At that time, there was little distinction between criminality, and criminal behaviour that was underpinned by mental illness, but a number of landmark cases in the mid-1800s drew attention to the differences between criminality and mental illness.

By far the most famous of these was the 1843 case of Daniel McNaughton. Acting under delusional beliefs that there was a conspiracy against him perpetuated by the Catholic Church and the Tory Government, he made plans to kill the Tory Prime Minster, Sir Robert Peel. Despite making elaborate plans to kill Peel, on the day in question he mistook Peel's private secretary, Edward Drummond, for Peel as Drummond left the Prime Minister's private residence. McNaughton followed Drummond out onto Parliament Street and in broad daylight, shot him several times in the back. Drummond died a few days later.

In an interview later, McNaughton spoke of being persecuted for a number of years. He described being driven to his act by absolute desperation. A number of notable physicians and surgeons gave evidence at his trial and he was found not guilty by reasons of insanity. Such was the public consternation at the finding that even Queen Victoria wrote to the Prime Minister with concern that McNaughton had been allowed to get away with a conscious act of murder. Nonetheless the verdict remained. McNaughton himself was admitted to Bethlem and later Broadmoor Hospital where he died some 20 years later in obscurity (Forshaw and Rollin, 1990).

That case and a number of others that followed led to what are now referred to in the United Kingdom as 'The McNaughton rules' which allow for individuals who have committed acts of violence while under the influence of a mental illness to be diverted away from the criminal justice system into the forensic mental health system. It was the beginning of a slow battle in which the distinction started to be drawn between criminality and mental illness.

The most significant development in this process for present practice was the passing in the United Kingdom of the Mental Health Act in 1959. As a piece of legislation it clearly made the assumption that individuals who had a mental illness could, once treated, be able to return to their previous lives. However, while this development was useful for the treatment of non-offending patients, the situation for mentally disordered offenders was not as innovative and by the late 1960s concerns were being raised that the treatment of mentally disordered offenders was less than acceptable.

The British Government sponsored a number of reports into the situation, the foremost of which was the 1975 report by the Butler Committee. These investigations had been prompted most probably by the case of Graham Young, a mentally disordered offender who had been released from Broadmoor Special Hospital with little or no provision for his community rehabilitation and supervision. Without community supervision he had gone on to commit two acts of murder and one of attempted murder.

Among the many recommendations of the Butler report was the subsequent setting up of a number of Regional Secure Units (RSU) around the United Kingdom. Such units now serve as a hub for forensic services within the various NHS regions. From within these hubs services radiate out into both the local NHS Trusts and other external agencies. They also serve the important function of being able to focus research activities on the unique and complex difficulties associated with such a population. In both Australia and New Zealand a similar system has been adopted, while in North America forensic mental health is dominated by state hospitals which fulfil a similar function, albeit with a wider range of services, all on one site.

Into this setting comes the clinical psychologist. Although ostensibly working with forensic issues, the development of Regional Secure Units systems was funded within the National Health Service and as such was staffed by clinical psychologists as opposed to prison psychologists, as they were then known. While the patients in these units had committed criminal acts, the overriding issue was not their criminality *per se*, but the degree to which their mental illness had contributed to that criminality. Thus clinical psychologists, with their wider training in working with psychological disturbances, were in a better position to meet the needs of patients in these forensic mental health services.

There is an important distinction to be made between forensic psychologists and clinical psychologists working in a forensic mental health field. For the purposes of this chapter, we are focussing mainly upon clinical psychologists who work within a forensic setting, however there are some areas of overlap between the two careers and it is worth exploring some of the differences and areas of overlap between the two subdisciplines.

Over the past 20 years forensic psychology has seen a meteoric growth in Masters and now Doctoral level taught courses. The educational pathways of the two subdisciplines tend to be somewhat different, with forensic psychologists undertaking the majority of their supervised clinical training within prison settings, whereas clinical psychologists will have had a wider range of experience working with many different types of client groups and facing different types of difficulties.

Today's forensic psychologist is primarily employed within the prison and probation services providing assessments and offending behaviour-related therapeutic programmes. They can also be found in some forensic mental health settings albeit in limited numbers. In contrast the forensic clinical psychologist is more usually found working with offenders who have a co-morbid disorder such as mental illness, personality disorder, substance abuse problems, and so forth. This may mean working in a Regional Secure Unit, but can also include working with community teams, prison 'in-reach' teams, child and adolescent forensic mental health services, learning disability forensic services, women's services, as well as the probation service. Thus the forensic clinical psychologist role is one that encompasses a wide repertoire of therapeutic knowledge and skills. Not only do they undergo the usual clinical doctorate training course, often with a specialist third year forensic placement, but, working in a forensic setting, be it secure hospital, prison, or in the community they require an understanding of the criminal justice system, court skills, theories of offending behaviours, and skills managing and treating clients with challenging behaviours. Many forensic clinical psychologists have become dual-qualified in both clinical and forensic psychology. For the purpose of this chapter, however, perhaps the most fundamental difference lies in the assessment, formulation, intervention, evaluation model of the clinical psychologist, something that is not as central to the training of the forensic psychologist.

A recent review of forensic clinical psychologists working within secure mental health settings found that the modal clinician had a caseload of between 6 and 20 inpatients and few outpatients. The review did not expressly study what proportion of their time was spent seeing patients or providing consultancy, although anecdotal experience of the authors suggests that more than 50% of the workload is taken up providing assessment and consultancy services other than direct therapeutic interventions.

In terms of the settings for clinicians, most clinical psychologists in the United Kingdom (and in North America, Australia, and New Zealand) will find themselves working in multidisciplinary teams that include, but are not limited to, a consultant forensic psychiatrist, an approved social worker, nurses, and occupational therapists. Currently, and for the past 20 years in the United Kingdom, the treatment of mentally disordered offenders has remained in a tiered system. Four Special Hospitals (Rampton, Broadmoor, Ashworth, along with Carstairs Hospital in Scotland) provide high security settings for mentally disordered offenders with the highest levels of risk of violence.

Outside these high security settings are the majority of mentally disordered offenders, situated within a range of NHS medium and low secure units, along with offenders managed by specialist community teams and general adult mental health teams as can be seen in Figure 10.1 below.

Further, within each of these general settings (as in all other areas of clinical psychology) there are also additional sub-specialty services, such as those for male adults, women, learning disabled individuals, and children, and adolescents. In line with current NHS guidelines, the psychologist working within each of these services needs to be aware of the best evidence-base currently available for the assessment and treatment of these groups, as there will be differences between the psychological requirements of each group. Thus, for example, a psychologist working within a forensic child and adolescent service would need to be aware of issues relating to the client's level of maturity and emotional development, which would influence both the assessment and treatment process. Similarly, for example, a psychologist working in a setting which caters solely to learning disabled individuals would need to take into account the client's intellectual and cognitive abilities in attempting to provide an efficacious services to these individuals. Thus, as with all other areas of clinical psychology, the exact nature of assessment, formulation, and intervention will be directly influenced by the needs and abilities of the specific client group, and interventions may have to be modified accordingly.

For many mentally disordered offenders, the point of entry into the system comes through court-diversion schemes moving them out of the criminal justice system, usually, but not always, into conditions of medium security. Depending upon their circumstances, illness, and level of risk, they may move to conditions of high security, or be rehabilitated into a community setting such as a hostel or supported accommodation. More recently there has been a growth in low secure rehabilitation services, which tend to cater

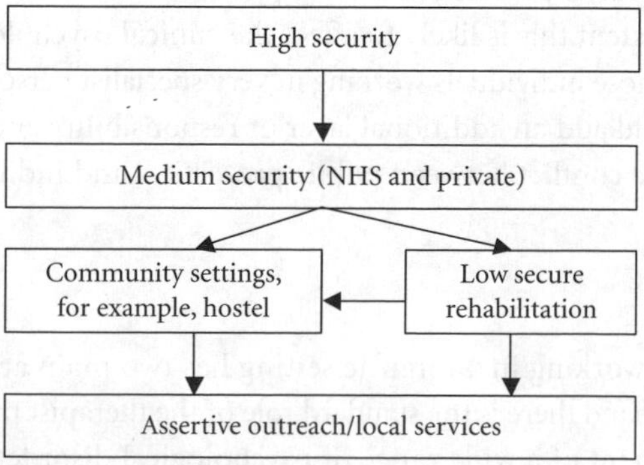

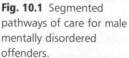

Fig. 10.1 Segmented pathways of care for male mentally disordered offenders.

for institutionalized individuals or patients who have specific deficits in daily living skills and social functioning, providing a bridge between conditions of medium security and the community. Equally there has been a growth in prison 'in-reach' teams that bridge the gap between prison health care services and NHS mental health providers.

Perhaps more than any other area of psychological speciality, forensic patients tend to provoke strong opinions and reactions from the general public. As in the example at the beginning of this chapter, popular culture still portrays individuals with mental disorders as being potential threats and there has been an increasing conflict between the need to treat a patient's distress, and the need to reduce the risk to the public. The distinction between mental illness and criminality remains a fine one in the eyes of the public. The public protection role, while not by any means central to the job, does have its effect. For instance it may mean that, unlike some other areas of psychology, clinical psychologists working in forensic settings may be more frequently presented with the challenge of motivating patients who do not wish to engage in psychology or change their behaviours, but may ultimately need to do so in order to regain their freedom or improve their quality of life. Alternatively it may mean working with individuals whose primary disturbance is not one of mental illness, but of personality, or behaviour (e.g. sexual offenders). The potential for ethical dilemmas in such work is an ongoing hazard, particularly when the mantle of responsibility for public protection issues is one that can conflict with the primary aim of clinical psychology training, being to help reduce an individual's distress.

Within the broader organizational context, developments that are likely to effect clinical psychologists working within forensic settings in the United Kingdom include the draft Mental Health Bill, which for the first time allows the possibility that a clinical psychologist may be an 'approved mental health professional' and may under the act have powers of detention, a role previously held only by medical professionals and approved social workers. It remains unclear to what extent this is likely to affect the clinical psychologist's role, as it may affect only those individuals working in very specialist personality disorder services, but would add an additional layer of responsibility and may add further impetus to the conflict between public protection and individual patient need.

The role in detail

The clinical psychologist working in a forensic setting has two main areas of responsibility. On the one hand there is the standard role of the therapist providing assessment and treatment of a wide range of psychological disorders and disturbances, albeit with a focus on criminogenic and risk issues. The second role, while having the same focus, relates to the duty to protect the public. However, as will become evident in this section, these are not mutually exclusive roles, but rather are both integral to the tasks carried out by forensic clinical psychologists.

Risk assessment and the problems with risk assessment

The term 'risk assessment' can apply to many things and, in mental health terms, to a range of behaviours including self-harming and suicidal behaviour. However, in the context of forensic work it is usually taken to mean an assessment of an individual's risk of engaging in offending behaviour in some form or another. The process of risk assessment in this context can be complex and multifaceted, which we aim to highlight in this section using the example of the risk of violent behaviour.

The process of risk assessment of violence has developed a great deal over the past 50 or so years. In the 1950s, 1960s, and 1970s the concept of formal risk assessment was not really considered, which appeared to be based on the belief that professionals were able to easily identify which individuals were dangerous and which were not merely on the basis of their training. However, a sea change in this view began following a naturally occurring experiment, which was taken advantage of by Steadman and Cocozza (1974). This 'experiment' centred upon the release of almost 1000 detainees following the successful appeal of Johnny Baxstrom in the United States that he was being detained unnecessarily and unlawfully, after which the United States Supreme Court released not only him, but also 966 other individuals. Steadman and Cocozza followed up 98 of the individuals released and found that only 2% of them subsequently violently offended, despite all of them having been detained on the basis that they presented a risk of doing so. This finding clearly highlighted the problem of the over-prediction of risk by professionals and the need for more robust and reliable risk assessment.

Although initially this finding led to some suggestions that forensic psychologists and psychiatrists may be best advised to stop providing risk assessments of this nature, Shah (1981) commented that 'To say something is difficult to do (namely, to achieve high levels of accuracy in predicting events with very low base rates) is *not* the same as asserting that the task is impossible and simply cannot be done' (p. 161). Such beliefs among some researchers led to the suggestion that, in order to enhance risk assessment for violent behaviour, it might be beneficial to use not only clinical judgement (as had been the case in the past), but also to include actuarial variables that had been demonstrated to be associated with dangerous acts. Such variables included previous violent acts, socioeconomic status and alcohol/drug abuse.

The view that to increase the reliability of risk assessment it was important to combine both clinical and actuarial variables eventually led to the development of risk assessment schedules such as the Violence Risk Appraisal Guide (VRAG), which attempted to cover both sets of variables. In using such schedules it was found that the accuracy of risk assessment could be substantially increased, which has led to the continued refinement of these instruments as they take account of research findings as they emerge. The most recent refinement of these instruments is the HCR-20, which consists of 10 'historical' items, 5 'clinical' items, and 5 'risk management' items. The HCR-20 remains in its relative infancy and, as such, the ability of this instrument to reliably increase the accuracy of risk assessment remains to be demonstrated, but the research on the VRAG would suggest that improving risk assessment in this manner is a most welcome development—especially given that in the past (without such instruments) the risk of violence was over-predicted and, therefore, many individuals would be unnecessarily detained. Indeed, such has been the confidence in the development of risk assessment in this direction, that versions of such instruments have also been developed for other types of offending behaviour, such as, sexual offending and abuse of spouses.

Overall however, despite these welcome developments, it has been argued that there remains a gap between the research findings and clinical realities (Webster and Bailes, 2004) and these commentators call for 'a renewal of emphasis on establishing scientist–practitioner models' (p. 25) in relation to the area of risk assessment. Indeed, despite the utility of such instruments it might be argued that while they can clearly guide risk assessment, they should not be used as an alternative to the construction of a formulation of an individual's offending behaviour, but rather as part of a multifaceted risk assessment process that includes actuarial variables.

Psychopathy and offending behaviour

One of the actuarial variables that has been found to predict future offending behaviour (both of a non-sexually and a sexually violent manner) is what has been termed 'psychopathy'. The notion of psychopathy deserves a special mention over and above each of the other actuarial variables identified as it has been shown to be associated with offending behaviour at least as well as, if not better than, any other single predictor of violent behaviour.

The notion of psychopathy, of which there is no widely accepted definition, is based on a number of characteristics which led to the development of the

Psychopathy Checklist-Revised (PCL-R) by Robert Hare, which is now used as the standard tool to assess an individual's level of psychopathy.

According to Hare (1996) psychopaths can be described as:

> predators who use charm, manipulation, intimidation and violence to control others and to satisfy their own selfish needs. Lacking a conscience and in feelings for others, they cold-bloodedly take what they want and do as they please, violating social norms and expectations without the slightest sense of guilt or regret.

Hare goes on to say that

> 'it is not surprising that . . . they are responsible for a markedly disproportionate amount of serious crime, violence and social distress in society.

However, despite the seeming ability of an individual's level of psychopathy to be able to predict future violent behaviour, it appears that not all psychopaths are detained in (or indeed are destined for) forensic institutions of some kind. According to Babiak (1995), psychopaths seem to be as well represented in the business and corporate world as they are in such institutions. It is possible, therefore, that a third variable known to be related to violent offending (such as socioeconomic status) may explain why some psychopathic individuals become violent offenders, while others may succeed in the world of business.

Overall, despite this, it is widely accepted that in a population of individuals who have a history of violence, their level of psychopathy can predict levels of future violence. This knowledge poses an ongoing difficulty for psychologists working in forensic settings. Not only are there no known efficacious treatments for such individuals, but there exists some research to suggest that engaging in treatment can increase the risk of reoffending in those deemed as psychopaths (Rice *et al.*, 1992). This remains an unresolved issue, although there are moves to try to solve this difficulty in the form of units which have been set up to contain and treat individuals with what has been termed 'dangerous and severe personality disorders', of which psychopathy occupies a central role.

Assessing offending behaviour

As with any other behaviour that would be assessed by a psychologist, the assessment of offending behaviour involves the collection of information from a variety of sources in order that a formulation of the behaviour of concern can be constructed and an intervention devised (where feasible) aimed at reducing an individual's level of risk of re-engaging in the particular offending behaviour.

The range of offending behaviours that psychologists working in a forensic setting might encounter are potentially innumerable, and vary in severity. For example, they can range from voyeurism and fetishism to serious sexual offences, such as rape, or from low level aggressive behaviour to manslaughter or murder. For this reason, this section will focus on the general issues related to the assessment of offending behaviour as an exhaustive list of issues related to all offending behaviours would not be feasible herein and, in any case, there are more commonalities than differences.

As in all other areas of clinical psychology, a central component of the assessment of offending behaviour is a clinical (and in this case, forensic) interview with the client. Similarly, in forensic cases a number of psychometric and/or psychological measures might be utilized to gain further and more detailed information about the client. However, one of the main differences between a clinical and a forensic clinical assessment is perhaps the greater emphasis in the latter placed upon the collection of information from additional sources, such as police records, victim statements, crime scene photographs, previous mental health assessments, the accounts of family and friends, nursing observations, and so on. The reason for this is that, as in other areas of psychology, while the individual's self-report is extremely useful, there may be a number of reasons why this self-report in a forensic setting is a distorted view of the individual's offending behaviour and his or her life more generally. Thus, for example, individuals may be extremely motivated to deny their offence, either because they are being assessed pre-trial or because they feel that admitting to and discussing the offence with a psychologist may prolong their enforced stay in hospital or for fear of future repercussions. Further, the individual's memory of the offence may be hazy (or, in some cases, non-existent) possibly due to the role of the symptoms of major mental illness in the offence, or the individual being under the influence of substances at the time the offence was committed. In addition, there may be some psychological defence mechanisms in place that are functioning to protect the individual against the realization of what they have done and what that may mean about them as individuals. Indeed, such defence mechanisms are particularly evident in those who have committed sexual offences. The individual may also be experiencing a great deal of shame associated with the offence and, until such time as the psychologist has built up a rapport with the individual and the individual has come to trust the psychologist, it is often not possible to discuss his or her offence with them.

Overall, however, a forensic clinical assessment would cover many of the areas that might be covered in a full assessment in any other area of clinical psychology. For example, a childhood and developmental history would be taken, as would a history of social relationships, mental health issues, and the individual's own perception of their symptoms and behaviours.

The differences between the two kinds of assessment occur when the offence becomes the focus. Thus, a forensic assessment would cover issues such as beliefs about and attitudes towards the victim type (e.g. children, women, or ethnic minorities), whether the individuals had fantasized about the offence, the antecedents of the offence, the degree and type of planning associated with the offence, the individuals' emotional and mental state at the time of the offence, the amount of force used, the individuals' view about the harm (psychological or physical) they may have caused the victim, and their immediate post-offence behaviour. In addition, during the assessment an extremely detailed account of the offence *per se* needs to be gained to aid with subsequent formulation.

It will be evident, given the information that needs to be gained during a forensic assessment, why individuals may be initially reticent to discuss their offence(s) with a psychologist. However, it can facilitate this discussion if the psychologist is open and honest about the purpose of the assessment and outlines the bounds of confidentiality at the outset—indeed, both of these are required ethically so that informed consent to the assessment can be given by the individual. It can also help if the psychologist has an open discussion with the individual about the possible pros and cons of engaging in the assessment, as this can help overcome some of the initial offence-related denial and motivate the individual to engage in the assessment process. It is only once this long assessment process has been completed that a formulation can be constructed to guide any subsequent intervention.

Psychosis and offending behaviour—treatment issues

On the basis of the assessment of an individual's offence that has been carried out, it should then be possible to construct a formulation of the offending behaviour in order to guide any subsequent intervention. As clinical psychologists working in the forensic arena are, more often than not, employed in mental health settings, such formulations will often include what is described as major mental illness; most frequently schizophrenia, bipolar disorder, delusional disorder, and atypical psychoses.

While the prevalence of major mental illness is relatively low in the general population (e.g. approximately 1% of individuals suffer from schizophrenia and approximately 1.6% from bipolar disorder), individuals who develop such disorders are more likely to be convicted of criminal offences than persons with no such disorder. Further, this difference between these groups is greatest for violent rather than non-violent offences. Acute episodes of such illnesses, which may have contributed to an individual's offending behaviour, can include marked distortions of reality (i.e. delusions), auditory hallucinations (usually consisting of the individual hearing voices speaking to them) and/or an extremely elated mood associated with bizarre behaviour. Anyone, or a combination of such symptoms may be related to an individual engaging in offending behaviour. For example, an individual who killed someone on the basis of experiencing command hallucinations instructing him or her to do so, and believing the person killed to be an agent of the Devil that had to be killed in order to save the whole of mankind, would be a clear example of the role of major mental illness in offending behaviour.

In response to offending behaviour that appears to be clearly linked to an individual's mental disorder, the criminal justice system often imposes a 'Hospital Order' so that the person can be compulsorily detained in hospital for treatment of their illness. However, the majority of individuals with major mental illnesses who have offended are resident in the community or will return to the community following a period of treatment and rehabilitation in hospital. While in hospital (and indeed in the community), the first line of treatment remains the use of antipsychotic medication. However, despite relatively recent advances in such medication which can result in a marked decrease in an individual's psychotic symptoms, such medications alone are rarely sufficient to treat an individual's offending behaviour and, it has been argued, should be seen as a prerequisite for the necessary psychosocial interventions required, the combination of which can be used to minimize the risk of reoffending. Such psychosocial interventions might include behavioural interventions aimed at specific behaviours rather than generalized improvement, skills training, help with living skills, and support to gain access to concrete needs (e.g. housing, money, and socialization opportunities). Thus, current perspectives on the treatment of mentally disordered offenders advocate a combination of medication management and psychosocial interventions in order to reduce the likelihood of reoffending, with such treatment characterizing both hospital and community care.

Non-psychotically driven offending behaviour—treatment issues

Of course, it is possible that, after a period of assessment and a subsequent formulation, it may become apparent that an individual's offending behaviour may not be directly linked to a major mental illness, but rather co-occurs with such illness. That is, the offence may not have been psychotically driven, but rather that the individual has a propensity to offend in a certain way, but also happens to suffer from a major mental illness. Indeed, in such individuals, anti-social attitudes might have been present from a very early age (which might be an indicator that the offence may not have been psychotically driven), but they have also developed a major mental illness later in life. One area of offending behaviour in which this is frequently found is in the area of sexual offending. For example, it has been found that no more than 5 per cent–8 per cent of rapists suffer from either a major mental illness, serious brain dysfunction, or a learning disability (Seghorn *et al.*, 1987).

If, following assessment and formulation, it is hypothesized that an individual's offending behaviour is not directly related to his or her mental illness, then the form of intervention would largely take the same format as that offered to individuals who do not suffer from such illness. Thus, keeping to the example of sexual offending, such individuals are likely to be offered a group intervention (most commonly based upon cognitive-behavioural principles) in order to reduce their risk of reoffending. The type of intervention offered to such sexual offenders, it is hypothesized, is best provided in such a group setting, since the challenging of the individual's views (which occupies a central role in such treatment) is seen as more credible if it is carried out by other offenders rather than by a therapist who will have no experience of having sexually offended. Further, not only is this seen as of greater benefit to the individual who is being challenged, but also to the person challenging as the latter, by doing so, may gain a greater understanding of his or her own offending behaviour.

In addition to this, such Sexual Offender Treatment Programmes (SOTP) are offered to a heterogeneous group of offenders (i.e. rapists, child sexual offenders, etc.) as it has proven difficult to classify such offenders according to their offence type, diagnostic criteria, or other systems in relation to their treatment needs. Indeed, it has been argued that it might actually be of benefit to mix different types of offenders within the same treatment programme as, despite them often believing that they differ from each other, they may benefit from realizing the distress that they have all caused to their victims, which is a central goal of such therapy.

The content of SOTPs covers the issues which are seen to be related to sexual offending. They most commonly include components focusing on denial, cognitive distortions, empathy training, social skills training, self-esteem enhancement, difficulties with intimacy, sexual preferences and, finally, a component on relapse prevention. However, it has been argued that the nature of this intervention needs extending to focus on individuals' schematic level beliefs (i.e. lifelong dysfunctional thinking patterns) in order to improve the efficacy of the treatment of sexual offenders, as the outcome studies (to date) of the traditional programmes have been mixed.

The consultancy role

Both the emphasis on public protection and the specialization of the forensic clinical psychologist has resulted in a situation where the psychologists' role as a consultant is as prominent as their direct therapeutic input. Figure 10.2 below outlines some of the varied consultancy contacts for a typical team psychologist working in a Regional Secure Unite (RSU).

As has been noted previously, the nature of the client group often prompts anxiety about their risk when such patients move from conditions of security to the community. In patients who are not mentally ill, but have other difficulties such as personality disorder or who have a history of sexual offending, the public protection role becomes even more prominent and this in turn increases the amount of consultancy to other agencies. Some of the difficulties that occur when trying to predict risk have been already outlined, but an added difficulty occurs when that risk has to be communicated sensitively to others. A difficult balance has to be struck between maximizing the patient's potential for successful rehabilitation, and communicating the likely risk such an attempt will incur. This is hampered by the lay impression of forensic patients that is sometimes perpetuated by aspects of the media and is little different from attitudes a hundred years ago. Equally, the development of public monitoring programmes such as the sex offenders' register brings the question of risk management and risk prediction to the forefront of the consultancy role.

An example of this can be seen in the development of Multi-Agency Public Protection Panels (MAPPPs). These meetings, formed in the United Kingdom as a result of the Criminal Justice and Court Service Act (2000) serve to bring

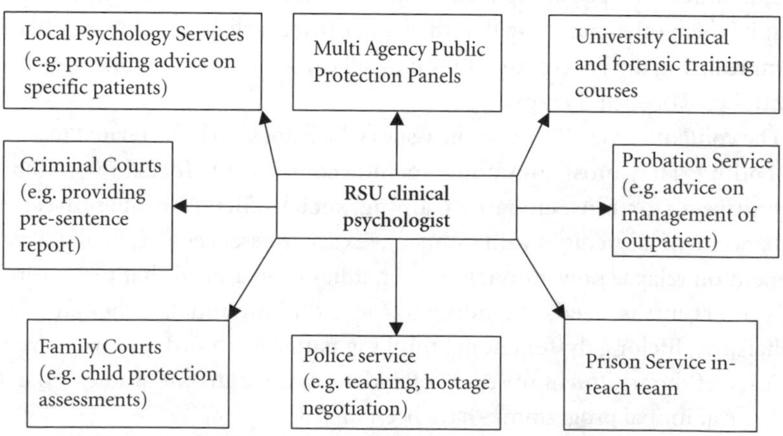

Fig. 10.2 Typical consultancy roles of an RSU clinical psychologist.

together the Police, Probation, Social Services, and Health Services to monitor and manage the potential risk represented by sexual offenders and other violent offenders. In 2003, the revised Criminal Justice Act included a specific duty by Health Services to be represented on such panels if they had an input.

At time of writing there are 42 MAPPPs in the United Kingdom managing nearly 40,000 individuals, approximately two-thirds of whom are registered sexual offenders, the rest being mainly violent offenders. For the psychologist, attending a MAPPP meeting can present some ethical difficulties. On the one hand, information has to be passed onto the MAPPP necessary for them to accurately assess the risk of the individual, but on the other hand, you as a clinician have to maintain rapport with your client. It may even be the case that your direct involvement in an MAPPP meeting may cause your client to distrust his or her therapist. In such a case such distrust may result in contempt, resentment, and anger and cause the therapeutic intervention to be ineffective, possibly even increasing the individual's risk to others.

The psychologist then has to carefully impart information about risk issues to the panel, without compromising professional ethics regarding confidentiality, ruining their relationship with patient, and also satisfying the needs of the panel, whose overriding priority is not necessarily patient care, but understandably, public protection. This is rarely an easy task.

Another area with similar difficulties is when the forensic clinical psychologist is called to assess a parent and advise Social Services or the Court about the parent's potential risk to their child. More often than not, the child has already been removed from the parent's care, sometimes voluntarily, but otherwise under an Interim Care Order, via the Children's Act (1989). The psychologist has the task of formulating an analysis of the parent's psychological functioning and parenting abilities. The complex interplay between history, environment, biology, social situation, and abilities that constitute parenting skills makes for difficult assessment, particularly since the parent will understandably try and present themselves in the best possible light, making their self-report inherently biased. The responsibility that comes with such work, particularly given the weight that can be placed on such reports by the Court, can be considerable.

As with any assessment of risk, the task is to predict the likely probability of a particular behaviour occurring, usually informed by past behaviours. Specific recommendations are often given in terms of such strategies as further assessments (e.g. a residential parenting assessment) or conditions regarding the gradual supervised reintroduction of parent and child. On rare occasions, the psychologist may feel that the potential risk to the parent outweighs the potential for benefit that contact might bring.

In the latter example, the psychologist may be called to Court to act as an expert witness. In family cases, the psychologist usually has to defend his or her report to a panel of magistrates or a circuit judge sitting in a family Court. This situation can prompt anxiety in Court-naïve psychologists, and even be an anxiety-provoking occasion for experienced expert witnesses. Crucially, the task is to convert the many probabilistic statements of the psychological report (e.g. 'It is likely that with continued drug use, Mr X will continue to bring his daughter into contact with situations that are likely to be harmful') into language that the Court can understand. While this includes a didactic teaching element, it is also a meeting of cultures. The legal system is, by its nature, built upon dichotomous elements (Guilty or Not-guilty). Psychology, on the other hand, particularly when behaviours are being predicted, tends to be built upon elements that exist on a continuum (e.g. 'It is likely that with increasing isolation from adults his age Mr X is more likely to present as a sexual risk to children'). It is also the case that the expert constrains his or her testimony to matters upon which they can prove their expertise. It is all too easy to be drawn into giving testimony on matters that are within the expertise of all human beings.

Forensic clinical psychologists can also attend Court as expert witnesses in criminal cases and it is worth noting that unlike family cases (which come under civil law), the criminal Court system has a different basis of evidence, tends to be more adversarial, and if they are indictable offences (e.g. murder, rape), usually involves trial by jury. The work of Professor Gisli Gudjonsson on the concept of suggestibility is a clear example of the impact that providing psychological testimony can have. As part of the appeals process for both the Guildford Four and the Birmingham Six, he was asked to assess the veracity of their admissions of guilt. In both cases he found that some of the individuals had admitted guilt as a result of yielding to strong interrogative pressure by the police. For instance, Carole Richardson was arrested in connection with the Guildford pub bombings, but at the time of her arrest was under the influence of Tuinol, a barbiturate depressant. She was kept for questioning for 4 days and was not allowed to contact anybody about her arrest. She was preoccupied about getting out of the police station and admitted her guilt out of fear and under pressure from police who she perceived as being completely confident of her guilt. She later admitted that she even started to believe that she was involved in the bombings while under such strong pressure. While she was arrested on 3 December 1974, she did not speak to a solicitor until 11 December, by which time she had confessed to her involvement.

As part of the appeal process, Gudjonnsson and his colleague James MacKeith were asked to examine the case and in the case of Carole Richardson they were able to show that she had a tendency to avoid conflict and confrontation when faced with pressure. They also questioned her mental state at the time of the police interview, given that she was suffering from barbiturate withdrawal. As a result of the reports, and along with other additional forensic evidence, the case was reopened by the Court of Appeal and in 1989, the Guildford Four were released after serving 15 years (Gudjonsson and Mackeith, 1992).

Obviously, few cases approach the impact that Professor Gudjonsson experienced, but the results of his expert evidence, and that of a number of other cases, have made psychological testimonies increasingly valued in the Court system. It is perhaps also important to note that while this chapter has primarily focused on the role of a forensic clinical psychologist working in a forensic mental health setting, there is also a role for clinical psychologists working both within the NHS, academia, and in private practice to provide forensic reports, assuming they have the necessary qualifications and experience.

Another area of consultancy with which forensic clinical psychologists have become involved, is in assisting the police in hostage negotiation situations. Certainly in the United States, psychological principles have been employed within the tactics used by police negotiators. The psychologist acts as consultant, along with other mental health professionals (such as a forensic psychiatrist), and might be asked to provide a psychological profile of a hostage taker, based upon whatever information can be made available at the time of the crisis. This profile can then be used to brief the police, who choose how to use that information to form a resolution strategy. This consultation is likely to take place within the highly pressurized environment of an actual hostage scene and is not therefore for the faint of heart. Currently there are probably only a small number of highly experienced senior professionals involved in such work.

As can be seen the consultancy role of the forensic clinical psychologist is considerable. There is grave responsibility, professionally, ethically, and morally to our patients, our profession, and ourselves as individuals to ensure that wherever possible the information we impart to others, particularly when it comes to risk issues, is accurate and as representative as it can be and moreover, that the degree to which it is likely to be valid is also communicated. Psychologists acting within the Court system act as objective assessors, independent of those who instruct them or are paying the bill. Similarly risk assessments must include statements regarding the validity of the information upon which that risk assessment is based.

The weight of such responsibility, along with the emotional nature of the therapeutic work, can take its toll. We consider personal reflection and supervision to be absolute essentials when working with forensic patients. Not only will such reflections enable you to protect yourself from the emotional impact of the work (which can be considerable), but also as importantly, it serves a vital function in ensuring that you do not become inured to the disturbances to which you are likely to be exposed. Finally, personal reactions to the sometimes morally abhorrent behaviours of our clients must be carefully managed and reflected upon in order to ensure that the patient, client, or service user is getting the best service they can.

Future developments for the forensic clinical psychologist

Among the new developments that may affect the forensic clinical psychologist in the United Kingdom at least, particularly those who work solely in the forensic mental health field, is the development of the Mental Health Act and its potential for clinical psychologist to act as lead clinicians. It remains to be seen to what extent such a role will develop or even if it will make its way into the final version of the act. There are arguments both for and against it, particularly when working with individuals with personality disorders for whom the psychologist is likely to be the lead therapist.

Also, within the forensic mental health world, there is an increasing focus on providing more graduated pathways out of the forensic service into the community. The closing of many of the old psychiatric asylums in the 1970s and 1980s have left many chronically ill individuals languishing in psychiatric units. These individuals struggle to fully partake in a culture that still tends to be dominated by a focus on return to the community, rather than one that focuses on maximizing quality of life. Equally, there seems likely to be an increasing focus on community respite for forensic patients who have previously earned the dubious moniker of 'revolving door' patients. Forensic clinical psychologists may increasingly develop a focus on helping patients gain community living skills, helping them to overcome the vicissitudes of life that contributed to the development of both their criminogenic backgrounds and their mental ill health.

Other developments include the separation of male and female services. Forensic services have been historically dominated by male service users (mainly due to the greater ratio of male offenders to female offenders) but dedicated female services have been a long time coming. Equally, specialist forensic mental health services for adolescents have only recently started to develop with a number of specialist units now in existence.

As has been noted throughout this chapter, there is also a growing emphasis on the public protection role that psychologists have. It is unclear to what extent this will continue to influence governmental policy. The debate currently rages about government proposals regarding individuals with 'dangerous and severe personality disorders' (DSPD). Psychologists are already taking a prominent role in the treatment of such individuals within custodial settings (e.g. the Peaks Unit, Rampton Special Hospital Authority), and it is likely that they will take an equally influential position in the development of DSPD community services. In such a case, the public protection role may also reach greater prominence.

Conclusions

This chapter has attempted to give an overview of the many roles that a forensic clinical psychologist can have. We have explored the historical context of the development of forensic mental health services and the role that clinical psychologists play in such services. We have examined the issues of assessment and treatment and the conflict between our role as therapists and as arbiters of public protection. It has been our intent to give as realistic view as possible of the difficulties that exist in such work in the hope that those who do pursue a career in this area, do so with their eyes and mind open. The work can be difficult and tiring, but it can also be exciting, challenging, and absolutely engrossing. We are constantly tested by some of the most complex behaviours demonstrated by human beings, and the opportunity for learning, research, and professional growth is extensive.

References

Babiak, P. (1995). When psychopaths go to work. *International Journal of Applied Psychology*, **44**, 171–88.

Blueglass, R. (1985). The development of regional secure units. In L. Gostin (ed.), *Secure Provision*. London: Tavistock Publications.

Forshaw, D. and Rollin, H. (1990). The history of forensic psychiatry in England, in R. Bluglass and P. Bowden (eds.), *Principles and Practice of Forensic Psychiatry*. London: Churchill Livingston.

Gudjonsson, G.H. and Mackeith, J.A.C. (1992). The Guildford Four and the Birmingham Six. In G.H. Gudjonsson (ed.), *The Psychology of Interrogations, Confessions and Testimony*. Chichester: Wiley.

Hare, R.D. (1996). Psychopathy: A clinical construct whose times has come. *Criminal Justice and Behaviour*, **23**, 25–54.

Rice, M.E., Harris, G.T., and Cromer, C. (1992). An evaluation of a maximum security therapeutic community for psychopaths and other mentally disordered offenders. *Law and Human Behaviour*, **16**(4), 399–412.

Seghorn, T.K. and Cohen, M. (1980). The psychology of the rape assailant. In W. Cerran, A.L. McGarry, and C. Petty (eds.), *Modern Legal Medicine, Psychiatry, and Forensic Science* pp. 533–51. Philadelphia, PA: F.A. Davis.

Seghorn, T.K., Prentky, R.A., and Boucher, R.J. (1987). Childhood sexual abuse in the lives of sexually aggressive offenders. *Journal of the American Academy of Child and Adolescent Psychiatry*, **26**, 262–7.

Shah, S.A. (1981). Dangerousness: Conceptual, prediction, and public policy issues. In J.R. Hays, T.K. Roberts, and K.S. Solway (eds.), *Violence and the Violent Individual*, pp. 151–78. New York: SP Medical and Scientific Books.

Steadman, H.J. and Cocozza, J.J. (1974). *Careers of the Criminally Insame: Excessive Social Control of Deviance*. Lexington, MA: Lexington Books.

Webster, C.D. and Bailes, G. (2004). Assessing violence risk in mentally and personality disordered individuals. In C.R. Hollin (ed.), *The Essential Handbook of Offender Assessment and Treatment*. Chichester, UK: John Wiley & Sons.

Chapter 11

Working in general medical settings

Gary Latchford

Introduction

Of the many different areas of academic psychology, health psychology has perhaps grown in popularity more than any other over the last 20 years. This is reflected in the establishment of a number of journals and organisations, and in its rise as one of the most popular topics for doctoral research projects in university psychology departments.

There has been interest, too, in practical applications, for example in predicting and influencing lifestyle change such as smoking cessation, and in examining and enhancing informed decision making by patients about medical treatments.

Within clinical psychology, using knowledge from health psychology to inform clinical practice for the benefit of patients with physical illness has come to be known as clinical health psychology. Although a new term, its roots go back many years. For example, clinical psychologists have long been involved in pain management.

Why has the situation changed? First, behavioural risk factors such as smoking and diet play an important role in major illnesses such as heart disease and diabetes, and lifestyle interventions are a crucial factor in prevention. Second, in many Western nations advances in medicine coupled with an ageing population has led to more patients surviving with chronic and debilitating conditions. With no cure available, the intervention instead focuses on symptom and disease management, and attempts to increase quality of life, which almost invariably involves psychology, for example in increasing adherence to medication. This emphasis on chronic disease management also links with a third development, an increasing acknowledgement by health services and professionals that patients need to be involved in how their condition is treated. This is clearly more ethical, and mirrors developments in increasing user involvement in mental health services. More than this, as many chronic conditions are in essence managed by the patients themselves (often responsible for taking medication several times a day), involving patients in their care also offers the possibility of increasing adherence and better outcomes. There is now good evidence that psychological interventions in health are cost-effective, reducing use of other health services (Kaplan and Groessl, 2002).

These developments inform recommendations and guidelines for treatment for a variety of conditions issued by national and international organisations, such as the National Service Frameworks for Coronary Heart Disease (2000) and Diabetes (2003) in the United Kingdom.

Hand-in-hand with this is a growing awareness among medical practitioners of the importance of psychological factors to many different aspects of medical care, from assessment of suitability for a medical intervention (e.g. cosmetic surgery), to support and management after onset of illness (e.g. cardiac rehabilitation). This has led to increasing demands upon clinical psychology services and an increasing number of clinical health psychologists specializing in psychological interventions with patients with physical illness.

The work and work settings of clinical health psychologists

In their work, clinical health psychologists use evidence based psychological interventions from clinical psychology and also draw upon research in health psychology with potential for helping to understand the impact of illness on individuals and informing therapeutic interventions. The work of clinical health psychologists is distinct from the emerging profession of health psychology, which does not involve face-to-face therapeutic work with patients, and the long-established areas of behavioural medicine and health promotion, which have applied psychological concepts to the practice of medicine and prevention of ill health, respectively.

Clinical health psychologists offer therapeutic and consultation services for patients and staff within a variety of healthcare settings (see Table 11.1.) Many clinical psychologists working in areas such as mental health will occasionally see individuals for whom health is an issue. Among those specializing in Health, some psychologists work in teams supporting the community care of patients with physical problems, such as physical disability or head injury. The majority, however, are based in acute hospitals, potentially providing a service to a variety of medical specialties. Such departments usually see patients across the age range from the very young to the elderly and psychologists will work with both inpatients and outpatients.

Table 11.1 Possible work settings of clinical health psychologists

Setting	Examples
Community	GP Clinic Unit for physically disabled adults Head injury team
Hospital	
Anaesthetics	Pain management Palliative care team
Women's services	Assisted conception unit Abortion clinic
Children's services	Paediatric intensive care Paediatric renal unit Cystic fibrosis unit
General medicine	Diabetes team Cardiac rehabilitation team Chest clinic Oncology (cancer) service
Surgery	Orthopaedic trauma ward Kidney transplant team Plastic and reconstructive surgery unit
Human resources	Staff counselling service Staff development unit
Strategic health authority	Health education unit Public health department

Inpatient referrals offer psychologists the opportunity to work with patients during a time when they may be particularly vulnerable or in crisis (e.g. hospitalization following a medical emergency). Such work can be particularly challenging. For example, carrying out a counselling session at a person's bedside, in ward day room or on a Haemodialysis unit, does not afford the privacy of more usual therapeutic settings.

A clinical health psychologist will normally spend much of his or her time working with individuals or groups, such as patients with chronic pain or recovering from a heart attack. It is not possible—or always appropriate—for a clinical health psychologist to see all patients where distress is a problem, and a productive use of time and skills is to offer consultancy on psychological care to colleagues in other professions, such as advising on assessment of depression and basic counselling skills. Clinical health psychologists may also make an impact at an organizational level, for example by involvement

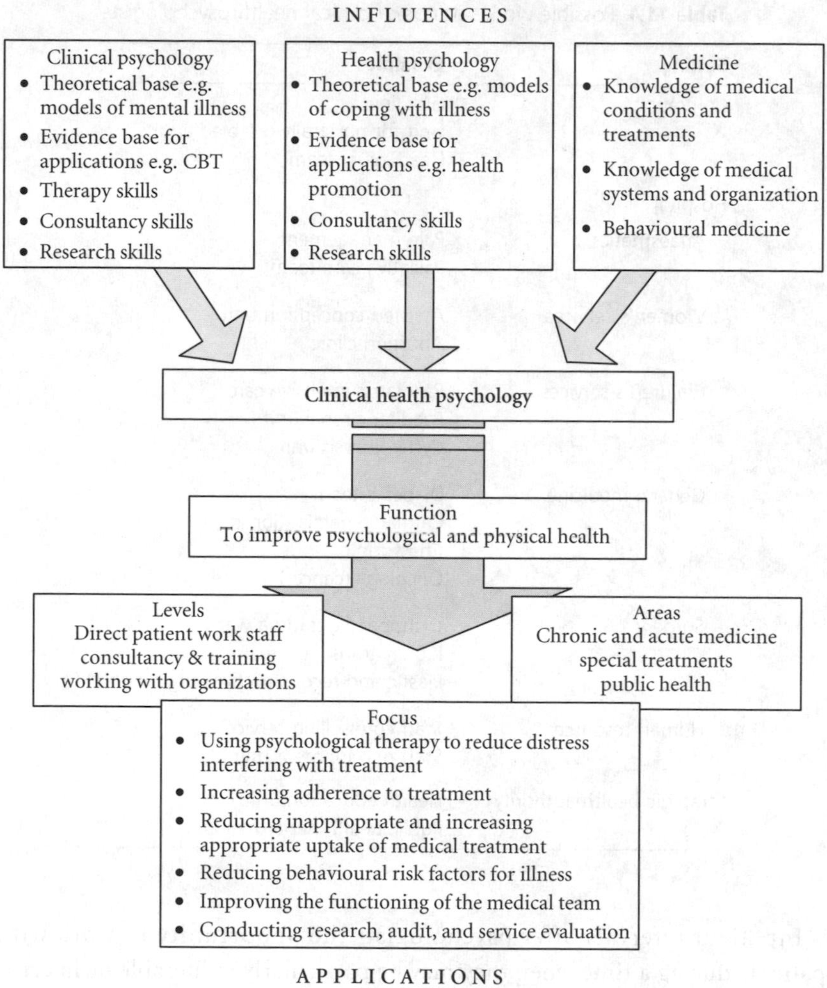

Fig. 11.1 Influences and applications in clinical health psychology.

in planning new services so that psychological aspects are taken into account.

Finally, clinical health psychologists are often involved in research projects in collaboration with medical and nursing colleagues, health and academic psychologists, or other members of the clinical team.

Figure 11.1 summarizes some of the influences (knowledge and skills) on the practice of clinical health psychology, the areas or setting in which practice is carried out, the levels at which interventions may be made, and the function and focus of those interventions.

The following sections in this chapter provide more detailed examination of these influences and applications.

Influences on practice—theoretical frameworks

Models from clinical psychology

Many of the core skills of clinical psychologists in assessing psychological state, formulating problems, and providing psychological interventions are similar when applied in a health setting. Psychotherapies such as Cognitive Behaviour Therapy (CBT), with some adaptation, are very suitable for work in health settings (e.g. White, 2001), but there are also important differences. For example, distress may be seen as a reasonable and rational response to a serious illness and it is unrealistic and probably counter productive for a therapist to aim to eliminate it completely. At the same time, some responses to ill health are maladaptive and influenced more by fear or previous history than an understanding of the implications of the current illness. There are many published examples of systematic adaptations of psychotherapies for specific health conditions, most notably—and successfully—CBT for pain management.

Models from health psychology

Models from health psychology may help to map out an individual's response to an illness. Taylor's model of coping with serious illness (1983) focuses on the meaning of the illness to the individual; Leventhal's self-regulatory model (Leventhal *et al.* 1980) sees people as active problem solvers, building up a picture of their illness and what they need to do to cope with it, and then evaluating their efforts. He proposes that the picture is informed by emotional and cognitive representations of the illness. The structure of cognitive representations he proposes is now well known, and involves five dimensions:

1. *Identity*: beliefs about the identity of the illness, based upon symptoms (e.g. pain), concrete signs (e.g. bleeding), and labels (e.g. heart attack).
2. *Consequences*: perceived physical, social, economic, and emotional consequences of the illness (e.g. difficulty walking, loss of employment).
3. *Causes*: perceived causes (e.g. heredity, environment) including internal and external attributions.
4. *Time line*: the perceived time frame for development and duration of illness (e.g. short or life-long).
5. *Controllability*: extent to which the illness can be controlled by the individual or an external agent.

Understanding a patient's perceptions or beliefs about his or her illness and its treatment is very important since these will in part determine an individual's response to both.

A general model

While a range of theoretical frameworks at different levels of specificity are necessary depending upon the problem focus, setting, or context, there is also a need for a general framework for theorizing and thinking about health and illness. The biopsychosocial model (Figure 11.2) was proposed by George Engel in 1977 as a response to the biomedical model of disease, which had dominated medicine for many years.

According to Engel (1977), a more satisfactory model would broaden the focus from biology to take into account social, psychological, economic, and environmental factors that contribute to health and illness. He argued that an acknowledgement of these influences was essential for effective medical practice, since doctors must be able to assess the role of these factors if they are to successfully diagnose a patient's condition, plan an effective treatment, and gain the patient's trust to enable treatment to be carried out.

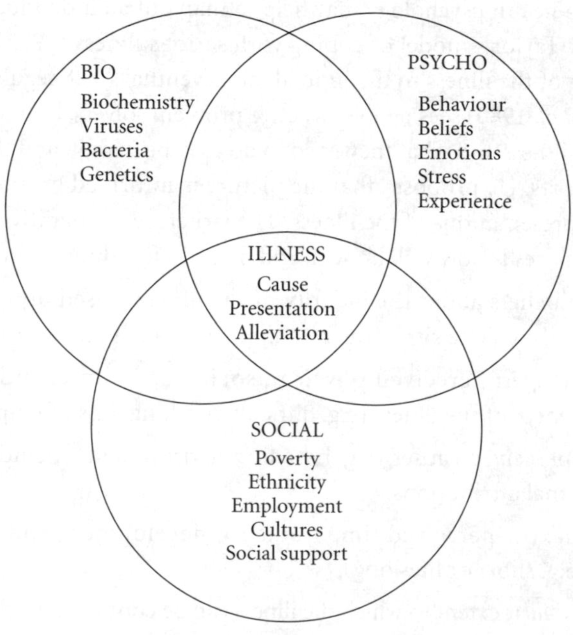

Fig. 11.2 A graphical representation of the biopsychosocial model of health and illness.

Though rarely cited directly, the biopsychosocial model underlies much of the practice of all clinical psychology. In health, the wide variations in morbidity and mortality in different segments of the population are clearly influenced by socioeconomic circumstance. Factors such as wealth and culture have been referred to as 'superhighways for disease', though the nature of the relationship is complex. The association between socioeconomic status and health cannot be totally attributed to variations in unhealthy behaviour such as smoking, for example. Similarly, social support is known to be an important factor influencing good outcome across a range of physical and mental health problems.

These seemingly academic issues are of great importance in the practice of clinical health psychology since the discipline must draw upon models that emphasize both social and psychological influences on health. In addition, if interventions in clinical health psychology are to be widely effective they should be capable of operating at individual, family, organizational, and community levels, which take account of the multiplicity of variables contributing to ill health.

A suggested synthesis

Working with those with psychological and physical health problems is complex. How someone copes with an illness is a product of many factors, including their social and cultural background, and their beliefs and expectations concerning their illness. A person's resources are also important, and are likely to affect how well they cope with an illness. This includes personal resources such as self-esteem and financial security, and social resources, such as family relationships, social support networks, and social stresses. As in psychotherapy, successful formulation needs to take into account antecedents in the person's history, including the events that have shaped their lives and may be influencing their interpretation of current events. In health, it is also important to take into account the history of health problems, current treatment and prognosis, and to consider interactions between all of these factors. For example, the loss of freedom a patient experiences after a lower limb amputation may also trigger emotions associated with earlier losses, such as loss of a parent during childhood. It is important to acknowledge this in the context of therapy. Finally, it should be remembered that an illness might strike at any time in someone's life. One person may be in the middle of a depressive episode, another about to become a parent for the first time. There is clearly an important interaction between events triggered by an illness and other concurrent events.

Clinical health psychology in practice

Clinical health psychologists may be referred many different kinds of problems. Some examples of different kinds are given in the short vignettes (see Box 11.1).

Box 11.1 Short vignettes

1 Ahmed is 53 and is married with three children. He smokes 30 cigarettes a day, and works as an architect. He enjoys his job, though he often works long hours. He has recently been diagnosed with lung cancer. Since the diagnosis he has become very withdrawn. He becomes very distressed when attending hospital appointments and is not sure whether he can face the chemotherapy he has been offered.

2 Joanne is 17 and has cystic fibrosis (CF). She has failed to turn up for a number of appointments at the regional CF unit that she has attended throughout her childhood. Staff worry that she is not taking the medication she needs to help her control the condition. They cannot understand why she does not attend and feel annoyed by her behaviour. Joanne hates having CF and the time and effort it takes every day to have all of her medication. She enjoys socializing with friends at the weekend and tries to forget about having CF so she can feel 'like everyone else'.

3 Janette is 47, married with two children. She is concerned that her heart is not right. She has attended Casualty three times in the last 12 months, fearing that she was having a heart attack. On one occasion she was admitted for a week but tests found no organic problem. Her mother died from a heart attack 12 years ago.

4 Alan is 46 and has had health problems for 8 years. His father and older brother both died of heart attacks in their early forties. Alan has had three heart attacks and a stroke. He has nerve damage in both feet due to poor circulation. He also smokes and has an alcohol problem, admitting to drinking perhaps 12–20 pints of lager each night. The medical team are concerned that his drinking may shorten his life expectancy considerably.

5 Dorothy has just seen her GP for the results of tests following a period of ill health. The GP has told her that she has type 2 diabetes, gave her some tablets and some recommendations about treatment. This came as an awful shock. Her aunt had diabetes and she remembers her

Box 11.1 Short vignettes (*continued*)

having a difficult time. She is so upset she misses most of what the GP says, but thinks he insisted that she lose weight. Dorothy doesn't see how this is possible, and is anyway too upset to think about that right now.

6 The team at a large hospital looking after patients after a heart attack are concerned that many don't come back after they leave hospital to attend rehabilitation classes, particularly women and those from ethnic minorities. They ask the psychologist in the team to lead a research project to find out what factors influence this and what may be done to increase attendance.

Assessment and treatment of individuals

Psychotherapeutic work with individuals utilizes models from clinical and health psychology in building up a complex formulation of the presenting problem. As described above, interventions are usually taken from the practice of clinical psychology and may be applied very successfully in physical health.

In terms of assessment, there is much overlap with other areas of clinical psychology. Clinical health psychologists will always use interview and observation. They will often use idiographic tools such as diaries to examine the frequency of illness-related problems or variations in mood (such as pain levels or anxiety during medical procedures). A variety of nomothetic instruments are also useful. Some of these may be taken directly from clinical psychology, such as measures of anxiety and depression, though care must be taken in interpretation where a symptom may have a psychological or physical cause—fatigue is a symptom of both depression and multiple sclerosis, for example. Other assessments tend to be used exclusively in health, and may be measures of concepts such as quality of life or social support which may be used with any patient, or designed for specific illness groups, such as the Cancer Worry Scale and the Diabetes Treatment Satisfaction Scale.

Interventions with teams

An important issue in clinical health psychology is to decide on the most appropriate level at which to intervene. Sometimes the level of distress in an individual patient precludes any other intervention until individual work has been completed by the psychologist. Clinical health psychologists are a scarce resource so where problems are common (e.g. anxiety in patients following a heart attack) it may be most appropriate to intervene at a ward or unit level.

In practice, many clinical health psychologists work as a team, offering individual work with patients where indicated, collaborative work with colleagues (such as co-facilitating a psycho-educational group for newly diagnosed patients), advice to colleagues on psychological care of individual patients, and training for other staff on psychological issues. In some instances a patient referral may be more indicative of staff difficulties within a ward or unit than the individual patient's problems. Staff who are overworked or under pressure temporarily may find it more difficult than usual to deal with patients who are demoralized by setbacks in treatment. In such instances, interventions with staff may be more helpful than direct treatment of the patient.

Interventions with organizations

Finally, to have the most impact on the experience patients have of a service, it is important for clinical health psychologists to exert some influence on how services develop at an organizational level. This includes advising national bodies drawing up guidelines for treatment on psychological aspects, for example in diabetes. It also includes advising hospitals of the psychological implications of new innovations in treatment, such as the potential increase in patients' anxiety caused by a move to day surgery (where patients do not stay overnight), and the need for good pre-surgical assessment and preparation. It also includes the need to be involved in developments in the community, whether looking at ways of increasing hospital attendance by some groups such as ethnic minorities, or examining ways that psychological aftercare in the community following hospital treatment can be maintained so that there is continuity of care.

Applications—the focus of clinical health psychology interventions

Perhaps the major difference between clinical psychology in mental health and physical health settings is in the focus of interventions. In that improving psychological well-being will be common to both, there is clearly much overlap. In specifics, however, they may be quite different. In general medical settings the focus for medical interventions is usually the control or cure of physical illness, using a variety of chemical, surgical, and physical means. In common with other health practitioners in this setting, clinical health psychologists may use their psychological skills and knowledge to attempt to affect outcomes for patients in terms of improved physical health or quality of life.

Table 11.2 summarizes the key areas for the focus of psychological interventions in clinical health psychology, which are described in detail in the sections that follow.

Table 11.2 Focus and level of interventions with selected examples

Focus	Level	Examples of intervention
Psychological distress interfering with treatment, recovery, or quality of life. (e.g. depression and anxiety following a heart attack)	Individual	Psychological assessment and therapy
	Team	Training other staff on psychological aspects of care, including recognition of psychological problems.
	Organization	Advising on provision of psychological care (e.g. psychological component in services for patients after a heart attack).
Poor adherence to medical treatment. (e.g. adolescent patient with diabetes needing regular insulin injections)	Individual	Psychological therapy, e.g. using self-monitoring techniques, removal of barriers to adherence, goal setting, and rewards.
	Team	Training staff in counselling skills to improve interactions with patients, advising on managing care, co-facilitating patient psycho-education groups for newly diagnosed.
	Organization	Investigate staff methods for dealing with non-adherence. Advising on new methods based on psychological principles.
Inappropriate uptake of medical treatment. (e.g. patient with non-cardiac chest pain attending emergency clinic)	Individual	Psychological therapy as an alternative to medical treatment (e.g. anxiety management)
	Team	Input to other staff (e.g. advice on managing patients and indirect therapy work)
	Organization	Advising on organization of services, increasing knowledge of psychological problems, and establishing referral routes to psychology
Behavioural risk factors for illness. (e.g. alcohol abuse in patient at risk of stroke and heart attack)	Individual	Psychotherapy/counselling for lifestyle change
	Team	Input to other staff on psychological approaches to lifestyle change (e.g. teaching motivational interviewing techniques)
	Organization	Advocating health promotion interventions within community settings
Increasing the effectiveness of the medical team. (e.g. poor communication with patients)	Individual	Support and supervision for individual team members
	Team	Providing training for the team, e.g. on improving communication skills, facilitating support group for team.
	Organization	Survey communication skills across the organization and produce recommendations for training.

Table 11.2 *(continued)*

Focus	Level	Examples of intervention
Research, service evaluation, and audit. (e.g. audit of cardiac rehabilitation, research into factors influencing attendance)	Individual	Evaluate clinical outcome of own caseload
	Team	Collaborate with team on audit of entire service, collaborate with colleagues on theoretical research project, advising on psychological aspects of physical illness and treatment, theoretical conception and assessment.
	Organization	Identify appropriate benchmarks for service and review audit procedures.

Tackling psychological distress interfering with treatment, recovery, or affecting quality of life

A common experience of those suffering from physical illness is loss of control. In some conditions, this is reinforced by symptoms that are painful or debilitating, which may prevent or interfere with functions of normal life such as employment or social activity. It may also be reinforced inadvertently by medical intervention such as periods of hospitalization or treatment regimens that are intrusive or difficult to follow.

Individuals bring their own style of coping to their attempts to manage the threat of illness. They may also bring pre-existing psychological problems that may potentially interfere with treatment. This may be relatively straightforward, such as needle phobia in someone who requires injections as part of treatment, or complex, such as someone with a history of depression and loss facing up to the losses engendered by a serious illness.

Even without pre-existing psychological problems, anxiety and depression are common reactions to physical illness. Particularly at risk are those with life threatening or debilitating chronic conditions such as cancer or renal failure. The impact of less serious conditions—and an interaction with existing psychological vulnerabilities—should not be underestimated, however, for example in dermatological conditions such as psoriasis.

Distress may have a significant impact on the course of a patient's illness and the effectiveness of treatment. Distress may prevent discharge from hospital, for example, or impair a patient's ability to engage in treatment. Most commonly, it may reduce patients' ability to cope with their illness, having a significant impact on quality of life. In some cases, distress may continue to lower quality of life even after a medical intervention has been successful.

An important concept when considering the impact of an illness on an individual is its intrusiveness. This refers to the extent to which the illness interferes with activities of daily living. End-stage renal failure, for example, may require patients to have several hours of dialysis treatment three times a week and also severely restrict their fluid intake. In general, the more intrusive the illness, the greater the risk of distress or psychological problems, though there may also be large individual differences. For example, someone whose self-esteem is largely bound up with sporting prowess or position at work may find a condition that limits this more difficult to cope than someone with the same condition but a different self-image.

The example of coronary heart disease

One example of a major life-threatening disorder is coronary heart disease, one of the major causes of premature death in the Western world. In this condition the arteries supplying the heart with blood are narrowed by plaques of fatty substances such as cholesterol (a process known as atherosclerosis). This results in reduced blood flow and can lead to a sudden complete blockage of an artery. A blockage causes the death of the heart muscle being supplied by that artery; this is known as a heart attack.

There are now well-established protocols for treatment of a heart attack, an important part of which is attendance at multidisciplinary 'cardiac rehabilitation' featuring graded exercise and education classes about topics such as diet and stress. Where individuals are distressed, psychology has a crucial role in successful rehabilitation, having a significant impact on mortality (Linden, 2000). In fact, there is widespread agreement that psychological factors are crucial to quality of life in heart disease. Psychological state (such as anxiety) as a risk factor is more controversial, though there is strong evidence of a link between depression and early death after a heart attack (Frasure-Smith and Lesperance, 2003).

The role of psychological factors can be seen clearly in relation to recovery in the example shown in Case Study 1.

Case Study 1: Coronary Heart Disease

Bill is 69, and married with three children who all have families and live nearby. He recently had a first heart attack, and seems to have been quite depressed since. He has attended hospital with his wife. They confirm that he wakes early in the morning, has low appetite, low mood, and has been staying in at home. In fact, since the heart attack he has left the house only to attend hospital appointments. He has not even walked to the newsagents, 3 minutes away.

The psychologist determines that there is no previous history of psychiatric problems. Bill worked in a glass factory until retirement at 65, and still sees people he used to work with. Until the heart attack, he was extremely sociable, going to a working men's club three or four nights a week to see friends. Overall, he felt that life was good. He was financially secure, going on holiday every year with his wife.

Bill has good resources in terms of practical and social support. The heart attack was the first ill health he has ever suffered, and it has left him overwhelmed with anxiety about having another. The psychologist asks Bill to keep a diary of his activities, thoughts, and feelings, and finds that Bill often reports being very anxious, and then worrying about worrying in case this triggers another heart attack. Bill is always checking himself for signs of illness. Bill is avoiding leaving the house because he is afraid of having a heart attack when out. He is comforted a little by having his wife with him, but has avoided seeing friends and now finds the prospect of being in a group quite frightening.

The psychologist works with Bill and his wife on an intervention with a cognitive and behavioural component, determining Bill's beliefs about a heart attack and challenging misconceptions (e.g. that worry will bring on another heart attack) and tackling his avoidance through graded exposure to leaving the house and resuming socializing.

After a brief intervention Bill has resumed most of his previous social activities and is no longer depressed or anxious.

Following a heart attack it is often possible for patients to improve their physical fitness even beyond pre-illness levels, yet many continue to lead restricted lives. Moreover, there is no simple relationship between the severity of the heart attack and the extent of the patient's recovery afterwards. Beliefs about the heart attack are crucial—patients who erroneously believe that any stress or exertion may bring on another heart attack will avoid many activities, and may put themselves at risk of depression. Patients' beliefs are known to be some of the best predictors of recovery, such as their subjective belief about the cause of their heart attack ('causal attribution').

Psychological distress is also predictive of patient recovery. Although for the majority, levels of anxiety and depression fall during the recovery process, for a significant minority (around 30%) high levels persist. Patients with raised anxiety or depression are less likely to return to work, are more likely to be hospitalized, and once hospitalized are more likely to have increased lengths of stay.

Prolonged psychological stress of this nature in patients with physical illness is an important focus of intervention for clinical health psychologists. Psychological states such as depression and anxiety have many implications for successful delivery of treatment. Patients may not feel motivated to participate in an intervention such as physiotherapy, for example, and may neglect important self-care tasks such as taking medication. In addition, the relationship between patient and health professional is inevitably placed under greater pressure, and there is a risk that communication will be adversely affected.

Also important in this area is predicting those who are most likely to show such sustained reactions. For some patients, psychological problems existed before they became physically ill, but for others, facing stressful events with few social supports or resources is the crucial issue. The presence of good social and family support systems have been found to be predictive of good psychological adjustment in patients with cancer, rheumatoid arthritis, diabetes, as well as those recovering from coronary heart disease. For this reason some clinical health psychologists have attempted to focus interventions on improving social support via community or family networks.

Tackling poor adherence to medical treatment

Surveys of medical practitioners indicate that one of the most distressing features of their practice is poor adherence—the failure of patients to follow medical advice or carry through treatment regimes that have been prescribed. This may be shown in many ways including failure to keep appointments, premature dropping out of treatment regimes, discharge from hospital against medical advice, or a failure to take medication as prescribed.

Adherence is a major problem—estimates suggest 50 per cent of prescriptions are not taken by patients, which in a chronic illness can result in serious physical complications.

Why is adherence so poor?

Adherence is the product of an interaction between three factors:

1. The treatment—what we expect patients to do.
2. The health professional—what and how they communicate with the patient.
3. The patient—their beliefs about their illness and the treatment, and their cognitive and emotional state.

Adherence is worse if the treatment is particularly intrusive into the patient's life, particularly if it is painful or has unpleasant side effects, and if it involves behaviours with personal or social meaning. Adherence will be poorer if the work the patients have to carry out involves tasks that are difficult to do, complicated and hard to understand, offer no immediate feedback on whether they have been done correctly, and offer no immediate benefit—instead they are to prevent symptoms getting worse.

Similarly, if the health professional does not explain the treatment in a way that ensures the patient has understood, they are likely not to adhere.

Finally, there are many factors in the patient that influence adherence, including their beliefs about the severity of their illness, the effectiveness of the treatment and the risks of non-adherence, and their confidence in being able to adhere. An important distinction is between patients not adhering because they do not know what to do or because they choose not to do it. Some may choose not to be fully adherent in an attempt to minimize the intrusiveness of their illness on their life. Others may be influenced by partly unconscious psychological processes such as extreme fear of their illness, meaning that they feel better not thinking about it and avoid reminders of it, such as taking medication. Still others may be influenced by mental health problems such as an eating disorder, which can be very serious in conditions where food intake is monitored and medication may affect weight.

In Type I diabetes, for example, in which the body lacks insulin to break down sugars in food, the person has to monitor food intake and self inject with insulin in the right amounts and at the right time. Insulin usually has to be injected several times a day for the rest of the person's life, or diabetes quickly becomes life threatening. In addition, if the amount of sugars in the blood is not kept down to a recommended level, the person faces an increased risk of a number of secondary complications (including blindness) at a later age. Even with the threat of secondary complications, many people with diabetes struggle to follow the suggested treatment, a pattern repeated in many chronic illnesses. Case Study 2 illustrates some of the complexity in adherence problems in diabetes, and a psychological intervention to tackle them.

Case Study 2: poor adherence

Christine is 43. She has had type 1 diabetes since she was 11. Her control has always been very poor. She has had a difficult relationship with her hospital consultants in the past, but has usually attended for appointments. This year it has become clear that she is developing serious complications of diabetes due to her poor control: she now has some retinal problems and has developed the first stages of heart disease. She is married and has two children, aged 9 and 11. She was upset in clinic this week and was referred to a psychologist.

The psychologist explores with Christine her ambivalence about adhering to her treatment, and her feelings about diabetes. Christine says that she has never let diabetes stop her from 'getting on with my life', and sees avoiding injections of the insulin she needs as a way of 'beating it'. She has a wide circle of friends, but reports feeling very unconfident. She is very concerned about her appearance, and a fear of putting on weight has led her to avoid insulin (which can lead to weight increase) in the past. She now feels very guilty that her past behaviour may have led to complications in her health, but still finds it difficult to talk to her consultant.

The psychologist talks with Christine about her feelings about herself, and works with her on increasing self-esteem. When Christine agrees, they together look at her adherence. Christine weighs up the pros and cons of changing, and opts to try a different way of 'beating diabetes' in gaining good control and minimizing the intrusions of symptoms in her daily life. They use as a behavioural approach, setting goals and rewards for behaviour change and generating strategies for potential difficulties. They also explore her feelings of guilt, talk about her experiences of having diabetes as a young child, and consider her avoidance as an understandable reaction to a threatening disease. Finally, they look at ways of making her consultations with medical staff more productive, looking at their behaviour and her reactions and ways she could be more active, such as asking questions and writing down notes.

Christine still feels scared by the diabetic complications she faces, but her control has improved tremendously, and she understands and accepts the poor control in the past without blaming herself too much. Finally, she attends clinics regularly and her consultant reports that she is more assertive and much more involved in her own care.

Poor adherence, often confounded by problems adjusting to a diagnosis of an illness, is a common reason for referral to a clinical health psychologist. Individual work may focus on the beliefs of the patient, and an exploration of the emotional impact of the illness. Psychologists may also influence adherence by offering consultancy to colleagues on ways of improving communication with patients, and contributing to behavioural skills training for patients in managing the practical aspects of adhering to a treatment regimen.

Intervening to prevent inappropriate medical treatment and facilitate appropriate uptake

Preventing inappropriate uptake of treatment

Patients presenting with multiple unexplained complaints represent a huge problem for the health services. It is estimated that up to half of all medical outpatients in the United Kingdom experience bodily symptoms that cannot be explained in terms of organic pathology, and in half of these cases there is underlying anxiety and depression.

In a smaller number of patients, these problems become chronic. Around 5–7% of the primary care population in the United States meet the criteria for a diagnosis of somatization disorder—a condition in which psychological problems are presented as physical symptoms such as fatigue, dizziness, and pain. For some patients this takes the form of hypochondriasis or health anxiety, a disorder in which the patients become preoccupied with the possibility that they have a serious disease. The usual response from medical practitioners is to offer reassurance. Unfortunately, this seldom has any lasting effect, and in many cases such patients will often press for further consultations and investigations, all producing at best a temporary relief from worry.

The financial consequences of treating this group of patients may be huge. US estimates suggest that their health care costs are nine times the national average. However, apart from these financial considerations, research has also shown that patients with somatization problems report greater disruption to quality of life than most other chronic conditions.

Research in the United States and the United Kingdom reveals that the psychological nature of these problems tends not to be detected by staff in general medical settings. Patients are often put through timely and expensive diagnostic tests that produce no useful findings, just further disruption to the patient's life.

A related and sizeable group are patients who experience symptoms of a panic attack and turn to their general practitioner or hospital accident and emergency department, afraid they are having a heart attack. These cases of non-cardiac chest pain can also occur in patients who have previously had an actual heart attack, but are so afraid of a reoccurrence that they misinterpret anxiety symptoms. These patients require a psychological rather than a medical intervention.

Somatization disorder is not the only reason for inappropriate medical treatment. Another, rarer group of patients have dissociative disorders (or conversion reactions). These patients unconsciously present with quite dramatic symptoms that at first appear to mimic an organic disease. Sometimes this is easy to diagnose, but more often the presentation of such patients is very ambiguous.

Other reasons for inappropriate medical treatment include factitious disorders such as Munchausen's syndrome. In this rare but challenging condition patients present to medical practitioners with a variety of faked and self-induced symptoms in themselves, or in a variant (Munchausen's by proxy) in their children. When challenged (often after lengthy investigations and treatments) they may present at a different hospital with a new identity. A single patient may cost the health service many hundreds of thousands of pounds.

A small group of patients with body dysmorphobia (delusions about a body part, such as the size of the nose) often seek medical treatment such as plastic surgery for their perceived deformity. The needs of such patients are never met by medical intervention, the focus of the delusions simply shifting to another body part. Rather than relief, medical intervention can induce disappointment followed by anger and resentment.

A major role for clinical health psychologists working in medical settings is the assessment and treatment of patients with these problems. Also important is assisting other staff to recognize such conditions and the development of coordinated systems of medical care to avoid multiple and inappropriate medical interventions. In cases of Munchausen's, for example, it is important to facilitate good communication between all medical staff involved in the patient's care to present a clear and united message to the patient.

Facilitating appropriate uptake of treatment

Another important role of clinical health psychologists is in facilitating the appropriate uptake of medical treatment. This might involve working in an area where some groups are under-represented in a service, for example participation of some ethnic groups in cardiac rehabilitation classes. The psychologist might work with other members of the team in considering possible barriers to seeking treatment and ways to reduce them.

Clinical health psychologists are increasingly being involved in assessment of suitability for surgery, such as living related donors for kidney transplants, in which the psychologist is asked to determine the motivations of the donor, and spinal cord stimulation surgery for pain management, in which the psychologist is asked to assess psychological suitability for the treatment.

Contributing to prevention of illness (behavioural risk factors)

The most common causes of death in the nineteenth century were infectious diseases such as tuberculosis, which were tackled by medical interventions such as vaccination, and public health interventions such as sanitation. The interventions proved to be extremely successful, but have arguably left a less helpful legacy in the tendency to turn to medicine for a cure for all diseases.The diseases responsible for most deaths in the Western world in the twenty-first century are very different, however. Diseases such as coronary heart disease, stroke, and cancer are caused not by a single bacterium or virus, but are multiply determined. More than this, an important determinant is the actions of the individual, for example, whether they smoke, whether they drink alcohol, what they eat, and how much exercise they get. Smoking, for example, is the single biggest risk factor for a number of diseases, and accounts for 30% of all deaths from cancer.

For this reason lifestyle factors are an important consideration for primary prevention (helping to prevent someone from becoming ill) and secondary prevention (helping someone who has developed an illness from suffering a recurrence). Clinical health psychologists working in a range of settings from primary care to acute hospitals cannot fail to address these important domains. In this, they need to work closely with a number of other health professionals including public health physicians, physiotherapists, dieticians, and experts in health promotion.

Occasionally a clinical health psychologist may be involved in prevention work directly with a patient. More commonly, they may contribute to this work through consultancy with a team, such as in cardiac rehabilitation, where they may advise on principles of behaviour change and issues that may affect it. Lifestyle change can be a complex undertaking for some individuals. Stress may be a confounding issue, for example, often being related to smoking and alcohol consumption, and an important barrier to change. In these situations stress management can be an important part of a successful multidisciplinary intervention.

Contributing to the effectiveness of the medical team

As we have seen, the biopsychosocial model makes it clear that the treatment of ill health is not an impersonal, biological undertaking. Just as psychological and social factors can influence the occurrence of illness, so they can influence its treatment. The role of the patient's beliefs and behaviour has already been discussed, but it is also important to consider the social context of treatment. This includes the physical and social environment of health care settings such as the architectural arrangement of a clinic (e.g. the provision of areas with privacy) and social milieu of a hospital ward (e.g. the perceived approachability of staff).

A patient's first impression of a service is often through written communication. This can be important, and how appointment letters are written can have an impact on attendance. Information leaflets, too, may be important in offering appropriate reassurance and information.

The physical environment is important both to outpatients and those staying on a ward, and to the staff for whom it is a place of work. Poor design may make the patient disoriented and increase work demands on staff. Shabby and out-of-date buildings have a damaging effect on staff morale and the confidence patients have in the service treating them. In addition, the policies and procedures used in the service can have direct effects on patient care. If little attention is given to the patients' journey through the system, their needs for information and the potential impact of changes or delays, for example, their psychological well-being, is likely to suffer. As with other colleagues in the team, clinical health psychologists should be aware of these issues and seek to address them at the appropriate level. Clinical health psychologists may work alongside nursing and other staff to find ways of improving ward procedures and facilities. Using patient views to introduce individual choice and a sense of control during hospital inpatient stays or treatment can be important in improving health outcomes.

Communication with patients

A key aspect of treatment is communication with health care professionals. Poor communication is the most commonly cited complaint by patients about the health service. Patients report not feeling listened to, and not understanding what the health professional has said. This does not just lead to less satisfaction; poor communication has been linked empirically to increased distress and less adherence. Without good communication skills, the knowledge of the health professional is redundant—they are unable to provide information on the condition to the patient, nor elicit their commitment to participate in the treatment. On the patient's part, they are often very anxious during health consultations, they may need time to gather their thoughts and ask questions, and their anxiety may interfere with their ability to recall the content of the interview afterwards.

The solution to these problems is for health professionals to be aware of the psychological and emotional state of the patient; to ask them if they have any questions using open rather than closed questions, to check out their understanding of each new piece of information given, and to write down anything important and give it to the patient to take away. As professionals with good skills in communication and the assessment of emotional states, clinical health psychologists have an important role to play in training and supporting the team in developing these skills. A particularly useful approach is 'Health Behaviour Change Counselling' (Rollnick *et al.* 1999), an adaptation of Motivational Interviewing, an intervention used in addictions. This approach includes techniques from client centred counselling such as open questions ('how are you?' rather than 'are you well?') and reflection (repeating back summaries of what a patient has just said). It provides a useful approach to tackling lifestyle change and adherence problems in patients with physical illness, and also offers a template for good communication between a professional and a patient.

An additional influence on communication is the emotional state of the health professional. Poor communication may sometimes reflect the disquiet of the health professional in giving distressing information about a diagnosis, for example. Over the last few years, communication skills have become an important part of basic medical training, particularly in breaking bad news. Clinical health psychologists involved in medical education and research in doctor–patient communication have played key roles in this area.

Emotional support of medical colleagues

Clinical health psychologists also have a role in providing emotional support to colleagues in other health professions. Staff who feel unsupported by work colleagues or managers can find it difficult to provide supportive care for patients. High level of stress amongst health professionals is now a widely acknowledged problem, particularly amongst medical doctors, where rates of addiction and suicide are significantly above the national average. Staff with high stress levels are more likely to be dissatisfied with their job and show more absence through sickness than those with lower stress levels. Moreover, there is evidence that job satisfaction in health professionals is an important predictor of job performance, patient satisfaction with treatment, and patient adherence. The importance of this issue has led to a national initiative to address workload for junior doctors in the United Kingdom.

High workloads can have an adverse effect on the social context of health care. It can lead staff to use apparently less time-consuming methods of care that actually reduce patient choice and control and reinforce dependency. Staff may feel unable to spend time in supportive conversations with patients. If harnessed, staff attention and positive expectations can be a powerful factor helping to motivate patients who are in pain or distress, or coping with the disabling and restrictive consequences of disease.

Conducting research and audit

The ability to plan, conduct, and interpret research is fundamental to the practice of clinical psychologists, who are the only health service professionals for whom research skills are a core part of pre-qualification training. Clinical health psychologists therefore have a potentially important role to play in a health service committed to evaluating the effectiveness of treatment, and developing more effective approaches.

Much of this research activity is in collaboration with colleagues from other professions. Sometimes they will be asked for methodological advice on research with no psychological aspects. More often, clinical health psychologists have a role in ensuring that psychological aspects of research questions, for example evaluating the impact of a new intervention, are given due consideration and are adequately assessed. There is now a widely held appreciation of the importance of psychological issues in many aspects of health and health research, and clinical health psychologists are increasingly being asked to collaborate in research by adding a theoretically grounded understanding of psychological factors.

Another equally important aspect of research is that conducted at a local level to improve the effectiveness of a service. This again may often be in collaboration with other colleagues, for example in evaluating a multidisciplinary pain management programme. Service research normally takes one of two forms: service evaluation or audit. Service evaluation looks at the structure of services (e.g. appointment systems), processes (e.g. communication with patient or referrer), or outcomes. For example, a service evaluation project might look at whether the ethnic minorities being treated by a service such as pain management are representative of the population served. Audit projects compare aspects of a local service to well-established guidelines giving some indication of what might be expected. For example, an audit of a cardiac rehabilitation programme might compare national standards derived from research evidence to what is offered locally.

Finally, an aspect of service research growing in importance is user involvement—getting users' perspectives on current or planned services. Clinical health psychologists have a useful role in advising on methods for obtaining users' views—such as focus groups or Delphi studies—and in helping to put the ideas into practice.

The future

It is an exciting time to work in clinical health psychology. The last 10 years have seen a surge of interest in this specialty within clinical psychology, especially in North America where some have argued that it represents the future of clinical psychology.

This interest has been backed up by a growing body of research and evidence of clinical- and cost-effectiveness, and a growing acknowledgement amongst colleagues in other health professions of the role of psychology in illness and treatment. The future will undoubtedly see this strengthen. In the industrialized nations, spending on health is likely to be increasingly dominated by chronic illnesses such as diabetes, where the majority of patients are effectively self-administering their own treatment. This will bring into ever more focus the need for a collaboration between health professional and patient, to take account of patients' perspectives when planning or improving services, and to help them take more control over their own health. This emphasis also entails an appreciation of the physical and psychological factors influencing an individual's ability to cope, and interventions to help. Clinical health psychologists are already contributing to these developments, and have an important role to play in facilitating patient-centred health care through working with individuals, teams, and organizations.

Developments in medicine hold the potential to improve the prognosis for many with health problems, but new interventions often generate new moral and ethical dilemmas with psychological consequences for those involved. The expertise of psychologists is increasingly called upon in planning new services. For example, when considering the impact of a new rapid-access diagnostic service for heart failure (a condition that often has poor prognosis), it is important to consider the reactions of the patients to the news, and what support will be available to them. In some areas, the importance of psychology is being recognized in national guidelines: recognizing the stressful nature of infertility treatment and the difficult treatment choices that couples are required to make, the Human Fertilisation and Embryology Authority in the United Kingdom place a legal requirement upon Assisted Conception Units to provide counselling services to all couples entering treatment programmes.

Though it is impossible to predict the future of clinical health psychology with complete confidence, the rise of this specialty during a time of major attempts to control public spending on health does give testament to both the enthusiasm of psychologists and the positive views of health purchasers.

Reflections and conclusions

Clinical health psychology can be one of the most exciting and rewarding areas in which to work as a clinical psychologist. There are many opportunities for research and clinical work in a variety of areas with a range of patient groups.

This work can be demanding in many ways, however. It can be intellectually demanding, requiring the psychologist to be aware of relevant literature in clinical and health psychology, and, especially, medicine. It can also be emotionally demanding: the stories of people facing serious illness are often extremely upsetting. In addition, more perhaps than in any other area of clinical psychology, the nature of the clinical material can have personal resonance. Put simply, everyone gets ill, including psychologists, and everyone has friends or family who become ill. There are two dangers in the reaction to this emotional content: that the psychologist blunts their emotions and becomes less effective, or become overwhelmed by emotion, and unable to work. As in other areas of clinical psychology, the solution lies in good support and supervision, and the ability to reflect on the impact of the work.

On the other hand, the range of work in clinical health psychology is vast, the type of problems fascinating, and the promise of making a real difference to someone at what may be one of the lowest points of their life very rewarding. From newborn babies to patients facing a terminal illness, the health care system is witness to the whole spectrum of human experience. For the clinical health psychologists working within it, there are few more stimulating places to see and influence psychology in action.

References

Engel, G. (1977). The need for a new medical model: A challenge for biomedicine. *Science*, **196**, 129–36.

Frasure-Smith, N. and Lesperance, F. (2003). Depression and other psychological risks following myocardial infarction. *Archives of General Psychiatry*, **60**, 627–36.

Kaplan, R. and Groessl, E. (2002). Applications of cost effectiveness methodologies in behavioural medicine. *Journal of Consulting and Clinical Psychology*, **70**, 652–856.

Leventhal, H., Meyer, D., and Nerenz, D. (1980). The commonsense representation of illness danger. In S. Rachman (ed.), *Medical Psychology*, Vol 2. New York: Pergammon Press.

Linden, W. (2000). Psychological treatments in cardiac rehabilitation: Review of rationales and outcomes. *Journal of Psychosomatic Research*, **48**, 443–54.

Rollnick, S., Mason, P., and Butler, C. (1999). *Health Behaviour Change: A Guide for Practitioners.* Sydney: Churchill Livingstone.

Taylor, S.E. (1983). Adjustment to threatening events: A theory of cognitive adaptation. *American Psychologist*, **38**, 1161–73.

White, C.A. (2001). *Cognitive Behaviour Therapy for Chronic Medical Problems.* Chichester, UK: Wiley.

Further reading

Kaptein, A.A. and Weinman, J.A. (eds.) (2004). *Introduction to Health Psychology*. Oxford, UK: Blackwell.

Llewelyn, S. and Kennedy, P. (eds.) (2003). *Handbook of Clinical Health Psychology*. Chichester, UK: Wiley.

Chapter 12

Working with physically disabled people

Paul Kennedy

Special care must be taken to avoid overemphasis on the pathologic that leaves one inadequately sensitised to stabilising and maturity inducing factors.
(Beatrice Wright, 2005).

Introduction

Clinical psychologists aim to work in partnership with service users, providers, and planners to ensure, enable, and maximize the fullest access to, and participation in, physical, psychological, social, and vocational domains. The prevalence of disability increases with age and as people live longer, many more people will experience a longer period of their life in a state of limited physical functioning. Much of health care expenditure is associated with the care and management of chronic disease and disability. There is a growing recognition of the contribution individuals can make to their associated morbidity and mortality. In the United Kingdom there has been a significant growth in the number of clinical health and rehabilitation psychologists working in the National Health Service (NHS). Historically, the contribution of clinical psychologists to people with physical disabilities was to assess psychopathology, but now clinical psychologists contribute not only to the management of mood and adjustment disorders, but also contribute to rehabilitation planning, assist with the amelioration of psychophysiological aspects, and have taken the lead in developing a variety of self-management and resilience enhancing techniques. Before discussing this contribution further, it would be helpful to describe the terms most commonly used, summarize the main causes, and outline the incidence and prevalence of the major conditions involved.

Definitions

The World Health Organization has reformulated its model of disability (WHO, 1999) and proposes a model of disability that distinguishes between body functions and structure (impairment), activities (capacity to perform and limitations) and participation (capacity to engage and restrictions in wider social domains). It also recognizes the interaction of the above with contextual environmental and personal factors. Environmental factors include physical, social, and attitudinal constructions which may maximize or minimize the impact of the disability. Personal factors refer to the individual's background with respect to age, gender, ethnicity, and experiences. This is a widely used model of disability which has served as a framework to understand and identify the physical, psychological, and social impact of disease, acquired injury, and congenital disorders. While Imrie (2004) develops the proposition that the WHO model provides a coherent, if uneven account of the competing conceptions of disability, it does require further clarification with respect to biopsychosocial factors and disability definitions.

Prevalence of physical disability

Changes in demographics, more effective treatment plans and health policies have contributed to the large constituency of people with disabilities requiring rehabilitation. According to the Health Survey for England (2001) 18% of men and women aged 16 and over reported having one or more of five types of disability (locomotor, personal care, sight, hearing, and communication) and 5% of adults were found to have a serious disability. Overall, just over half (55%) of men and women with any disability had one disability, a third had two disabilities, and about a tenth had three or more disabilities. In the oldest age group, 85 and over, 7 in 10 of men and women were disabled. The most commonly reported type of disability was locomotor disability.

In view of the wide variation in type and cause of disability, it is difficult to summarize the life cycle experiences. For example, spina bifida is a congenital condition which affects individuals throughout their lifespan, whereas the age of onset of asthma tends to be by the age of 8–12. In conditions such as osteoarthritis, rheumatoid arthritis, and multiple sclerosis, increasing age is positively associated with greater physical disability. Disability can also result from accidents such as in spinal cord injury and traumatic amputations, and may also result from degenerative neurological disease and cerebral vascular accidents. While there are many people born with disability or acquire their disability in adolescence or young adulthood, the prevalence of severe disability within the UK population remains stable until the age of 60; from

Table 12.1 Major conditions causing physical disability

Condition	UK Prevalence	Causes
Neurological	1.5 million people	Stroke, epilepsy, Parkinson's disease, multiple sclerosis, motor neurone disease, muscular dystrophy, cerebral palsy, spinal cord injury
Musculoskeletal	3 million people	Osteoarthritis, rheumatoid arthritis, systemic lupus erythematosus, juvenile arthritis, osteoporosis, fractures and injuries
Sensory	1 million have significant sight loss	Congenital, glaucoma, diabetes, retinopathy, otitis media, presbycusis, meningitis
Chronic respiratory	5% of population	Cystic fibrosis, asthma, emphysema, chronic bronchitis

then there is a considerable increase in the prevalence, severity, and range. In general, there are four broad conditions that account for most of the physical disabilities in the United Kingdom. These are illustrated in Table 12.1.

Not surprisingly, the conditions listed above create a range of functional problems that impair general, physical, psychological, and social functioning. These conditions can cause problems related to movement, reaching, and dexterity. Other problems include difficulties with vision, hearing, and communication, and other people can experience distressing problems associated with continence, behavioural disorders, and impaired consciousness. The extent of functional loss will depend on the severity of the condition and chronicity.

The clinical context

Before describing the role of the clinical psychologist while working with people who have physical disabilities, it is important to highlight the general rehabilitative context within which these services are provided. Rehabilitation is defined as a process of active change by which a person who has become disabled acquires the knowledge and skills needed for optimum physical, psychological, and social functioning. Physical rehabilitation also refers to the application of all measures aimed at reducing the impact of disabling and handicapping conditions and enabling disabled and handicapped people to achieve maximal social integration. The disability movement in Britain prefers not to use the term 'people with impairment', or 'handicapped people' and prefers the use of the generic term 'disabled people'. It is important for rehabilitation services to be user- and community-centred with the emphasis on the rights of individuals to make choices and take control of their own lives from a range of options.

Most organized physical rehabilitation teams have clinical psychologists as part of their team or have access to clinical psychology resources. Many of these teams are based both in hospitals and the community and are funded by the NHS via hospital and community trusts and general practitioners. Clinical psychologists are also employed in specialist centres, for example, spinal cord injury rehabilitation centres, specialist centres for people with hearing and visual disabilities, services for people with muscular skeletal disorders and neurological impairment (see also Chapters 11 and 13). Input is provided at all stages of the process and includes specialist services for children, adults with acquired injuries and disabilities, and people living in the community. Clinical psychology services are provided to hospital based populations, outpatients, community rehabilitation facilities, health centres, general practitioner surgeries, and in the person's home.

The psychological problems

Emotional aspects

There is a growing body of research evidence that clearly documents the emotional impact of these chronic conditions. Psychological distress, usually in the form of anxiety and depression, has been found to be higher in people with physical disabilities such as multiple sclerosis, rheumatoid arthritis, and spinal cord injury. There is also a significant body of evidence from a variety of conditions that have highlighted that there is little relationship between the extent of the physical disability and degree of psychological well-being (Dupont, 2005; Kennedy, 2006; Mangelli *et al.*, 2002).

Depression can emerge in response to perceived losses, and anxiety can occur when people perceive that their existing coping strategies are insufficient to meet unknown future demands. These may emanate from the sudden onset, continued chronicity, or ongoing deterioration of the condition. Some people experience considerable guilt in response to their inability to perform roles and responsibilities associated with relationships, families, and in pursuit of vocational goals. Others may feel angry in response to a sense of unfairness, injustice, and frustration. While many people understand the organic condition that caused their disability (although this is not always the case) it may be difficult to integrate change, alter expectations, and manage the consequences within their particular context.

Adjustment and adaptation

Depending on the onset, severity, and chronicity, the condition will normally require considerable adjustment and adaptation. There are a number of psychological theories which help us understand these complex processes and include the biopsychosocial model (Engel, 1980), the Coping with Stress paradigm (Lazarus and Folkman, 1984) and the various phase or stage theories for which there is little empirical evidence (Wortman and Silver, 1989). Adaptation is a process whereby the individual conceptualizes the nature of his or her condition, considers the implications, acquires new skills for old goals, relinquishes unattainable goals, and re-establishes previously held life goals. Adjustment is theoretically conceptualized as the end point of the adaptation process. Here the person assimilates the functional limitations associated with the disability and continues to develop in personal, social, and vocational spheres. However, when thinking about adaptation, it is important to distinguish adaptations to disabilities associated with a traumatic event such as a spinal cord injury and adaptations that are associated when the onset is gradual and insidious. Wright (1983) suggests that adjustment to disability entails the following: enlarging the scope of one's values; containing the effects of one's disability; sub-ordinating physical concerns; and transforming values based on comparison with others into values placed on one's own assets and strengths.

In anecdotal and clinical reports, denial is often referred to an important component of the psychosocial adaptation process. It is conceptualized as either a phase in the process or a psychological mechanism to minimize distress. Often it refers to denial of outcome, (e.g. 'I will not go blind' or 'I will walk again'), functional limitations, or chronicity. Historically, denial was viewed within the psychoanalytic perspective as an unconscious defence mechanism. However, more recently, denial is conceptualized within an information processing model. Here, it is viewed in the short term as an adaptive strategy to minimize seriousness, prevent the person from being overwhelmed, and facilitate assimilation to the permanency and change. Therefore this may well have adaptive significance in the short term but there is some evidence that denial in the longer term is associated with increased morbidity and dysfunction.

The disabling environment

When considering the contribution of clinical psychology within this context, it is important to remember that the experience of disability is not solely a condition of the individual. From the perspective of disabled people, the negative experiences of disability, such as architectural and social inaccessibility, are physical or social creations in a society geared by and for able-bodied people. This is not to deny the personal experience of disabling conditions, but to highlight the impact of a world designed for non-disabled living. Therefore, the creation of more enabling physical, psychological, and social environments can change the experience of disability. The Professional Affairs Board of the British Psychological Society in 1989 produced a document entitled Psychology and Physical Disability in the National Health Service which criticized the lack of coordination, poor communication, and discontinuity of services for people with physical disability. It also drew attention to the limits of using the medical model which puts undue focus on medical treatment and fails to address emotional, personal, and social aspects of disability. This report recommends that clinical psychologists should be available in each health district (now Trust or Authority) to provide specialist skills in assessment and intervention with people with disabilities, their carers, and other staff. It proposes that psychological expertise should be sought in the analysis of, and the solutions to, health problems of people with disabilities and that services should be provided in the context of active partnership with persons with a disability, the family, and professionals. Recommendations are also made to encourage the development of psychological services, the extension of training for clinical psychologists, and the priorities of psychological research and disability. Despite the date of this document, much of its recommendations remain current.

The history of physical rehabilitation (and indeed clinical psychology) is relatively short and tied to the major conflicts of the twentieth century. Services in the early part of the twentieth century focussed on the level of impairment and the restoration of functional abilities. However, since the Second World War, and in response to the assertions of the Independent Living Movement, rehabilitative services have needed to address personal efficacy, emotional issues, social factors, and vocational opportunities. Also in the twentieth century, the pattern of physical illness afflicting developed economies has changed considerably. In the early part of this century, acute and infectious diseases were the leading cause of death, and have now largely been controlled by the advances in biomedical science. There is now a growing population of people with chronic illness and disability where psychologists can play an important role in: modifying health related behaviour such as adherence to medical regimens; managing psychological distress; minimizing the negative consequences of disability; using psychological techniques to prevent the exacerbation of symptoms (chronic pain management); and the promotion of healthy behaviour and illness prevention (see also Chapter 11). Physical rehabilitation services aim to enable people with disability to live with dignity, to maximize their potential, and minimize disabling experiences. Clearly services need to optimize functioning, self-care, and autonomy. Services need to recognize the comprehensive needs of the person with disability, which will include requirements for alterations in accommodation, legislation to maximize employment and educational opportunities, acquire necessary illness-related health care skills, and a wide range of needs to include mobility, assistive technologies, and care management. It is also important to remember that disability occurs within a social context, normally a family, and depending on the extent and onset, may influence the issues associated with roles and responsibilities.

The role of the clinical psychologist

Clinical psychologists provide a broad range of services to people with disabilities. As mentioned, these services are provided across a range of sites from acute treatment centres to an individual's home. Services are provided on a one-to-one basis with individuals, couples, families, and groups. Clinical psychologists also make a contribution to service planning, organizational aspects, management, and administration. It is helpful to conceptualize the work of clinical psychologists with physically disabled people in three ways. First, the contribution to assessment and formulation; second, the contribution to treatment and intervention; and third, the wider societal and contextual contribution.

Assessment and formulation

Assessment with this population may serve a variety of purposes. Assessments are generally used as part of assessing individual needs, to help in the formulation of intervention techniques and treatment planning and outcome evaluation.

Needs assessment

Survival is conditional and people must take specific actions to fulfil needs. The onset of disability will trigger a re-examination of need. Clinical psychologists provide standardized and objective assessment of the nature and severity of disability with individuals and patient groups. This can include broad health status, type assessments such as the Sickness Impact Profile, or more specific assessments such as the St. George's Respiratory Questionnaire. Other assessments may focus on the assessment of mood disorder such as the Hospital Anxiety and Depression Scale, functional limitations such as the Functional Dependence Measure, and psychosocial impact such as the Psychosocial Adjustment to Illness Scale. Available measures include the Acceptance of Disability Scale, the Ways of Coping Scale, and the Multidimensional Pain Inventory. In addition to these psychometric instruments and rating scales, psychologists can also assess problems by direct observation. Behavioural assessment techniques include a variety of behavioural rating scales, time sampling techniques, and naturalistic observations such as behavioural mapping.

In adopting a more objective approach to assessment, clinical psychologists can assess the extent of psychological distress within an individual or a patient group. For example, between a quarter and one-third of people who are chronically disabled have levels of anxiety and distress and score above mild clinical caseness. We also know that while much of this disturbance is amenable to treatment, most remains untreated. Assessment can also help with individual treatment planning and the organization of general services. Behavioural observations have been proved to be both reliable and valid and can help with a range of issues which could include the assessment of an individual's capacity for independent living in an independent living unit, and levels of patient activity and engagement in treatment and rehabilitation centres.

Assessment for formulation and interventions

Assessments are carried out to answer questions, and formulation and intervention provide the rationale for these questions. Assessments which help in formulation may include identification of behavioural risk factors as in the acquisition of pressure sores and the identification of negative assumptions following acquired disability. Questionnaires, self-report, and self-monitoring techniques are helpful in assessing antecedent conditions, responses, and consequences in a traditional Cognitive-behavioural therapy (CBT) formulation. The assessment of individual appraisal and coping responses also helps by identifying propensities to engage in emotional focused and problem focused coping strategies. Lazurus and Folkman's (1984) transactional model has had a major impact on the current conceptualization of coping with chronic disability. In this model, the patient's coping responses are determined by their appraisal of the degree of threat posed by an illness and the resources available to help them cope. These assessments can help identify adaptive coping strategies which are useful in many chronic conditions. In general, strategies that include the processes of acceptance, reframing, planning, and utilization of social support have been found to be adaptive, while behavioural disengagement, mental disengagement, and alcohol and drug use ideation are associated with increased distress and disability. Many formulations require multifactorial assessments. This is not surprising given the comprehensiveness of the biopsychosocial prospective. These assessment techniques can help in the prediction of problems and in some cases help in the prediction of morbidity and, indeed, mortality. For example, a brief self-completed questionnaire assessing instrumental activity of daily living was sent to an elderly sample living in the community, which proved to be a significant predictor of mortality independent of demographic or other social factors over a 4-year period (Reuben *et al.*, 1992).

Assessing outcomes

Despite health care providers possessing humanitarian principles, there is a growing recognition of the need to acknowledge the competition for resources. Clinical psychologists have access to a range of measures that provide evidence of the effects of intervention and progress of patients over time. These can include observer based assessments such as needs assessment checklists (Berry and Kennedy, 2003), the Barthel Index or standardised interviews and questionnaires such as the Sickness Impact Profile, the SF-36 (Short Form 36 Health Survey Questionnaire) and the Nottingham Health Profile. In today's health care systems where evidence based approaches, outcome assessments, and evaluations have greater emphasis, clinical psychologists have an important role in ensuring that psychological outcomes are placed on the agenda, and that the effects of interventions which most directly address patients concerns are recognized.

Outcomes are the result of interventions. Examples of outcome include employability, performance of activities of daily living, and satisfaction with quality of life. Outcome measures are used to demonstrate that particular goals have not only been identified, but also achieved. Historically, professionals working with disabled people have defined independence in terms of physical functioning, whereas clinical psychologists equate independence with social and psychological autonomy and the enhancement of control.

Assessment of social and vocational issues

Social support serves as a general resistance resource in the management and recovery of illness and disability. It is important not only to assess the quantity of social support, but also its perceived quality. An example of an assessment tool that incorporates both is the Social Support Questionnaire (Sarason and Sarason, 1983). This tool has a sub-scale which assesses both quantity and quality. Access to employment is important for those of working age. When Sir Ludwig Guttmann (who set up the first treatment and rehabilitation centre for people with spinal cord injuries) was asked to define rehabilitation, he said it was to make the person 'a tax payer'. This highlights the importance for clinical psychologists to contribute to the assessment of vocational needs and training. The vocational impact of disability is assessed in many of the sub-scales assessing quality of life and psychosocial impact. Other tools include vocational preference checklists and attainment scales.

Other assessments

Clinical psychologists also have access to a range of psychometric and psychophysiological techniques for assessing a variety of sensory and somatic aspects of disability. This would include questionnaires assessing pain intensity such as the McGill Pain Questionnaire and various visual analogue scales, and psychophysiological measures such as monitoring electromyographic activity in specific muscles. Many people with physical disabilities have concurrent cognitive difficulties which will include problems with memory, concentration, and attention. A comprehensive description of assessment techniques is presented in Chapter 13 and other clinical health related assessment tools are described in Chapter 11.

Whatever the assessment tool, clinical psychologists recognize the necessity to select reliable and valid measures when assessing psychological aspects of disabling conditions. When deciding on self-report measures, an essential question concerns the appropriateness of the measure for the psychological factors to be assessed. There is also the need to consider whether the measure has been applied to people with the condition under review. Some somatic aspects of physical health problems may impair the reliability of the measures. It may also be necessary to consider the time taken for completing an assessment, as fatigue is an important factor. There are few sound multidimensional measures, but the World Health Organization—Quality of Life measure, General Health Questionnaire, Psychosocial Adjustment to Illness Scale, and the Sickness Impact Profile are general useful measures of psychosocial adjustment. Good measures which are specific to disability are rare, but the Arthritis Impact Measurement Scales are an excellent exception.

In addition to formal psychological assessment, effective formulations require information on personal background and developmental histories. Previous psychological vulnerabilities, resilience factors, and coping need to be identified. Threat, loss, and challenge perceptions will help explore individual responses. Additionally, behavioural and cognitive based ABC functional analyses are fundamental to effective formulations. The examination of archival records, such as medical and rehabilitation notes will also be useful.

Approaches to treatment and interventions

Case Study

Martin, a young man aged 22, acquired a traumatic spinal cord injury as a result of a road traffic accident which rendered him paralysed from almost the neck down. He was unconscious for 40 minutes and reported a post traumatic amnesia of 2 days. During the initial acute phase of his treatment, nursing staff reported that he seemed to be coping well. Two weeks after he was mobilized in his wheelchair, he was approached by a trained key worker who administered the needs assessment to help him conceptualize and prioritize his new needs. Goal planning meetings were arranged in association with the key worker and the key members of the rehabilitation team. These occurred every 2 weeks, whereby new targets were set and he was provided with feedback on achievement.

A month after his rehabilitation he joined the Coping Effectiveness Training Programme which he attended for 4 weeks. During these sessions he was taught the relationship between appraisal and effective coping, and when events were appraised as being uncontrollable, emotion focused strategies were encouraged, while problem focused strategies were advocated for controllable aspects of the disability. Other practical management situations were discussed in the group, such as how to manage a bladder accident, and a lot of information and concerns were shared about the consequences of the injury and the impact of disability. Assessment of mood state and coping strategies before and after the programme demonstrated a reduction in anxiety and an increased use of adaptive coping strategies. After Martin had spent his first weekend home as part of his rehabilitation programme, he raised concerns about not having sufficient information concerning sexual aspects of his disability. Both Martin and his partner were seen on three occasions and provided with sexual counselling, which contained information on the nature of the changes, and specific suggestions were given on how to maintain an erection, change positions and deal with problems. This was supplemented by giving him the patient information booklet on Sexuality after Spinal Cord Injury.

Intervention services are provided across a number of levels, including provision of a treatment programme to an individual or family, and the organization of rehabilitation planning within a health care system, thereby challenging myths within the sociocultural environment for research or policy making. Services are provided in a variety of settings. Disabled people are referred to psychology services in primary health care teams, adult mental health services, community mental health teams, or acute or specialist hospitals. Hospitalization occurs when aspects of the disability can no longer be managed within the home environment and when specialist investigations or treatments are required.

It is important for a clinical psychologist to become familiar with the medical and organic factors of the disability, as well as the psychosocial. When an inpatient is referred, it is good practice to become familiar with the available information on the medical condition on the ward. When a patient is confined to bed, it is important to be careful when entering the patient's space that permission is sought and an attempt is made to sit next to the patient rather than hover above their bed. The clinical psychologist will then explain their role to the patient, and their brief, to assist the patient in managing the stress associated with their disability, hospitalization, and/or other emotional concerns.

A major source of stress in hospital is the investigations and treatment which may involve pain and uncertainty of outcome. However, when the concerns of hospital patients have been examined, many of their worries are unrelated to the hospital environment and often concern family well-being and issues irrelevant to personal health. It is important to spend time with disabled persons to understand their needs and concerns. It may also be appropriate for the psychologist to act as an advocate on behalf of the patient with other members of the team, explaining major concerns and sources of misunderstanding. Patients in hospital depend on staff for their care and treatment and there are high levels of dissatisfaction with the amount of treatment they receive. Many patients report having difficulty in understanding their medical condition and the prognosis. There is growing evidence that patients, regardless of the severity, or indeed the terminal nature of their condition, report positive aspects of being given the diagnosis.

In addition to ensuring that accurate and accessible information is provided, clinical psychologists also help the team understand and normalize emotional reactions to disability. Postural, mobility, and illness factors may require that the disabled person be provided with therapy or treatment in a non-traditional environment, such as while on bed rest or lying in a prone trolley. It is then even more important to work on maximizing eye contact and posture symmetry. The clinical psychologist may also have to acquire skills in managing some medical problems, for example, chest suction for people on ventilation. In emergencies, they may be required to provide assisted breathing, pressure relief, or empty the patient's leg bag. These are just some of the specific issues that clinical psychologists working with disabled people may have to address.

Individual therapy

Given its theoretical underpinnings in learning theory (classical, operant, and social) and the science of cognitive psychology (information processing and schematic analysis) CBT has entered this century with a broad range of empirically validated and effective treatments. CBT is a common intervention for the management of emotional concerns of disabled people. The CBT perspective suggests that there is a reciprocal inter-dependence of feelings, thoughts, and behaviour. Turk and Meichenbaum (1994) characterized five central assumptions of treatment. First, individuals are active processors of information rather than passive reactors to environmental contingencies. According to the Cognitive Behavioural Model, each person's perspective is based on his/her idiosyncratic attitudes, beliefs, and unique schemas. Behavioural responses are elicited from significant others that can reinforce both adaptive and maladaptive modes of thoughts, feelings, and behaving. In this perspective, anticipating the consequences are as important as actual consequences. The second assumption of their more constructivist perspective is that thoughts can elicit or moderate affect and physiological arousal. The third assumption recognizes the reciprocal relationship between the individual and the environment. The fourth requires that interventions should not focus exclusively on changing thoughts or feelings or behaviours, but that successful interventions should target each, and not one to the exclusion of the others. The final assumption emphasizes the role that the individual has as an active agent of change or maladaptive modes of responding. Patients with chronic disability, no matter how severe and despite common beliefs to the contrary, are not helpless pawns of fate. They can become instrumental in learning and acquiring more effective modes of managing the consequences of their disability within our socially created disabling environments.

Case Study

Mary had become progressively more disabled with her rheumatoid arthritis. She had consulted her GP who was concerned about her current mood state and level of depression. She was seen in the health centre by the clinical psychologist who provided her with a treatment plan consisting of eight sessions of Cognitive Behavioural psychotherapy. The two major initial problems were severe depression and chronic pain. A number of other issues were explored as Mary's two children had recently left home and she had given up employment in a local school because of ill health. Negative thoughts included 'I'm just going through the motions of life', 'nobody needs me anymore', 'my husband and friends will reject me'. Intensive cognitive behaviour therapy challenged these assumptions by exploring the evidence for and against, and examining alternatives. In the first two sessions, Mary was taught relaxation techniques and was encouraged to pace activity to help with the management of pain. It was also important to work at developing distraction techniques and recreation opportunities. Reframing attributions from helplessness and hopelessness to resourcefulness and confidence and altering catastrophic thinking patterns were also important components of the intervention. This restructuring enabled Mary to become more aware of the role of thoughts and emotions in potentiating and maintaining distress and physical symptoms. Therapy aimed to help Mary manage the consequences of the pain rather than the pain *per se*. During the final sessions, self-monitoring charts were used to reinforce treatment success, and relapse prevention was discussed to help Mary identify potential risk situations and responses that may be necessary for successful coping.

Generalization was helped by developing specific plans for specific situations and being able to develop these plans generally. Two months after treatment Mary, who had not been looking forward to her Silver Wedding celebrations because of anticipated problems such as not being able to organize, not being able to dance, etc., had developed a plan to cope by preparing, pacing, and planning.

However, CBT is not a panacea, and more powerful and prolonged interventions are required to yield long-term significant change with clients who have severe chronic conditions. Many of the perceived losses are unchangeable and are not a function of cognitive distortions or irrational beliefs. Here, coping appraisal training is important. The patient is encouraged to develop emotion-focused strategies such as positive reframing and acceptance for those aspects of disability which are unchangeable, and to acquire problem-focused coping strategies to manage those consequences of the disability that are capable of being changed. This intervention technique will be discussed later in the chapter when discussing group approaches.

Cognitive Behavioural therapy procedures have been successfully applied to diverse clinical populations. The two clinical populations that have received most research attention are those suffering from anxiety and depressive disorders (see Chapter 4). A number of randomized control trials have demonstrated the efficacy of this approach for the management of depression, generalized anxiety disorders, and social phobias. Emotional distress in disabled people is formulated using the same CBT treatment conceptualizations as those for able-bodied people. It is, however, always important to acquire an understanding of the specific disabilities to help in establishing rapport, preparing individuals for therapy, and engaging them in the treatment process. Other cognitive-behavioural techniques include modelling, exposure based treatments for anxiety, challenging distorted beliefs via evidence seeking, and behavioural experiments. Activity scheduling may be particularly helpful as many chronic conditions are associated with change in activity levels. Cognitive monitoring and challenge may also help identify core distortions and processes that may exacerbate the impact of injury, disease, and disability. In this area the modification of negative thinking may not be the focus of treatment, rather the management of such thoughts maybe a more realistic treatment goal. The challenge for the therapist is to integrate established techniques with the idiosyncratic aspects of a physical condition while retaining fidelity to the model and respecting the individual's experience.

Another example of individual theory based psychotherapy is Rodin *et al.*'s (1991) integrated psychodynamic approach for the treatment of depression in people with chronic medical conditions. They advocated three phases that would begin with facilitation of grief and mourning. Here, people are encouraged to express feelings of loss and bereavement. The next phase explores the individual's understanding and personal meaning of the disability. At this point, the severity of the impairment is linked with the individual's belief system, prior experience, and premorbid personality characteristics. The therapeutic process finishes by the achievement of a sense of mastery over feelings associated with the chronic condition. In general, psychoanalytically based, psychodynamic therapeutic interventions are characterized by assisting the person with an acquired disability or chronic condition to gain insight into the impact of the disability on their present conflicts, anxieties, and vulnerabilities.

In addition to the more theory-based approaches, many clinical psychologists work within humanistic and general counselling frameworks. The goals of these interventions are similar to those previously discussed and often incorporate information giving and emotional support. Typically, these interventions assist in enabling the client to deal with the personal meaning of the disability and explore issues associated with loss, suffering, acceptance, and coping. Disabled people are encouraged to describe their feelings and integrate the meaning and reality of the loss. Whatever the therapeutic approach, clinical psychologists recognize the importance of providing an opportunity to ensure that disabled people are seen in accessible environments and free from disturbance during psychotherapy. Once contact and rapport is established and the therapeutic rationale explained, exploring and influencing can begin. This is often done with a combination of questioning, information giving, and problem solving. This is then monitored and evaluated and the therapeutic process is terminated by mutual consent.

Sexual counselling

Clinical psychologists are often involved in helping individuals and couples explore sexual needs and concerns. Many professional and disabled groups express concern that sexual themes continue to be an area neglected within the health service, often based on the assumption that disabled people do not have sexual needs, wishes, and rights. There is general consensus that the P-LI-SS-IT (Permission-Limited Information-Specific Suggestions-Intensive Therapy) developed by Annon (1974) provides a useful framework for organizing sexual counselling. This model has four levels of intervention, each increasing in sophistication. Permission giving is the first level and relates to the general responsiveness within the therapeutic context to discuss sexual issues and concerns. Limited information is provided depending on the person's ability and level of concern. Patient information booklets are useful and should be available upon request. With the next stage, specific suggestions are offered to the individual and partner, and suggestions include advice on positioning, comfort, and relationship issues. People with more complex sexual difficulties may require more intensive therapy such as sensate focus techniques. In the United Kingdom, a London-based organization called Sexual Problems of Disabled People (SPOD) helps by providing telephone counselling, professional training, and information.

Some disabling conditions may directly affect genital functioning. Secondary complications, such as respiratory failure, spasticity, and pain may also affect a person's ability to engage in sexual activity. In both static and progressive conditions, fatigue, anxiety about causing damage, and the side-effects of medication may also impair sexual function. Clinical psychologists assist in this area by examining the physical, emotional, and relationship issues involved. Many couples require advice in resuming activity, challenging unhelpful attitudes, and exploring alterative methods.

Behaviour modification

Clinical psychologists have used behaviour modification techniques to manage a number of problems within rehabilitation environments. Operant behavioural techniques have been used to increase the frequency of pressure lifting in spinal patients and classical conditioning techniques have been used in the management of hypotension. Reinforcement contingencies have helped in managing problems with treatment adherence and underpin many of those rehabilitation programmes based on goal planning and goal setting. Extinction may be used to reduce the frequency of inappropriate target behaviour by withdrawing reinforcement. Modelling and role play techniques are effective strategies for problem rehearsal and competency management.

Biofeedback

Some clinical psychologists use biofeedback to help in the management of mood disorders and more specifically to reduce levels of functional impairment. Clinical psychologists have worked with occupational therapists and physiotherapists to use electromyography (EMG) to manage problems associated with foot drop, shoulder dislocation, and maximizing muscular function in weak muscle groups. Here, the therapist's expertise is combined with the psychologist's awareness of systematic observation and use of operant behavioural techniques.

Skills training

As an adjunct to many of the psychotherapeutic interventions mentioned, clinical psychologists are involved in relaxation training skills and assertiveness and social skills training. Relaxation training can take the form of traditional Jacobsonean relaxation training, but as this is contra-indicated in many disabled people (e.g. people with chronic rheumatoid arthritis, spinal cord injury, and muscular paresis), autogenic relaxation training can be provided which focuses on using imaging techniques. Relaxation training is designed not only to help individuals learn a response that is incompatible with muscular tension, but as an additional coping skill which can be used to strengthen the disabled person's belief in exerting control. It has a value in the reduction of generalized arousal, enhancing control, and reducing the experience of disability.

Assertiveness training is important and may help people re-establish roles and responsibilities and gain control. Assertiveness training can also include the use of role models and behavioural rehearsals to assist people anticipate behaviours and rehearse problem-solving strategies. These are more usefully implemented on a group basis and clinical psychologists have organized such self-management and social skills groups in hospitals and in day centres in the community.

Interventions with families

Families play an essential role in health care across the lifespan. There is growing evidence of the critical role families have in health beliefs, risk behaviours, and adherence issues. There is also evidence that involving family members in health risk intervention trials improves success. Smith *et al.* (2004) found that solicitous family responses to expressions of pain were positively associated with higher levels of pain and disability. Kerns and Weiss (1994) used a cognitive behavioural model of family functioning to underpin interactions, which aim to increase self-management, improve communication, and promote problem solving skills for medical needs. Clinicians are also involved in helping families renegotiate roles, encourage independence, and increase family, social, and recreational activities. Psychologists not only recognize the importance of therapy to increase family motivation and involvement, but that many non-disabled family members require support to help with their own adjustment issues. Disability occurs within a social context.

Group interventions

Problem-solving skills training and coping effectiveness training are more focused group intervention techniques. Group work, as opposed to individual therapy, has advantages not only in terms of cost effectiveness, but also in increasing the potential for learning and obtaining the support that comes from one's peers. In problem-solving training, individuals define their source

Table 12.2 Problem solving questions

Problem identification	What is the concern?
Goal selection	What do I want?
Generation of alternatives	What can I do?
Consideration of consequences	What might happen?
Decision making	What is my decision?
Implementation	Now do it
Evaluation	Did it work?–if not, retry

Source: Adapted from Turk and Salovey (see Nicassio and Smith, 1995).

of stress, or stress reactions, set a range of concrete goals, and consider a wide range of possible alternatives to attain these goals. Turk and Meichenbaum (1994) usefully summarize these problem-solving steps through seven specific questions. These are illustrated in Table 12.2.

Coping effectiveness training is a development from Lazurus and Folkman's (1984) transactional model of stress. It utilizes cognitive methods to appraise the stressor and identify the changeable and unchangeable aspects. When these demands are perceived to be amenable to change, a problem focused strategy is applied, whereas in situations where demands are appraised as not changeable, individuals utilize emotion focused strategies. Coping effectiveness training (CET) consists of a series of group learning sessions aimed at helping people deal with the demands resulting from acquired disability. It is generally based on the idea that coping has two functions: (1) to alter the problem causing a distress, and (2) to regulate the emotional response to the problem. Once changeable aspects have been identified, the individual is trained to utilize problem focused strategies. For those which are unchangeable, the person is trained to utilize emotion focused strategies.

Kennedy *et al.*, (2003) identified a number of coping strategies that were associated with positive adjustment that included accepting the reality of the injury occurring, having available high levels of quality social support, having the capacity to engage in positive reappraisal, and engagement in planned problem solving. Maladaptive coping strategies associated with poor adjustment included behavioural and mental disengagement, alcohol and drug-use ideation, denial, escape-avoidant coping strategies, focusing on and venting of emotions, and low social support. They effectively used a coping effectiveness training programme to improve skills for assessing stress, teaching coping skills and provided an opportunity for interaction with others who had similar disabilities. The intervention consisted of seven, 60–75 min sessions run twice a week in small groups of six to nine people. The concept of stress was introduced in the first session and attempts were made to normalize stress reactions. The need to develop the ability to think critically about how one appraises and copes with situations was also emphasized. The second session covered appraisal skills and the third session problem solving, which included working through several realistically based scenarios commonly experienced by people with spinal cord injuries. In the fourth session, the connections and distinctions between thoughts, feelings, and behaviour were examined with the inclusion of work on pleasant activity scheduling and relaxation. Session five was concerned with increasing awareness of negative assumptions, thoughts, and expectations and how to challenge them. The final two sessions described the meta-strategy for choosing appropriate ways of coping and increasing social support. This treatment package demonstrated significant reductions in mood disturbance especially depression, and enhanced the belief that the consequences of this disability were manageable.

In addition to the psychological framework previously discussed, groups also enable participants to share positive and negative experiences of disability, discuss disability-related problems, and encourage the normalization process. Many community rehabilitation services provide essential opportunities for people to discuss the emotional and practical aspects of being disabled. Many groups utilize shared experience to endorse effective coping, increase confidence, and perceive self-efficacy. In summary, group interventions have been shown to reduce mood disturbance, improve social functioning, and facilitate adaptation.

Contribution to the health care system

In addition to individual, group, and family interventions, clinical psychologists make a significant contribution to organizational and health care systems. They are often involved in ensuring awareness and recognition of psychological issues in hospital-based ward rounds, community case conferences, and health care planning groups. However, it needs to be remembered that much of the focus of rehabilitation effort is on changing behaviour. Clinical psychologists recognize the importance of incorporating behavioural change principles in many aspects of health care provision. Goal planning provides a systematic framework for doing this. This is a 'soft' form of behaviour modification that is applied by clinical psychologists across many rehabilitative settings, both in the community and in hospital.

In understanding behaviour, goal directedness is critical. The common features of goal directed action include those which are generated within the individual, have a significant association with the management of need, and recognize the interplay between physiological, cognitive, and environmental factors.

Rehabilitation is a process of active change by which a person who has a disability acquires the knowledge and skills for optimal physical, psychological, and social functioning.

There are many variants in goal planning, but they generally share the following elements. The first principle of goal planning is participant involvement. Practice that is client-centred, rather than therapist-centred, recognizes the need to engage a disabled person throughout the rehabilitation process as an active participant. Secondly, all disabled people have strengths that can be identified and it is the therapist's role to build on these strengths. These strengths not only compensate for loss of function, but enable maximum control and independence. By emphasizing needs rather than disabilities, goal planning identifies difficult areas and explores ways in which these can be realistically tackled. A similar approach is described in working with people with learning disabilities in Chapter 9. The third component indicates that goals need to be set by the disabled person in collaboration with the therapist. The values and choices of the client will dictate the goals to be achieved, as well as the targets or the small steps which will be taken along the way. This time scale for achieving these targets may vary from weeks to months. When setting goals it is important to specify who (i.e. the disabled person or multidisciplinary team member) will be carrying out the activity; what (i.e. specifies the behaviour required); under what conditions and how often the activity should take place. A goal must be about behaviour, it needs to be clear, refer to the disabled person's behaviour where possible, and specify who will do what, under what conditions, and to what degree of success. This approach to task analysis is fundamental to behavioural programming, whereby long-term goals can be broken down into smaller steps or targets which are tailored to the needs of the individual. Social reinforcement provides the essential flux that incorporates meaning to goal planning meetings.

Psychologists often utilize more formal assessments such as Needs Assessment Checklists and behavioural indicators to set standards and monitor progress in rehabilitation. Standards are statements of best practice and provide a benchmark to compare services. These behavioural indicators which express qualitative and quantitative aspects of intervention can also be used for audit purposes.

In view of the wide range of needs which may arise from the many forms of disability, it is clearly beyond the capacity of any one professional to have expertise in all areas. Disabled people need to draw upon the skills, knowledge, and support of the multidisciplinary team or rehabilitation professionals. Most physical rehabilitation teams will be composed of medical doctors, nurses, physiotherapists, and occupational therapists, and can include clinical psychologists, speech therapists, social workers, discharge planning coordinators, and care managers. Goal planning alerts each professional to the specific needs with which an individual requires help.

Goal planning is a behavioural process to maximize engagement in rehabilitation. Research has demonstrated that the best predictor of post-discharge behavioural or medical status is engagement in a comprehensive rehabilitation programme. Many goal planning programmes utilize a key worker as part of this process to empower and involve the disabled person. The key worker generally coordinates, advocates, and supports the individual within the rehabilitative process. This approach to rehabilitation planning not only provides a safety net for disabled people, but also highlights gaps in services and unmet needs. Duff *et al.*, (2004) conclude that their goal planning system demonstrated the capacity to reflect individual need, and could potentially lead to more efficient rehabilitation and the identification of care pathways within clinical areas. It also supports the rehabilitation team in minimizing role ambiguity and role conflict which can undermine team effort, essentially demonstrating needs and achievements over disability and losses.

In addition to organizing and training in goal planning, psychologists also provide teaching and training in many other related issues. Typically, this would include education about the specific psychological needs of a disabled group, adaptation issues, as well as the provision of basic training on approaches to counselling, social skills, and assertiveness. Training can also be provided to support risk assessment and promote prevention strategies. Clinical psychologists contribute to the teaching and training of other professionals involved in rehabilitation. Many academic and professional courses incorporate teaching on psychological needs in order to underpin practice with general psychological sensitivity and responsiveness.

Legislative and health policy context

In promoting the philosophy of care that recognizes the full range of individual needs rather than the functional limitations, clinical psychologists acknowledge the influence of progressive legislation and policy making on the experience of disability. The Swedish Fokus Schemes, Collectivhaus in Denmark and the Het Dorp in Holland informed policy makers on the need to provide a more community focused, local and integrated service for disabled people. In many developed economies, disabled groups have collectivized, such as the British Council of Organisations for Disabled People (BCODP) to influence legislation and ensure accessible transport, prevent discrimination, and promote integrative social change. In the United Kingdom, the 1995 Disability Discrimination Act (Stationary Office, 1995) made it unlawful for people with disabilities to be discriminated against in areas of employment, and accessing goods and services. The requirements of the act were extended in 2004 to trade organizations and qualification bodies. This enshrines in legislation the rights to access facilities for disabled people on all storeys of new, non-domestic buildings, and provides new rights in areas of employment, obtaining goods and services, and in buying or renting property.

The British National Health Service (NHS) has incorporated research experience that patients with chronic conditions are more than the recipients of care and can be enabled to take more responsibility for the treatment and management of their condition. The Expert Patient model (Department of Health, 2001) developed Lorig *et al.*'s (2000) self-management programmes to promote greater patient participation in service delivery and planning. Other NHS National Service Framework documents set out clear guidelines incorporating psychological needs and services for a range of index conditions, such as Coronary Heart Disease, Long Term Conditions, and Diabetes.

Research

As part of their portfolio of skills, clinical psychologists offer significant research skills which can range from pure research endeavours, to service evaluation and audit. Research can also challenge outdated orthodoxy (e.g. requirement for mourning), and provide people with information on psychological impact and adjustment processes. It can also be used to identify the psychological processes associated with effective coping, promotion of resiliency and enable more realistic expectations of future management possibilities. Researchers have explored elements of theoretical models of impact and coping and helped identify factors such as social support that can buffer against the adverse impact of disability. Service evaluation can help identify procedures and services which are most effective in managing needs. The dissemination of psychological research findings and knowledge through publishing and presentations at scientific and professional meetings is an important professional responsibility.

Conclusions

In summary, there are an increasing number of clinical psychologists involved in providing services to disabled people. There is also a growing number of people for whom chronic conditions and physical disabilities are a common experience. This group of people will require an increasing proportion of health care expenditure. Clinical psychologists contribute to the management of these needs by combining theory and practice in integrated health care delivery systems. They do this by utilizing objective and standardized approaches to assessment, the implementation of scientifically based clinical intervention strategies, and collaboration with health service users to support informed choices. They participate at many levels ranging from the individual, the family, and health care systems, providing individual psychotherapy, group work and developing client-centred care, and goal planning. They can continue developing co-management approaches, such as the expert patient models, and integrate more with primary care providers. They also contribute by disseminating knowledge to health care professionals, providers and the general public. They possess a broad portfolio of skills which also includes education, training, and research. While a lot has been achieved, there is yet more to be done to ensure that the needs of disabled people are recognized and that they become active participants in the rehabilitative process. Clinical psychologists have professional responsibility to ensure the evidence base of their interventions and need to compete effectively for resources for service developments and research. New partnerships need to be established on a trans-disciplinary basis to deal with the complex multisystems involved. Many myths have yet to be challenged to ensure that the needs of disabled people are effectively addressed. Psychologists are well placed to respond to these challenges in this millennium.

References

Annon, J.S. (1974). *The Behavioural Treatment of Sexual Problems*, Vol. 1. Honolulu: Enabling systems incorporated.

Berry, C. and Kennedy, P. (2003). A Psychometric Analysis of the Needs Assessment Checklist (NAC). *Spinal Cord*, **41**, 490–501.

Duff, J., Evans, M.J., and Kennedy, P. (2004). Goal planning: A retrospective audit of rehabilitation process and outcome. *Clinical Rehabilitation*, **18**, 275–86.

Dupont, S. (2006). Medical Topics: Multiple Sclerosis. In S. Ayers, A. Baum, C. McManus, S. Newman, K. Wallston, J. Weinman, and R. West (eds.), *Cambridge Handbook of Psychology, Health and Medicine*. Cambridge: Cambridge University Press.

Department of Health. (2001). *The Expert Patient: A New Approach to Chronic Disease Management for the 21st Century*. London: Department of Health Publications. www.ohn.gov.uk/ohn/people/expert.htm

Engel, G.L. (1980). The clinical application of the biopsychosocial model. *American Journal of Psychiatry*, **137**, 535–44; Frank R.G. and Elliott T.R. (2000) *Handbook of Rehabilitation Psychology*, American Psychological Association.

Health Survey for England (2001). *National Centre for Social Research and the Department of Epidemiology at University College London*. Department of Health: The Stationery Office.

Imrie, R. (2004). Demystifying disability: A review of the International Classification of Functioning, Disability and Health. *Sociology of Health and Illness*, **26**, 287–305.

Kennedy, P. (2006). Medical topics: Spinal cord injury. In S. Ayer, A. Baum, C. McManus, S. Newman, J. Weinman, K. Wallston, and R. West (eds.), *Cambridge Handbook of Psychology, Health and Medicine*. Cambridge: Cambridge University Press.

Kennedy, P. Duff, J., Evans, M., and Beedie, A. (2003). Coping effectiveness training reduces depression and anxiety following traumatic spinal cord injuries. *British Journal of Clinical Psychology*, **42**, 41–52.

Kerns, R.D. and Weiss, L. (1994). Family influences on the cause of chronic illness: A cognitive-behavioural transactional model. *Annals of Behavioural Medicine*, **16**, 116–21.

Lazarus, R.S. and Folkman, S. (1984). *Stress, Appraisal and Coping*. New York: Springer.

Lorig, K., Fries, J.F., and Fries, J.E. (2000) *The Arthritis Helpbook: A Tested Self-management Program for Coping with Arthritis and Fibromyalgia*, 4th Edition. Reading, MA: Da Capo Press.

Nicassio, P.M. and Smith, T.W. (1995). *Managing Chronic Illness: A Biopsychosocial Perspective*. Washington: APA.

Mangelli, L., Gribbon. N., Buchi, S., Allard, S., and Sensky. T. (2002). Psychological well-being in rheumatoid arthritis: relationship to disease variables and affective disturbance. *Psychotherapy and Psychosomatics*, **71**, 112–16.

Psychology and Physical Disability in the National Health Service (1989). *Partnership, Participation and Power: Report of the working party of the British Psychological Society Professional Affairs Board*. Leicester: BPS Publications.

Reuben, D., Rubenstein, I., Hirsch, S., and Hays, R. (1992). The value of functional status as a predictor of mortality: Results of a prospective study. *American Journal of Medicine*, **93**, 633–9.

Rodin, G., Craven, J., and Littlefield, C. (1991). *Depression in the Medically Ill: An integrated approach*. New York: Brunner/Mazel.

Smith, S., Keefe, F.J., Caldwell, D.S., Romano, J. and Baucom, D. (2004). Gender differences in patient-spouse interactions. *Pain*, **112**, 183–187.

Sarason, I.G. and Sarason, B.R. (1983). Assessing Social Support: The social support questionnaire. *Journal of Personality and Social Psychology*, **44**, 127–39.

The Disabilities Discrimination Act 1995. Regulations 2003. London: HMSO.

Turk, D.C. and Meichenbaum, D. (1994). A cognitive-behavioural approach to pain management. In P.D. Wall and R. Malzack. (eds.), *Textbook of Pain*. London: Churchill Livingstone.

World Health Organisation (1999). *International Classification of Functioning, Disability and Health (ICFDH-2)*. Geneva, Switzerland.

Wortman, C.D. and Silver, R.C. (1989). The Myth of Coping with Loss. *Journal of Consulting and Clinical Psychology*, **57**, 349–57.

Further reading

DeGood, D.E., Crawford, A.L., and Jongsma, A.E., (1999). *The Behavioural Medicine Treatment Planner*. New York: Wiley.

Frank R.G. and Elliott T.R. (2000). *Handbook of Rehabilitation Psychology*. Washington: American Psychological Association.

Llewelyn S. and Kennedy P. (2003). *Handbook of Clinical Health Psychology*. Chichester: John Wiley and Sons.

Wright, B.A. (1983). *Physical Disability—A Psychosocial Approach*, 2nd edn. New York: Harper and Row.

Chapter 13

Working in clinical neuropsychology

Katherine Carpenter and Andy Tyerman

Introduction

Clinical neuropsychology is concerned with people whose thinking, behaviour, or emotions have become disrupted as a result of brain damage. Such neuropsychological changes often have a major effect on the person and their lifestyle, occupation, and family relationships.

Clinical neuropsychology has its own specialist knowledge base of neurology, neuroanatomy, and brain–behaviour relations. However, it still involves work with people with their own everyday life events and stresses who experience psychological problems (such as anxiety and depression) similar to those in mental health settings, in addition to their specific neuropsychological changes.

The clinical neuropsychologist needs the expertise to make sense of what can be bizarre and frightening experiences for patients (such as their not being able to remember anything from one day to the next, or not being able to recognize their family by seeing their faces but only on hearing them talk). However, sensitivity and understanding is also required to treat patients with these problems as a whole person in a family and life context not just as a dysfuntional brain. During the course of recovery the professional role may evolve from that of an expert assessor/advisor to a trainer or guide in rehabilitation, to that of a mentor or facilitator in long-term personal, family, and social adjustment.

Neuropsychological impairment

Neuropsychological impairment is extremely varied, encompassing a wide range of difficulties in cognitive function, behavioural control, and emotional responsivity. These neuropsychological changes are often experienced alongside a range of physical and sensory effects of neurological conditions such as paralysis, loss of balance and co-ordination, visual field deficits, loss of sensation, headaches, fatigue, and epilepsy.

After generalized damage to the brain the most common cognitive difficulties are with attention, concentration, memory, and reduced speed of information processing. After focal damage (such as stroke and tumour) more specific deficits may be seen in motor skills, visual perception, spatial judgement, language function, etc. Disruption of executive function (i.e. higher level reasoning, planning, problem solving, and self-awareness and self-monitoring), which are very common after severe head injury, are of particular importance as they affect insight, understanding, use of compensatory strategies, and capacity for long-term adjustment. The realization of changes in cognitive skills that we usually take entirely for granted can be a bewildering and immensely frustrating experience.

A wide range of behavioural and emotional changes may be experienced, reflecting an interaction of primary neurological damage and secondary psychological reactions to neurological illness/injury and its effects. Common primary changes are of increased irritability, disinhibition, impulsivity, emotional lability, mood swings, and aggressive outbursts. A wide range of emotional reactions may also be experienced such as frustration and anger, fear and anxiety, depression and loss of confidence/self-esteem.

Some common causes of neuropsychological impairment are shown in Table 13.1. An important distinction is made between relatively circumscribed lesions such as those caused by a stroke (where a blockage or constriction of an artery results in loss of blood and oxygen to a particular area) or a penetrating missile injury (such as a bullet wound), and diffuse brain injury

Table 13.1 Causes of neuropsychological impairment

Alcoholism
Anoxia (lack of oxygen)
Benign tumours (e.g. meningioma)
Cerebrovascular accidents (e.g. intracerebral haematoma, stroke, subarachnoid haemorrhage)
Dementias (e.g. dementia of Alzheimer's type, multi-infarct dementia)
Degenerative diseases (e.g. multiple sclerosis, Parkinson's disease)
Epilepsy
Head injury
Hydrocephalus (excess fluid in the ventricles of the brain)
Infections (e.g. AIDS, herpes simplex virus encephalitis)
Malignant tumours (e.g. metastatic carcinoma, glioma, astrocytoma)
Poisoning (e.g. carbon monoxide following a suicide attempt)

caused by a head injury, a progressive degenerative process (such as Alzheimer's disease), or a subarachnoid haemorrhage (in which an artery ruptures explosively driving blood into the space around the brain causing widespread damage).

Neurological conditions differ markedly in both onset and course. Some conditions (such as anoxia, head injury, and stroke) are of sudden onset, infectious conditions (such as encephalitis and meningitis) may develop over periods of hours or days, whereas others conditions (such as tumours, movement disorders, or the dementias) evolve very gradually. Some conditions (such as head injury and anoxia) are single episodes followed by recovery and adjustment, others (such as epilepsy and multiple sclerosis) may be intermittent and others progressive (such as cerebral tumour and the dementias). As such, while some people with a neurological condition require acute hospital care, followed by rehabilitation and community support, others may require limited input in the early stages of the condition but increasing medical, psychological, and social care as their condition progresses.

Neuropsychological services

In the United Kingdom approximately 300–400 clinical psychologists have specialized in work with people with acquired brain damage and their carers. They work in a range of settings and at different stages in the pathway of care from acute to community.

Neuropsychologists working with people at their first point of contact with services, either as out-patients or on admission to hospital, are usually located in a hospital-based neurosciences centre. These centres bring together specialists such as neurologists (concerned with medical aspects of central nervous system disorders and their treatments) and neurosurgeons (similarly concerned with what surgery can contribute to management). Much of the work carried out in such units involves emergency treatment or investigation of very sick or at-risk patients. Many patients will be struggling with serious physical illness or impairments, such as paralysis down one side of their body, and will not have had time to take on board the longer-term cognitive effects of their condition. Neuropsychologists work closely with medical and nursing staff but often need to see patients again as out-patients at a 'post-acute' stage, when many of the acute medical features have settled and cognitive and emotional changes become much more relevant.

Up to the 1990s clinical neuropsychologists working in rehabilitation in the United Kingdom were based primarily within a few specialist regional in-patient neurological rehabilitation centres catering for people with severe and multiple disabilities or in specialist centres in the independent sector for persons with severe behavioural problems. More recently clinical psychologists are increasingly working within generic physical disability teams, within local neurorehabilitation teams or specialist community brain injury or stroke rehabilitation services. There are also a number of specialist residential, out-patient, and community rehabilitation services which focus specifically on the cognitive, behavioural, and/or vocational needs of people with acquired brain injury.

The role of the clinical neuropsychologist varies markedly across acute, rehabilitation, and community settings with acute neuropsychology and post-acute/community rehabilitation services operating as distinct areas of practice, typically attracting clinicians with different interests and skills working with an overlapping but contrasting range of conditions at different stages in the care pathway. In illustrating our work in this specialist area we shall first consider the acute neurological/neurosurgical setting and then move on to the rehabilitation and community setting.

The acute neurology/neurosurgery setting

The patients

Patients present at all ages and a good working knowledge of the developmental context is important especially for the younger ones. Detailed comprehensive assessment needs to take account of any sensory or perceptual disturbance, any problems with movement or posture, and any episodes of altered awareness (faints, blackouts, funny turns), as well as the more usual areas of premorbid medical/psychiatric history. This is important because neurological disorders tend to present with a complex interplay of cognitive, emotional, behavioural, and physical features. These interact with each other and may affect assessment or measurement of any one component. For example, if you are testing a patient's verbal memory by reading him or her a short paragraph and asking the patient to tell it back to you, and he or she is suffering from tinnitus (ringing in the ear), then this may affect the patient's attention, making the test less valid as a test of verbal memory.

Medical context

Trainee psychologists are often surprised by what can seem an intimidating 'Casualty' or 'ER' type environment in the acute setting. Neuropsychologists need to be flexible in switching between a medical model, which allows them to communicate rapidly with medical colleagues, and more meaningful and ecologically valid psychological models which may have greater relevance when helping patients and their carers try and make sense of their experiences.

In-patient clinical work is often constrained both by competing demands (such as pressure on beds resulting in a short hospital admission with patients being transferred some distance to a more local district general hospital) and by the general level of 'unwellness' of patients.

Parallel investigations

Clinical neuropsychology at the acute end is best thought of as one of a number of investigations available to the neurologist or neurosurgeon coordinating care of the patient. Psychometric test results must be interpreted in the context of overall formulation of the case and in the light of parallel investigations. History taking is 'the cornerstone of neurological diagnosis' (Donaghy, 1997), with many disorders being diagnosed on clinical grounds and examination confirming information anticipated by the history. The explosion in scanning techniques over the past 15 years has radically altered the role of neuropsychology in relation to other specialties. Computed tomography (CT) involves X-rays and is particularly good at detecting blood (e.g. a blood clot). Magnetic resonance imaging (MRI) exploits the different radiofrequency signals produced by the protons in tissue molecules which are first lined up by a powerful magnet and then displaced by radio waves. MRI is much more sensitive for imaging the substance of the brain and has replaced CT scanning for routine clinical work (see Figure 13.1). It is less invasive than CT but

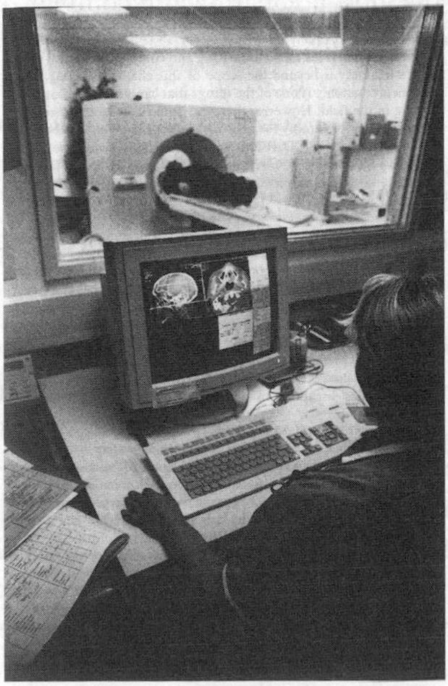

Fig 13.1 Structural imaging of the brain (MRI)

very noisy, 'a bit like lying on a building site' said one patient, and can feel claustrophobic. CT and MRI allow us to look at neuroanatomy and pathology in the living brain, which means that localization of pathology is no longer so central for psychology. Cerebral blood flow techniques, positron emission tomography (PET) and functional MRI (fMRI), allow us to observe the dynamic metabolism of the working brain. This will be increasingly crucial for our understanding of brain–behaviour relations. For example, if a non-brain damaged subject is speaking, does the region thought to mediate spoken language output (Broca's area) 'light up' on a PET scan? Similarly if a patient with a significant lesion in Broca's area identified on CT brain scanning can still speak, what area 'lights up' when a PET study is done (Ogden, 1996)? Neurophysiology, which measures electrical brain activity using electro-encephalographs (EEGs) and evoked potentials, is particularly important in the diagnosis of epilepsy.

Other disciplines which impact on neuropsychology are medicine (e.g. endocrinology and diabetes; neuro-oncology; plastics, reconstructive and cranio-facial surgery; ENT; geratology; psychiatry), physiotherapy, speech and language therapy, and occupational therapy.

Neuropsychological context

Functional neuroanatomy

The human brain is the most fascinating and complex biological system and its anatomy is beyond the scope of this chapter. Feeling woolly about neuro-anatomy is one of the things that can put psychologists off working in the field. However there are some excellent and readable sections on neuroanatomy for neuropsychologists (Andrewes, 2001; Lezak, 1995) and interactive CD ROMs will increasingly be on the market (Johnson & Becker, 1999). A basic knowledge is adequate for many purposes and work in the area necessarily brings increasing familiarity.

Neuropsychological terminology

Similarly, somewhat impenetrable technical terminology for syndromes can be off-putting. Although unnecessary jargon should be avoided where possible, jargon is often a useful shorthand between clinicians for what would otherwise be a complex phenomenon or concept to express. One or two pointers can help. Many terms are derived from Latin and their meaning can be worked out. Strictly speaking any label with the prefix *a-* denotes loss of a function, as opposed to the prefix *dys-* denoting partial impairment, although the two tend to get used interchangeably. So, *amnesia* means memory loss, d*ysphasia* means disruption of speech or language.

Underlying concepts and assumptions

It is worth bearing in mind a few key tenets which underpin much of the way neuropsychologists think. Cerebral dominance refers to lateralization such that either the right or the left side of the brain is specialized for a particular function. In the vast majority of right-handers (>92%) and in a large proportion of left-handers (69%) speech, language, and verbal memory are represented in the left 'dominant' hemisphere. In contrast the right hemisphere is predominant for tasks involving stimuli that cannot be easily put into words, such as visual memory, visuo-spatial function, interpretation of emotional expression, and probably attention. There is a subtle interplay between specialization and functional plasticity, whereby areas of the brain can apparently take over functions for which they are not normally thought to be specialized, at least sometimes following brain damage in childhood. Making inferences about normal brain function from the study of brain-damaged patients assumes that a patient's brain was previously normal and this may not always be the case (e.g. following early insult such as epilepsy). As Ogden (1996) points out, it also presupposes we know what 'normal' is when there is individual variation and evidence that the same lesion does not always lead to the same impairment.

Neuropsychological assessment

Clinical interview

Neuropsychological assessment usually involves an appointment lasting from two to five hours. With adults, a comprehensive semi-structured interview first reviews a wide range of factors relating to the patient's views (and those of a close relative) on the medical, social, and educational/occupational background, presenting problem and current symptomatology. This includes the following:

- previous or concurrent treatment (especially for epilepsy, learning disability, head injury, alcoholism);
- previous psychiatric/psychological history, medication, significant recent stressors (e.g. bereavement, crime, financial/work pressure);
- mental health screen (e.g. mood, appetite, sleep, sexual interest, drive, headaches);
- sensory-perceptual screen (i.e. vision, hearing, touch, smell, taste);
- movement-posture screen (i.e. weakness, paralysis, incoordination, gait, balance);
- cognitive screen (concentration, orientation, new learning, organization, reasoning).

As with any other interview, the psychologist is constantly developing a hypothesis and looking for disconfirming evidence, as well as making qualitative observations on aspects such as insight, comprehension, speech, mental state, etc.

Psychometric testing

A standard battery of tests can be administered. However most neuropsychologists adopt a more flexible approach (Lezak, 1995; Goldstein and McNeil, 2003), often using certain core tests plus other tests, sampling specific cognitive domains as and when appropriate. Neuropsychological tests are aimed at sampling behaviour in one or more cognitive domains, such as general intelligence, visuospatial perceptual ability, language, memory and concentration, attention, and higher order skills such as planning and so called executive function. As is common in many standard forms of measurement, the scores obtained by an individual on a test (measurement) of a particular psychological characteristic or process are compared with the average score obtained by a comparable group of individuals, usually the same age and from the same general population. The average of the comparable group is calculated and an individual score is expressed in terms of its departure from the group average. This allows one to take into account, for example, the fact that younger people tend to remember more than older people, and similarly that brighter subjects should remember more than those of more limited ability. An estimate is made of the patient's level of *premorbid* ability both on the basis of education and occupational attainments, and from their performance on more 'crystallized' components of cognitive performance (for example, lexical knowledge or knowledge of word meanings which is more robust in the face of neurological and neurosurgical conditions). In addition to quantitative indices, qualitative observations on test performance are also made. Standardized questionnaires may also be included to assess health-related quality of life and mood.

A standard assessment should include a measure of premorbid function (e.g. the National Adult Reading Test; the Wechsler Test of Adult Reading); a measure of general intelligence (e.g. the Wechsler Adult Intelligence Scale III); orientation (e.g. the Wechsler Memory Scale III protocol); verbal memory tests, including immediate and delayed recall of both narrative material and unrelated words (e.g. the Adult Memory and Information Processing Battery—Story Recall and List Learning); a non-verbal memory test (e.g. the Rey Complex Figure Test and Recognition Trial); attentional and 'executive' tests as appropriate (e.g. the Test of Everyday Attention, the Stroop Test, Trails A and B; the Wisconsin Card Sorting Test); and verbal fluency (e.g. letters F, A, S and animals) and additional language tests if appropriate.

Choice of test instruments obviously needs to take into account any sensory, motor, or linguistic constraints on the person. Where English is not the first language, more non-verbal tests of global ability (e.g. Raven's Standard Progressive Matrices) may be helpful, although cultural and ethnic differences still need to be taken into account both in administration and interpretation. Many of the widely used tests (e.g. the Wechsler Adult Intelligence Scale III, Wechsler Memory Scale III) have been translated into other languages, but the proviso remains that in general the normative data on which they are based remain North American.

Testing is an area that can seem dry to the uninitiated. In fact this is far from the case. Cognitive evaluation involves what is effectively a series of controlled behavioural experiments in which as many variables as possible are controlled. A skilled neuropsychologist needs to be capable of developing and maintaining rapport with a patient while coaxing them through what can be an exacting set of tasks. Imagine being faced with a bright person, perhaps a company director or medic, in the early stages of an insidious dementing process; extracting the greatest amount of information possible from a minimum of testing, which protects the dignity of the patient, is an undoubted challenge. Quiet, well-lit surroundings without any undue distractions or interruptions are preferable to maximize the patient's performance; quite an opposite set of conditions are obviously required if one is accessing a patient's capability of returning to a stressful job in a busy open-plan environment.

Neuropsychological report

A full written report is prepared following assessment and usually comprises sections on the medical background, personal history, clinical presentation, neuropsychological evaluation, and conclusions. Reports vary according to the audience for whom they are written. Internal reports in an acute neurology/neurosurgery setting tend to be succinct with cross referral to other medical reports. Rehabilitation reports often serve as a contract between the patient, their carers, and the interdisciplinary rehabilitation team and, as such, may use a goal setting model. A good report should appropriately convey the clinical problem and its context, together with a detailed description of the test results and findings and their interpretation, with a clear distinction between fact and observation and inference and interpretation. A good report should also not be merely descriptive, but should provide a clinical opinion in relation to the underlying referral question. Medico-legal reports, usually required for personal injury cases following traumatic brain injury in a road traffic accident for example, need to be comprehensive and intelligible to a non-specialist and should include an opinion on likely prognosis.

Purpose of assessment

In the acute setting the emphasis is on differential diagnosis, evaluation of outcome of intervention (e.g. drug treatment or operation), monitoring of change, and early identification of cognitive sequelae. All the information is taken together and interpreted in the light of the questions to be answered. These obviously vary from patient to patient but include the following: is there evidence that the patient's cognitive function has been adversely affected from a previously higher premorbid level? Is the pattern of deficits consistent with the known pathology and medical variables? Does the test profile reflect focal pathology or a generalized decline? What are this person's current strengths and weaknesses? Are their deficits likely to progress or improve? What is the likelihood of this person being able to return to their previous employment or academic study? and so on.

Case Study

Mrs Freeman was a 58-year-old former nurse referred by a neurologist, with progressive memory loss over 3 years. On interview she presented well socially and appeared relatively intact at least in conversation for a short period of time; she also had limited insight and tended to deny any difficulties. When she talked more freely, about her family for example, she had some difficulty in expressing herself. Spending more time with her, the difficulties became more apparent. She was forgetful during the assessment and sometimes lost the thread of what she was saying. Her husband, who accompanied her, gave various instances of her confusion, disorientation, and memory loss at home. He was clearly searching for an alternative explanation for his wife's problems to the possibility of a dementing illness, and spoke of lead in their water pipes and the fact that they had lived abroad for many years. There was no evidence of depression although she appeared mildly anxious.

On testing it became clear that her intellect and memory were severely deteriorated. An estimate of premorbid ability based on her current single word reading (National Adult Reading Test) was 'high average' (110) in line with her nursing background, but Verbal (86) and Performance (74) quotients on the Wechsler Adult Intelligence Scale III fell in the 'low average' and 'borderline' ranges respectively. Her range of subtest scores showed a typical pattern often seen in dementia, of adequate scores on more 'crystallized' components of intelligence, such as vocabulary and general knowledge, and severely impaired scores on speed of information processing, visuo-constructional ability and abstract verbal reasoning. She was able to repeat 9 digits forwards but only 4 backwards suggesting a deficit in auditory 'working' memory (confirmed on other tests). She was unable to give the date or say where she was. When read a short story (Adult Memory and Information Processing Battery) she was unable to remember more than a few words from the last sentence immediately afterwards, and half an hour later could remember nothing of the story. Her copy of a complex geometric design (Rey Complex Figure Test) was spatially distorted and incomplete, and after half an hour she was unable even to recall having done the copy and instead drew an elephant. Further testing confirmed diffuse generalized loss of cognitive function including memory.

Dementia is usually due to incurable disorders such as dementia of the Alzheimer's type or multiple cerebral infarctions. An important aim of parallel investigation is to uncover reversible causes. Pseudodementia due to depression can be treated; however such patients usually show more concern and insight into their memory loss in addition to symptoms of depression. Mrs Freeman turned out to have changes on brain imaging consistent with the neuropsychological test profile and suggestive of dementia of Alzheimer's type. Intervention involved sensitive feedback, support, and advice to the family on managing the problems. This straightforward case has been used for clarity, however diagnosing advanced dementia is not difficult whereas diagnosing early dementia can be. In addition, depression and dementia are by no means mutually exclusive since elderly patients often become depressed when they are beginning to lose their mental faculties.

Interventions

Intervention in the acute setting can be tantalizing and frustrating because the turn-over of in-patients is high and because a specialist tertiary neuroscience centre may serve a population of 2–3 million, many of whom live some distance away. Specialist services (such as epilepsy surgery) are often supra-regional. Most work is necessarily time-limited, post-acute, out-patient follow-up.

Interventions are generally either neuropsychological rehabilitative procedures, or cognitive or behavioural treatments derived from mental health work. Rehabilitation is not as fully developed in acute neurology/neurosurgery as it should be; detailed assessment of the problems forms the basis of (limited) goal planning, education, and information-giving, and introduction of palliative coping strategies and techniques (such as a watch with an alarm, sticky-backed notes, a diary, Filofax or personal organizer, routine). Neurological/neurosurgical patients with emotional or behavioural problems may require a range of techniques, such as cognitive therapy for depression or anxiety (especially post-traumatic stress disorder), anger management, progressive muscle relaxation, sexual and relationship counselling, management of pain, etc.). Brain surgery is always a major life event. Sometimes the problems pre-date the neurological condition but are exacerbated by it or need tackling because they interfere with recovery; sometimes they are the direct result of an underlying neurological/neurosurgical condition (such as a frontal brain tumour or head injury). Either way they are often best dealt with by a neuropsychologist who is experienced with the neurological context and the constraints of memory loss, language difficulty, dysexecutive symptoms, sensory and perceptual problems, seizure activity, etc.

Consultation and team work issues

Neuropsychology cannot be useful clinically without liaison with parallel disciplines in the neurosciences. However it is important not to overestimate others' knowledge about neuropsychological variables: what often seems straightforward advice to us may be invaluable to the referrer. Liaison is particularly relevant in paediatric working. It is also crucial to understand that paediatric neuropsychology is not simply adult neuropsychology applied to children, and that a thorough grounding in general paediatric psychology, in the developmental context, and in cognitive development is key.

Case Study

Tom was a bright sparky 8-year-old boy who was referred from the children's neurosurgery ward because the nursing staff felt his parents were having difficulty coping. He had been admitted 6 weeks earlier to have a tumour removed which turned out to be benign. He had a stormy post-operative period with a fluctuating temperature, vomiting, headache, and general unwellness. This was due to inflammation (but not infection) of the meninges, the membranes covering the brain, which is a relatively common condition but unusual in this case in that it lasted longer than 2–3 weeks. Tom had improved and was more bright and cheerful since insertion of a drain to reduce the pressure of cerebrospinal fluid on the brain. Intervention involved seeing both Tom and his parents on the ward, as well as nursing staff, to assess the problem and intervene appropriately. Nursing staff felt Tom's parents were excessively anxious and 'difficult', by which they meant they were hostile and made constant and unrealistic demands. The parents had undergone a prolonged period of stress and uncertainty and felt their questions and concerns about Tom were being ignored by staff. Intervention involved daily sessions with the parents on the ward for a week to offer support, allow ventilation of feelings, provide medical information, problem-solve better coping strategies, and mobilize resources for their management of Tom. Work also involved liaison with ward staff to help re-frame interaction with the family more positively. On discharge, contact with the family continued. Tumours like Tom's do not normally result in any significant intellectual changes but affect balance and coordination, including fine coordination such as handwriting, and concentration. Advice needed to be given both to the parents and to Tom's school when he was ready to return, and encouragement to manage him as normally as possible (not easy when a child has been such a source of worry for so long). A full neuropsychological assessment was carried out at 3 months and results on Tom's strengths and weaknesses and the sequelae in terms of attention and coordination were discussed with Tom, his family, and teachers.

Research and audit

Research in the acute setting is at the sharp end of clinical practice and, in the current pressured NHS environment, predominantly aimed at evaluating outcome (cognitive status, functional disability, and health related quality of life). The British Medical Research Council, together with local Research and Development Committees, is concerned to enhance the quality of randomized clinical trials in the neurosciences and the potential future contribution of neuropsychologists in this area is considerable.

Rehabilitation/community settings

Most people with a neurological condition return home following acute care in the neuroscience and/or general hospital. However, some are transferred to a specialist in-patient rehabilitation centre and a few to a nursing home or residential care. Once back into the community some will continue to be seen for rehabilitation in hospital out-patient departments or through hospital outreach teams, some will be referred to local rehabilitation teams, and others to specialist neuro-rehabilitation services.

In rehabilitation and community settings, most referrals will be of people with head injury, stroke, or multiple sclerosis. As noted, the different pathology across neurological conditions results in a contrasting profile and course of disability. Furthermore, onset peaks at different stages in the life cycle: typically, head injury affects the young single adult; multiple sclerosis, the married person with a young family; and stroke, the older adult with grown-up children. The impact on the person and the family is therefore very variable, depending upon the specific pattern of disability, individual coping resources and personal, family, and social circumstances. In outlining the role of the clinical neuropsychologist in rehabilitation and the community we shall review the personal, social, and family impact of neurological conditions and the process of rehabilitation.

Personal, social, and family effects

The complex array of neurological disability often has far-reaching effects upon the person and their family, friends, and employers/work colleagues. While recovery and adaptation may continue over several years (particularly after traumatic brain injury) many will be faced with restrictions in independence, work, leisure, social, and family life. These restrictions are often shared by members of the family who may experience great stress in caring for and supporting the person with the injury, often amidst marked changes in family relationships, roles, and functioning.

Personal impact

As noted, a wide range of emotional reactions may be experienced by people with a neurological condition such as frustration and anger, fear and anxiety, depression and loss of confidence/self-esteem. For some this may be an early reaction to the trauma of neurological illness/injury, the loss of skills, roles, and control over one's life, the slow pace of progress and the uncertain extent of future recovery. For others, anxiety, depression, and loss of confidence may surface only later when the person has developed greater insight and/or attempted but struggled to resume former family, work, and social roles.

Independence

Neurological disability often results in a loss of independence: the need for assistance in personal and domestic care for those with severe physical disability; guidance and supervision for those with marked cognitive or behavioural changes. Others may be independent in their daily care but be unable to travel independently, or need help from the family in making decisions or in managing their financial affairs.

Occupation

Return to education, training, or work represents a major challenge for people with a neurological condition. Reduced cognitive and motor speed, limited concentration, unreliable memory, headaches, and/or fatigue render many uncompetitive. Others face more specific restrictions e.g. visual deficits may preclude driving; communication or executive difficulties may exclude managerial positions; poor behavioural control is unlikely to be tolerated in the workplace; emotional vulnerabilities may restrict the ability to cope with pressure or responsibility.

Leisure and social lives

Many with neurological disability face restrictions in their leisure activities, sports, cycling, and walking may be precluded by physical disability or impeded by an inability to drive; activities such as chess or bridge may be limited by poor memory, concentration, and reasoning; reading will be limited by visual/perceptual deficits. The person may also feel less inclined to pursue an active social life due to lack of confidence, low mood, intolerance to noise, or difficulty in contributing to conversations. Friends may struggle to cope with the changes in personality and behaviour: the irritability and aggression; the repetitive nature of conversation; and impulsivity, disinhibition, and general loss of refinement in social skills. As such, many friendships fall by the wayside, often resulting in social isolation. When this includes boy- and girlfriends, there may be a considerable degree of sexual frustration.

Family effects

Neurological disability also has a major impact upon the whole family, who are often left to cope with little support, especially where the person is left with subtle changes in cognition and personality, which may not be apparent to extended family and friends. Many primary carers experience considerable stress and distress. As life is tailored to meet the needs of the person, the occupational, leisure, and social lives of other family members often falters. Relationships with partners often become strained: physical disability may disrupt household routine and shared activities; cognitive impairment may limit conversation and companionship; changes in personality may alter the dynamics of the relationship; behavioural difficulties may cause both embarrassment socially and tension or threat within the relationship; changes in arousal may disrupt sexual relations. Spouses may also find the behaviour of their partner incompatible with that of a sexual partner. Spouses often struggle to cope with competing needs of work, home, partner, and children, feeling trapped in a relationship they no longer find rewarding. Some couples adapt positively, others remain close but with less intimacy and fun in the relationship, but for some the extent of disability is such that the relationship breaks down.

The consequences of neurological disability are therefore potentially devastating for the person with major restrictions in independence, occupation, leisure, and social life. This is often mirrored by substantial psychological and social impact upon the family, with couples often experiencing relationship and sexual difficulties. The challenge for rehabilitation services is to ensure that people with a neurological condition achieve and maintain optimal recovery and to facilitate long-term personal, family, vocational, and social adjustment. Clinical neuropsychologists have a vital role to play in the rehabilitation process and are increasingly leading community rehabilitation services.

Assessment

The complex long-term needs after neurological illness/injury require specialist and detailed assessment to clarify the nature of disability and plan rehabilitation. Whilst formal testing of cognitive function is undertaken routinely, supplementary assessment of emotional state and behaviour are often required either on initial assessment or during the course of rehabilitation. The fundamental principles of neuropsychological assessment are described above for the acute setting. In rehabilitation the focus of assessment tends to be more functional, in identifying strengths as well as weaknesses, in clarifying rehabilitation needs and potential and in monitoring recovery. In this respect the results of formal neuropsychological testing need to be considered alongside self and family reports, observations of both nursing and rehabilitation staff, and parallel assessments completed by other professionals.

In rehabilitation, neuropsychological assessment is commonly undertaken as part of an integrated multidisciplinary assessment process. This will routinely include medical, nursing, occupational therapy, physiotherapy, and speech and language therapy assessments, as well as neuropsychological assessment. In community brain injury services, clinical neuropsychology often plays a leading role in identification of overall needs on initial assessment, with neuropsychological testing a core component of both rehabilitation and specialist vocational assessment programmes (Tyerman, 1997).

Feedback of complex neuropsychological test results to the person (who frequently lacks insight and is quite defensive) and to the family (who may be understandably protective) is a highly skilled and challenging task. This can be undertaken separately or as part of integrated feedback of team assessments. The main purpose of feedback is to provide a framework of understanding, to explain the results and their implications and to engage the person positively in rehabilitation.

Interventions

The identified needs require a broad range of psychological interventions including: cognitive rehabilitation; behavioural management; neuropsychological counselling or psychological therapy; long-term psychotherapy; and specialist family interventions.

Cognitive rehabilitation

Core interventions are likely to include an explanation of cognitive function and specific cognitive impairment. This may be followed by re-orientation exercises, re-construction of lost memories, computer-based work on core skills and/or strategies to help compensate for skills deficits. Teaching about cognitive difficulties and general strategies can often be undertaken in group settings. In the longer term, the focus often shifts to exploring alternative ways of organizing tasks and limiting demands to cope with long-term difficulties, for example in the work place. Regular reviews and formal re-assessments are vital to monitor progress, review rehabilitation strategies and goals, and guide resettlement, especially in managing return to education or employment.

Behavioural management

Behavioural management is most commonly required after acquired brain injury. Early in recovery, people with brain injury are often restless and agitated and may display disinhibited, sometimes aggressive behaviour on the ward. Nursing and rehabilitation staff may require expert assessment and advice from the clinical neuropsychologist about the management of difficult behaviour. In some cases a psychiatric opinion and medication may be required on a temporary basis to manage severe behavioural problems.

When major problems persist a formal behaviour modification programme may be required. In extreme cases referral to a centre specializing in the management of severe behavioural problems may be appropriate.

Neuropsychological counselling/ psychological therapy

The course of recovery after neurological illness/injury is usually both uncertain and protracted. When the person is aware of his or her difficulties there may be fear, anxiety, and a profound sense of loss. When the person lacks insight there may be confusion, frustration, and aggression. Specialist neurorehabilitation counselling (e.g. provision of information, explanation, negotiation/monitoring of goals, promotion of insight/ realistic expectations, and resettlement planning) may serve a vital function in guiding and supporting the person through the complex process of rehabilitation and resettlement. This may be provided directly by psychologists or by other experienced rehabilitation staff, drawing on psychological expertise as appropriate. While individual neurorehabilitation counselling, ideally combined with person-focussed discussion/support groups, will meet many of the emotional needs of people with a neurological condition, some require individual psychological therapy. This will commonly include anxiety management, anger management, help with depression, post-traumatic stress counselling, and help with alcohol/drug abuse. Standard interventions are often ineffective in this context and have to be adapted both to compensate for the cognitive constraints of persons with neurological illness/injury and to take into account any loss of emotional and behavioural control.

Long-term psychotherapy

Given the complex nature of neurological illness/injury, it is not surprising that some struggle to adjust to long-term disability, particularly when cognitive impairment has reduced the capacity for self-appraisal and problem solving. In the confusion of the present and the uncertainty about the future, there is a tendency to cling to the illusory security of the past. Common difficulties in adjustment include: preoccupation with lost skills/roles with a failure to recognize remaining potential; a striving for an unattainable degree of recovery; repeated failure and loss of confidence/self-belief; social withdrawal due to fear of loss of emotional/behavioural control; strained family relationships; and social isolation. Individual psychotherapy, adapted to the neuropsychological constraints of the individual, offers a structure within which to assist the person forward in making sense of changes in themselves and their lives; in reviewing strengths and weaknesses; in identifying, clarifying, and prioritizing unresolved issues; and in finding the strength and direction through which to start to re-build their lives.

Working with families

It is vital to include the family as fully as possible in the process of rehabilitation. Whenever possible a family member should be included in initial interviews about past history, early recovery, and current problems, particularly when the person struggles with memory, and/or lacks insight into current difficulties. It is equally important to include the family in feedback of test results, to help the family to understand the nature and implications of difficulties and the rationale for proposed rehabilitation. Thereafter close liaison with the family is essential both to receive feedback about progress at home and to explain ongoing rehabilitation strategies which can then be reinforced at home. However, it is vital not to view family members as therapists, and great care is required not to add further to the stress on family members and/or alter the dynamics of family relationships. The needs of families warrant attention in their own right, as family members may themselves be in need of specialist advice and support in coping with the impact both upon themselves and the family as a whole. Relatives highly value the provision of specialist family services comprising individual counselling, relatives' educational workshops, follow-up workshops, and specialist couple/family counselling (Tyerman, 1997).

Interventions in rehabilitation and the community are therefore many and varied. For example, the core interventions provided within the Community Head Injury Service in Aylesbury are detailed in Figure 13.2. These will be illustrated with a case example.

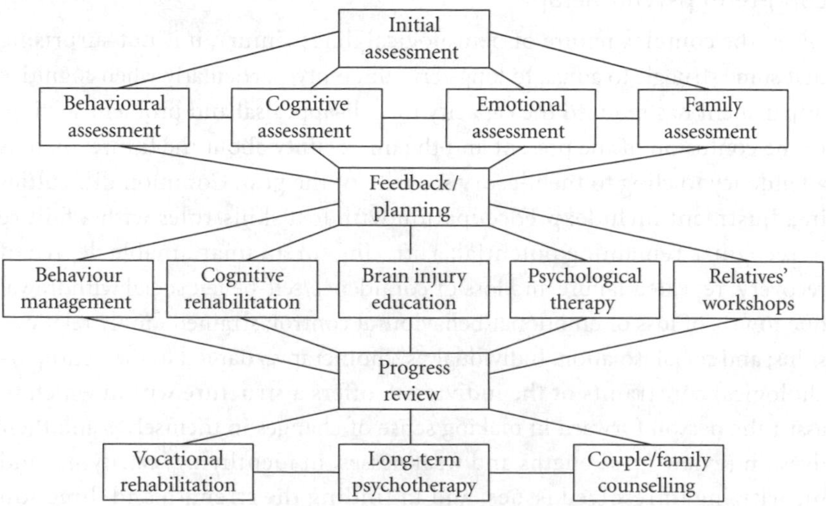

Fig. 13.2 Neuropsychological rehabilitation: A service example.

Case Study

Jeremy, a professional man in his late thirties, was living with his wife and 4-year-old daughter when he incurred a very severe head injury and orthopaedic injuries in a road traffic accident. He was admitted unconscious to his local general hospital where his level of consciousness gradually lifted but he remained in intensive care for 18 days and in hospital for 9 weeks.

Assessment: Jeremy was seen for initial assessment at 5 weeks post-injury. He had no recall of his accident or of the preceding few weeks and had only recently emerged from a post-traumatic amnesic state. At this early stage he was aware of some of his physical disability (fatigue, slurred speech, reduced vision) and cognitive difficulties (speed, memory, expressive language) and changes in emotion/behaviour (irritability, frustration, aggression, disinhibition, mood swings, and depression). His wife reported his major problems as his obsession with returning home, lack of insight, aggression, disinhibition, being overly talkative, and very self-critical. A neuropsychological assessment confirmed substantial cognitive impairment of a generalized nature: reduced general intellectual ability; word finding difficulties; visuo-perceptual difficulties; markedly reduced speed of information processing; and impaired verbal memory. He reported a low self-concept but no significant anxiety or depression.

General rehabilitation: After feedback of assessment results, Jeremy commenced an out-patient rehabilitation programme 2 days per week comprising: psychological therapy; occupational therapy; physiotherapy; and a weekly cognitive rehabilitation group programme. Our initial goals were to improve right hand/arm function, to improve constructional skills and to work on word finding and memory strategies. Individual psychological therapy sessions concentrated on emotional support and understanding of the rehabilitation programme. As he progressed, the focus of psychological input shifted to planning/organization skills and improving insight, awareness, and understanding. A neuropsychological re-assessment at 7 months confirmed substantial progress but speed of information processing and psychomotor speed remained below average and marked impairment of verbal memory persisted. At 10 months he felt that he had improved physically, cognitively, and in behaviour but acknowledged that he remained irritable and liable to lose his temper at home. He was by now becoming more aware of the range of his psychological difficulties, but with increased insight came a mild degree of anxiety and a high level of depression.

Vocational rehabilitation: At 9 months Jeremy joined a specialist vocational rehabilitation programme, attending a weekly work preparation group, two community vocational rehabilitation activities, individual project work, individual neurorehabilitation counselling and a weekly personal issues group. In groups he was noted to be outspoken, dominating and, at times, insensitive and dismissive of others. However, if criticized or feeling threatened, he tended to opt out of discussions. On individual project work he found it hard to accept guidance from staff and demonstrated marked difficulty with planning. By 16 months he reported that he had been 'terminated' from his former job and felt 'bitter' about the lack of contact with former colleagues. In line with progress, the emphasis gradually shifted from rehabilitation activities to individual project work, to a desktop publishing course and voluntary work. At 2 years post-injury he started a voluntary work trial at local printers—he coped well with technical skills, but had difficulty in planning and creative design work. After 6 months he started a second part-time work trial but this did not develop into a job as he had hoped. At 3 years post-injury he realized that he was not able to cope with the pressure of paid employment and decided to continue with part-time voluntary work. While our view was that he had the skills to work in a part-time supported capacity, this was not acceptable to him at that time. It was agreed that he would continue to work in a voluntary capacity, but that we would keep the door open in case he wished to seek paid employment in the future.

Couple Counselling: During rehabilitation Jeremy's wife was supported regularly by a specialist social worker. At one year the family situation was causing great concern with his wife reporting that he was preoccupied with the effects of his head injury and not coping with family life. He was noted to be irritable, frustrated (especially by his inability to drive and loss of independence), unable to discuss family matters without getting irritated, and verbally aggressive if challenged or criticized. He was intolerant of noise and unable to cope with the pressures of a young family—tending to opt out and take refuge in his computer. His relationship with his daughter was causing concern—not dealing well with discipline and struggling to cope with her demands or join in her play. Both partners rated the relationship as having 'very severe problems' with low levels of intellectual, emotional, and sexual intimacy. Over the next 2 years we sought to guide and support the couple in understanding the family impact of the head injury, in managing his anger, in re-building his relationship with his daughter, in facilitating open communication, and in supporting their relationship. A major challenge was to use specialist neuropsychological knowledge and skills to help him to compensate for his cognitive difficulties in order to participate productively in couple counselling. (He found it difficult to appreciate others' views—tending to dominate discussions, interrupt frequently, and see issues categorically from his own perspective.) While the couple remained somewhat distant with little sharing at a personal level and no physical intimacy, couple counselling served to contain confrontation and stabilize/support strained family relationships under extremely difficult circumstances.

Individual psychotherapy: As the lack of feelings of intimacy was a major long-term concern, Jeremy was offered exploratory sessions of psychotherapy. Unfortunately, the indication from these sessions was that he was not holding back on emotional intimacy or sexual arousal due to anxiety and/or lack of confidence, but rather that he was not experiencing any such feelings as a direct result of his injury. He did not appear ready yet to deal with the more sensitive issues in his marital relationship, remaining preoccupied with the effects of his head injury on himself. He appeared largely unaware of the impact of his expressed lack of feelings of intimacy upon his wife and further discussions focused on helping him to appreciate the impact of his injury, behaviour, and the current situation on his wife and family, as well as himself.

Follow Up: When followed up at 4 years post-injury Jeremy had continued with his part-time voluntary work and appeared somewhat more settled and relaxed. This was reported by his wife to have eased slightly the stress and friction within the family, although significant family tension remained and his wife continued to receive support. He was at this stage resigning himself to his residual disability and associated family, vocational, leisure, and social restrictions. Support for his wife continued on a regular but infrequent basis. The offer of further sessions of psychotherapy to assist him in long-term personal, family, and social adjustment remains open, as and when he wishes to take this up.

The above example illustrates the wide range of psychological interventions that may be required, in this example working continuously to promote recovery and adjustment over 4 years: individual/group cognitive rehabilitation; individual/group neurorehabilitation counselling; anger management; vocational rehabilitation; family education and support; couple counselling; and long-term psychotherapy. Such interventions are usually integrated within an interdisciplinary rehabilitation programme.

It is equally important to work in partnership with other health services (i.e. general hospital; specialist neuroscience services; and general practitioners) but also with other agencies: with Social Services to secure appropriate day care and residential care; with Jobcentre Plus to address vocational needs; with Education services for those wishing to continue with former or alternative studies; with voluntary agencies in distributing information, in providing specialist day care and in supporting families. Working in partnership, we can offer many people with neurological disability and their families the opportunity to optimize recovery and adjustment and, thereby, lay the foundation for a gradual rebuilding of their lives.

Conclusions

While sometimes thought of as overly academic, clinical neuropsychology is a rich blend of specialist neuropsychological expertise and core clinical psychology skills. We hope that we have conveyed a flavour of this fascinating and challenging area including something of the similarities and differences with other specialties. We hope too that we have provided an insight into the complex pathway of care from diagnosis and assessment in the acute setting, through rehabilitation of skills and behaviour, to the promotion of long-term personal, family, and social adjustment in the community.

While operating within a common neuropsychological framework, the nature of the work and core skills differ in emphasis across acute, rehabilitation, and community settings. As such, clinical neuropsychologists are a disparate group with different settings attracting practitioners with contrasting interests and skills. A basic grounding in neuropsychology is provided in clinical psychology training but practitioners need to develop their specialist expertise. The British Psychological Society Division of Neuropsychology was established in 1999. A number of post-qualification courses are now available, including two paediatric neuropsychology courses. Formal training via one of these, and a further post-graduate qualification, is now required for practitioner full membership of the division.

This is an exciting time in the neurosciences with major technical advances in *in vivo* imaging, image-guided neurosurgery and work on implants and neuronal plasticity. Computer technology also offers major potential benefits for those struggling to cope with neurological disability, but the challenge is to make such advances accessible to those with neuropsychological impairment. Advances in technology will hopefully extend the range of medical treatment and rehabilitation options. This will increase the need for specialist neuropsychological expertise.

Currently, services for people with neurological disability are patchy and disjointed with many identified gaps. However, services for people with neurological disability are increasingly supported by the development of national clinical guidelines, for example for head injury, multiple sclerosis, and stroke. The National Service Framework for Long-term Conditions (Department of Health, 2005), which focuses specifically on neurological conditions, sets national standards of care across the NHS and Social Services. This will hopefully provide a long-awaited opportunity for the development of coherent service provision for people with neurological disability over the next 10 years. Clinical neuropsychologists will need to play a major role in such developments.

References

Andrewes, D.G. (2001). *Neuropsychology: From theory to practice*. East Sussex: Psychology Press.

Department of Health (2005). *The National Service Framework for Long-term Conditions*. London: Department of Health.

Donaghy, M. (1997). *Neurology: Oxford Core Texts*. Oxford: Oxford University Press.

Goldstein, L.H. and McNeil, J.E. (2003). *Clinical Neuropsychology: A Practical Guide to Assessment and Management for Clinicians*. Chichester: Wiley.

Johnson, K.A. and Becker, J.A. (1999). *The Whole Brain Atlas on CD-ROM*. Philadelphia: Lippincott Williams and Wilkins.

Lezak, M.D. (1995). *Neuropsychological Assessment*. New York: Oxford University Press.

Lishman, W.A. (1997). *Organic Psychiatry: The Psychological Consequences of Cerebral Disorder, 3rd edn*. Oxford: Blackwell Scientific Publications.

Ogden, J.A. (1996). *Fractured Minds: A Case-Study Approach to Clinical Neuropsychology*. New York: Oxford University Press.

Tyerman, A. (1997). Head injury: community rehabilitation. In C.J. Goodwill, M.A. Chamberlain, and C. Evans (eds.), *Rehabilitation of the Physically Disabled Adult*. Cheltenham: Stanley Thornes.

Further reading

Anderson, V., Northam, E., Hendy, J., and Wrennall, J. (2001). *Developmental Neuropsychology: A Clinical Approach*. Hove: Psychology Press.

Broks, P. (2004). *Into the Silent Land: Travels in Neuropsychology*. London: Atlantic Books.

Clare, L. and Wilson, B.A. (1997). *Coping with Memory Problems. A Practical Guide for People with Memory Impairments, Their Relatives, Friends and Carers.* Bury St Edmunds: Thames Valley Test Corporation.

Cull, C. and Goldstein, L.H. (eds.) (1997). *The Clinical Psychologist's Handbook of Epilepsy: Assessment and Management.* London and New York: Routledge.

Goldstein, L.H. and McNeil, J.E. (2003). *Clinical Neuropsychology: A Practical Guide to Assessment and Management for Clinicians.* Chichester: Wiley.

Halligan, P., Kischka, U., and Marshall, J. (eds.)(2003). *Oxford Handbook of Clinical Neuropsychology.* Oxford: Oxford University Press.

Schacter, D.L. (2001). *How the Mind Forgets and Remembers: The Seven Sins of Memory.* London: Souvenir Press.

Chapter 14

Working with others

Tony Lavender and Sarah Allcock

Introduction

The ability to work effectively with others is an essential part of a clinical psychologist's role. The focus of this chapter will be on working with other professionals, organizations, and communities rather than with clients themselves as this aspect of a clinical psychologist's work has been covered more fully in earlier chapters. The tasks undertaken by the majority of health and social care services are complex and require that professionals are able to work together in a sophisticated manner in order to provide an effective service. This involves working with people from a diverse range of backgrounds, both in terms of professional and sociocultural factors. No one individual or profession has all the necessary skills to meet all of the needs of any client group or, in many cases, of an individual client.

Working with others also has the advantages of facilitating the coordination of a client's care, management of workloads, and provision of support and learning between colleagues. It also enables establishment of common priorities for professionals working with a particular client group, assisting with decisions about resource allocation, and organizational and service development. There is also evidence that working as part of a team can improve the performance of an individual team member (Pilling, 1991) and provide the most effective way of delivering care (Borrill *et al.*, 2000).

This chapter will begin with an outline of the contexts within which clinical psychologists work including services in which they work, the range of professionals and other staff with whom they work, and how government policy influences the contexts within which they work. Then five levels at which clinical psychologists work with others (adapted from Bender, 1991) will be outlined and examples given. These include direct work with another professional, work as a team member, consultation work with a client focus, consultation work with a team or organizational focus, and finally consultation work with a community focus. Finally conclusions will be drawn about current roles and future developments.

Context

The range of services within which clinical psychologists work is wide and growing. Consequently the services described here are not exhaustive but rather a sample of where clinical psychologists currently work. Clinical psychologists may, for example, work in any of the three tiers within Adult Mental Health Services. These are: primary care (which involves working services where people have first contact with the Health Services such as GP surgeries); secondary care (this includes services where primary care staff have referred patients because they do not have adequate resources or expertise to provide help, these services include Community Mental Health Teams and/or Acute inpatient psychiatric wards); or tertiary services (these are highly specialist services such as Assertive Outreach Teams and Therapeutic Communities usually for people with the most severe mental health problems). However they may also work with adults in a range of other services including forensic services (including outpatient settings, in secure units, and prison services), neuropsychology services (which includes people presenting with a range of neuropsychological problems or within a specialist service, such as a head injury unit), and drug and alcohol services to name just a few. Clinical psychologists working with children may similarly work in services at four levels: tier one (schools and community services); tier two (in GP surgeries); tier three (Child and Adolescent Community Mental Health Teams); or tier four (inpatient services) as well as some specialist services, such as those for Looked after Children or Sure Start. Services for older people and people with learning disabilities require clinical psychologists to work in day care centres and residential homes as well as multidisciplinary community teams. Clinical psychologists also work in health settings (such as general acute hospitals, specialist services such as pain management, and spinal injuries units) and increasingly in health promotion work.

Applied psychologists are chartered psychologists who work in a range of services and with a variety of client groups and now include those working as clinical, counselling, health, forensic, occupational, educational, and neuropsychological psychologists. A survey of applied psychologists in England in 2002 indicated that the majority of psychologists work in Adult Mental Health (35%) followed by Child (13%), Learning Disabilities (12%), and Older People (6%) (Lavender *et al.*, 2005). In the United Kingdom while clinical psychologists have expanded in numbers most rapidly, the other applied psychologies are also developing and it is now not unusual for different applied psychologists to also find themselves working together in the same service.

Within all the services clinical psychologists are required to work with a wide range of professionals. These include clinical colleagues, such as doctors, nurses, social workers, occupational therapists, and a variety of different therapists and other professionals, as well as staff who may not be professionally trained but who may have a wealth of experience and are often in closest contact with the client (e.g. mental health support time recovery workers). Specialist therapists that a clinical psychologist might be working with include speech therapists, physiotherapists, psychotherapists, family, art, and music therapists. Other professionals might include health visitors, teachers, and police officers. Within each of these professional groups there is often a wide range of roles that members of each group may take. For example, nurses' roles can vary from providing the daily care of a client's physical needs on acute medical wards, to the provision of specialist therapy (e.g. Cognitive Behaviour Therapy) within which they may have a high level of training, to expertise in community mental health teams, to managing an entire team or service. Furthermore, it is not only clinical colleagues with whom clinical psychologists need to be able to work effectively but also service managers, finance directors, and administrative colleagues, including secretaries, information technology staff, and human resource personnel.

The vast majority of clinical psychologists in the United Kingdom work in public sector contexts, mainly the health service, but also social services, prison services, the voluntary sector, and police. Governments and the policies they generate have a significant influence on these service contexts in two major ways. First, government policy has a significant impact on the structure of organizations within which psychologists work. For example, all NHS hospitals in the United Kingdom are currently administered as part of NHS Trusts, while GP surgeries are all part of Primary Care Trusts (PCTs). In a recent policy change (DOH, 2001), PCTs now directly receive over 70% of the NHS budget and commission services from a range of providers, including NHS Trusts. This has given them great power to influence services provided, including psychology. Second, government policy has a significant influence on the type of services that can be provided and there has been a significant trend to insist that psychological interventions are an essential part of service provision. This has resulted, in part, from the increasing evidence for the effectiveness of psychological interventions in relieving the psychological distress of service users (e.g. Roth and Fonagy, 2004). This demand for psychological interventions to be made available can be seen in the National Service Frameworks developed for many service areas, in particular mental health and children's services (DOH, 1999, 2004). The current political/government context has proved to be fertile ground for the development of applied psychology.

Professionalization, networking, and team working

An important issue that successive government policies have tried to address over the last two decades is the need for greater networking and team working in the NHS. Networking involves professionals working for different organizations, with potentially different tasks, but with the same client group, and sharing information to serve the client's interests. Examples include: a doctor explaining the results of medical tests which may have implications for understanding a client's psychological state to their psychologist; a psychologist talking to social services about their concerns about a child who, for example, may be caring for an ill or disabled parent; or a meeting between professionals from health, education, and social services to monitor the effectiveness of the local child protection procedures.

In contrast, team working involves different professionals working together in the same organization and with the same task. For a team to function effectively its members need to be clear about their purpose, goals, and values which, ideally, should be coherent and agreed. However difficulties can arise in team working which have often been characterized as professional staff (doctors, nurses, psychologists, occupational therapists, social workers, etc.) operating in a way that benefits the development of the profession rather than the service. It is argued that this professional self-interest mitigates against operating collectively and co-operatively to the benefit of the team and the client.

This represents a rather simplistic view but nevertheless contains some elements of truth. Working with other professional groups who have different training, based on different assumptions, can be challenging. Thus the highly biologically focused doctor or nurse may act with certainty about genetic and biological factors and deny the relevance of most psychological factors. The psychologist may find it difficult to acknowledge the benefits of medication. This complex mix of beliefs about the nature of the problems that the clients are facing means that it can be difficult for the different professions to come together to produce a coherent and agreed plan for the client.

Another important set of related organizational issues that can impact on team working concern the exercise of leadership, management, power, and authority (Schein, 1987). 'Leadership' involves behaviour by some members to determine the purpose and values of an organization. 'Management' involves the behaviour of members to ensure that the organization's purpose and values are achieved. 'Power', refers to the ability to control/influence the behaviour of others, and 'authority' the amount of influence that is legitimately granted to a particular job role. In many health care organizations the lack of clarity about these roles can lead to problems in team working. For example, in many community mental health teams the leadership of the team is not clear. Often there are disputes about whether the leader is the manager of the team (often with a nursing or social work background), the consultant psychiatrist (i.e. the lead doctor), or another member of the team (e.g. psychologist). This can all make team working rather complicated. In such situations a more collective form of leadership is often required, but teams can struggle to find ways to resolve the leadership issues. Psychologists can become as lost in this issue as other team members but they may also have the skills to help resolve such problems (see section on consultation with a team or organization focus later in the chapter).

Psychologists have particular issues in relation to leadership, management, power, and authority because they rarely arrive in an organizational position where their leadership, management, and authority are very clear. This means that their ability to influence others (i.e. power) is often dependent on their ability to manage interpersonal relationships and perceived usefulness to clients and the team. Clinical psychologists are also generally perceived as reasonably high status, which is in part a result of the level of professional/ academic qualifications and pay compared with many other team members, and in part due to their long history in the NHS compared to other applied psychologists. This status carries with it a certain amount of power but unless the psychologists can prove themselves in terms of team relations and clinical utility, this source of power, or ability to influence others rapidly dissipates.

This complex set of issues has, at times, led psychologists to doubt the value of team working. Modern services however are destined to be delivered by teams and unless psychologists learn to work constructively in teams it is unlikely that psychologists will have a significant impact on services in which they work. Many psychologists of course do make very positive contributions and the rest of the chapter illustrates how this can be done.

Levels of working with others

It is possible to identify five levels at which clinical psychologists work with others. However, no matter at which level, the approach remains guided by the clinical psychologist's core competencies of engagement and assessment, formulation, intervention, evaluation, and communication within a framework of ethical, professional, and reflective practice (BPS, 2003). In the following sections, the type of work involved at each level will be described with some examples to illustrate practice.

Direct work with other professionals

The needs of many clients are too complex to be met by one professional and so two or more professionals often find themselves working with the same client. This can be structured in two ways: parallel work and co-working.

Parallel work

Parallel work is where two or more professionals are working with the same client at the same time but in different contexts. For example, the evidence base suggests that a combination of antidepressant medication and psychological therapy are more effective in treating depression than either of these alone (Roth and Fonagy, 2004) and so it is common for adults within a community mental health team to be seen by both a psychiatrist for medication and a clinical psychologist for psychological therapy.

Similarly, clients may be working with professionals from more than one service or agency, as in the example below:

Case Study

Jake was a 5-year-old boy referred to the Child and Adolescent Mental Health team by the family's Health Visitor due to severe behaviour problems. Jake, his mother, Karen, and baby sister, Chloe, were seen for an assessment by the Clinical Psychologist in the team. Karen was very grateful for the appointment as she had been struggling with Jake's behaviour since Chloe's birth 6 months previously. If she was occupied with Chloe or simply exhausted and trying to rest, Jake would demand her attention and, when he did not get it, throw violent tantrums which placed himself and the family's belongings at risk. Karen was scared to leave him alone with Chloe in case he harmed her but often had to leave Chloe to attend to Jake. She had recently been very concerned that Jake was beginning to exhibit similar behaviour at his new school and, on one occasion, Jake had spent almost the entire day alone in the headteacher's office to prevent him getting in more trouble. Karen described feeling low in mood since Chloe's birth and was aware that she was not giving Jake the time and attention he needed. She had suffered from post-natal depression briefly after Jake had been born, thought that she may be experiencing similar symptoms again, and was concerned that other people, particularly Jake's school, would think her a poor mother. Her husband Simon worked long hours and was often away from home for days at a time. Simon was concerned about Jake's behaviour and his wife's low mood but often felt too stressed and tired to be actively involved in looking after the children.

The clinical psychologist formulated Jake's behaviour as an expression of his unhappiness about the loss of his mother's undivided attention, since his sister's birth coincided with his mother's depression and his starting primary school all at the same time. As his temper tantrums succeeded in attracting the attention both of his mother at home and his teacher in school, Jake's behaviour was being positively reinforced.

With the family's agreement, the clinical psychologist referred Karen to Adult Mental Health Services for assessment of possible post-natal depression. Karen and the clinical psychologist worked together to devise a behavioural programme in which Jake would be rewarded for behaving well while his tantrums would not be reinforced. They agreed that

Karen and Jake meet for a few sessions to help Jake engage actively in changing his behaviour using externalization techniques (where the problem is redefined as something external to the child allowing the child to join with their family in overcoming it).

The psychologist also contacted Jake's primary school and met with his teacher. Together they worked out how to adapt these ideas for school. The teacher devised a behavioural programme which they agreed with Jake and Karen before putting into practice. After a few initial hitches, Jake's behaviour improved dramatically. While he was still slightly envious of his sister, when the clinical psychologist met with him for the last time, he was proud of himself for having successfully beaten the tempers.

One of the issues that can arise in this sort of work is the coordination of care. Put simply each professional must have an understanding of what the other is doing so that different professionals/services avoid providing the same service or do not mistakenly assume the other is providing a service. Carefully coordinated services are vital in providing high quality care. The lack of coordination has resulted in some tragic outcomes for service users, their relatives, and members of the public. In the above example it was important that the clinical psychologist was in contact with the school and did not just assume that they would put a behavioural programme in place.

Ethical issues frequently arise in such work, including informed consent and confidentiality. Thus, in the above example, the psychologist was careful to seek the family's consent before contacting other agencies. In addition, the psychologist worked with the school to facilitate their ability to manage Jake's behaviour without passing on confidential information, such as information about Karen's post-natal depression.

Co-working

Sometimes a client may benefit from seeing more than one professional at the same time and in the same context. Sometimes this is to prevent the client having to undergo unnecessary assessments, such as when a risk assessment is needed by both a Mental Health Team and a Social Services Department or when a client's needs appear to fall between the boundaries of two services. In both examples the cooperation of different services provides easier access for the clients to the most appropriate service to meet their needs.

At other times clients may benefit from therapeutic work involving seeing more than one member of a team at the same time. For example, family therapy approaches often require that one or more of the family therapist's colleagues act as a 'reflecting team'; therapeutic groups are often run by more than one professional who may or may not be from the same professional background; partnership/marital and sexual therapy is similar; and many brief therapy consultation models advocate co-working of two different professionals.

These approaches have the advantages of enabling clients' problems to be viewed from multiple perspectives, thereby facilitating a richer formulation and a broader understanding of possible ways of intervening. In order for these approaches to be effective, clinical psychologists need to be able to develop close working relationships with colleagues in which there is shared understanding of the purpose of the work alongside respect for differences between each other's approach.

A brief example of marital therapy illustrates this.

Case Study

A couple in their mid-thirties were seen by a female clinical psychologist and a male social worker after an assessment by the psychologist had indicated significant relationship problems, including lack of communication, poor sexual relationship, and significant anxiety about the relationship breaking down. It was decided that seeing a male and female therapist could be helpful in terms of avoiding unbalanced gender alliances in the therapy. A series of six fortnightly sessions were held. The first involved taking a history of each individual up to the point where they met and the second a history of how they met and how the difficulties had emerged. This process served to throw light on their difficulties in communication, failure to listen (both would frequently interrupt), and a tendency to blame rather than understand. The therapists helped the couple to notice this and asked them during the second session to report their understanding of the other's point of view. Between the second and third sessions the wife phoned the psychologist saying things were getting worse and she was becoming more anxious. An individual session was arranged and the wife recounted a period 3 years ago when the relationship had not been going well and she had an affair. The husband did not know and she was feeling increasingly that she needed to tell him and regain the honesty in the relationship, but was afraid the relationship would break up. They discussed how, the way the relationship was currently going, this was indeed likely and the wife appeared to be coming to the conclusion that she must talk to her husband about the affair. In the third joint session it was clear nothing had been said and the couple struggled to describe their current difficulties. The social worker had observed how the husband had been very guarded when discussing previous difficulties and asked if there was something difficult to say. After some silence, the husband said he knew his wife had been involved in an affair but had not wanted to say because he was angry and thought if he raised the issue the relationship would collapse. His wife broke down at this point. The husband then said he had wanted to punish her by attacking her verbally but that it was destroying the relationship. The remaining sessions were spent in working with them to rebuild and repair the relationship. There was a strong sense in this work that the two therapists of different gender had facilitated the communication in a way that may have proved more difficult for a therapist working alone.

Work as a team member

As with many health and social care professionals, the majority of clinical psychologists now work as members of multidisciplinary teams. In these teams they adopt a number of roles which are also shared by other team members, including:

- Direct work with clients for assessment and intervention. While a clinical psychologist may be unique in terms of their training in multiple therapeutic models (behavioural, cognitive, systemic, psychotherapeutic, and community perspectives) many other members of the team may also have training in the same models, such as psychoanalytic psychotherapists, cognitive-behavioural therapists, and family therapists, while other colleagues may have completed such training in addition to their original professional qualifications.
- Participating in meetings to discuss the needs of clients. These may include meetings to decide whether referrals will be accepted by the team and to assess their urgency, or to decide which clients will be seen by which team members, or to give and receive advice about ongoing client work.
- Acting as a care coordinator for clients who have more complex needs requiring the involvement of several professionals and/or services. The care coordinator takes responsibility for managing the network of professionals involved and ensuring that the client's needs are being met.
- Participating in meetings to discuss the management, functioning, and needs of the team such as team business meetings, team building days, and working groups for specific projects.
- Representing the team to other services and agencies. This may be in relation to a particular client, such as when a representative from a community team is asked to attend a case conference at an in-patient unit or social services department, or in relation to service development, such as a working group to develop projects that will operate across service boundaries.

There are also a number of skills and roles that clinical psychologists may be particularly competent to undertake. Perhaps one of the most unique skills in relation to direct work is the use of formulation to bring together demographic and personal information about the client, with psychological theory and research evidence, to provide a coherent psychological understanding of the client's problems. This formulation is then used to inform the nature of any intervention. Such an approach contrasts with a medical approach where the focus of any assessment is on identifying symptoms or a group of symptoms that lead to a particular diagnosis.

Research and audit are also often carried out by clinical psychologists as part of their role within a team. Clinical psychologists' training is strong in this area. Carrying out research and audit involves a great deal of work with colleagues not only in designing and carrying out the project, but also in following through communicating about the results and ensuring any implications/recommendations are implemented. The example below is intended to illustrate this.

Case Study

A Community Adult Mental Health Team had been operating with a number of vacancies for some months as a result of which clients were having to wait almost a year to be seen. The team felt this was unacceptable and established a working group to devise possible solutions, including a clinical psychologist, family therapist, and senior house officer (SHO) on a 6-month placement as part of her training in psychiatry. The group looked at the numbers of referrals, the number of people in the team, and the number of people being discharged from the service. They decided that the only way for the team to see people sooner was to work with clients for less time. Both the family therapist and the clinical psychologist had learnt about Brief Therapy Consultation Models as part of their training. The clinical psychologist undertook a literature review that encompassed the theoretical background of the approach and the results of outcome studies. The group discussed how the model might be implemented in their team and presented the idea to the rest of the team who were very interested but had concerns about the needs of clients being adequately met. A 6-month pilot was agreed. The psychologist disseminated the literature review to the rest of the team and established a discussion group for colleagues to share their questions and experiences. The psychologist also arranged a system whereby records were kept about the outcome of each case and clients were sent questionnaires about their views of the new service. After 6 months an audit was conducted by the SHO as part of her training which was supervised by the clinical psychologist. The results were overwhelmingly positive and, after presentation to the team, it was agreed the model would be adopted as routine practice. The waiting list reduced to 6 months and other teams in the Trust began to express interest in the approach, following which the clinical psychologist and family therapist agreed to present the model and audit to others in the Trust and at a conference.

Consultation with a client focus

The next way that clinical psychologists work with other professionals is by consulting with them in order to improve the service provided to clients. Clinical psychologists can consult at different levels, the first of which has an individual client focus and can be either guidance (i.e. advice and practical suggestions) or supervision.

Guidance

Clinical psychologists may be asked by a team to provide advice regarding a particular client, either to help them understand the client's needs from a psychological perspective, or to design and implement an intervention. For example, clinical psychologists may be asked to provide guidance for staff in a hostel for people with long-term mental health problems about the experience of caring for particular residents or, as in the example below, to help staff in a care home for people with severe learning disabilities devise an intervention to assist with a resident's behaviour.

Case Study

Harry was a 45-year-old man with severe learning disabilities who had been living at Spring House residential home for 6 months. Before that he had lived with his parents. He had moved after the sudden death of his father and because his mother feared that she would be unable to manage caring for Harry alone. The clinical psychologist was contacted by Harry's keyworker for guidance on how to manage Harry's behaviour. In particular he was stealing food from the kitchen, eating one or two mouthfuls, and then leaving the rest. When the staff challenged Harry about his behaviour he simply giggled; consequently he was viewed as being deliberately uncooperative and was becoming increasingly unpopular amongst both staff and residents. The psychologist agreed to collect some background information, meet with staff to come to an understanding about what was underlying Harry's behaviour, and devise an intervention.

The clinical psychologist read Harry's notes, observed him in the home, and contacted Harry's mother to find out about him before he moved to Spring House. This suggested that, while Harry's overall ability level fell within the severe learning disability range, his social skills were significantly more advanced. In Spring House Harry spent most of his time alone. He seemed to get frustrated in his attempts to communicate with other residents, who were not as socially skilled, while the staff were so busy meeting the needs of less able residents that the only prolonged contact they had with Harry was when he went into the kitchen to help himself to food. Harry's mother said his father used to spend a lot of time with Harry, taking him for walks and to the pub regularly. She also said that Harry had always liked his food and had enjoyed helping her prepare family meals.

The clinical psychologist then met with the staff team and shared this information with them. From this followed a new understanding of Harry's behaviour, as being a method of gaining the social contact and pleasure in food that he had lost since his father's death. The psychologist explained how challenging behaviour could be understood as communication and could be reinforced by the reactions received.

The staff became much more aware of how much Harry's life had changed since his father's death and felt more sympathy and less anger towards him. It was decided to reinstate Harry's walks and visits to the pub with his keyworker, and a plan was agreed whereby Harry would be able to help preparing tea and snacks for other residents thereby having contact both with food and staff. A month later the keyworker reported that, not only was Harry's behaviour much improved, but now he was also very popular amongst the residents, bringing them drinks and sitting with them when the staff were occupied.

In such work the clinical psychologist will try to ensure that staff are enabled and empowered by the advice. In the best examples of such work, staff are left feeling both able to deal with the particular client and also to generalize the learning to working with other clients. It is however important for the psychologist not to lose their humility when meeting experienced colleagues from other professions from whom they need to draw guidance and advice.

Supervision

Clinical psychologists can also be asked to offer supervision to other professionals or other clinical psychologists on their work with clients. This can be done individually, such as supervising the work of a community psychiatric nurse who is keen to develop skills in Cognitive Behaviour Therapy, or of a cognitive behavioural therapist who is struggling with their feelings towards a particular client and wanting an opportunity to think about the impact of psychodynamic processes. Alternatively clinical psychologists might offer group supervision to a staff group trying to deal with their work in particular health care settings (e.g. residential homes, day care services, or therapeutic communities), or in particular therapies in which the psychologist has some expertise. The advantage of group supervision is that it enables the use of the processes and skills within the group, and also can be more cost-effective in offering more people supervision in a limited amount of time.

In addition to providing supervision clinical psychologists are expected to receive supervision about their own work. Indeed it is now a British Psychological Society requirement that psychologists engage in their own supervision in order to continue to practice. This supervision is often provided by other clinical psychologists but it is now quite common for supervision to be provided by a broader range of professionals, including other applied psychologists and specialist therapists.

Consultation with a team or organizational focus

Health and social care is increasingly being provided by teams of professionals (Borrill *et al.*, 2000). Working as part of a team can not only be enjoyable and provide the most effective way to deliver care, but can also run into difficulties, most commonly arising because of teams' lack of clarity about their main task and the roles required by individuals to complete that task (such as those discussed at the beginning of this chapter). They can also arise as a result of problematic dynamic processes between members of the team that prevent the teams from completing their tasks. Clinical psychologists can be asked to provide consultation to teams where they are not a member (i.e. as external consultants) or to provide consultation to a team where they are a member (i.e. as member consultants). This later role is quite problematic particularly if the difficulties are about the dynamics of the team, as the psychologist is likely to be contributing to those problematic processes. In this short introduction to consultation work with others we will discuss and provide an example only of external consultation.

Case Study

A clinical psychologist known for his work with teams was asked to facilitate an away day for a team of 17 professionals to look at problems they were facing. The team provided an in-patient assessment service for older people with mental health problems suspected to be suffering with the early stages of dementia. The psychologist decided that, if there were difficulties, it would be better to understand them before agreeing that such a facilitated day was the most appropriate way to address the problems.

The psychologist met three team members (the psychiatrist, the clinical psychologist, and the senior nurse) nominated by the team to discuss issues prior to the away day. A number of issues emerged as problematic during the course of this discussion. It was clear that there had been difficulties about the leadership of the team for 6 months, since the time when the current team had been formed from the merger of two teams. The two teams had previously existed to cover two different geographical areas but had been forcibly merged into a single team covering the two areas, plus an additional area. They also had lost a number of long-standing members of staff and were having difficulty recruiting. Morale was described as low.

The psychologist negotiated with the three team members that the problems facing the team were unlikely to be solved in the single away day and asked if the team might consider a series of events (a mixture of days, half days, and some individual consultations) over a period of 18 months. After taking this back to the team, an agreement was reached. The first phase of the work was to help the team develop a shared understanding of the present situation and to identify what aspects were most problematic. This was done using a mapping exercise, at a whole team meeting, where all members were asked individually to put their difficult issues on small cards and then, with the help of the psychologist (facilitator), created a map on a large wall of the collective issues/problems. Most problematic issues identified included rivalries and fighting between the two old teams, lack of clarity about leadership roles within the team, and the way they were unable to agree on a common approach to clients referred to the service.

Sessions were organized for the team to develop a vision or clear view about how they wished the team to work in each of these areas and then to check whether they had the resources to deliver. As each of these issues were tackled the team developed a new way of working together, began to meet the goals set by the wider organization (the NHS Trust) and to feel more positive about each other. The psychologist's role was essentially to facilitate the development of the team by helping them define the nature of their primary (main) task, to explore how best to achieve this and, along the way, help them to identify and address the destructive group processes that had arisen in the team. At the end of the 18 months, while some difficulties in recruitment remained, the team was receiving positive feedback from the NHS Trust, had developed a common way of assessing clients, were meeting regularly to review their work and reported significantly improved morale.

The example described above focuses on work with particular teams in an organization. An increasing number of more senior clinical psychologists now work with entire organizations or significant parts of large organizations. This work and approach is somewhat similar to that described with teams and usually extends over a significant period. This work is called organizational process consultancy (Schein, 1987) and aims to help foster the development of a healthy organization by encouraging key members of the organization to address key transformational factors that concern the purpose and overall functioning of the organization (i.e. leadership, values, strategy, and impact of developments in the external world) and the transactional factors that concern the day-to-day operation of the organization (i.e. policies, procedures, ways of completing the primary task, organizational structure, capacity, capability, and motivation of staff). Working with staff on helping them to identify those factors that are being dealt with poorly and then using their skills and knowledge to address the identified problem is becoming an increasing part of the work of senior psychologists.

Consultation with a community focus

The role of clinical psychologists in working with whole communities is becoming increasingly important, particularly for communities where traditional services are less accessible perhaps because people within that community are unaware of the service and do not therefore request support from it. Other groups may be underreferred by professionals in the community such as GPs, schools, community doctors and nurses, and social workers. For example, it is estimated that only 15% of dementia sufferers are referred for professional help (Bender, 1991). Finally a community may believe that a service is not relevant or suitable for their particular sociocultural group. For example, some ethnic groups may find that the traditional approach of mental health services to phenomena such as hearing voices directly contradicts their own understanding of the causes and meanings of these phenomena.

Consultation at a community level requires that the clinical psychologist takes a person-in-context perspective in which the focus is as much on the context and its impact on the individual as on the individuals themselves. Orford (1992) suggests that the main principles of consulting at a community level are to help people understand the connection between social and economic reality and states of health and well-being, to help them join together with others with similar realities to give voice to this understanding, and finally to help the community engage in collective action to change these realities. Bostock and Beck (1993) describe the following example.

Case Study

A clinical psychologist working in primary care joined the local Community Forum which had been set up to develop a cohesive approach to improving the area by addressing the concerns of local people in a part of Nottingham at a time when the city was bidding for

City Challenge status. However, the regular attendees at the forum were nearly all professionals and there was concern that there was not enough representation from the local residents. So it was decided that a survey of local people's opinions should be made and that this would have two goals: to gain knowledge about issues in the area which people thought affected their physical and psychological health, and to encourage active engagement between the forum and members of the local community.

The clinical psychologist advised on an appropriate methodology to achieve these goals and all of the members of the forum took part in semi-structured interviews with 123 people in the local community. The clinical psychologist analysed the results which were then presented at a Public Meeting. People who had participated in the research were invited as was a local councillor. The meeting was also widely advertised in the community. Twenty-eight local residents attended. At the meeting a number of small groups worked on developing ideas to tackle the concerns raised in the research and, as a result of this, the structure of the forum was changed to a network of small groups concerned with different issues with a steering group managing organizational issues. The small groups have worked on projects, such as, getting local teenagers' views about leisure facilities, pursuing the development of specific sites for children's play areas, setting up a parents' and toddlers' group, employing someone to set up Neighbourhood Concern groups, and writing a local resource directory for parents and young children. The clinical psychologist involved herself in the group looking at play and play provision. More than 100 local people became involved in the small groups and several community representatives were appointed to posts within the City Challenge organization, which went on to provide funding for many of these projects.

This work involves clinical psychologists working with a range of professionals and others who had not traditionally worked with NHS professionals. These include local self-help groups, local education college staff, community workers, residential association members, housing association staff, and local counsellors. This new area of working is gathering momentum as clinical psychologists' awareness grows of the power of the social context to influence people's psychological health.

Conclusions

It should be evident that the work of the clinical psychologist involves much more than working on a one-to-one basis with clients. Not all psychologists are involved in all the levels described in this chapter but all are significantly involved in working with other people. Modern health and social care is delivered by teams and networks of professionals, and psychologists have to learn to work cooperatively and effectively with these others. It should also be evident that the scope of the discipline is expanding fast from its roots, in terms of the type of therapeutic work, the type of clients, and the range of 'others' with whom they work. The future looks positive as long as clinical psychologists continue to see the work 'with others' as an integral part of what they do and a part to which they have an enormous amount to contribute.

References

Bender, M. (1991). Levels of service delivery: An extension and elaboration. *Clinical Psychology Forum*, Oct, 15–19.

Borrill, C., West, M., Shaphiro, D., and Rees, A. (2000). Team working and effectiveness in health care. *British Journal of Health Care Management*, **6**(8), 364–71.

Bostock, J. and Beck, D. (1993). Participating in social enquiry and action. *Journal of Community and Applied Psychology*, **3**, 213–24.

British Psychological Society (2003). *Criteria for the Accreditation of Postgraduate Training Programmes in Clinical Psychology*. Leicester: British Psychological Society.

Department Of Health (1999). *National Service Framework: Mental Health*. London: The Stationary Office.

Department Of Health (2001). *Shifting The Balance Of Power Within The NHS*. London: The Stationary Office.

Department Of Health (2004). *National Service Framework for Children, Young People and Maternity Services*. London: The Stationary Office.

Lavender, A., Gray, I., and Richardson, A. (2004). *Survey of Applied Psychologists in England*. Leicester: BPS Publications.

Orford, J. (1992). *Community Psychology: Theory and Practice*. Chichester: Wiley.

Pilling, S. (1991). *Rehabilitation and Community Care*. London: Routledge.

Roth, A. and Fonaghy (2004). *What Works for Whom*. London: Brunner Routledge.

Schein, E. (1987). *Process Consultation*. Wokingham: Addison Wesley.

Further reading

Division of Clinical Psychology (2004). *Working in Teams*. Leicester: British Psychological Society.

Hayes, N. (1997). *Successful Team Management*. London: International Thomson Business Press.

Schein, E. (1987). *Process Consultation*. Wokingham: Addison Wesley.

Chapter 15

Working in cross-cultural and international settings

John Hall

Introduction: The European and North American beginnings of psychology

The formal discipline of psychology began as essentially a western European science. The subject matter with which it deals was originally drawn from a range of backgrounds, with an appeal to philosophy from classical Greece, and to the empiricists Locke and Hume in the eighteenth century, founded against a background of nineteenth-century European physiology and psychophysics, and nourished with mostly American empirical evidence. The conventional dating of the beginnings of academic psychology in 1879 in a laboratory at Leipzig only underlines this point.

As the nineteenth century moved to the twentieth, individual nation-states established national psychological bodies, the first two of which were the American Psychological Association in 1892 and the British Psychological Society in 1901, and psychologists set up international meetings. The initial World Congresses of Psychology, starting with the first in Paris of 1889, and then successively in London, Munich, Paris, Rome, and Geneva in 1909, all continued to give the clear message that psychology as an international movement was firmly based on western European and North American foundations. The first psychological laboratory was German, the first psychometric tests were French, and the first widespread use of psychological screening tests was carried out in the United States during the First World War. The early development of clinical psychology accordingly reproduced this Euro-centric view, with, for example, the items of intelligence tests assuming education within a western Judeo-Christian culture.

During the succeeding century, the world has changed. Former undeveloped colonial countries have become independent major international economies. Chinese is now the second most common world language, and the majority of Spanish speakers are in South America. The range of world cultures can be encountered in a variety of ways. First, directly by travel to other countries, and also directly by migration, so that in many of the founding psychological nations there are now significant ethnic minorities, often reflecting past economic and colonial links. Second, world cultures are also encountered indirectly through television and other media. All of these cultures have their own health beliefs and traditions of personal and social relationships and of health care, that may be linked to particular religious or philosophical views of personhood and the body.

Nonetheless, the predominant image of psychology continues to be conveyed by American psychology, both because the majority of the leading journals and textbooks are American, and because of the dominance of English as the most accessible second language. American psychology and European psychology continue to be ethnocentric, although in recent years there have been some interesting and stimulating explorations of other ideas, for example the applications of ideas of the Russian writer Vygotsky into developmental psychology, and from there into clinical psychology through the model now promoted in Cognitive Analytic Therapy. Nevertheless, psychology remains by and large dominated by Western discourse. Berry *et al.* (1992) suggest that from a perspective of cross-cultural psychology, there are four levels of ethnocentrism:

- the use of culturally inappropriate questions or stimuli;
- the use of culturally specific methods;
- culturally specific conceptualization and formulations;
- choice of research topics and applications that are culturally specific.

One factor commonly identified by psychologists working in non-Western cultures is the tension between the individualistic assumptions of Western psychology and the collective philosophy of the countries in which they work. This suggests a number of responses. First, applied psychologists should search for any primary data obtained by indigenous psychologists working in the community of origin of a presented client or patient. Second, primary data-collection and research in a new host country must encompass the range of cultural backgrounds within a society, and the research methods and questions asked must be sensitive to those differing backgrounds. Third, the applications of that research must equally take account of the range of cultural backgrounds, and of the limitations of available research when no primary data at all may be available for a particular cultural sub-group.

Understanding cultures

The term 'culture' encompasses a number of different aspects. Culture may be seen as a framework, or set of guidelines, within which we negotiate our relationships with others. It may be seen as a process by which that culture is transmitted. Also it may be seen as a communication system, spoken and written, non-verbal and symbolic, which has a shared significance for all members of the cultural group. Culture is not simply about ascribed group membership on the basis of these aspects; it is also an issue of felt identity.

Cultures are many-layered and exist at a number of levels. For people outside a culture, a language, a form of diet, types of clothing, and sets of customs and beliefs may define the culture. Within a culture, more subtle cues indicate not only regional differences within the culture, but convey messages of relative status, function, and locality. In between these, members of other cultures may understand some of the more subtle cues, but not all of them, and so may miss finely nuanced words and gestures. One key cue is that of spoken language. For psychologists, language is of central importance as a tool for applied work, so misunderstanding of a language becomes a major obstacle in understanding others.

Psychology as a profession has its own culture, which is transmitted both through the initial first degree, and through subsequent professional training. Professional training as a clinical psychologist in Britain is unusual in comparison with most other training for health care professions, in that the initial degree is non-vocational, while other professions typically start vocational training relatively soon after leaving school. Part of the philosophy of psychology, as an independent discipline, is to encourage an enquiring critical approach, which is itself a cultural expectation, and which may then result in tension with the explicit and implicit task- and role-expectations of other health care professionals.

Most of those cultural expectations are learned silently, often by modelling senior members of a profession, and by tacitly absorbing the rules for professional advancement and progression. Professional organizations, by their very nature, exist to promote the development of that profession, which may imply at least some competition with other professions, and thus potential role conflict with members of those other professions. Part of an awareness of cultural factors in clinical work should therefore include an awareness of the culture of the individual professionals themselves.

Cultural variation within Britain

Within the indigenous British population there are significant varieties of culture, often tied to wealth and status. The concept of social deprivation is now widely used to describe multidimensional variations in the resources and quality of the social environment, taking account of, for example, levels of income, levels of educational attainment, and quality of housing. Using such indices, it is possible to compare the relative degrees of social need at the level of individual electoral wards, and these are known to have a significant association with rates of mental disorder. This means that in identified areas of major British cities, it is possible to target psychological resources, along with other resources, to meet those higher levels of need. However, this then creates an ethical dilemma, in that giving people psychological skills to cope with unacceptable conditions may be seen as colluding with the continuation of those conditions.

There remain significant variations between England and the other home nations in terms of culture. Some of these are explored in the chapters of Bhugra and Littlewood (2001), who explore issues of cultural differences in Ireland and Wales. Irish people are often not seen as immigrants, but they are in fact the largest single migrant minority ethnic group in England, and have a social profile similar to other disadvantaged groups in England. They have higher rates of unemployment, and have higher levels of suicide and self-harm, and higher levels of psychiatric admissions, than the indigenous English population. Issues for Welsh people include that of language. In some rural areas of Wales, Welsh speakers form up to 80% of the population, but it is unlikely that psychological therapies will be available to many of them in the Welsh language.

For both of these groups the fact that they are 'invisible' as immigrants because of their skin colour, and because they are native speakers of English, conceals the reality of the levels of discrimination that certainly Irish people experience. This includes the risk of mis-diagnosis on the basis of stereotyping, for example the over-diagnosis of Irish women as alcoholic. There may also be cultural differences in their expression of distress, reflecting lower levels of social support in an English setting.

The most common cultural factor considered is that of ethnicity or race. The ethnic composition of Britain in 2002 (excluding Northern Ireland) was 53 million white (including both British and other white) out of a total population of 59.3 million, or 89%. The remaining 11% of the population was made up of 2.3 million of Asian origin (of whom 1 million are Indian), 1.8 million Black, and 500,000 people of mixed ethnicity.

The 2001 census included, for the first time, a voluntary question on religion, and 92% of the population chose to answer the question. Forty two million of the population chose to identify themselves as Christian, but this overall figure conceals a wide variation in individual belief and practice, and does not clarify the differences between the major denominations. Where psychologists themselves may have no personal understanding of religious commitment and practice, they may underestimate its influence in those of the host English, Irish, and Welsh communities with strong Christian beliefs.

Nearly 1.6 million identified themselves as Muslim, and the next three most frequently mentioned faiths were Hindus (560,000), Sikhs (336,000), and Jews (267,000). These labels also conceal variation in the personal meaning of a religious affiliation, and gloss over the frequency of religious pluralism.

This ethnic and religious variation is not distributed evenly. So while some rural areas (and some areas of previous heavy industry) in Britain have only about 1% of their population from ethnic minorities, other urban areas (typically sections of large cities) may have over 50% of their population from ethnic minorities. These differences may translate into complex local patterns linking members of individual ethnic communities to particular types of employment and to very local groupings of shops and places of worship, or they may translate into a dispersed pattern of distribution wholly assimilated into the local community.

Intersecting with these dimensions of culture are those factors affecting people of all ethnicity and language, such as understanding of disability, and sexual orientation. For people with a severe disability such as Multiple Sclerosis, belonging to self-help groups can also create a sub-culture. Deafness is an example of a condition that is invisible, that has a language of its own (sign language), and that offers membership of a positive community and culture. Differences of sexual orientation are tolerated differently within cultures and religious groups, and raise questions of whether or not to declare that orientation, even when it is a central part of a person's identity. People with mental health problems are often perceived negatively within many cultures, and the 'social exclusion' that results, by making it more difficult for people with mental health problems to remain in work, and more difficult to access community services and support networks, only further compounds those problems. It is also unclear how, and if, services should be offered differently to these various cultural groups, and to what extent membership of such groups is or is not more salient than membership of other groups, such as ethnic or religious communities.

The increase in the number of refugees and asylum seekers in Britain in recent years is still not well documented, and local health authorities may be uncertain about the numbers of refugees resident. A significant proportion of refugees have distressing histories. They may have been subject to torture, the women raped, and apart from their own experiences, they may have seen members of their families killed, quite apart from surviving possibly years of oppression and exploitation. Understanding their needs is complicated by the fact that their English may be very poor, and they may be illiterate in their own language.

These patterns of cultural variation in both the host communities and in immigrant communities are common throughout many European countries. Most of the variation in immigrants has been due to either past colonial activity by that country or economic migration, with political refugees being a more recent group. France had extensive colonies in both Africa (with Algeria being part of metropolitan France) and the West Indies, so that 8% of the population of France is now Muslim. Spain had South American colonies, Portugal African colonies, and the Netherlands Indonesian colonies. Just over 2% of the population of Australia are of Aboriginal and Torres Strait Islander origin, and 13% of the population of New Zealand are of Maori origin, with a further 5% from other Pacific islands.

Cultural differences then exist not only within most European countries, but also between them, so that understanding of our own indigenous beliefs and culture must be broadened alongside a widening international perspective. An applied psychologist must then be aware of and accept differences both between and within cultures, including differences of social structure and intimate relationships, faith traditions, language traditions, patterns of help-seeking behaviour, as well as sexual orientation and behaviour.

An issue of special concern is how accessible mental health services are to members of black and minority ethnic communities. The British Department of Health has focused on what needs to be done at a national level to improve the equity of services, and a number of guidance documents now exist (such as the detailed consultation document published in 2003). The documents emphasize the importance of engagement with the local communities, which will lead in turn to improvement in the information available to both commissioners and providers of services, so that in turn services can then be more appropriate and responsive. Three aspects of services are highlighted as of special concern, these being suicide, pathways to care, and acute in-patient facilities. Research carried out in Britain suggests that specific communities are at high risk in each of these areas. Thus there is a particularly high risk of suicide in young women born in India and East Africa, and in Irish-born men. As far as acute in-patient services are concerned, African and African-Caribbean patients are at increased risk of admission to high secure facilities, and are more likely to perceive in-patient care negatively. These examples illustrate how good epidemiological information can help to plan services more equitably, and to plan the provision of psychological services within that overall framework.

All of these factors influence the practice of applied psychology in health and social care settings, by helping to understand the individual person, quite apart from understanding any distressing or disturbed behaviour. It may be foolish to assume that Western systems of formal diagnosis and classification can be applied to all the problems presented by cultural minorities.

Two often-quoted examples of 'culture-bound' or 'culture-specific' syndromes are amok and koro (Jilek 2000). Amok describes a phenomenon originally referring to those heroic warriors in Malayan epics ready to die in battle. The amok reaction observed in Malayo-Indonesian men refers to a specific dissociative syndrome, which is preceded by a state of tension, experienced in conjunction with interpersonal situations which are perceived as involving 'loss of face'. An upsetting incident then triggers an altered state of consciousness, followed by the sudden random occurrence of aggressive acts. The amok run ends with either attempted suicide or exhaustion, following which the perpetrator may claim amnesia for his deeds. This is very different from the way in which the term is used colloquially to describe any episode of unprovoked attack, usually involving young men under the influence of alcohol or other substances.

Koro describes the subjective experience of shrinking of the penis in men, and of the breasts in women, associated with transient acute anxiety, originally reported in China and South-East Asia. Since this is perceived by the local community as possibly leading to impotence or death, the community will then attempt what are believed to be life-saving measures, including holding the genitals manually or by applying special instruments. It is not surprising that colonial physicians working in South-East Asia were struck by this phenomenon, and it was an obvious opportunity for psychoanalytic speculation and explanation. Koro also manifests itself in other cultures, and major epidemic outbreaks of koro have occurred within recent decades.

Both of these examples illustrate, in perhaps extreme form, the problem of trying to understand unusual patterns of behaviour in the terms of Western psychology. The question as to whether or not the person displaying these patterns of behaviour also suffers from any formal mental health problems has to be separately established. It is likely that a person presenting with these or other culture-bound syndromes will already have been in contact with native healers, or at least had an explanation offered to them in terms of their traditional beliefs.

It is not possible to make simplistic assumptions about the needs of an individual based on knowledge only of their ethnic origin or faith. That person may have been in the country for only a few weeks, or they may be a second or third generation immigrant whose life has been spent wholly integrated into their local British community. The cultural challenge for clinical psychologists is then three-fold:

- to understand their own professional culture
- to understand the range of cultures within the indigenous community, of which they may or may not be a member
- to understand the range of cultures of those from other countries of origin, of which they also may or may not be a member

This challenge has major implications. It implies understanding a range of aspects of language, understanding health beliefs, and understanding the assumptions made about intimate and familial relationships, as a component of understanding health and social care needs. It assumes an understanding of the route by which an individual has arrived at an NHS setting, after perhaps a complex route involving the use of traditional healers. It assumes that it is possible to negotiate treatment aims that are acceptable to both user and provider, and so to provide services that meet their needs.

The experience of working within other cultures

An increasing, but still proportionally small, number of psychologists have themselves worked in other countries, and a number of accounts of their experience have appeared in Clinical Psychology (formerly Clinical Psychology Forum). The writers have described their experiences as voluntary workers, as trainees, or as trained clinical or health psychologists. British clinical psychologists may choose to work in another country for a variety of motives, not just the experience of living in another country. Some psychologists may be working with a non-government organization (NGO) to improve standards of health care, or to meet the needs of refugees and those in crisis. Others may be working explicitly to support the development of training courses designed to meet the needs of those countries.

Apart from understanding the presented problems in their cultural context, it is also important to understand something of their potential patients' expectations of the health and social care system, both in terms of how to access it, and what it will deliver. They will have no experience of anything like the British primary care system, where the family doctor, and increasingly his or her colleagues from other professions, are gatekeepers to health care. They are instead likely to be accustomed to either a simple payment system in which you buy what you want, and that may include a 'gift' to the doctor or nurse, or a system embedded in their own culture, where the native healer has a recognized place in the community, sanctioned by community leaders.

In terms of the countries where they have worked, these first-hand accounts cover three main sets of circumstances. First, psychologists may be working in countries with well-developed health care systems, such as western Europe or Australia. Second, they may be working in politically stable countries with health care systems that provide a range of services but with a low overall level of resource. Third, they may be working in countries that are either politically unstable, such that there are high numbers of refugees, or are extremely poor, or both and consequently have significant proportions of the population who are traumatized, displaced from their national communities, and without basic food, water, and shelter.

As an example of the third set of circumstances, Fawcett and Refaat (2000) described their work in 1999 with refugees from Kosovar who had fled across the border to Albania. They provided workshops to Albanian and Kosovar nationals who were active in refugee work, and supported the key workers directly involved. Fawcett and Refaat point, however, to the dubious value of bringing in Western professionals when they know nothing of local language and culture, and question in any event the logic of applying an individualistic approach to trauma which is the result of widespread and sustained disruption to a large population. They conclude that the available evidence on what best to do under such circumstances is contradictory, and they discuss the ethical dilemmas in such settings, such as the fact that the imported psychological experts themselves expect logistical support and food, when those with whom they are working have none.

These reports convey something of the realities of both understanding the culture, and coming to terms with the implications of that culture for working practice. Common issues are the very low staffing levels and considerable lengths of time it takes to reach services such as clinics, so not surprisingly the severity of presented problems on first contact can be grossly more disturbed than in routine British practice. It is not uncommon for it to be customary for several members of the family to attend a clinic together, with whoever is identified as the patient. Family members may commonly stay at a hospital whenever a person is admitted for any sort of condition, and then become key members of the care team themselves.

Alongside the use of Western modes of healing, patients may in parallel be using traditional folk-healing procedures. These are highly varied, but common characteristics include:

- a holistic integration of several physical, psychological, spiritual, and social modalities of treatment
- ritual acts, in which images and objects acquire a symbolical value

- identification of the affliction by a divination process
- heightening levels of emotional arousal, with possibly cathartic abreaction
- purifying measures to reduce or eliminate 'pollution' which may include special dietary or abstinence requirements or prescriptions

In other countries, native healers may well prescribe allopathic drugs, of known effectiveness, alongside their native procedures. Native healers may themselves have been brought up in a family of native healers, and may be shrewd observers of their clients, and with their knowledge of the cultural background, can be a major therapeutic force.

The international nature of clinical psychology as discipline and profession

Within a positivist tradition, one of the requirements of psychology as a science is that results are replicable. This implies that the outcomes of psychological experiments in one country should be replicated in another country. If it is true that cultural factors affect psychological performance, then the field of social psychology should reveal such effects.

This hypothesis was put to test by Smith and Bond (1999) in their text concerned with cultural influences in the field of social psychology. They reviewed a number of studies in the field, including classic studies such as those of Milgram and his colleagues on obedience to authority, and examined the differences in outcome when those studies were replicated in other countries. They comment on the considerable variation in the percentage of research participants who were deemed 'obedient', from 65% overall for Americans, to over 90% for Spanish students, and between 16 and 40% for two groups of Australian students. They point out that a phenomenon such as compliance to authority depends on the social context which defines the meaning of the orders given, and to the accompanying difficulty in constructing experiments which control for those different meanings.

In another chapter, Smith and Bond examine the interpretation of facial displays of emotion, as shown in photographs of faces carefully posed to depict different emotions. They showed that the level of inter-cultural agreement varied considerably between two experimental conditions. When participants were asked to rate the photos in terms of names of emotions using Western terms, translated into their own language, there was a high level of agreement. When, however, the participants were asked to describe the emotions in their own words, the levels of agreement were much lower, and they varied sharply between the emotions, with joy and surprise being consistently recognized, but with interest and shame being the least consistently identifiable. This particular example, although not immediately related to clinical work, does suggest that the accurate identification of more extreme emotional states across cultures could be very difficult.

The importance of Smith and Bond's approach is two-fold. First of all, it challenges uncritical application of experimental psychological findings from one culture to another. Second, it casts doubt on the validity of constructs of cultural variation such as educational level and socioeconomic status, and encourages us to search for correlated psychological factors that may be more generalizable from one culture to another.

International psychological communication

Academic and professional psychologists communicate with each other in a number of ways. Most of the time they communicate in writing, traditionally on paper, but increasingly this is now done by electronic means. Conventionally, results of primary research have been communicated by scientific journals. Systematic reviews and meta-analyses are relatively new additions to the historically more important textbook as the main ways in which results of individual studies are criticized and integrated. However, since the most prestigious academic journals tend to be American, the biases of American editors will affect the selection of articles for publication.

With the increased attention paid to the statistical power of a study, it becomes more difficult to assemble sufficient participants in a study to achieve statistically robust outcomes, and hence multicentre clinical trials are becoming more important as well as being much more expensive to coordinate. This is difficult for poor countries to afford, as well as being more difficult to achieve in smaller countries.

A further twist to this bias is apparent in the Research Assessment Exercise (RAE) currently evaluating the research carried out in British universities and colleges. In 2001 for example the grading achieved by departments was related directly to the research funding available to that department from public funds. Each academic department could be awarded up to a maximum grade of 5*, meaning that within that department, the attributed 'quality' of research equated to attainable levels of international excellence in more than half of the research activity submitted, and to attainable levels of national excellence in the remainder.

In this exercise, psychology was considered as a separate subject field, but it included human experimental psychology, biological psychology, and applied psychology, within which clinical psychology was included with counselling and forensic psychology. But of course the standard of international excellence was partly determined by the journal in which the research was published, with American journals heading the list of academic prestige. In the 2006 RAE, clinical psychology has been separated out from the rest of psychology and has been allocated to a group including neuroscience and psychiatry. The consequences of this remain to be seen, but at the very least, it can lead to high levels of pressure on clinical psychologists working within academic departments that are driving towards high levels of research excellence, and illustrates the point that political factors may bias the nature of research carried out in different countries.

Psychologists also meet at international conferences. These are important opportunities for psychologists from different countries to meet face-to-face, and their value should not be under-estimated for this opportunity. However, they arc costly to attend, and although bursaries may be available for participants from poorer countries, invariably conference delegates are likely to be from more affluent countries. If the balance of contribution from poorer and smaller countries is to be addressed, it requires significant support from wealthier countries for delegates from poorer countries.

Clinical psychology practice in other countries

Clinical psychology in Europe

Since Britain joined the European Community in 1971, the decisions of the European Parliament and Commission have progressively impacted on British legislation. Article 27 of the Treaty of Rome of 1957 was implemented in 1991, which provides for mutual recognition of professional qualifications in member states. This is leading to the positive consequence of convergence in standards of health care, and the potential for freer movement within the community of citizens, and thus of health workers. However, most health care systems in Europe have more of a mixed economy that in the United Kingdom. This is reflected in more variation in funding systems, with a combination of state health insurance, voluntary additional health insurance, and direct fee-for-service arrangements. Re-imbursement schemes vary, with the individual citizen possibly paying a higher proportion of the cost, but with more genuine choice of provider. Provider agencies are more varied, with a mix of municipal state and regional agencies. University hospitals and hospitals, as well as by independent practices may also be run by religious bodies.

While there is considerable ambivalence within Britain about the level of control exercised by the European Commission, and although the mechanisms of delivery may vary, there is broad support in at least the north-western nation states of Europe for some form of welfare state and for public health and social care provision. Thus the development of clinical psychology and related disciplines has been guided to some extent by similar philosophies about the role of psychological therapies.

This has led to increasing convergence in the training standards across Europe for applied psychologists. This has been facilitated by the European Federation of Professional Psychologists Associations (EFPPA), which was founded in Germany in 1981, when 12 national psychology associations signed the statutes. There are now (2005) 30 member associations, representing some 110,000 psychologists. The member organizations of EFPPA are concerned with promoting psychology as a profession, particularly in applied settings, with emphasis on the training and research associated with practice.

The influence of the EC treaty requirements, and of EFPPA, together mean that flexibility of movement of psychologists between EC countries is now much easier than before. However, the requirement of fluency in the language of another country has limited the amount of movement that has taken place. As a generalization, more migration of professional psychologists to Britain has taken place from the countries of north-west Europe (such as Germany and the Netherlands) than has taken place from southern Europe. This may also be because the theoretical orientation more dominant within southern Europe has been psychoanalysis, in contrast to the relatively greater dominance of cognitive approaches in the United Kingdom.

Clinical psychology in other English-speaking countries

The American Psychological Association (APA) is the largest association of psychologists in the world. It has 150,000 members, all of whom have doctoral level degrees. The APA does not support the use of the term 'psychologist' for those working at Masters' level, such as counsellors and clinicians. The APA includes 53 professional divisions, and publishes nearly 50 journals, among them the prestigious Journal of Experimental Psychology, as well as the Journal of Abnormal Psychology, and the Journal of Consulting and Clinical Psychology. It has an office of international affairs that produces a Psychology International newsletter, which regularly has a short note on psychology in other countries. Although the APA was for many years the only national body for psychologists, the tension between applied and scientific psychologists in the United States led to a breakaway organization being formed, the American Psychological Society, in 1988. This represents those psychologists who see themselves primarily as scientists, and now has 14,000 members, larger than many other national psychological societies.

Voices are not lacking within the APA pointing to the need to diversify the profession of psychology in the United States, before it 'becomes obsolete and irrelevant to diverse populations in the United States', as phrased in one article in the American Psychologist. In 2004, the APA council adopted a resolution on culture and gender awareness in international psychology, as part of its effort to ensure that it is relevant to the predicted increasingly diverse American population.

Other examples of clinical psychology in English-speaking countries are Canada (which is strictly speaking bilingual), Australia, and New Zealand. The Canadian Psychological Association (which is itself bilingual, and hence is also called the Societe Canadienne de Psychologie), follows APA practice in training fairly closely, as Canadian psychologists can then work in the United States.

The Australian Psychological Society has over 14,000 members. After the Second World War, a number of British psychologists emigrated to Australia, and so it is not surprising that a number of aspects of clinical psychology practice are similar to that in Britain. There are currently three modes of generic training in clinical psychology. There is still a training route via supervised practice, without attending a university course, similar to the former British 'in-service' training system, which was discontinued in the United Kingdom in 1982. There are then two university training routes, one via a 2-year full-time M.Psych. course, and the other via a doctoral training of either a 3-year D.Psych. or a 4-year Ph.D. route. However, all these post-graduate training routes require significantly fewer hours of supervised practice than the British training system. It is also possible to train directly as a clinical neuro-psychologist, without the requirement to have supervised practice in any other specialties.

The New Zealand Psychological Society has over 800 full members. Interestingly the society logo incorporates a Maori strap line on its web-site. Their approach to training is similar to the Australian model. Atchison (2003) describes the process of applying to work as a clinical psychologist in New Zealand, and the general requirements she lists are similar to those likely to be required of any psychologist looking to work abroad. These fall into two categories, the first being satisfying any immigration or work regulations, which in the case of New Zealand means obtaining a work permit from the New Zealand High Commission. The second and more complicated part of the process is obtaining registration with the New Zealand Psychologists Board. This essentially involves satisfying the board that the applicant possesses an adequate training, and so requires the submission of documentation such as academic transcripts, evidence of eligibility for membership of the psychological society of the country of origin, confidential references, a detailed CV, and a police check. In fact it sounds very similar to what someone has to do to obtain work in Britain, and the warning is given that this can take several months to sort out.

There is no record of the ethnic or national background of clinical psychologists working in Britain, but there are a number who have lived and studied abroad before moving to Britain. These include those from western Europe (including a significant number from the Netherlands), and those from Australia, New Zealand, and South Africa. A small number of early British psychologists were themselves from overseas, including some of those who made major contributions to research, training, and the development of the profession, most notably Hans Eysenck from Germany, and May Davidson, Monte Shapiro, and Jack Rachman from South Africa. Interestingly very few American trained psychologists moved to Britain.

Clinical psychology elsewhere in the world: examples

For a number of years the training course in clinical psychology at the University of Hong Kong was directly accredited by the BPS, but this is no longer the case. In a number of countries, the main resources in applied psychology have been directed towards educational psychology, and this is the case, for example, in Vietnam. The psychological influences on Vietnam were French prior to 1945, and from 1953 included Soviet textbooks, reflecting the changes in political influence prior to independence in 1945.

The recent development of clinical psychology in Japan has been unusual, as described by Shimoyama (2004). Prior to the Second World War, Japan had developed indigenous models of psychotherapy, such as Morita therapy, and some psychometric tests and psychoanalytic ideas were introduced. After the war, client-centred counselling was introduced from the United States, and an Association of Clinical Psychology was founded in 1964. This was then dissolved in 1973 because of radical objections to the possibility of oppression that professional registration might engender. The association was then re-founded in 1982 with an orientation towards Jungian psychology and individual psychotherapy.

However, the growth of problems such as truancy and bullying led the Japanese Ministry of Education to introduce a counselling system into schools. Hence an attempt to address problems in the education system drove the development of clinical psychology in Japan, just as it did in Britain in the 1940s. Increased awareness of other social problems, such as terminal care in hospitals, has now become the driver to expand psychology further, along lines similar to clinical psychology in Britain, although the distinction between clinical psychology, counselling, and psychotherapy is harder to make in Japan. Crucially, the previously dominant intra-psychic psychotherapy model has been seen as less relevant to the pressing social problems of Japan, while a model closer to eclectic or integrative counselling is now being seen as more appropriate.

Because of time and resource constraints, the new training model that is being developed in Japan is limited to 2 years, but has involved a very careful option appraisal of the theoretical and practice skills needed to meet local demands. This option appraisal has included considering the relevance of British, European, and American training and practice models. Since there has not been a tradition in Japan of scientific research in these fields, there is no local evidence-base to guide key decisions. This Japanese development is a unique example of the recent growth of an indigenous profession akin to clinical psychology in an economically highly developed country. Interestingly, part of the thinking in Japan derives directly from the previous edition of this book, which Shimoyama and colleagues translated into Japanese as part of their research into the best way forward for Japanese clinical psychology.

India is similar to Japan in having an intellectual tradition for thousands of years that linked together both metaphysical systems and systems of treatment such as ayurvedic medicine and yoga. Academically this tradition was hidden beneath Western ideas, until during the 1960s a need to develop an indigenous psychology was felt, both to relate psychology to that pre-existing intellectual tradition, and also to create a better fit with the pressing national problems of poverty, and the continuing impact of the caste system (Jain, 2005). Just as the University of Tokyo has been a key player in change in Japan, so the All India National Institute of Mental Health and Neurosciences at Bangalore has contributed to the redefinition of both training and research for clinical psychologists in India.

Conclusion

Both academic and applied psychology have been heavily influenced by the broader western European philosophical and scientific traditions from which they emerged. In their application to social problems, including health problems, they have similarly reflected Western priorities of need, ideas of the nature of disease, and preferred methods of intervention.

This bias has meant that the concerns of even existing low-status and minority groups within European countries have not been given the priority they deserve. Even less have the problems of newly arrived citizens of these countries been first understood and then addressed. When Western applied psychology has then been exported to countries with pressing problems of poverty, massive social dislocation, and very low availability of psychologists, then the need for a radical re-appraisal of how psychologists can meet those needs is apparent.

A positive approach to working with people from other cultures would then involve:

- Understanding the most pressing psychological needs of those communities
- Understanding the language used to describe those psychological needs and concerns, without imposing on that language meanings that may be absent
- Understanding their pre-existing philosophical and religious formulations of the nature of personhood, the meaning of some categories of unusual behaviour, and valuing the treatments that derive from them
- Developing forms of intervention, and means of service delivery, that do not depend on large numbers of highly skilled (and expensive to train) psychologists

This represents an enormous challenge for clinical psychology, but one which must be addressed if clinical psychology is to contribute effectively both internationally and across cultures within a nation.

References

Atchison, L. (2003). A six-month locum clinical psychology post in New Zealand. *Clinical Psychology*, **22**, 40–2.

Berry, J.W., Poortinga, Y.H., Segall, M.H., and Dasen, P.R. (1992). *Cross-Cultural Psychology: Research and Applications*. Cambridge: Cambridge University Press.

Bhugra, D and LittleWood. R. (2001). *Colonialism and Psychiatry*. Oxford: Oxford Universiy Press.

Department of Health (2003). *Delivering Race Equality: A Framework for Action. Mental Health Services Consultation Document*. Department of Health, London.

Fawcett, G. and Refaat, R. (2000). Were Kosovar refugees a suitable case for treatment? *Clinical Psychology Forum*, **118**, 18–21.

Ithugra, D. and Littlewood, R. (2001). *Colonialism and Psychiatry*. Oxford: Oxford University Press.

Jain, A.K. (2005). Psychology in India. *The Psychologist*, **18**, 206–8.

Jilek, W.G. (2000). Culturally related syndromes. In M. Gelder *et al.* (eds.), *New Oxford Textbook of Psychiatry*. Oxford: Oxford University Press.

Shimoyama, H., Resnick, R.J., and Norcross, J.C. (2004). On the development of clinical psychology in Japan. *The Bulletin of Psychological Consulting Room*, School of Education, University of Tokyo, **26**, 78–101.

Smith, P.E. and Bond, M.H. (1999). *Social Psychology Across Cultures*. New York: Allyn & Bacon.

Further reading

Ithugra, D. and Littlewood, R. (2001). *Colonialism and Psychiatry*. Oxford: Oxford University Press.

Smith, P.E. and Bond, M.H. (1999). *Social Psychology Across Cultures*. New York: Allyn & Bacon.

Chapter 16

Conclusion: Working in changing contexts and changing practice

John Hall and Susan Llewelyn

This final chapter draws together a number of themes that emerge from the preceding chapters. It provides, first, an overview of the contextual, social, and policy issues which have an impact on clinical psychology as a profession, and which have been described in many of the chapters. It then considers the conceptual, professional, and ethical responses of clinical psychology to these issues, leading to potential changes in modes of practice.

We are attempting to gaze into a crystal ball in this chapter, which is of course likely to be doomed to failure, as nobody can accurately read the future. Nonetheless, we think these themes reflect many of the points made by our contributing authors, writing from their very varied and different experiences. The chapter represents an attempt to understand the range of complex forces which either currently or in the future will probably have an impact on the development and practice of clinical psychology.

Psychologists in the frontline

An important theme running through this volume has been the growing presence and influence of applied psychology in general, and clinical psychology in particular, in many spheres of health and social care. This in turn creates a potential new challenge, however. In previous decades it was more feasible for psychologists to appear almost invisible, possibly protected by psychiatry, yet now clinical psychologists are becoming better known both to the general public, and to health and social care policy makers and planners. This exposure in the media and elsewhere, and their involvement in a much wider range of services, means that both individual clients and purchasers are asking for particular types of treatment, such as Cognitive Behavioural Therapy (CBT), and will express disappointment if their expectations are not met. At the same time, the public at large is still not clear exactly what it is that we do, or how we do it.

In tension with this lack of awareness is the ready availability electronically of self-help material and information that means that at least some clients are much better informed than in the past, and have access to an array of support systems and opinion via the Internet. This new technology has also brought opportunities to clinical psychology, such as the possibility of providing online or remote-access therapy for groups who have mobility difficulties or who come from rural locations. Nevertheless, others will have little or no access to any of this, through poverty, age, or disability. This disparity around access to knowledge and other resources is likely to grow in our society, and may have a variety of implications for the future work of clinical psychologists, as it will for all involved in health and social care.

Implications of this improved but patchy awareness include the need to respond positively to increasing demands for services, even where resources remain limited, with the attendant need to decide how best to distribute those resources. There are now increasing demands for accountability for all health care professions, and more emphasis on the cost-effectiveness of treatments, which are not likely to go away. What all this means is that we require better ways of consulting with our stakeholders, who include both service users and those who commission and pay for our services, and we will need to develop more accessible and briefer treatments. We cannot hide from our own responsibility to consider how best to deliver psychological therapies to communities, and thus as a profession we need to pay much closer attention to our public relations.

Changing contexts

Demographic and cultural changes, and service provision

Most of the chapters in this book have made reference to the need for psychologists to be aware of the social and cultural context within which they work, especially when seeking to intervene therapeutically. Many aspects of society are changing, including the ethnic and cultural balance within communities in many parts of Britain and Europe, with the associated differing patterns of family life and structure, all of which impact on professional work. This has already influenced the range of settings in which services are delivered, which are now immensely more varied than even 10 years ago. For example, clinical psychologists are now likely to be found working via interpreters with diverse linguistic groups in community clubs, or intervening with young offenders who are in the care of social services and who have multiple mental health problems, or providing supervision for specialist nurses working in hospital clinics who provide counselling in connection with genetic disorders. Intervention with all these groups demands sensitive and flexible awareness of cultural and professional differences, as well as self-awareness on the part of the psychologist around their own beliefs and cultural expectations, that they are inevitably bringing into the relationship with the client.

Another significant change is the age structure of the population. As the proportion of older people in Western Europe increases, and most of them retain good physical health for longer periods of their life-span, the services will therefore have to adapt. Increasingly services are considering adopting a total life-span approach to individual development as a basis for organizing the delivery of services, so the cut-off age of 65 is no longer a psychologically meaningful indicator of 'old age'. Having said that, increasing age is linked to an increase in the numbers of people suffering from chronic illnesses, who in turn may not be able to care for themselves, and this too must affect the work of our profession, and our relationship with carers, both family members offering informal care and the paid carers, and is also reflected in the increasing diversity in the characteristics of paid carers. Hence work with older adults is growing in terms of numbers served, in the range of people involved, and is becoming more diverse in scope. In contrast, the age structure of many Asian countries, for example, includes very high proportions of children. Clinical psychology services will need to adapt to ensure age-appropriate provision for all these groups, and to enable transitions between those services that remain age based to ensure equity of provision.

All of these changes contribute to what are now termed the health needs of a population. The concept of need has replaced earlier Poor Law concepts such as obligation, eligibility, and perhaps rights. Beveridge, in his 1942 report, laying the foundations for the NHS, did not talk about 'needs', but talked about 'giant evils'. The very language in which we phrase the needs of a population, and the policies which are intended to meet those needs, conveys assumptions that may require challenge.

Problems do not occur alone or in isolation

Conventionally, medical textbooks have described different clinical syndromes, such as depression and anxiety, as being separate. In practice, however, one condition or problem may lead to another over time, and crucially, one individual may be coping with more than one problem at a time. This is particularly true for the kind of difficulties often presented to clinical psychologists, for instance:

- where the increased level of severity of one condition is associated with an increased probability of another condition (such as the increased likelihood that a person with a more severe learning disability will also have a physical disability, of which epilepsy is an important and disabling example);

- where an individual has two (or more) separate conditions which interact with each other in their impact on the individual (such as the increased risk of at least episodic disturbed behaviour when a person has both a severe mental illness and is also drinking alcohol to excess).

This occurrence of co-morbidity is not limited to clinical conditions, but extends to associated social or environmental factors. At the population level, living in a socially deprived community, in a family without adequate social support, increases the risk of psychological or behavioural disturbance. An example is that the poorer the levels of educational and occupational attainment a person has, the greater the probability of them having a more severe mental illness. Greater severity usually implies greater complexity of presenting problems, and clinical and social co-morbidity usually complicates and limits the effectiveness of many interventions.

Unfortunately the research evidence base for the treatment outcome of any intervention does not often take account of multiple problems, so the more complex a problem, the greater the likelihood that there will be difficulties in attempting simply to extrapolate from existing research. This clearly has implications for the aspiration of clinical psychologists to work as evidence-based practitioners. At times, and with many client groups, psychologists working with the most distressed and disturbed people will be using techniques for which there is no clear guideline or manual. Hence creativity, as well as the skills of reflective practice and critical thought, are crucial to helping those with the most severe problems.

Working in changing health and social care systems

Clinical psychologists, as any other professionals, work within a social and political context. A major factor affecting that context is the demand for a professional service and the position of a single profession to supply that demand. In line with the economic language of that statement, the position of clinical psychology within the overall demand for health and related social care will depend on the prosperity of the country. The recent 2001 World Health Organisation Annual Report, which was dedicated to mental health, shows that the proportion of a nation's health-care budget dedicated to mental health becomes greater as the country is more prosperous. One-third of all countries in the world devote less than 1% of their public health budget to mental health, although neuropsychiatric problems constitute 12% of the total global burden of disease. Clearly a very focused strategy for psychological services would be required under those circumstances.

For more developed economies, another factor is the extent to which health and social care is provided predominantly through public, or private, funding. Most European countries have a mixed health economy, with a range of providers and a mix of funding systems. Britain is atypical within Europe in the high proportion of provision through both public funding and through public agencies (although that proportion may reduce). In the United States the impact of managed care, where Health Maintenance Organizations linked to health insurance schemes now control funding for a large part of clinical psychology practice, is instructive and may have implications for British practice. Accordingly, the profession of clinical psychology in Britain is highly dependent on public health policy and on the skill mix required in public services. The way in which public health, for example, both as a profession and as a service, has been marginalized in Britain since about 2002 gives a warning that high levels of investment in training and posts for an individual profession is not automatic.

A simple analysis of the rate of change of public policy in Britain regarding both the structures and processes of health care delivery indicates how crucial it is that clinical psychology is sensitive to these changes. Since the inception of the National Health Service (NHS) in 1948, which as discussed in Chapter 1 was effectively the inception of the profession of clinical psychology in Britain, the overall structural framework remained the same until 1974 and was then essentially stable until the introduction of the NHS Trusts in the early 1990s. Since then however there has been an increasing rate of change in the hierarchical relationships between the lowest levels of provision, through the intermediate levels, to the current dominant position of the Department of Health. During the British general election campaign of 2005 the detailed structure of the NHS was itself a party political issue.

Successive changes have occurred over the past 10 years, from the experiment of individual GP practices holding their own budgets, through to the creation of large geographical administrative units of about 70 District Health Authorities (DHAs) in England, which were then slimmed down to 28 and then 12 Strategic Health Authorities, as well as reducing the numbers of Regions from 14, down to 8, and then abolishing them entirely. Alongside the changes in configuration of NHS Trusts (the administrative unit actually delivering services), all this has meant a profound destabilization of health service management at every level.

The changes have not been confined to management processes. There have been changes of equal magnitude in regulatory and monitoring arrangements, from a starting position where the DHA was both manager and monitor, to the current separation of those functions. What was the Commission for Health Improvement became the Health Care Commission in 2005 and monitoring of the policy targets set out in the range of National Service Frameworks produced from 1999 has become both extremely detailed and prescriptive.

All of these changes mean that the profession of clinical psychology needs to be constantly aware of the nature and impact of policy. National policies may be inconsistent and may not match with either local need or evidence. The profession should then be capable of constructive and informed critique of policy, rather than adopting a negative complaining posture.

Who chooses?—the tension between user, professions, and funders

There is a fundamental struggle between the individual with health care needs, the professional groups setting out to meet those needs, and the agencies funding services, regarding who should influence individual choice of health care and whether those choices should be regulated. In a state where the government is itself the major funder—as in Britain—then there is a risk that the needs of the individual may be subordinated to government policy. Although in a large Western-style representative democracy, a government claims to govern by mandate of the people, when populations are in tens of millions (as in many nation states of Western Europe) it is often difficult for the voice of the individual to be heard. Nonetheless, there are signs that individuals are now becoming more empowered in this tension, through better education and changes in technology so service users can have access to the information previously held only by professionals, and in Britain paradoxically by some state encouragement of that empowerment. Important contributors to this movement have been those professionals, including clinical psychologists, who are themselves committed to that empowerment.

Two instructive examples of user involvement can be seen. The first is in the research field, where there is an increasing (and some would say remorseless) drive towards research subjects, now rightly called research participants, demanding full information and free consent as a condition for their participation. These demands are mediated by more complex research ethics procedures, all of which have dramatically changed the form of research and the ease with which it is carried out. So for example, the extent of side effects is now a significant measure of the effectiveness of any new drug. The implications of this for clinical psychologists is that research studies now need much more careful planning and may require user participation in design. Insistence that participants should not be used unless the study clearly has scientific merit may also affect the ability of psychologists to carry out some forms of study unless stringent criteria around numbers and consent are met.

The second example is in the health and social care planning field, where there is increased pressure from both users and carers to be involved in individual and community care decisions. The implications of user-led issues, and of a strengthened user/consumer voice, and the new concept of the 'expert patient', are likely still further to change relationships between professional psychologists and users—and psychologists themselves are increasingly declaring themselves as users too.

Changing practice

Reconceptualizing the challenge

Although as a profession clinical psychology initially developed at the behest of and in some senses was even nurtured by sections of the medical profession, particularly by those working in child health and psychiatry, clinical psychologists have always been willing and eager to challenge 'medical models' of ill health and to articulate alternative, non-medical frameworks for understanding distress. Sometimes these challenges have been heated and relatively unproductive, and have not resulted in any major changes in how most people are treated, even though they may have pointed adroitly to serious limitations in the medical model.

One development, which has however been particularly influential in recent years, has been the elaboration and gradual adoption of coping and recovery models, both in psychiatry and in clinical health psychology. The work of Bentall and others, for example, as described in Chapter 5, has opened up ways of helping people with psychotic experiences psychologically, which were not conceivable given a medical model of psychosis. Likewise, the work of Kennedy and others, as described in Chapter 12, allows psychologists to make a real difference through rehabilitation and the use of a variety of cognitive techniques, thereby facilitating effective methods of coping with conditions such as spinal cord injury. These ideas are truly psychological, and are unlikely to be the focus of most medical practices where the predominant aim is to cure.

Another example of a major reconceptualization of the nature of clinical problems is given by the World Health Organisation's development of the International Classification of Functioning, Disability, and Health (ICF), replacing their earlier International Classification of Impairment, Disability, and Handicap. ICF describes how people live with their health condition, and is a classification of health related domains that describe body functions, structures, activities, and participation, within an environmental context. While it complements the International Classification of Diseases (ICD), it looks beyond disease, and does not depend on specific diagnosis.

These examples show how new ways are emerging for describing and understanding people's distress, and ways of coping with that distress, using psychological and social, not medical, terms. The constructional approach to helping people with learning disabilities, and the interest in well-being espoused by positive psychology, suggest approaches to interventions that are not problem focused but solution focused. The language and ideas that psychologists use are important in themselves, as they underpin what we do to help others.

Ethical issues in clinical practice

Another recurrent theme throughout the book has been the importance of ethical issues. Most contributing authors have pointed to the idea that integral to the work of clinical psychologists should be an awareness of the ethical, moral and cultural context within which clinical practice occurs. Any form of clinical intervention in the lives of others involves responsibility to act in that person's best interests and those interests of the wider community. This demands sensitivity and judgement where there may be no easy answers.

The problem lies in the fact that ethical principles often appear to contradict each other, and that acting ethically in one way may sometimes apparently mean acting unethically in another. For instance, as psychologists we should always respect the confidentiality of information given to us by patients, but on occasions we may have to betray that confidentiality if by doing so we may be able to prevent a greater harm. A good example of when this might happen is if a client provides information to the psychologist which suggests that a child may be at risk, in which case the psychologist has no choice but to pass on that information to Social Services, even if the client has expressly requested this should not happen. Another example is when we may not wish to cause distress to a client, but if we are to be truthful, we may have to give them upsetting information.

It is important for psychologists to recognise that, during the course of clinical work, we almost inevitably are given privileged access to people's vulnerabilities, and it is essential that the trust with which this access is granted is only used for the benefit of clients. Through their training, clinical psychologists gain the ability to influence the future of individuals, families, and services, and this influence is probably unavoidable, even if the psychologist seeks to minimize this. In the vast majority of instances, psychologists aim to work collaboratively with clients, and to assist them in being able to make decisions according to their own values. As far as possible, the client should therefore always be able to choose what their goals are, what sort of treatment they want, and to be able to end treatment if they so wish.

Nonetheless, any action always has ethical consequences, and it may not always be possible to inform clients fully about possible consequences of treatment. For example, in individual CBT a psychologist may inadvertently affect a woman's choice to leave an unhappy marriage through encouraging her to develop assertiveness skills, hence promoting her ability to act independently for the first time. Likewise, in a situation with limited resources, the decision to offer a service to any client group will probably involve not offering that service to another. The psychologist must be able to take or accept responsibility for such difficult choices.

Because of the pervasiveness of ethical concerns in clinical work, it is vital that psychologists are mindful of the need to obtain valid consent from clients for all their interventions whenever possible. This is not always as easy as it seems, as many clients (such as those with profound learning disabilities or suffering from advanced dementia) are not able to give informed consent, while others may not be fully aware of the consequences of entering treatments. They may encounter issues that are unwelcome or distressing, or not realize that therapy might lead to significant but unexpected life changes, as noted in the example above concerning assertiveness skills. Psychologists therefore need to pay careful attention to providing as much information as possible to clients (or their relatives or carers) to ensure consent, or where this is for some reason impossible, to consult with experienced colleagues.

A similarly essential aspect of clinical work is the need to maintain appropriate boundaries, which allow clients and psychologists to work safety and respectfully together. Given their position as recognized professionals, clinical psychologists inevitably have more power than clients, and it is imperative that this power is used for the benefits of clients, not the psychologist. While almost everyone would agree with the importance of behaving ethically and would very probably always wish to behave in an ethical manner, people do still sometimes find themselves acting unethically and abusing their power and privilege. For the vast majority of practitioners this is probably because of a lack of thought about ethical issues in all aspects of conduct and the difficulties we as humans sometimes have of being self-critical of our own behaviour.

For example, the most common breach of ethical principles is that of confidentiality. Without wishing to betray someone's confidences, a psychologist who is struggling with their own emotional reactions when working with a difficult clinical situation may not be able to resist the temptation to tell a partner or friend about the client, or may even wish to tell others about a particularly funny or sensational aspect of a client's life, primarily to entertain or inform others. Although this is potentially a very serious breach, an even more serious breach can occur when the psychologist puts their own needs, for example, for friendship or personal gain, ahead of the interests of the client. Here, for example, a psychologist might be tempted to accept inappropriate gifts from a client or even to develop a close personal and sexual relationship with a client who initially approached the psychologist for therapeutic help. Such situations are always harmful for clients.

In Britain the British Psychological Society (BPS) currently requires all Chartered Psychologists to act in accordance with a Code of Conduct, which lays down certain key principles, including the importance of acting in the interests of the recipient of services, to be competent in the performance of professional duties and the need to respect evidence. For clinical psychologists the Society's Code is further elaborated by the Division of Clinical Psychology's Professional Practice Guidelines, which provides a helpful framework for ethical practice. All Chartered Psychologists must act according to this framework and the Code, or they may be subjected to disciplinary proceedings by the Society.

The statutory Health Professions Council (HPC), set up by Act of Parliament, may in due course take responsibility for regulating the conduct of all applied psychologists in Britain. Similarly the American Psychological Association and the Australian Psychological Society have codes of ethics covering similar areas and registration procedures, which in the case of both countries are carried out by state bodies and not by national bodies. All of these Codes are designed to protect the public and to ensure that psychology as a discipline and the regulatory bodies are not brought into disrepute.

There are a number of key underlying components of most ethical codes, including those of the BPS and the HPC, which relate closely to culturally pervasive perspectives on ethical behaviour. These include the importance, at the very least, of doing no harm, and if possible, of doing good to others, and of promoting the autonomy of others. Other key principles include the need to promote justice, to maintain confidentiality, to be truthful, trustworthy and fair, and to promote safety.

Ethical thinking is however much more than just awareness of codes of conduct. It involves a commitment to a promotion of behaviour which is respectful of others, and to acting in accord with one's own personal values at the same time as being conscious that we now live in a multicultural society where values are not always shared. It also involves accepting that ethical decisions are often difficult, and that hard decisions may need to be made which are complex and may be unpopular. At root, it involves psychologists taking personal responsibility for their own actions, having personal integrity, being sensitive to the context in which they live and work, and having both respect and compassion for others. 'Good moral character is more important than mere conformity to professional standards' (Anderson and Kitchener, 1998, p.97).

Teamworking, family working, and community working

Another clear theme that has been echoed throughout this book is the importance of the relationships that clinical psychologists have with others in teams, families, and community networks. Modern health and social care is almost always delivered through or with others, most of whom are not clinical psychologists. Changing demography and patterns of morbidity, as well as new technologies, mean that in the future more and more health and social care will be delivered in close liaison with service users and their families, or will be provided through multidisciplinary teams. Good, positive working relationships are vital, and are effectively a prerequisite for psychologists to influence the quality of health care provided to many clients and their families.

Achieving this effectively is not always as easy as it sounds. Communication with families and carers needs sensitive awareness of difference and diversity, and the ability to attend simultaneously to differing perspectives held by different family members or clients. Working with teams requires similar sensitivity and flexibility, as well as the ability to work with differing theoretical perspectives and different organizational structures. If handled well, this can be used to great advantage.

In Chapter 14, Lavender and Allcock point to the frequent ambiguity in the organizational position of clinical psychologists, resulting from lack of clarity about their lines of authority within health and social care, combined with their relatively high status because of training and other factors. As a result, the ability of psychologists to function effectively in teams, and have influence, depends to quite an extent on them being able to manage interpersonal relationships well and to demonstrate their perceived usefulness to clients and their teams. They also suggest, however, that if psychologists are unwilling or unable to establish good working relationships and to demonstrate clearly what they can contribute, then their ability to have any major influence over provision for clients quickly dissipates.

No one is going to champion the views of clinical psychologists just because they are clinical psychologists. It has to be the responsibility of the profession and its practitioners to show how psychology can in practice contribute to client welfare and the alleviation of suffering. Primarily this has to be done by working and communicating with others, who will not necessarily share the same values or place the same emphasis on the scientist-practitioner model, or the same wish to understand people's psychological functioning in context.

Being able to listen, empathize, assess, and formulate clearly and effectively are all skills as necessary for teamworking as they are for working with individual clients or families. Likewise the willingness to communicate is essential in both types of work, which in turn implies the ability to be adaptable and flexible. Team working improves the quality of most decision-making processes, as well as offering support to practitioners. Families and communities have the potential of being able to intervene or support clients for longer and in more personally informed ways than psychologists ever can. An understanding of the dynamics of teams and families and how best to facilitate their functioning is therefore a key skill for all clinical psychologists, but also enriches the discipline and its potential.

Independent professionals?

The very idea of 'profession' assumes the possession by that group of a set of knowledge or skills that are not only unique to that group, but are also socially valued, and to some extent protected. Historically three main professions have held dominant positions in Western Europe: the clergy, medicine, and the law. When looking at their development, the concept of 'semi-professions' is instructive, whereby a claim of encompassing knowledge enabled a superior profession to assume control of another, as for example where physicians and surgeons controlled herbalists and apothecaries, and where barristers had access to the higher courts denied to solicitors. During the mid-nineteenth century, new groups of professions arose on the basis of technical knowledge, such as engineers and architects, where, because of risk to the public from negligence, the state authorized their protection, either by Act of Parliament or Royal Charter. Similarly new scientific groups and societies arose, as scientific disciplines themselves were also defined.

In all of these developments it is possible to discern the intermingling of meeting public need, improving standards of practice, protection from malpractice, and mutual self-protection. An element of trade unionism, and restrictive practices, was, and is, never far away. The professionalization of psychology has exhibited all these features. Gradually the position has arrived whereby 'professions' are defined in two interlocking ways. First by knowledge, techniques, and expertise, which include issues of control of social relationships, accountability, and autonomy. Second, by explicit and implicit values and ethics, which relate to the socialization processes of that profession, and the implicit social consensus between and within professional groups; and to the ethics of practice.

However a profession defines itself, the actions of any profession are still open to public scrutiny. In Britain the issue of professional protectionism was first tackled by opening up legal practice in the higher courts to solicitors. This government intrusion into the world of professionalism was at least in part legitimated by the real inadequacy of most professional complaints procedures, where the public perception was that professional procedures protected professional interests, rather than that of the client or customer.

Viewed from a historical perspective, professional psychologists have been late entries into an organizational world where the rules were not only set, but were beginning to be challenged. Applied psychologists of all varieties have thus been effectively intruders into pre-existing professional communities: clinical psychologists into a medically led community; educational into a head-teacher-led community; forensic into a prison governor-led community. This has inevitably led to conflicts, but also to questions around regulation. Occupational psychology is probably an exception, in that business has typically been more open to entrepreneurial individuals of any background going to the top.

More specifically, within the health field, clinical psychology has held an anomalous position with respect to the dominant profession of medicine and the increasingly assertive profession of nursing, and with respect to the other grouping, previously known as Professions Supplementary to Medicine and now as Allied Health Professions. Clinical psychology has always been vulnerable to that anomalous position and must now face up to the realities of the new situation, with the probable requirement of regulation through the Health Professions Council and the accompanying loss of some elements of professional independence.

With much more wide-ranging UK and European legislation also protecting consumers, and remedies for complaints being available though routes other than via professional and other regulatory bodies, all professions have less self-control than they had before. The goal of being an independent profession may now be illusory. One of the implications indicated in the previous sections on ethics and teamworking, of course, is that in any event being an independent profession is an undesirable goal from the patient perspective. The most important attributes of a clinical psychologist then become the values and principles they bring to their work, the quality of their relationships with others, and their technical knowledge and practice skills.

The skills of clinical psychologists: The future of training and skills sharing

It is undoubtedly the case that a major factor underlying the substantial growth in the numbers of clinical psychologists over the last two decades has been the quality of trained psychologists, who have been judged by employers to be able to contribute effectively to health and social care provision. The NHS funds training because it thinks that trained clinical psychologists are competent and can play an important role in the delivery of care. One important contributor to this position has been the high calibre of trainees, arising from the popularity of clinical psychology as a career choice amongst the most able graduates. The coordination between training courses in achieving a high level of quality in their educational and practice training provision has underpinned this. The standardization of training at three-year doctoral level has been crucial here, combined with agreement over benchmark statements, accreditation, and quality assurance processes.

The future of the present form of training is however less clear. It may be that other models of training will be developed, partly because of cost pressures, and partly because of questions over the necessity for generic training, given the demand for services in some specific areas. For example, some people have raised questions about the possible return of an apprenticeship model in specific areas of work, while others have talked of reinstating shorter or more flexible routes to training. A number of other professions, including medicine, physiotherapy, and teaching, have all recently developed accelerated or semi-apprenticeship models of training, alongside conventional modes of training.

Another key pressure has been to encourage multi-professionals working through shared learning initiatives, by which professionals are encouraged to learn, and so to work, more closely together. Clinical psychologists have been encouraged to participate in this agenda, through contributing to multi-professional training courses and services. Government pressures to employ, group together, and reward practitioners according to the skills they have, rather than the disciplines they come from, can also be seen in operation through several structures. 'Agenda for Change' is the common pay system now being put in place for most NHS employees. The Knowledge and Skills Framework encourages all practitioners to develop their competencies as part of their individual development plans in connection with ongoing Continuing Professional Development (CPD) programmes, seen as being required throughout the professional career of an individual. The Skills Escalator encourages people to develop their skills and move more easily between professions and types of employment. The implications of all these pressures on clinical psychology as a profession have yet to be seen.

Whatever the future for pre-qualification training, the current emphasis on lifelong learning and on CPD will undoubtedly continue. Many chapters in this volume have pointed to the central role of psychologists here, both in developing their own competencies and those of other psychologists, as well as helping to develop those of other professions. An ongoing debate concerns whether or not the dissemination of what we often see as 'our' psychological skills and approaches, to other, possibly less expensive professional groups, is both sustainable by those other groups and is a helpful move for our profession. Some claim that we are thereby promoting our own professional redundancy. Others point out that not only is there no shortage of psychological distress in health care, our tasks as scientists and practitioners should include the development and dissemination of effective strategies of assessment and intervention. Whatever view is taken, most psychologists in practice see their role as including the need to supervise and encourage good psychological practice by others, and to encourage a psychologically informed approach to health and social care. Hence many see the role as supervisor and trainer as a central one.

Assigning psychological resources

An issue not addressed in the individual chapters (although hinted at in Chapter 1) is how best to assign psychological resources across a range of populations and settings within a particular locality. The way in which psychological services in Britain have developed historically is that funding for additional staffing has often been to provide posts for a named team or service, or funding has been earmarked in line with a national requirement. In this way marked variations in staffing can develop, which do not relate to variations in identified need or to levels of demand or activity. The fact that psychological services in primary care, secondary-level services such as community learning disability or mental health teams, and tertiary services such as neurosurgery or forensic mental health, are funded through entirely different budgets means that an individual can experience very different levels of access to psychological services simply by moving from one age-group service to another, or from one clinical service to another clinically adjacent service (such as moving from a community rehabilitation team to an inpatient unit for the same condition). In this way the continuity of care of an individual may be seriously disrupted.

This issue has been addressed for mental health services in general by Thornicroft and Tansella (2004), who in a series of papers have expounded a model of what they term 'balanced care'. Their model derives from work carried out for the Health Evidence Network of the European Regional Office of the World Health Organization, and incorporates evidence from countries with widely differing levels of health resource, taking account of three differing levels of resource, covering, low- medium- and high-resource levels. This model makes a number of assumptions about services, which include the desirability of providing them close to home, which are responsive to disabilities as well as symptoms, are related to the priorities of users themselves, and are coordinated between health professionals and agencies.

This model sets out the range of service components to be expected at each level of resource, building up from a 'primary care with specialist back-up' variant for low resource areas, and a 'specialist/differentiated services' variant for highly resourced areas. While their model has some limitations, it does offer a planning matrix within which psychological resources could be planned and assigned according to available evidence, and some of the evidence they quote (such as that relating to the employment of people with mental health problems) is directly relevant to the work of clinical psychologists. As psychological resources and access to psychological therapies improve, the question of how to assign those resources equitably over localities, conditions, and service components emerges as an important issue.

New ways of working

It is often claimed that the clinical psychology profession needs to keep up to date, and to innovate. But what does innovation really mean? How can we ensure that the profession sustains the creativity which has underpinned its rapid growth?

For the editors of this volume, the answer has to lie in the thoughtfulness and ingenuity of its recruits, using their scientist-practitioner training in combination with sensitivity and ethical awareness as implied by the reflective-practitioner philosophy. The research and evaluative role of clinical psychologist becomes key here, as psychologists strive to develop, apply, and appraise the applicable knowledge base from a foundation of clinical experience. As David Smail once said, as clinical psychologists who have regular contact with the intimate details of people's lives and their distress, we should really *know* what we are talking about. As researchers we need to listen carefully to our clients, as well as our theories, and use their experiences to lead us to ask sensible questions, and hence to develop effective interventions that meet their needs where possible.

Besides their research and evaluative role, however, clinical psychologist also need to develop their roles within systems, especially given that those systems are always in need of effective leadership. Psychologists need to develop their capacity for strategic thinking and influencing service developments, for the sake of both the providers and recipients of services. In the past we have perhaps been able to use our small numbers to limit our responsibilities here, but we are surely well placed now to try to ensure that the client remains at the centre of health and service care. The skills needed to do this are not far removed from our clinical skills. What we need are the professional confidence and interpersonal skills to use opportunities to further awareness of psychological issues within health care, and to develop creative solutions to the complex and changing problems which an applied setting will always produce.

References

Anderson, S.K. and Kitchener, K.S. (1998). Nonsexual posttherapy relationships: A conceptual framework to assess ethical risks. *Professional Psychology: Research and Practice*, **29**, 91–9.

Beauchamp T. and Childers, J. (1994). *Principles of Biomedical Ethics*, 4th edn. New York: Oxford University Press.

British Psychological Society (2002). *A Code of Conduct for Psychologists*. Leicester: BPS.

Division of Clinical Psychology of the British Psychological Society Professional Practice Guidelines, 1995, Leicester, BPS.

Thornicroft, G. and Tansella, M. (2004). Components of a modern mental health service: A pragmatic balance of community and hospital care. *British Journal of Psychiatry*, **185**, 283–90.

World Health Organization (2001). *The World Health Report 2001: Mental Health—New Understanding, New Hope*. World Health Organization, Geneva.

Appendix 1

How to train as a clinical psychologist in the United Kingdom

All clinical psychology training in the United Kingdom is carried out at doctoral level, and is aimed to achieve the attainment of the three integrated components of academic, research, and clinical competence. There are 28 university-based programmes which provide training in close collaboration with the NHS, and all applications are processed though the Clearing House based at Leeds University. Candidates are able to apply to up to four courses, and an application form is provided by the Clearing House, copies of which are then distributed, together with confidential references supplied independently from referees of the applicant's choosing, to their nominated four universities. A standard fee is payable to the Clearing House for an information handbook and application forms, and for processing all forms to universities. Information on all courses, including selection procedures, course staff, curriculum, entrance requirements, and other relevant details, is provided in the handbook, and candidates are recommended to read this carefully before making applications. Further information is available from the Clearing House, 15, Hydc Terrace, Leeds, LS2 9LT, telephone 01 14343 2737. The website also provides helpful information including answers to frequently asked questions, at www.leeds.ac.uk/chpccp.

Given that all training is funded by the NHS, candidates should be aware that most courses are unlikely to select candidates who are unable to demonstrate a strong likelihood that they will continue to work in the NHS after qualification. Candidates from overseas are also required to have a work permit throughout the training period. All courses are committed to equal opportunities legislation, and seek to be particularly encouraging to candidates with disabilities, or who come from ethnic minorities.

Psychologists who have qualified overseas as clinicians, or who have qualified in other areas of applied psychology, are also able to apply for the British Psychological Society's Statement of Equivalence in Clinical

Psychology. This statement is recognized by the NHS as allowing subsequent appointment as qualified clinical psychologist, at a level equivalent to a doctorate awarded in the United Kingdom. All candidates are invited to apply to the Society's Committee for the Scrutiny of Individual Qualifications (CSIQ) for an assessment of any individual requirements which they may need to complete under supervision before being issued with a statement. Further information is available from The British Psychological Society, St Andrew's House, 48, Princess Street, Leicester, LS1 7DR, telephone 0116 252 9555. The BPS website also provides helpful information including answers to frequently asked questions, at www.bps.org.uk.

Appendix 2

Working as a clinical psychologist abroad

For anyone intending to work as a clinical psychologist in another country outside the United Kingdom, the procedures to follow will be broadly similar to that in the United Kingdom, but will vary in detail. If you want to work in a voluntary capacity, or to work without having direct person-to-person contact, the requirements will usually be less stringent. It may also be possible to arrange an observer-status position. For those wanting employment, as well as needing to supply a full CV, and provision of references, in general the receiving country will probably also require:

Evidence of professional qualification. This will involve you in producing university and BPS membership documents, and possibly transcripts of university courses, and evidence of clinical placements and internships. You may be required to show evidence of being in 'good standing' with the BPS/HPC (i.e. to show you have not been struck off!) You may have to submit certified translations of some documents.

Formal approval of professional qualifications. This may involve approval by either or both of the national psychological associations, or the relevant government departments or ministries, depending on the registration procedures of the country concerned. EC Directive 89/48 requires EC member states to grant registration to citizens of other member states, but in practice different countries are at different stages of implementation for different professions.

Evidence of citizenship status. You may be asked to give details of your passport, any naturalization procedures, and police checks.

Residence and work permits. These are not required in EC countries. Evidence of citizenship status may be required in other countries to obtain these permits, and the embassy or high commission in Britain of the receiving country will provide details on how to apply.

Obtaining all of this documentation may take a considerable amount of time. You may have to pay for some documents, and you will have to pay a fee to the registration body. In other words, plan early! If you are travelling, and do not know in advance which country you may want to work in, the more of the above documentation you have with you, or can arrange to be faxed at short notice, the better.

More detailed information for a number of European countries is given on the website of EFPPA (the European Federation of Professional Psychologists Associations) at: www.cop.es/efppa. The office address of EFPPA is: Agora GalerijGrasmarkt, 105/18 B-1000 Brussel, Belgium. Information for other countries is given on the websites of the relevant country. For example, the website for the Australian Psychological Society (www.psychology.org.au) has a very clear section on the assessment of overseas qualifications. The APS is nominated as the national assessing body by the government of Australia, and an assessment of overseas qualification will cost A$600 (in 2005) and is likely to take 8 weeks.

Glossary

Adherence Extent to which a patient follows the course of treatment suggested by their doctor. This term is preferred over 'compliance' as adherence suggests collaboration, though some favour the use of the term 'concordance' for the same reason.

Advocacy Pleading, defending, or interceding on behalf of another. In psychological usage, it refers to advocacy on behalf of handicapped or disabled people (such as people with learning difficulties) to enable them to have access to a range of benefits within the complex welfare, social care, and health care systems, and to improve the quality of those systems as used by them.

Agoraphobia From the Greek 'fear of the market place'. Characterized by fear of being away from a place of safety, usually the home. Low self-esteem and excessive dependence on others are features.

Allopathic medicine Treatment of disease by inducing a condition opposing the disease (contrasted with homeopathic medicine).

Alternative and complementary medicine and psychologies Non traditional theories and techniques of disease and treatment, such as osteopathy and aromatherapy. The terms are often used interchangeably, although strictly alternative medicine refers to medical practices which are not acceptable to conventional medicine, while complementary medicine refers to practices which are compatible with (and not infrequently themselves practised by) conventional medicine. Alternative psychologies are based on a variety of doctrines and philosophies, often including elements from psychodynamic schemes of thought, neurophysiological studies, mystical or esoteric philosophies, and so-called unexplained phenomena.

Alzheimer's Disease See Dementia.

Amnesia Disruption of memory processes, either partial or total, including memory loss and impairment of new learning.

Anger management Programme of treatment designed to help people understand and control their feelings of anger. Developed by the psychologist Novaco, it is a skills training approach in three stages (monitoring anger experiences, acquisition of adaptive behaviour, and role play in simulated anger situations).

Anorexia nervosa Characterized by excessive dietary restriction, to the extent that weight is maintained below that expected for age and height. Preoccupation with eating, weight, and shape is also present.

Anxiety Feelings of apprehension and unease in response to real or imagined threat. Anxiety consists of: physiological reactions, such as increased heart rate, sweating, and trembling; behavioural responses, such as avoidance; and cognitive disturbance, such as worrying thoughts or frightening fantasies. There are a variety of clinical anxiety states, for example, generalized anxiety and phobic anxiety.

Applied behaviour analysis Applied behaviour analysis is the application to problems of social importance of the concepts and methods associated with the philosophy of science known as radical and operant behaviourism. Behaviour itself is its fundamental subject matter, and it is not an indirect means of studying something else, such as cognition or mind or brain.

Assertive outreach Form of community provision for adults with severe mental health problems who have difficulty in engaging with mental health services and are at risk of repeated admissions or of loss of contact with services, so structured and assertive support is maintained with them.

Assessment ***behavioural***: psychological measurement procedures which focus on the behaviour which is to be treated, or which is likely to change, at the time it occurs and without making any assumptions about underlying causes or variables. ***Psychometric***: psychological measurement procedures which measure assumed traits or characteristics, typically involving comparison of the patient with appropriate norms, and often conducted in a face-to-face assessment setting.

Psychological See 'Tests'.

Attention deficit hyperactivity disorder (ADHD) Category referring to children and young people whose behaviour appears impulsive, overactive, and inattentive, in ways which are inappropriate for their developmental age and which may hinder their social and educational progress. These difficulties may be underpinned by an inability to maintain effort over time to meet task demands.

Audit Process of comparing what a service actually does with what it should be doing, as stated in a policy or clinical guideline, which assumes previously specified objectives or procedures.

Autism (Autistic spectrum disorders) Condition characterized by communication, behavioural, language, and social deficits normally first occurring in early childhood.

Autogenic relaxation/autogenic training Self-initiated, imagery-based method of relaxation.

Agenda for Change Standard pay and conditions system applied to all NHS employees in Britain apart from doctors, dentists, and service managers, based on job evaluations, aimed at ensuring fair and non-discriminatory reward for work carried out.

Attachment Theory Set of ideas developed from the work of Bowlby, based on the importance of early emotional relationships, and the importance of relationships for biological survival. Now seen as central to much psychodynamic work and theories of child development.

Baseline Assessment, or results of an assessment, carried out before treatment has started and normally continued until the measure is stable or steady.

Behaviour therapy Method of psychological treatment developed in the 1950s, derived from experimental studies of conditioning and learning. The focus of treatment is an overt behaviour, using psychological principles to achieve specific behavioural goals. Often contrasted with psychodynamic psychotherapy, where the focus is more on achieving insight or personality change.

Behavioural phenotypes Aspects of development which are related to the presence of a genetic difference/anomaly, which can lead to specific vulnerabilities.

Benchmarks Series of statements defining particular and/or unique features of a profession or activity of a group or service, in comparison to others; may also refer to costs of a particular service in contrast to other, similar services.

Between-groups design Experimental design where two or more different groups are studied, one receiving the experimental treatment and the other(s) receiving control or comparison treatments. In some such designs all groups receive all treatments, but in a different order.

Binge eating disorder Characterized by recurrent episodes of binge eating in the absence of compensatory behaviours. Other key characteristics include eating much more rapidly than normal, eating until feeling uncomfortably full, and eating large amounts of food when not feeling physically hungry.

Biofeedback Process of learning to control autonomic body functions using visual or auditory cues, usually provided by electronic sensors applied to the body surface.

Biopsychosocial model Conceptual framework that recognizes the reciprocal relations among the biological, psychological, and social aspects of health and illness. In this model the onset, cause, and treatment of physical illness are best understood as involving each of these levels of analysis.

Body mass index Conceptual tool for indicating weight status in adults. Calculated by dividing an individual's weight in kilogrammes by their height in metres squared. Normal BMI range for adults is 18.5–24.9.

Bulimia nervosa Characterized by recurrent episodes of binge eating (during which large amounts of food are consumed with an associated sense of loss of control), and compensatory behaviours, such as self-induced vomiting, dietary restriction, or laxative misuse. As with anorexia, preoccupation with eating, weight, and shape is also present.

Case-management Provision of a single person or team to assume responsibility for long-term care and support to a client, regardless of where the client lives or which agencies are involved. The case manager works in the community, sometimes intensively, and serves as a helper, service broker, and advocate (see advocacy).

Cerebrospinal fluid Fluid filling the ventricles of the brain, the central canal of the spinal cord and all other areas in the skull and spinal canal.

Child abuse Serious physical, mental, or sexual assault, neglect, or exploitation of a child, by implication referring particularly to that initiated by someone (well) known to the child. Includes intentional acts of omission as well as repeated excessive violence and incest; being subject to abuse may lead to profound disturbance in later adulthood.

Chronic Long-term or lasting. For example chronic pain is used to refer to pain which persists after healing has taken place and serves no useful function.

Client-centred therapy Developed by Carl Rogers in the 1940s, CCT aims to help clients to explore their feelings in the context of a warm, empathic, and trusting relationship. Therapy is seen as personal growth rather than treatment, and the approach eschews specific techniques or procedures.

Clinical psychology Application of psychological theory and practice to a broad range of problems—mental and physical—for which people seek help.

Code of Conduct The British Psychological Society's agreed set of principles which define appropriate ethical conduct, to which all Chartered Psychologists must adhere, and the associated set of disciplinary procedures.

Cognition General term to cover all aspects of knowledge—perceiving, thinking, imagining, reasoning, etc. Contrasted with affect or feeling. It is maintained by some that all emotions are cognitively processed and by others that emotions are at times directly experienced.

Cognitive–Behavioural Therapy (CBT) Describes the combination of behaviour therapy and cognitive therapy in which, generally, behavioural procedures are used to change cognitive processes, and cognitive procedures are used to change behaviour. It is a more liberal form of behaviour therapy in the recognition paid to thoughts and beliefs in understanding and changing psychological problems.

Cognitive Analytic Therapy (CAT) Developed from the work of Anthony Ryle, as an integration of CBT and psychodynamic approaches. CAT is a brief problem focused therapy which aims to move clients on via insight and developing more effective strategies in interpersonal relationships, and is based on an understanding of people in relationships.

Cognitive Therapy Approach where the prime focus is on patients' thinking processes, with the goal of changing distorted or unrealistic thoughts and beliefs. Methods vary from Socratic argument to behavioural procedures.

Community psychology Application of psychological theory and practice to people living in natural communities, and to the problems encountered by people in these settings.

Compliance Process of following a treatment prescribed by a doctor.

Conditioning The process by which a particular response comes to be elicited by a stimulus, event, or object other than that to which it is the natural or reflexive response. **Classical conditioning** Association in time of a neutral stimulus (for example a bell) with a reflexive stimulus (for example food) so that a conditioned response (for example salivation) occurs to the neutral stimulus. **Operant conditioning** Process by which behaviour is modified by systematically varying its consequences (rewards and punishments). **Consultancy model** Indirect approach to professional work, whereby the consultant provides advice on the best way to proceed, rather than working directly with the client or problem.

Constructional approach Approach to a person's problems involving establishing new behaviours or re-establishing behaviours which have been lost. It avoids focusing on the removal of behaviour by whatever means. The 'constructional question' would be 'if you didn't have this problem, what would you be doing, what would you be like?' A constructional approach gives particular recognition to how a problem first occurred or developed or is maintained.

Control group Group of patients or people in all respects similar to the experimental group, except that they are not subjected to the treatment or condition that is being experimentally investigated.

Coping Adaptive way of dealing with stress or threats.

Coping skills training Problem-solving approach which first identifies cues and high-risk situations leading to temptation or relapse. Then alternative ways of dealing with these high-risk situations are systematically explored.

Counselling Helping relationship in which the counsellor seeks to enable the client to explore his or her concerns and to find ways of resolving them. Counselling is a form of psychological treatment, although generally its focus is on less disturbed clients and it often takes place in non-medical settings, for example student counselling.

Critical psychology Approach which questions assumptions about how psychology currently operates, particularly its acceptance of psychiatric assumptions, and which places emphasis on social and environmental influences/cause of mental ill health.

Cue exposure Approach to psychological treatment which involves deliberate exposure to those cues or high-risk situations which provoke desire or compulsion. Prolonged repeated exposure, whilst at the same time resisting temptation, leads to a gradual reduction in desire.

Cystic fibrosis Genetic conditions that causes the body to produce mucus in the lungs and pancreas that leads to life-threatening lung infections and prevents the normal breakdown and absorption of food.

Dementia Deterioration of intellectual judgement and emotional processes, often characteristic of old age or brain dysfunction, accompanied by social isolation and stigmatization. **Alzheimer's Disease** is a common form of dementia in old age.

Depression Feelings of sadness and hopelessness, and lowered bodily activity. Clinical depression is characterized by a marked reduction or increase in appetite, disturbances of thought and movement (these usually being slowed down or occasionally agitated), lethargy, poor concentration, feelings of guilt and self-blame, and general loss of interest in previously enjoyed activities.

Dialectical Behaviour Therapy (DBT) Intensive treatment comprising individual and group therapy, skills training, telephone contact, and a weekly consultation group for staff, aiming to develop clients' skills in managing feelings, behaviours, and relationships. Includes sessions on mindfulness, interpersonal effectiveness, distress tolerance, and emotional regulation.

Discrimination Ability to detect and make judgements on observed differences on functions, behaviour, and emotions. More complex discriminations are based on categorization and may be arbitrarily or socially constructed.

Disinhibition Lowering of inhibitions (particularly social ones) that occurs under the influence of diseases, alcohol, or other factors.

Down's (or Down) syndrome Chromosomal abnormality resulting in a characteristic pattern of functioning, ability, and physical attributes, normally linked to limited intelligence.

Dysphasia Disruption of speech or language processing.

Educational psychology Application of psychological theory and practice to educational methods, and to problems encountered by people in the educational process.

Evaluation Process of finding the value of a treatment, by formally determining whether it is effective, efficient, and acceptable, in achieving predetermined objectives.

Evoked potential Regular pattern of electrical activity recorded from neural tissue evoked by a controlled stimulus.

Family Therapy Treatment of a client or clients with their family, essentially seeing the identified patient's problems as a symptom of a family, not an individual dysfunction.

Formulation Development of an understanding of a person or situation based on psychological theories and evidence which in turn also informs intervention.

Forensic psychology Psychology as applied to the legal process; sometimes also used generally to describe the application of psychological theory to the assessment and treatment of offenders.

Functional analysis Analysis of the relationship between a key event, and the preceding, concurrent, and following events, to see if there is any association between them. If such an association is found this functional relationship can be used to develop a treatment strategy.

Graduate primary care mental health worker Category of mental health worker newly introduced into the NHS in the early 2000s, who has a graduate background, often but not necessarily in psychology, whose function is to provide a range of health promotion and therapeutic functions that may include work with 'simple' mental health problems.

Group dynamics Underlying processes assumed to operate in groups, often hard to observe, which may explain why people operate differently in groups than when alone.

Goal directedness Set of responses that can only be interpreted in terms of attainment.

Goal planning Systematic approach to setting goals, specifying who will do what, under what conditions, and to what degree of success.

Health belief model Developed by Becker, initially to predict whether people engaged in preventative health behaviour such as attending screening, but later applied to a wide variety of health settings.

Health Professions Council (HPC) Body established by the British Government to regulate most health care related professional groups apart from nurses, doctors, dentists, and which may include applied psychologists.

Health psychology Application of psychological theory and practice to the beliefs, behaviour, and experience of people relating to their health, both when they are well and when they are ill.

Hypertension Abnormally high blood pressure.

Hypnosis Altered state of consciousness in which the hypnotized person responds to external suggestions allowing events to be experienced as if they were actually occurring. It has been successfully used as an anaesthetic and analgesic in selected people, as a form of psychotherapy, and it has been closely studied by experimental psychologists.

Ideographic Refers to an approach to personality that stresses the unique characteristics of an individual.

Intelligence General mental ability and specialized abilities such as numeracy, verbal reasoning, and perceptual skills. There is a long-standing controversy over the extent to which general intelligence (called G) exists over and above a variety of specialized abilities. The Intelligence Quotient (IQ) describes a way of measuring intelligence using psychological tests.

Inter-group rivalry Phenomenon of antagonism between groups including stereotyping, idealizing own group, and belittling those in another group.

Jacobsonean relaxation training Progressive method of achieving relaxation based on repeated contraction and relaxation of muscles.

Knowledge and Skills Framework Framework specifying the skills and competencies required by NHS professional staff which should be developed by individuals who wish to proceed up a particular career ladder.

Learning Process by which knowledge and behaviour are acquired and understood. The laws of learning refer to basic principles formulated by psychologists in the scientific study of learned behaviour. Learning theory describes the body of theoretical knowledge on the processes involved in learning.

Learning disability/intellectual impairment The following definition has been proposed by the American Association on Mental Retardation in December 1990. '[Learning disability] is manifested as significantly sub-average abilities in cognitive functioning, accompanied by deficits in adaptive skills. These deficits in adaptive skills may occur in one or more of the following areas: communication, self-care, social skills, functional academics, practical skills, leisure, use of community, self-direction, work, and independent living. Adaptive deficits often coexist with strengths in other adaptive skills or other areas of personal competence'.

Magnetic resonance imaging (MRI) Non-invasive procedure that provides a detailed picture of body tissue.

Manic depression (also known as bipolar disorder) Major mental health problem in which the person may experience both manic and depressive episodes, at different times.

Mental Health Act Government legislation applicable in England and Wales that provides the legal framework for treatment, and which can be invoked to detain people with a mental illness for psychiatric treatment, against their will.

Meta-analysis Statistical method used to evaluate the results of large numbers of outcome studies and arrive at a figure that summarizes the overall effect (effect size). It has become the preferred method of assessing outcome in psychotherapy.

Milieu therapy Method of psychotherapy that arose in the context of institutional care of psychiatric patients. The total environment of milieu, including staff and patients, is designed to be a 'therapeutic community', conducive to the patients' psychological welfare and recovery.

Morbidity Nature and frequency of specific mental or physical conditions in the population, often expressed as the number of contacts or notified cases for every 1000, say, of the population.

Motivational counselling Approach to counselling which emphasizes a supportive, empathic relationship, a non-confrontational approach, exploration of the benefits of behavioural change, and helping a client to make choices about coping strategies and alternative activities.

Motivational interviewing Intervention using psychotherapeutic strategies and methods to diminish resistance, resolve ambivalence, develop discrepancy, and trigger behaviour change.

Multidisciplinary Group of people from a variety of professional backgrounds covering many different skills and who contribute to the care of an individual (or group of people).

Multiple sclerosis Progressive neurological disease which can cause a variety of different symptoms in sufferers, such as visual, motor, sensory, and cognitive impairments.

National Service Framework (NSF) Series of standards for specific high volume clinical services provided by the British National Health Service, the first of which were published in 1999, and now covering a range of conditions such as Coronary Heart Disease and Chronic physical conditions.

Needs, and need analysis In experimental psychology a need refers to a deficiency or lack in terms of a postulated goal, which may be physiological. It has acquired a secondary meaning in clinical psychology practice, referring to a lack of appropriate clinical service for a person with a health care problem. Need analysis consists of formally establishing the needs for psychological and health care of a population or an individual, examining normative, felt, expressed, comparative, and met and unmet need.

Neuropsychology Study of the relationship between brain structure and pathology, and behaviour and experience.

Neurosis Psychiatrically based term to describe personal difficulties including phobias, depression, and anxiety where the person has awareness and insight but finds it hard to change. Seen as less disabling than psychosis.

Nomothetic Refers to an approach to personality that stresses the characteristics of an individual that can be compared with others, usually with reference to an imputed personality dimension.

Normalization Use of culturally normative means to establish, enable, or support behaviours, appearances, and interpretations which are as culturally normative as possible (compare with social role valorization).

Obsession or obsessive-compulsive disorder Irrational idea or thought that persists against one's will. Often accompanied by ritualistic, compulsive behaviour, and high anxiety. Common obsessions are of checking, contamination, and harm to oneself or others.

Paediatric Medical specialty concerned with the treatment of children and adolescents.

Palliative care Treatment that aims to reduce symptoms or pain rather than providing a cure, associated with the care of patients with limited time to live.

Parkinson's Disease Syndrome characterized by tremor and loss of coordination and exhaustion, may be linked with dementia.

Person-centred planning Approach which places the focus on the person and aims to make services more responsive to the needs of the person.

Personality Integrated organization of the physical and psychological characteristics of an individual, including intelligence, emotionality, and social behaviour, in the way that the individual presents himself or herself to others. Personality traits describe general characteristics of the individual, for example impulsive, social, taciturn, etc. Personality types describe major patterns of personality, for example introvert, neurotic.

Personality disorder Pattern of deviant or extreme personality traits relating to beliefs and feelings about the self and others and control of behaviour that impairs the person's social functioning. Antisocial personality disorder is the form most commonly identified among offenders and violent people. Other forms, such as borderline or avoidant personality disorder, are common among people seeking help for social and emotional difficulties. The validity and utility of the term itself is hotly debated.

Phobia Intense fear and avoidance of harmless events or objects. There are a variety of specific phobias, for example of insects and animals, and also social phobias and agoraphobia.

Post-traumatic stress disorder (PTSD) Syndrome or set of presenting problems arising as a consequence of the experience of an unusual, sudden, and major threat or distressing event, such as serious harm to oneself or one's close family, or sudden destruction of one's home. The consequences may include intrusive distressing recollections of the event, recurrent distressing dreams, persistent avoidance of places and stimuli associated with the event, and persistent symptoms of increased arousal, such as disturbed sleep.

Primary Care Trust Organizational units within the NHS that were set up in 2002, that commission primary care health services, including family practitioner services, to communities of approximately 150,000.

Progressive muscular relaxation Widely used method of relaxation based upon repeated contraction and relaxation of muscle groups. Often used as part of anxiety management.

Prompts, physical and verbal A prompt is help given to a person so that they may complete a task. A verbal prompt is essentially an instruction or some spoken help; a physical prompt is manual guidance.

Pseudodementia Temporary drop in performance of intellectual functioning brought about by emotional conditions.

Psychoanalysis Method of psychological treatment, developed from the work of Freud, which focuses on the uncovering of unconscious conflicts by predominantly verbal means. Significant features of psychoanalysis include free-association, interpretation, and the development of transference (see **Transference**). Classically a lengthy and intensive therapy lasting several years, although briefer and less intensive forms have also been developed.

Psychodynamic Term derived from psychoanalytic theory, describing the interplay of mental and emotional forces and the way these affect behaviour and mental state.

Psychopathic disorder Medico-legal category in which abnormally aggressive or seriously irresponsible behaviour is attributed to 'a persisting disorder or disability of mind', usually interpreted in practice as a personality disorder. The term should be distinguished from the clinical concept of psychopathic personality, which describes a more specific form of personality disorder characterized by callous, egocentric, and impulsive traits, and which is similar to antisocial personality disorder.

Psychosis Serious mental health problem characterized by disordered thought processes, disturbance in emotion, disorientation in time, and sometimes delusions and hallucinations.

Psychotherapy General term for any treatment by psychological means designed to reduce personal distress, raise morale, or help reduce personal or social problems. Sometimes used to describe verbal methods of therapy in contrast to behaviour or cognitive therapy, although this distinction is not consistently used.

Psychotropic Term used of drugs with an effect on psychological function, behaviour, or experience. The term can cover a wide range of substances, but is usually taken to refer to those drugs most frequently used in psychiatry (for example major tranquillizers or antidepressants).

Punishment Describes the way the probability of a response is reduced by the presentation of an aversive consequence.

Questionnaire A list of questions seeking information about a person's attitudes, knowledge or traits, often self administered and thus easy to use and often used for surveys.

Rating Scale List of questions about a person which are judged or rated, typically by another person (the rater) about the extent to which they occur. The observation or rating procedure is usually well defined and structured.

Reciprocal roles Term used in CAT to describe positions in inter- and intrapersonal relationships, between people or between parts of the self, such as abuser-abused, contemptuous-contemptible, loving-loved.

Reflective practice Approach to professional practice (including clinical psychology) recognizing the limitations of the evidence base and the need to think critically and creatively how best to proceed, with awareness of one's own biases and prior experiences, and how this may impact on practice, as well as sensitivity to ethical considerations.

Regional secure unit (RSU) Health service facility providing services with medium levels of security for disruptive psychiatric patients and mentally disordered offenders, as a complementary facility to Special Hospitals.

Rehabilitation Procedures for helping disabled patients to return to society after illness and to maximize their general functioning. It is applied both to institutionalized psychiatric patients being returned to community settings and to physically handicapped people being helped to recover from or adapt to their disability.

Relapse prevention Term used to describe a component of cognitive-behavioural programmes, for those with conditions (usually mental health conditions) that may periodically deteriorate, that identify the warning signs of a relapse and educate the service user to recognize them.

Safety behaviours Actions or thoughts taken by the client to guard against experiencing symptoms or distress, such as holding onto a friend's arm when feeling anxious away from home, or neutralizing negative thoughts. These actions fail to provide a challenge to the symptoms, and hence effectively maintain it.

Schizophrenia Major psychiatric disorder characterized by disturbances of thought, flattened, or inappropriate emotions, delusions, and hallucinations, usually in the form of imagined voices. Tends to occur in young adults in acute form, and can become chronic.

Scientist/practitioner Aspirant approach to clinical psychology based on a cycle of assessment, consulting research evidence, applying this in practice to an individual case, evaluation and modification of the approach and the evidence base, in the light of the new evidence.

Self-monitoring Assessment procedures that involve people in recording their own behaviour by suitable charts or diaries, or by suitable physiological devices.

Service level agreement Non-financial contract often between two parts of a government-funded organization, which specifies the terms under which one or both parts will provide a service for the other, or the ways in which the two parts will relate to the other. This contract is not usually binding.

Service users Term now often used to describe patients, clients, and other recipients of health and social care services.

Single-case designs Experimental design where one person receives a series of treatments or conditions in a carefully planned sequence, with some conditions possibly repeated (but where the sequence minimizes the effect of early conditions on later conditions).

Social role valorization Enhancing the social role of people or groups of people at risk of being socially devalued. There is an important distinction between the valorization of the role of the person, and the value of the person themselves.

Social skills training Use of didactic procedures of modelling, role-playing, and feedback, to train people in 'social skills'. 'Social skills' refer to specific features of social behaviour that result in successful interaction. These range from specific non-verbal behaviours, such as eye contact or gesture, to complex patterns of interaction.

Special Hospital Maximum-security hospital for patients whose violent or criminal behaviour is deemed to require treatment under conditions of special security.

Stages of change model A number of stages are involved in behavioural change according to Prochaska and DiClimente. In the precontemplation stage, no changes are planned in the near future. The contemplation stage covers that period when costs, benefits, and ability to cope are being reappraised. In the action stage positive steps are being taken. During the maintenance stage vigilance is still relatively high, in an attempt to prevent relapse.

Statistical analysis Process of subjecting a number of figures to a particular analysis or manipulation (which may include correlation, analysis of variance, calculation of means) essentially to condense the figures to show some central characteristics and measures of spread of the data, and the nature of the association between two or more variables. The statistical significance of a result is the probability that the result could have been achieved by chance, or by random allocation, and is conventionally expressed at probability levels of 5, 1, or 0.1 per cent (or as 0.05, 0.01, or 0.001).

Stress Either unpleasant aspects of the external social and physical environment or the subjective response of the individual to their perception of threats and challenges arising from that environment.

Stroke Rupture or disruption in the blood supply to the brain, leading to a variety of symptoms depending on the areas of the brain affected, and the extent of tissue damage.

Sure Start UK government programme aiming to deliver the best start in life for children, especially in deprived areas, by bringing together early education, childcare, health and family support services, often by assessing and helping vulnerable parents to build and improve relationships with their young children. Sure start is also linked to initiatives to help mothers access employment.

Systemic approaches Approach based on an understanding of how parts of a system, family, or organization, work together and interrelate, affecting each other's functioning.

Tests (psychometric) **Attainment:** sets of standard questions or items designed to measure specific achievements or attainments, such as reading, and distinguished from the measurement or more general abilities. **Intelligence** sets of standard problems and materials designed to measure maximum general mental ability, or power of learning and understanding, and typically yielding an intelligence quotient (IQ). **Personality** either sets of standard questions relating to a person's own distinctive character, or normal mode of functioning, scored to yield measures of different personality traits; or sets of projective materials which are essentially ambiguous or neutral in meaning, the responses to which are assumed to reveal underlying traits or characteristics.

Time out Withdrawal of positive reinforcement for a particular behaviour (for example shouting, fighting) by taking the individual out of the environment where such behaviour is being reinforced. Often used in managing aggressive behaviour in children and adolescents.

Transference and Counter-transference

Transference Re-experiencing in therapy of significant relationship patterns; the projection onto the therapist of characteristics more properly those experienced with early significant others; **Counter-transference** Therapists' own feelings or reactions towards the client in therapy.

Triaging Assessment of a client or patient when they first seek help to determine quickly the severity of their problem, and what kind of help is likely to be most appropriate.

Validity Extent to which a measurement procedure assesses what it is supposed to assess. This somewhat circular definition may be clarified by distinguishing between face or content validity—the extent to which inspection of the form or content of the procedure shows it is appropriate; and empirical validity—the extent to which the procedure is consistent with the scores derived from another totally independent measure of the same phenomenon.

Index